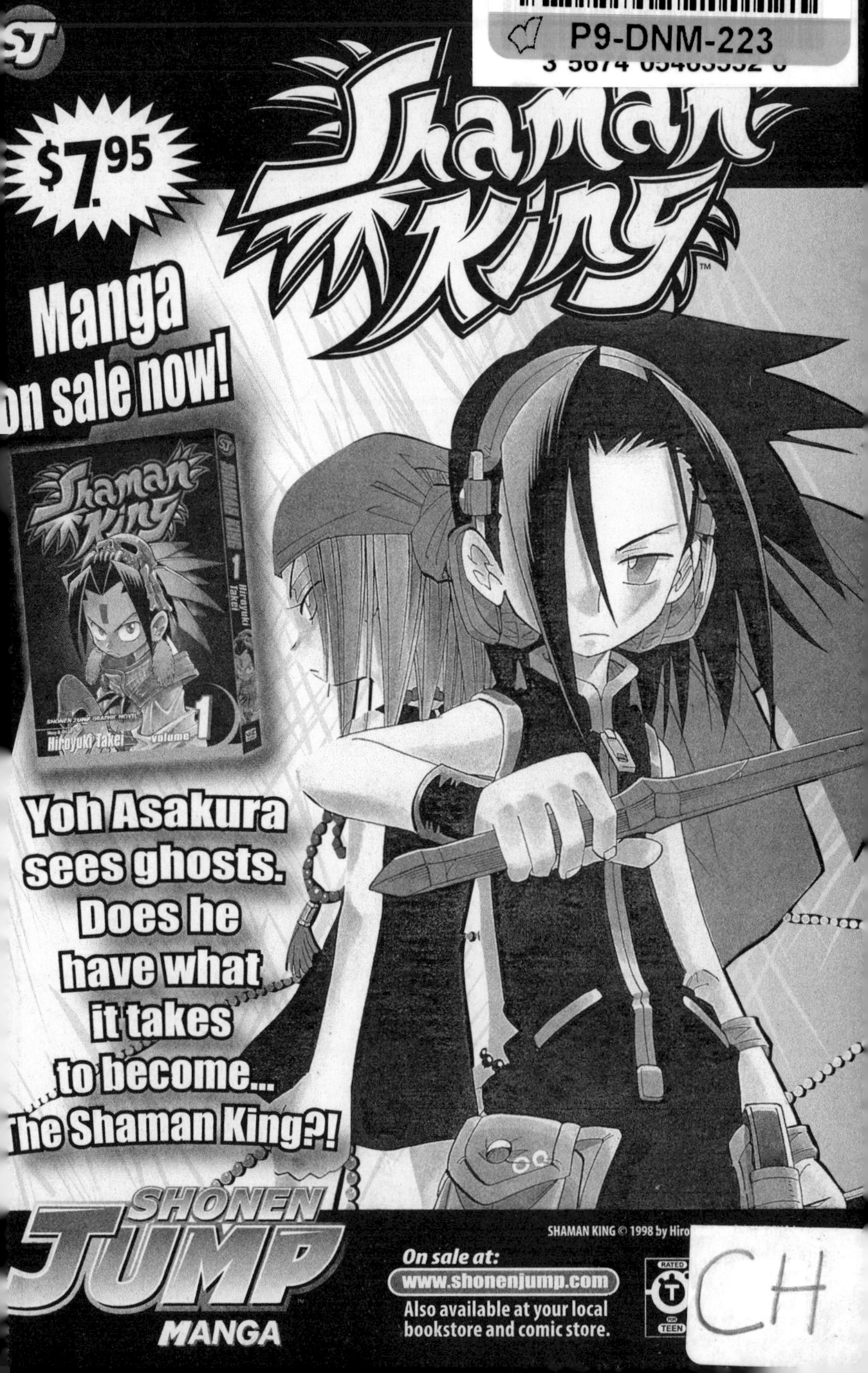
SJ
$7.95
Shaman King™
Manga on sale now!
Shaman King
SHONEN JUMP GRAPHIC NOVEL
Hiroyuki Takei
volume 1
Yoh Asakura sees ghosts. Does he have what it takes to become... The Shaman King?!
SHONEN JUMP MANGA
SHAMAN KING © 1998 by Hiro
On sale at:
www.shonenjump.com
Also available at your local bookstore and comic store.
RATED T FOR TEEN

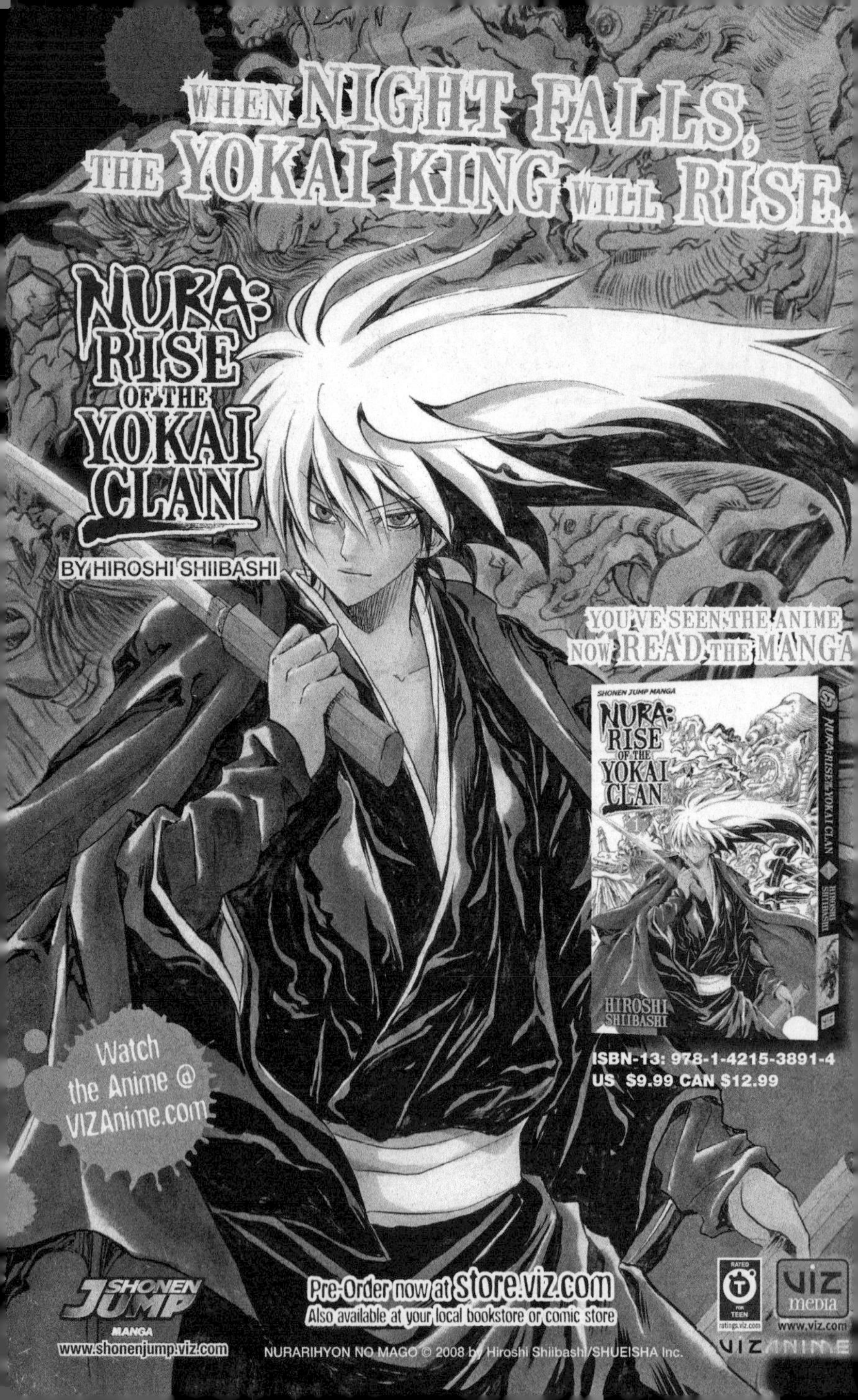
WHEN NIGHT FALLS, THE YOKAI KING WILL RISE.
NURA: RISE OF THE YOKAI CLAN
BY HIROSHI SHIIBASHI
YOU'VE SEEN THE ANIME NOW READ THE MANGA
SHONEN JUMP MANGA
NURA: RISE OF THE YOKAI CLAN 1
HIROSHI SHIIBASHI
ISBN-13: 978-1-4215-3891-4
US $9.99 CAN $12.99
Watch the Anime @ VIZAnime.com
SHONEN JUMP MANGA
www.shonenjump.viz.com
Pre-Order now at store.viz.com
Also available at your local bookstore or comic store
RATED T FOR TEEN
ratings.viz.com
VIZ media
www.viz.com
VIZ ANIME
NURARIHYON NO MAGO © 2008 by Hiroshi Shiibashi/SHUEISHA Inc.

TOO MANY OLD FOGEYS...

岸本斉史

I'm always in a quandary over who to draw on the cover of each graphic novel volume... but I usually choose characters that were very prominent in the storylines within that volume. But lately they've all been unsightly old fogeys*!!*

—*Masashi Kishimoto, 2011*

Author/artist Masashi Kishimoto was born in 1974 in rural Okayama Prefecture, Japan. After spending time in art college, he won the Hop Step Award for new manga artists with his manga **Karakuri** (Mechanism). Kishimoto decided to base his next story on traditional Japanese culture. His first version of **Naruto**, drawn in 1997, was a one-shot story about fox spirits; his final version, which debuted in **Weekly Shonen Jump** in 1999, quickly became the most popular ninja manga in Japan.

NARUTO VOL. 56
SHONEN JUMP Manga Edition

This graphic novel contains material that was originally published in English in SHONEN JUMP #108–110. Artwork in the magazine may have been slightly altered from that presented here.

STORY AND ART BY MASASHI KISHIMOTO

Translation/Mari Morimoto
English Adaptation/Joel Enos
Touch-up Art & Lettering/Inori Fukuda Trant, Sabrina Heep
Design/Sam Elzway
Editor/Megan Bates

Printed in the U.S.A.

Published by VIZ Media, LLC
P.O. Box 77010
San Francisco, CA 94107

10 9 8 7 6 5 4 3 2 1
First printing, May 2012

www.viz.com

THE WORLD'S
MOST POPULAR MANGA
SHONEN JUMP
www.shonenjump.com

SHONEN JUMP MANGA EDITION

NARUTO

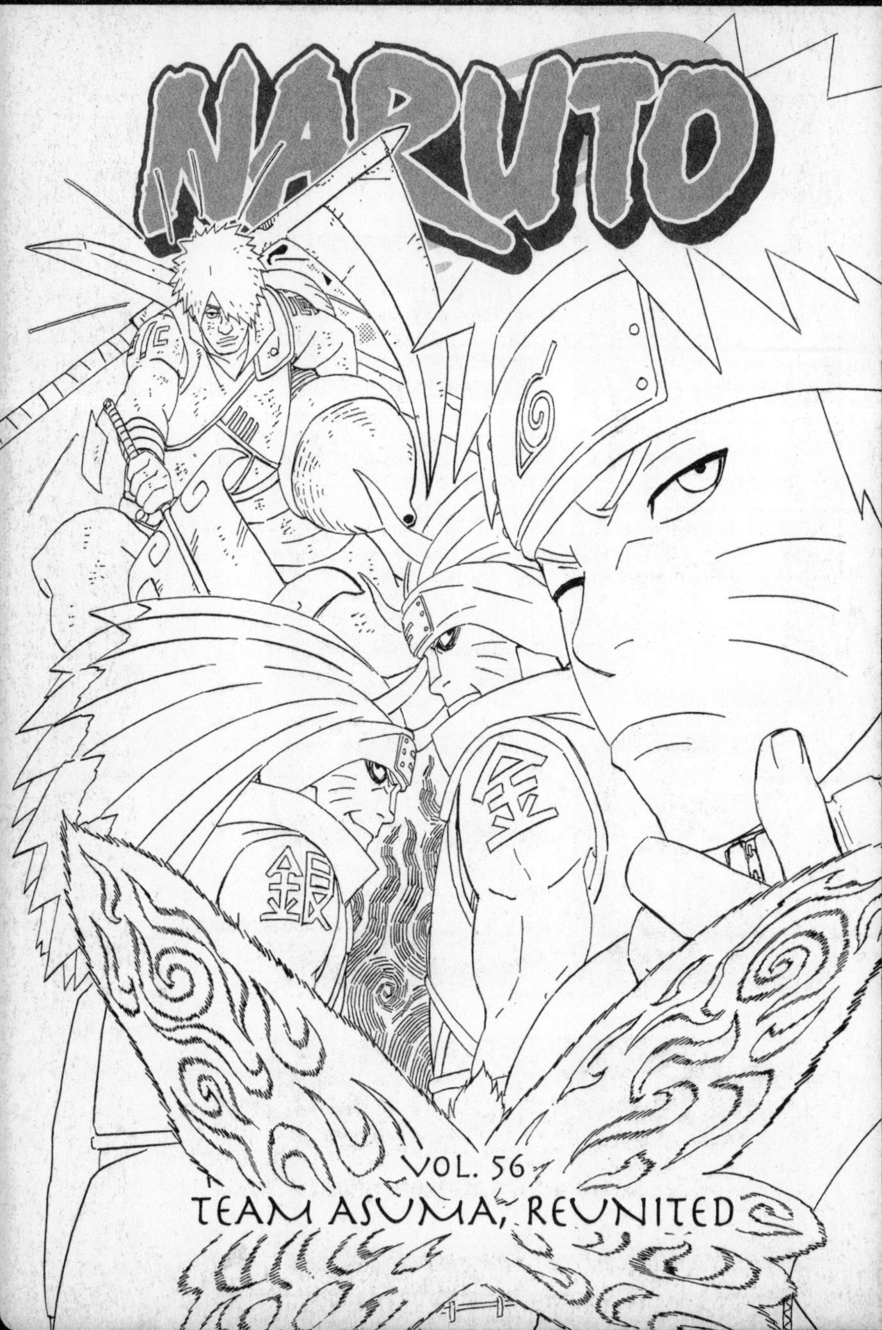

VOL. 56

TEAM ASUMA, REUNITED

CHARACTERS

Naruto ナルト

Sasuke サスケ

Kakashi カカシ

Sakura サクラ

Sai サイ

Yamato ヤマト

Tsunade 綱手

Gaara 我愛羅

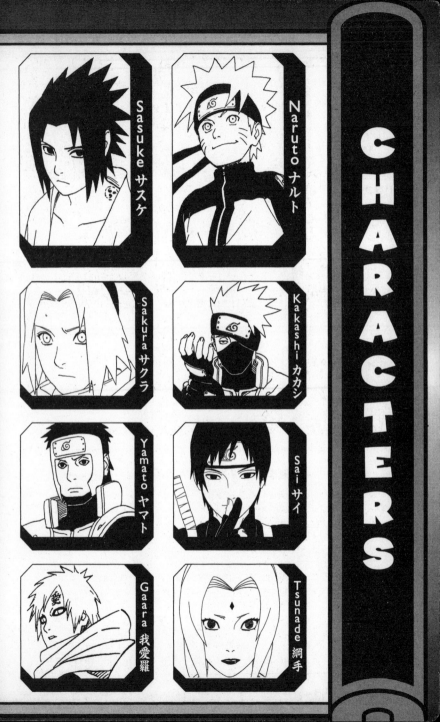

Mizukage 水影

Tsuchikage 土影

Raikage 雷影

Kabuto カブト

Zetsu ゼツ

Madara マダラ

Darui ダルイ

Killer Bee キラービー

Deidara デイダラ

━━━ **THE STORY SO FAR...** ━━━

Naruto, the biggest troublemaker at the Ninja Academy in the Village of Konohagakure, finally becomes a ninja along with his classmates Sasuke and Sakura. They grow and mature through countless trials and battles. However, Sasuke, unable to give up his quest for vengeance, leaves Konohagakure to seek Orochimaru and his power...

Two years pass. Naruto grows up and engages in fierce battles against the Tailed Beast-targeting Akatsuki. Elsewhere, after winning the heroic battle against Itachi and learning his older brother's true intentions, Sasuke allies with the Akatsuki and sets out to destroy Konoha.

Upon Madara's declaration of war, the Five Kage put together an Allied Shinobi Force. The Fourth Great Ninja War against the Akatsuki begins. Naruto continues training, still sequestered from the battlefield, while the Allied Forces fight harsh battles against the heroes Kabuto has resurrected. And do additional enemies threaten the main regiment of the Allied Forces?!

NARUTO

VOL. 56
TEAM ASUMA, REUNITED

CONTENTS

Number 525: The Kage Resurrected!!

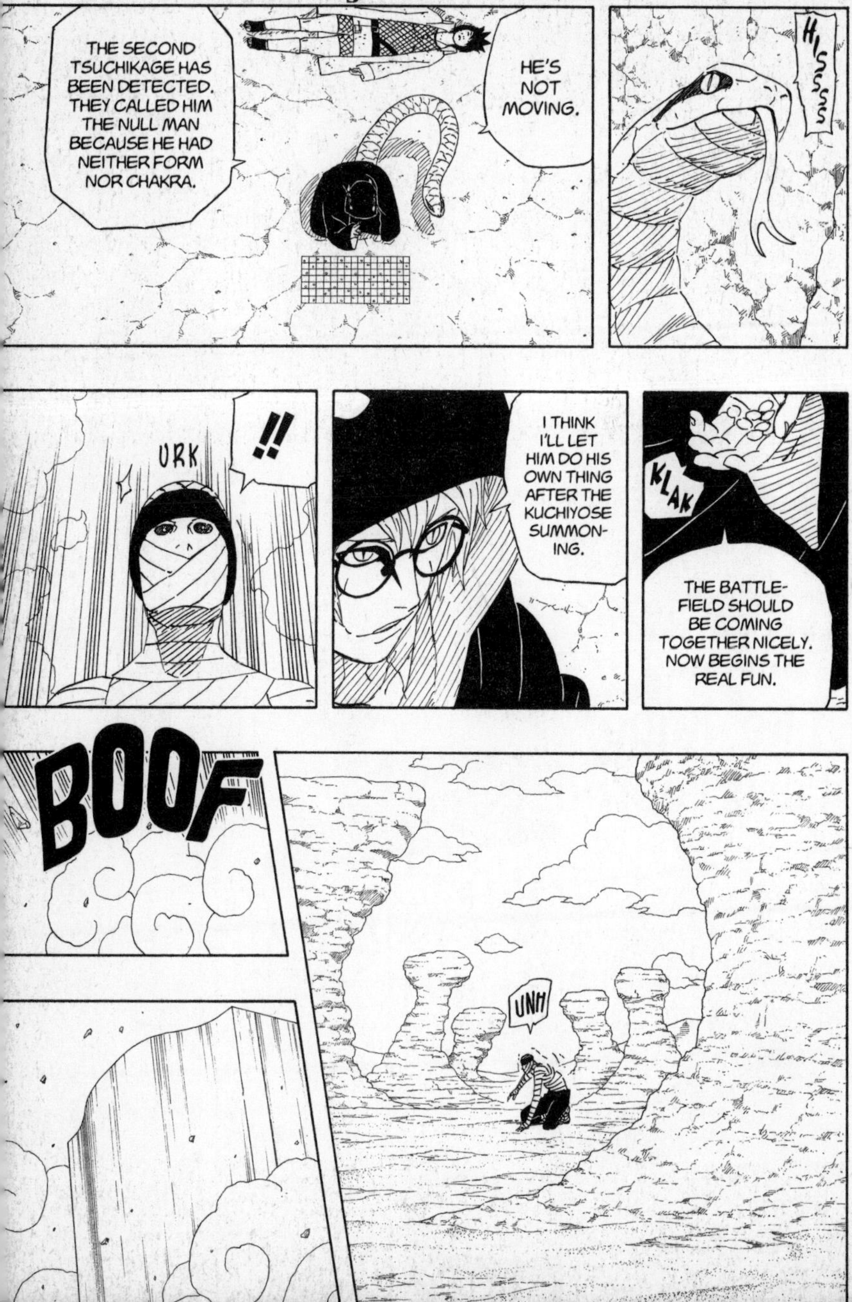

HISSSSS
HE'S NOT MOVING.
THE SECOND TSUCHIKAGE HAS BEEN DETECTED. THEY CALLED HIM THE NULL MAN BECAUSE HE HAD NEITHER FORM NOR CHAKRA.
KLAK
THE BATTLE-FIELD SHOULD BE COMING TOGETHER NICELY. NOW BEGINS THE REAL FUN.
I THINK I'LL LET HIM DO HIS OWN THING AFTER THE KUCHIYOSE SUMMON-ING.
!!
URK
UNH
BOOF

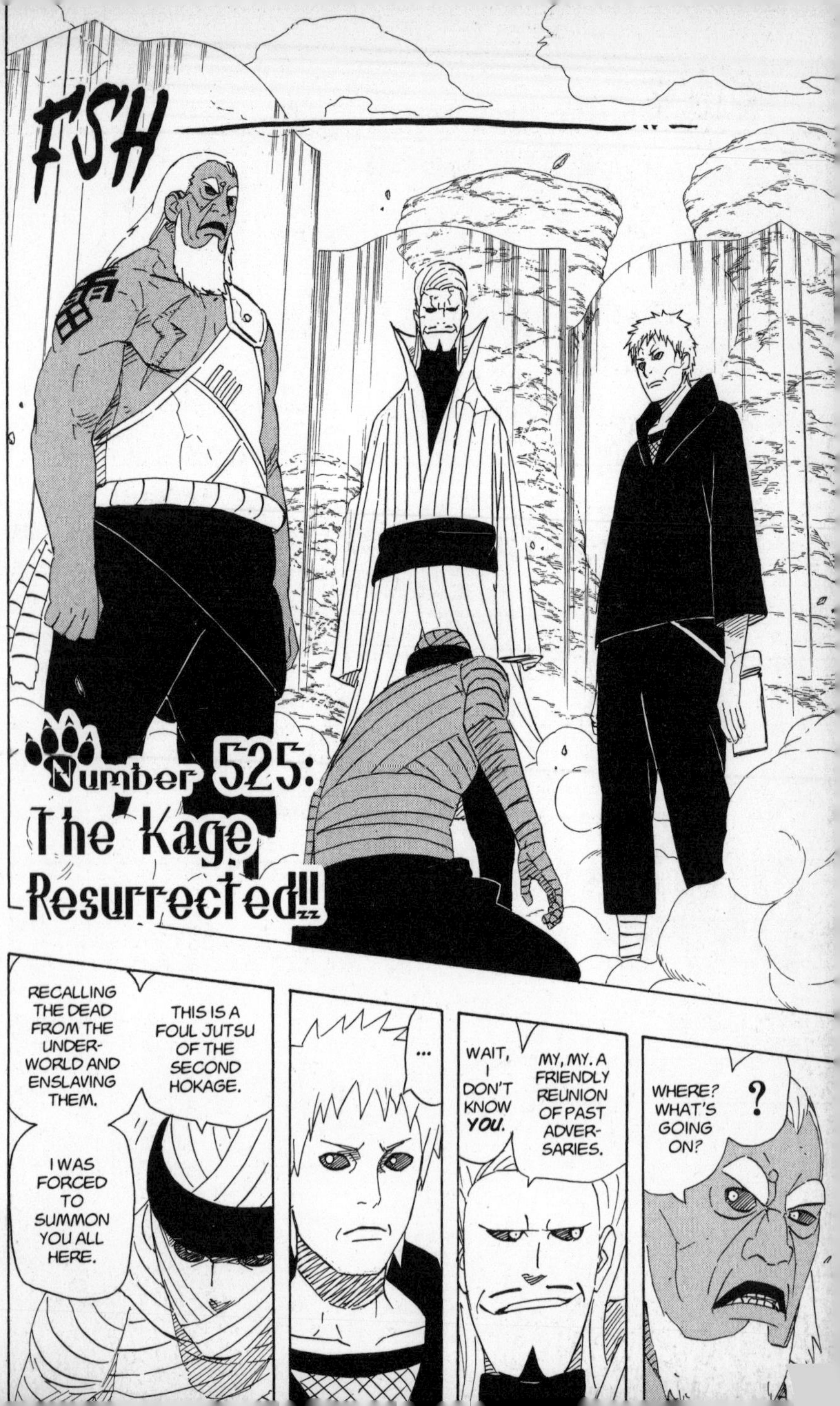
FSH
Number 525: The Kage Resurrected!!
?
WHERE? WHAT'S GOING ON?
MY, MY. A FRIENDLY REUNION OF PAST ADVERSARIES.
WAIT, I DON'T KNOW YOU.
...
RECALLING THE DEAD FROM THE UNDER-WORLD AND ENSLAVING THEM.
THIS IS A FOUL JUTSU OF THE SECOND HOKAGE.
I WAS FORCED TO SUMMON YOU ALL HERE.

READ THIS WAY

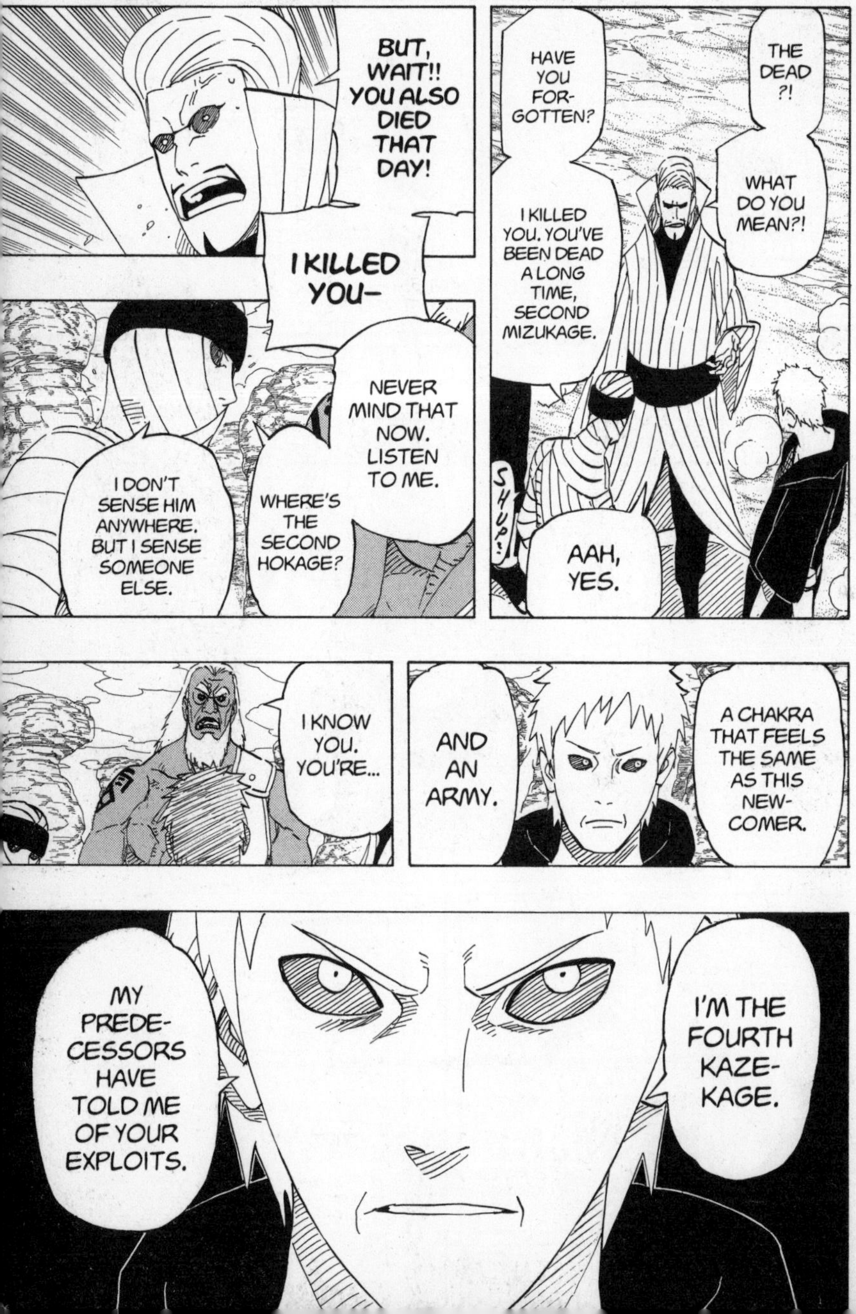
THE DEAD?!
WHAT DO YOU MEAN?!
HAVE YOU FORGOTTEN?
I KILLED YOU. YOU'VE BEEN DEAD A LONG TIME, SECOND MIZUKAGE.
SHUP!
AAH, YES.
BUT, WAIT!! YOU ALSO DIED THAT DAY!
I KILLED YOU-
NEVER MIND THAT NOW. LISTEN TO ME.
WHERE'S THE SECOND HOKAGE?
I DON'T SENSE HIM ANYWHERE. BUT I SENSE SOMEONE ELSE.
A CHAKRA THAT FEELS THE SAME AS THIS NEWCOMER.
AND AN ARMY.
I KNOW YOU. YOU'RE...
I'M THE FOURTH KAZEKAGE.
MY PREDECESSORS HAVE TOLD ME OF YOUR EXPLOITS.

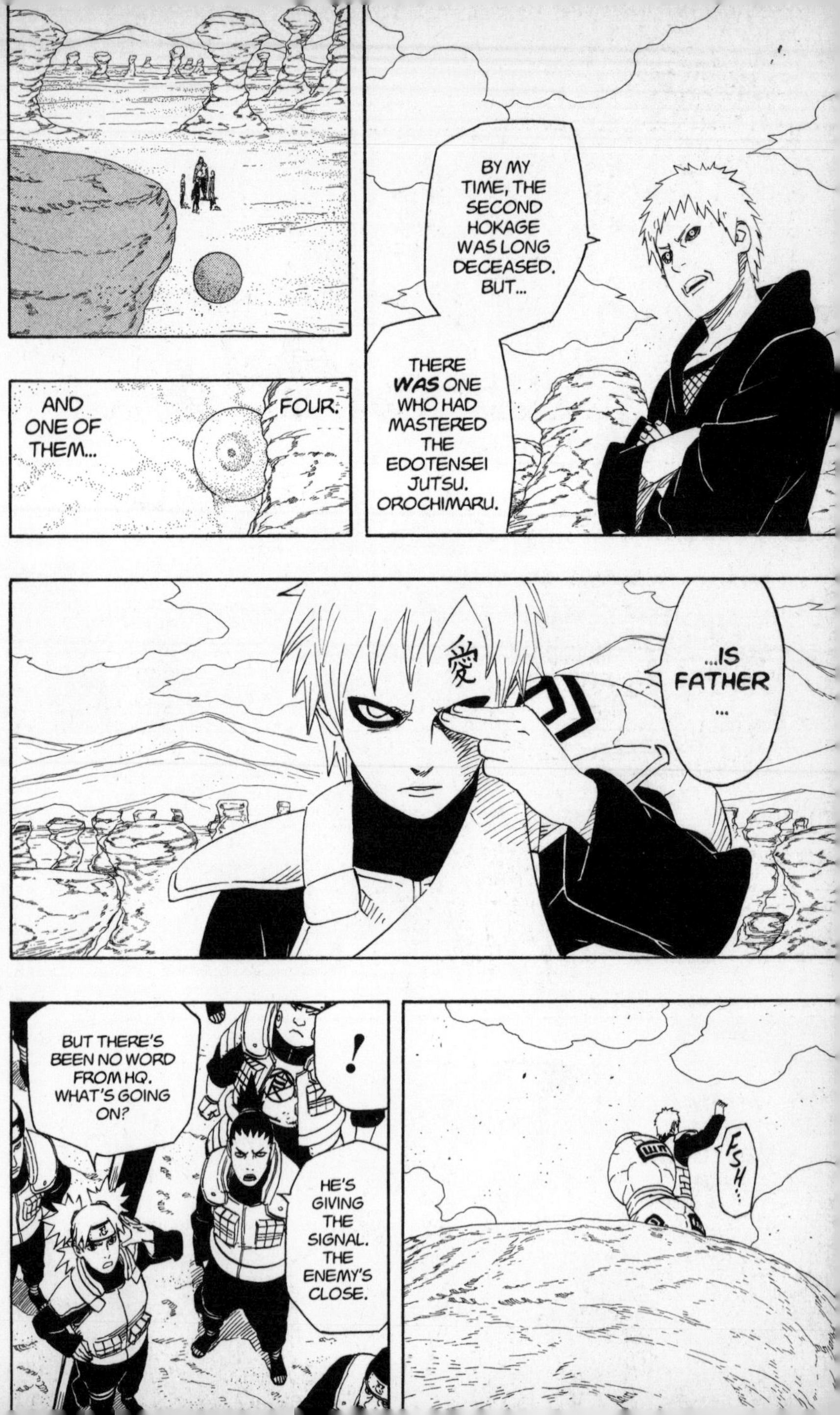
BY MY TIME, THE SECOND HOKAGE WAS LONG DECEASED. BUT...
THERE **WAS** ONE WHO HAD MASTERED THE EDOTENSEI JUTSU. OROCHIMARU.
FOUR.
AND ONE OF THEM...
...IS FATHER ...
FSH...
!
BUT THERE'S BEEN NO WORD FROM HQ. WHAT'S GOING ON?
HE'S GIVING THE SIGNAL. THE ENEMY'S CLOSE.

READ THIS WAY

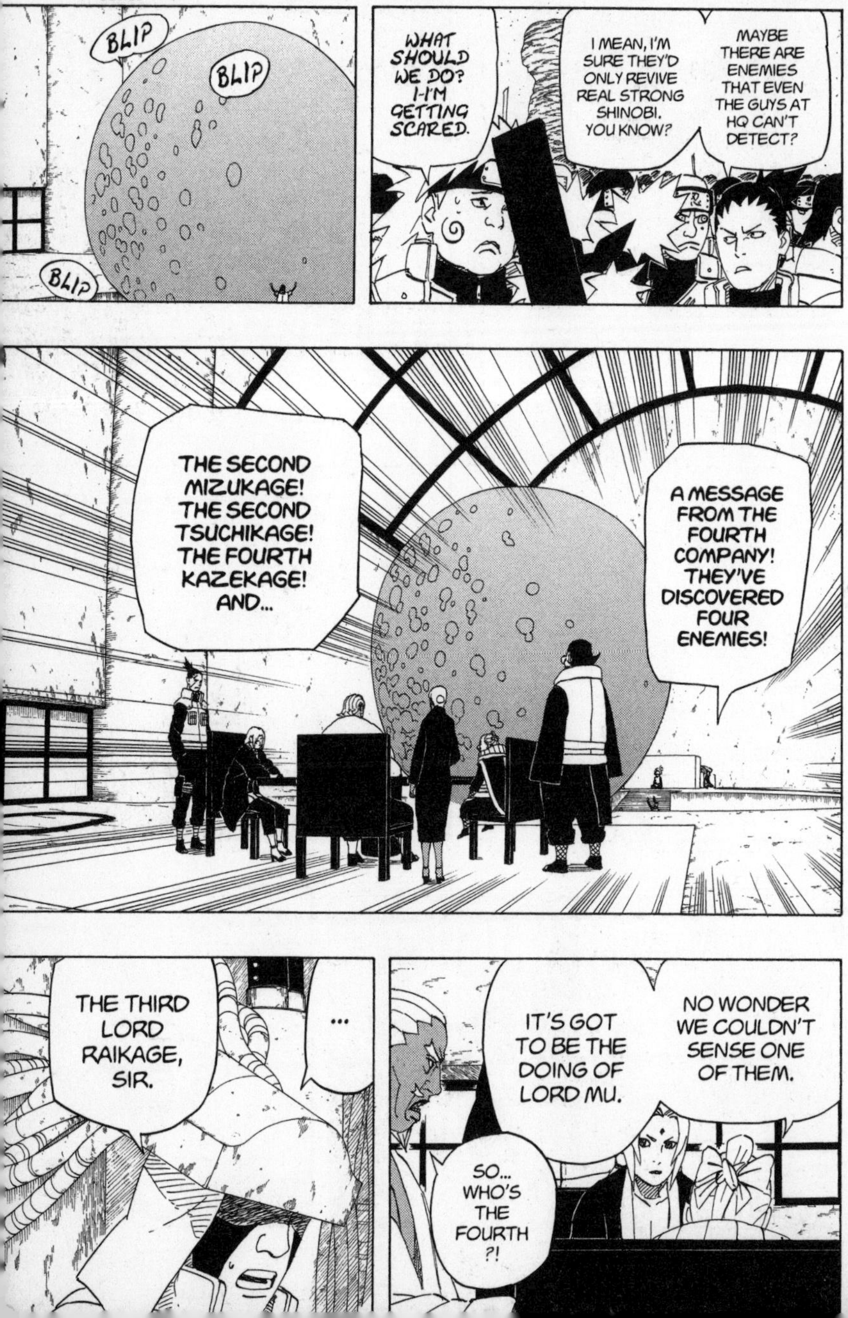
MAYBE THERE ARE ENEMIES THAT EVEN THE GUYS AT HQ CAN'T DETECT?
I MEAN, I'M SURE THEY'D ONLY REVIVE REAL STRONG SHINOBI. YOU KNOW?
WHAT SHOULD WE DO? I-I'M GETTING SCARED.
BLIP
BLIP
BLIP
A MESSAGE FROM THE FOURTH COMPANY! THEY'VE DISCOVERED FOUR ENEMIES!
THE SECOND MIZUKAGE! THE SECOND TSUCHIKAGE! THE FOURTH KAZEKAGE! AND...
NO WONDER WE COULDN'T SENSE ONE OF THEM.
IT'S GOT TO BE THE DOING OF LORD MU.
SO... WHO'S THE FOURTH ?!
...
THE THIRD LORD RAIKAGE, SIR.

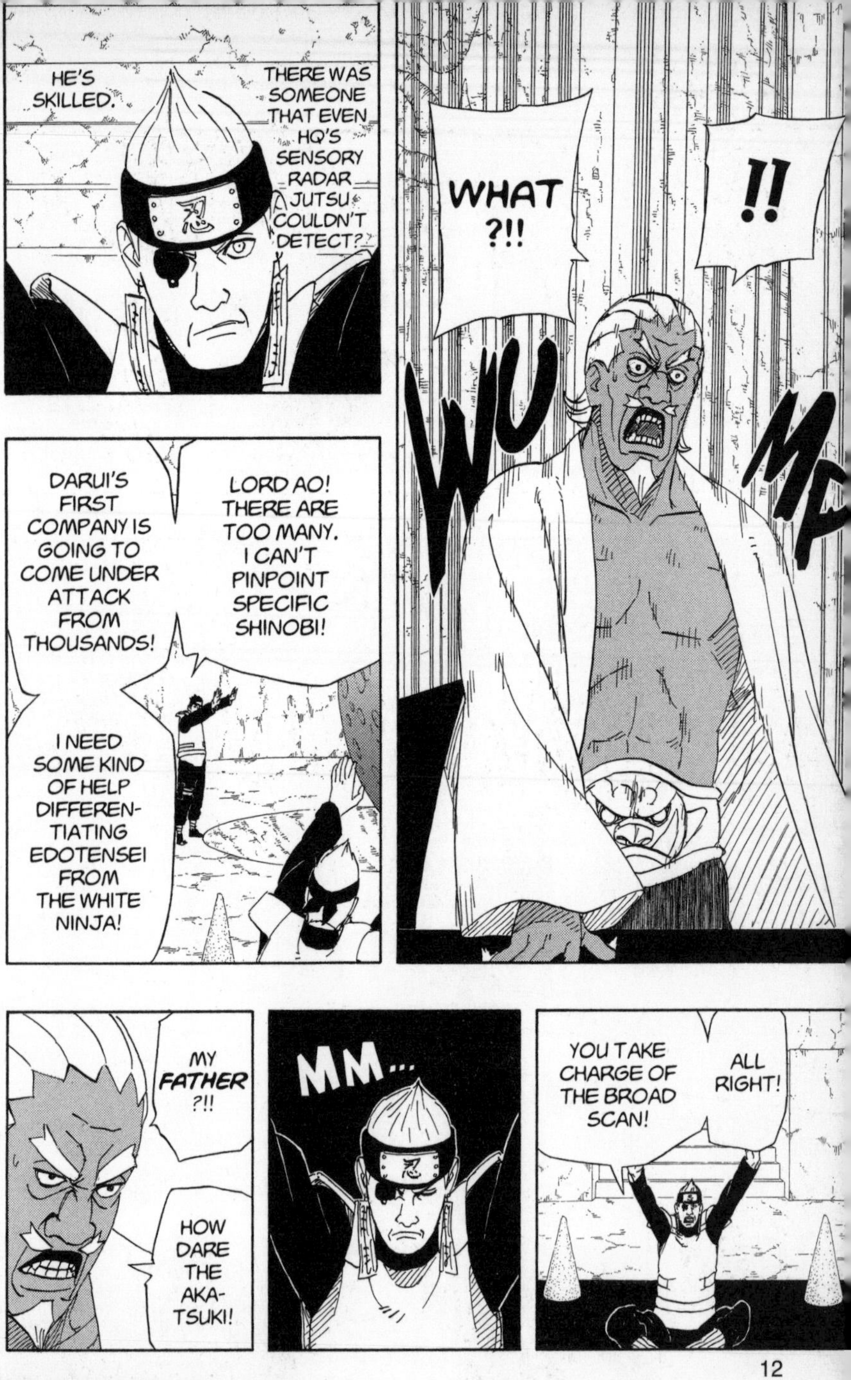
!!
WHAT ?!!
WUMP
THERE WAS SOMEONE THAT EVEN HQ'S SENSORY RADAR JUTSU COULDN'T DETECT?
HE'S SKILLED.
LORD AO! THERE ARE TOO MANY. I CAN'T PINPOINT SPECIFIC SHINOBI!
DARUI'S FIRST COMPANY IS GOING TO COME UNDER ATTACK FROM THOUSANDS!
I NEED SOME KIND OF HELP DIFFEREN-TIATING EDOTENSEI FROM THE WHITE NINJA!
ALL RIGHT!
YOU TAKE CHARGE OF THE BROAD SCAN!
MM...
MY *FATHER* ?!!
HOW DARE THE AKA-TSUKI!

READ THIS WAY

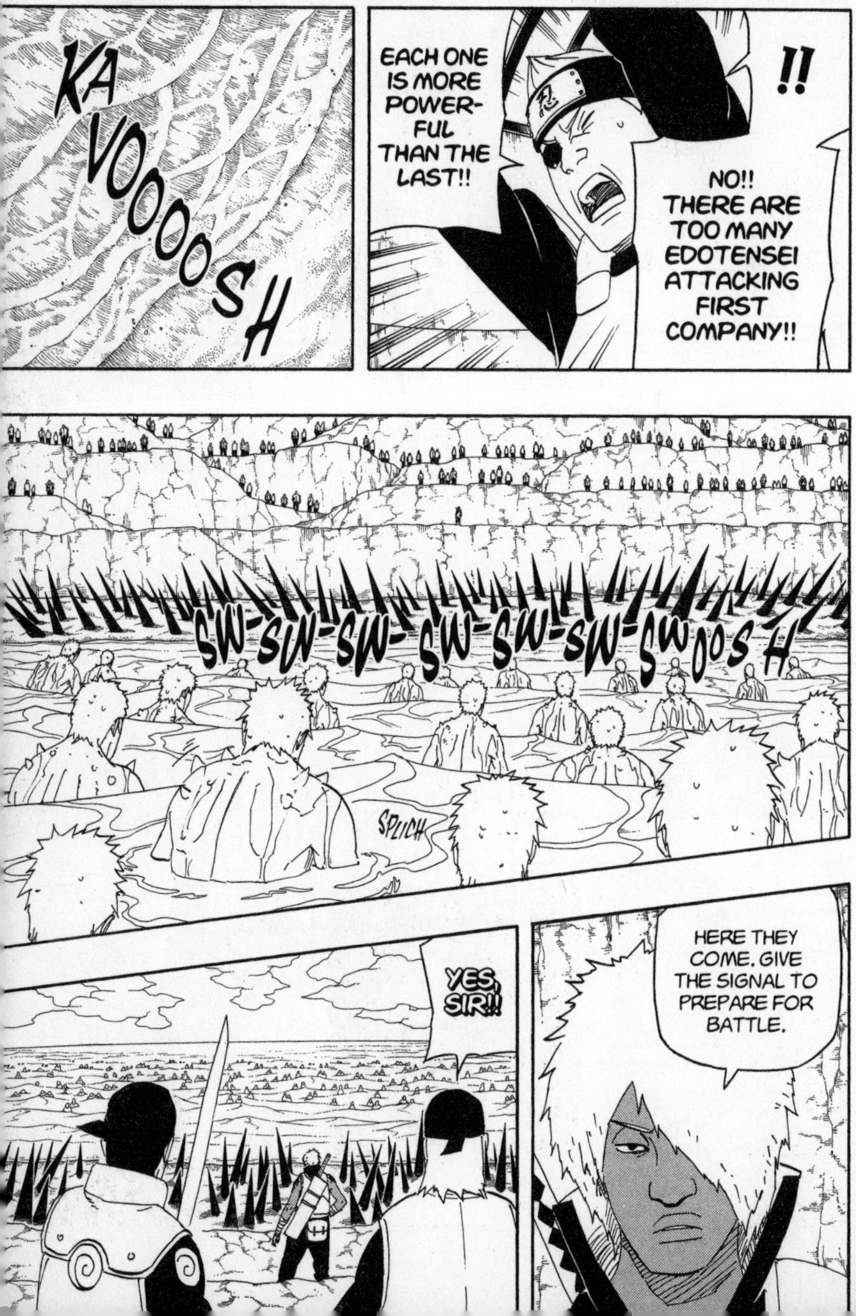
!!
NO!! THERE ARE TOO MANY EDOTENSEI ATTACKING FIRST COMPANY!!
EACH ONE IS MORE POWER-FUL THAN THE LAST!!
KA VOOOOSH
SW-SW-SW-SW-SW-SW-SWOOSH
SPLICH
HERE THEY COME. GIVE THE SIGNAL TO PREPARE FOR BATTLE.
YES, SIR!!

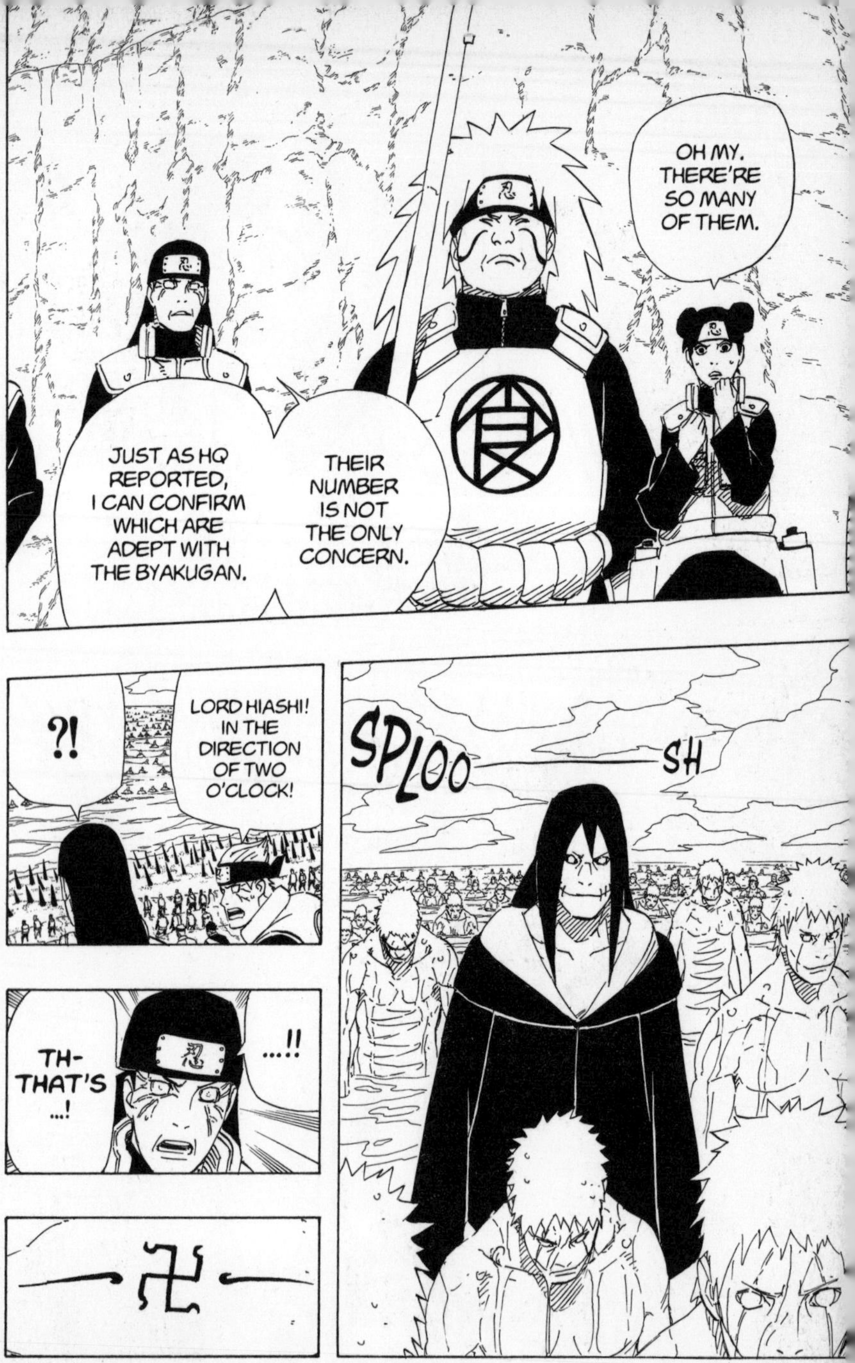
OH MY. THERE'RE SO MANY OF THEM.
THEIR NUMBER IS NOT THE ONLY CONCERN.
JUST AS HQ REPORTED, I CAN CONFIRM WHICH ARE ADEPT WITH THE BYAKUGAN.
SPLOO—SH
LORD HIASHI! IN THE DIRECTION OF TWO O'CLOCK!
?!
...!!
TH-THAT'S ...!

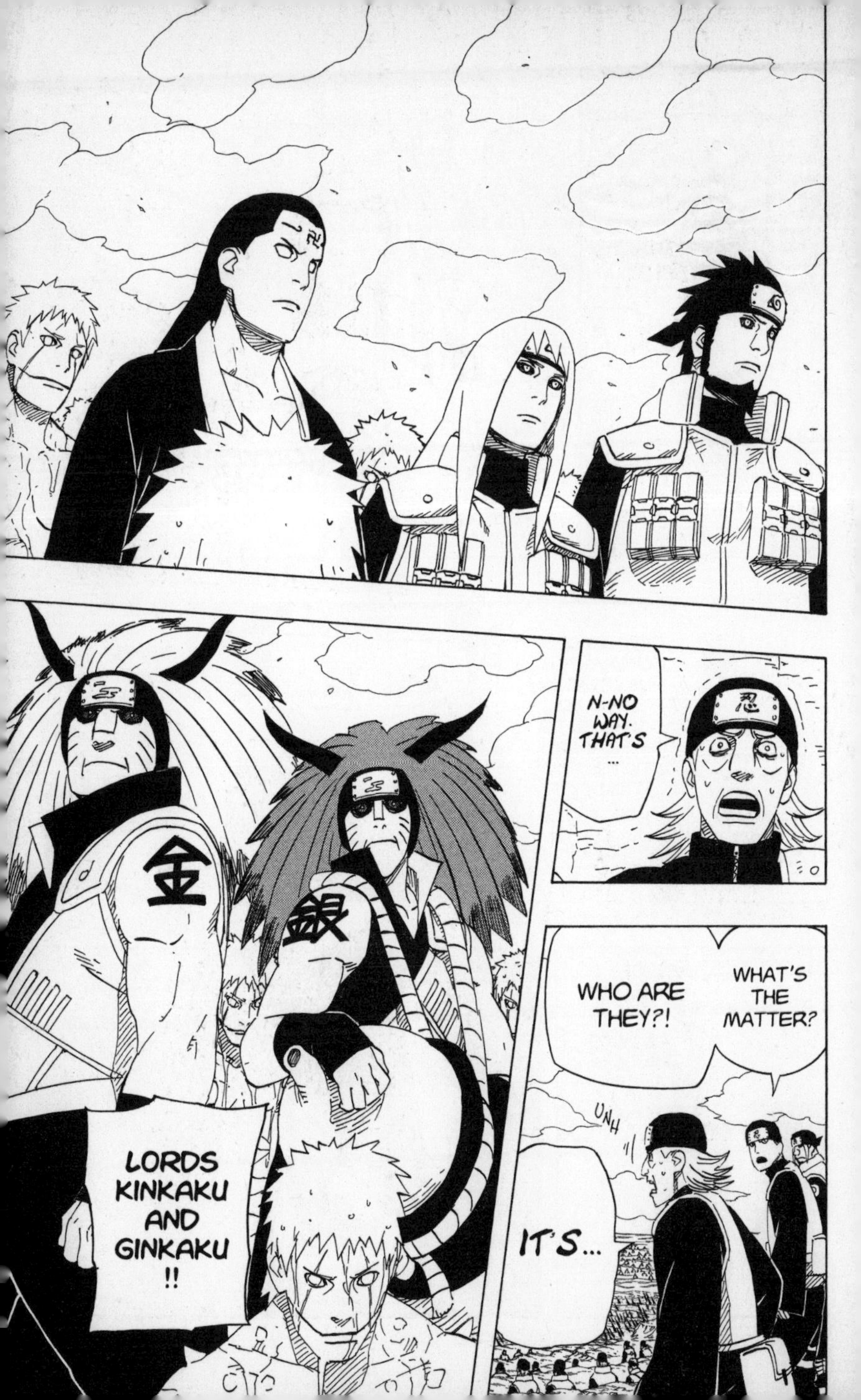
N-NO WAY. THAT'S ...
WHAT'S THE MATTER?
WHO ARE THEY?!
UNH
IT'S...
LORDS KINKAKU AND GINKAKU !!

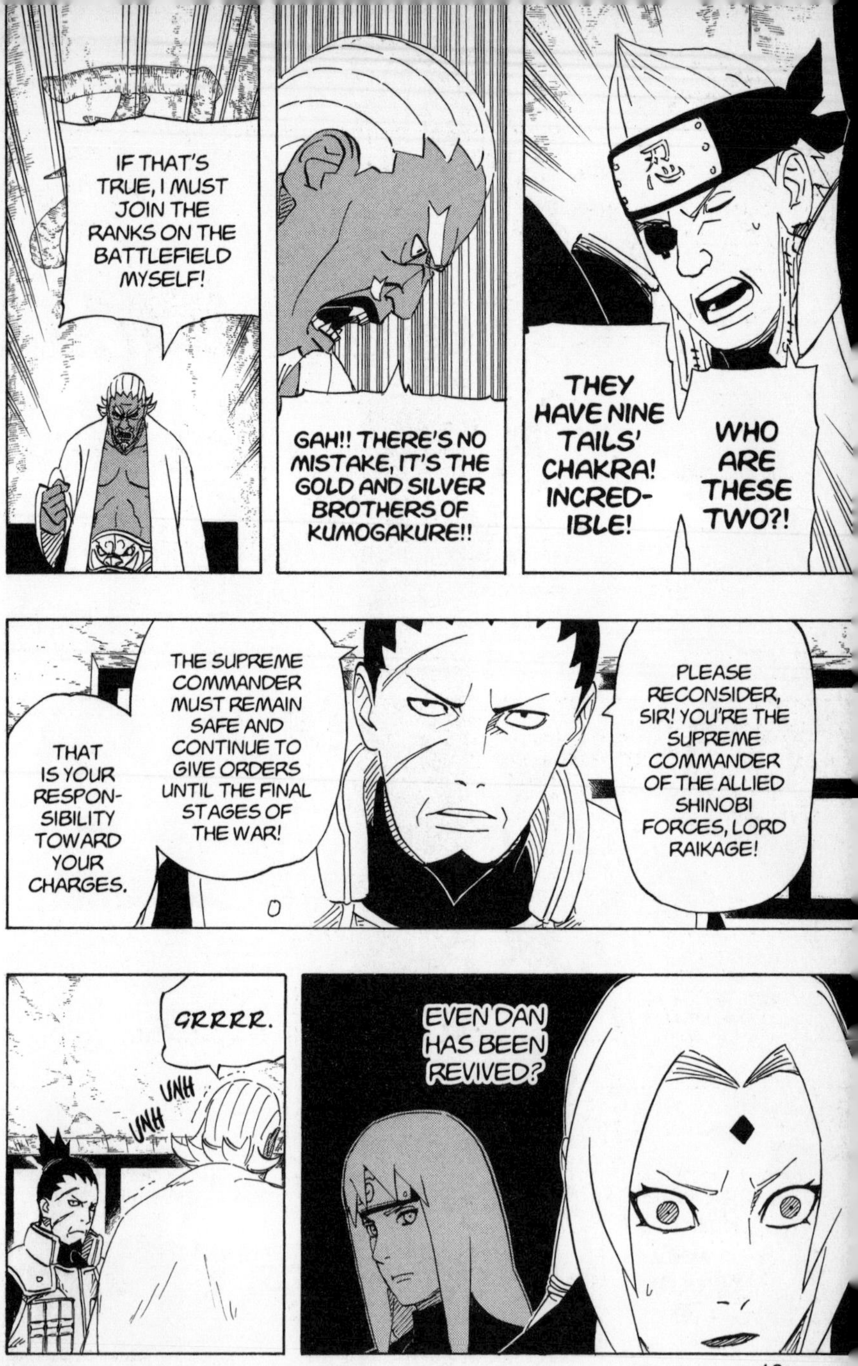
WHO ARE THESE TWO?!
THEY HAVE NINE TAILS' CHAKRA! INCRED-IBLE!
GAH!! THERE'S NO MISTAKE, IT'S THE GOLD AND SILVER BROTHERS OF KUMOGAKURE!!
IF THAT'S TRUE, I MUST JOIN THE RANKS ON THE BATTLEFIELD MYSELF!
PLEASE RECONSIDER, SIR! YOU'RE THE SUPREME COMMANDER OF THE ALLIED SHINOBI FORCES, LORD RAIKAGE!
THE SUPREME COMMANDER MUST REMAIN SAFE AND CONTINUE TO GIVE ORDERS UNTIL THE FINAL STAGES OF THE WAR!
THAT IS YOUR RESPON-SIBILITY TOWARD YOUR CHARGES.
EVEN DAN HAS BEEN REVIVED?
GRRRR.
UNH
UNH

READ THIS WAY

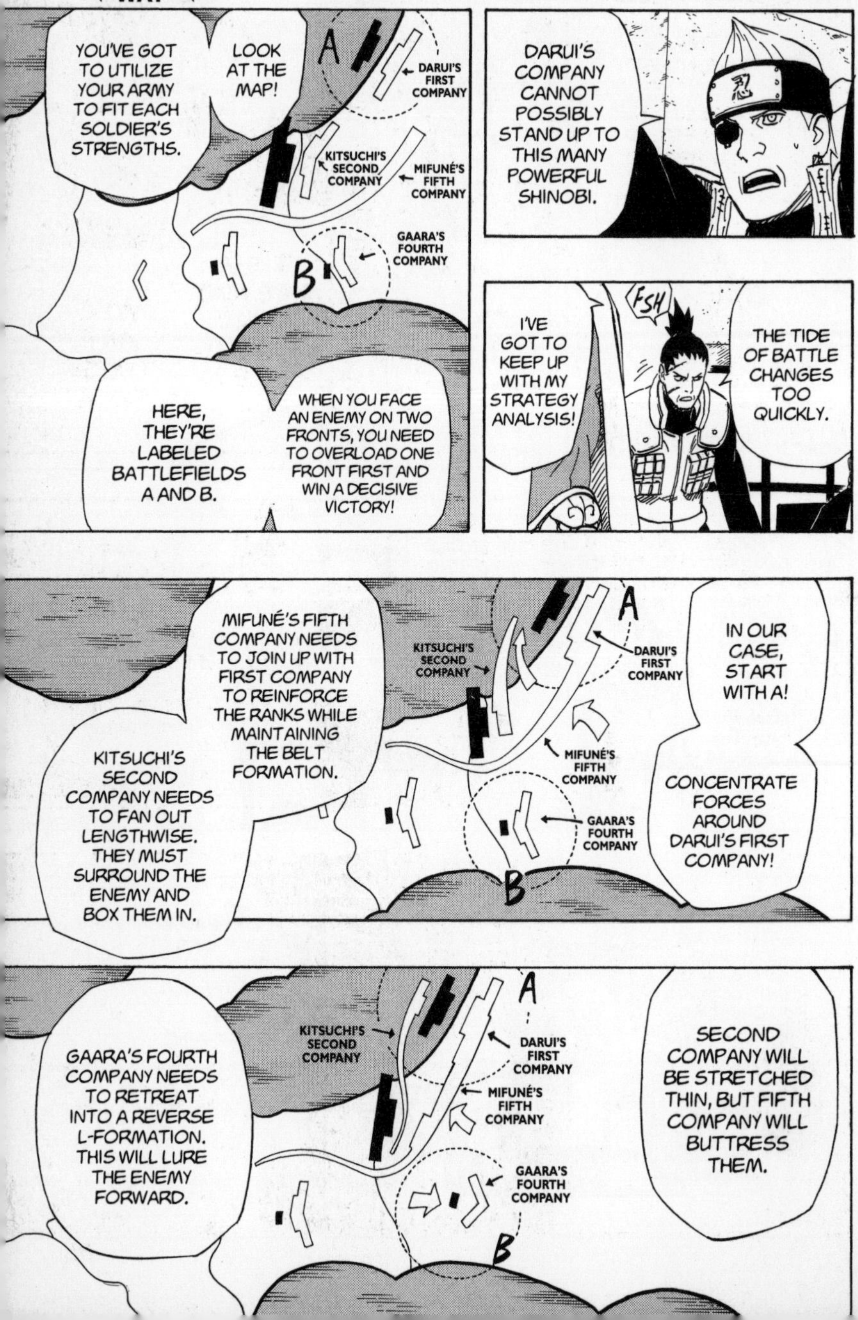
DARUI'S COMPANY CANNOT POSSIBLY STAND UP TO THIS MANY POWERFUL SHINOBI.
THE TIDE OF BATTLE CHANGES TOO QUICKLY.
FSH
I'VE GOT TO KEEP UP WITH MY STRATEGY ANALYSIS!
LOOK AT THE MAP!
YOU'VE GOT TO UTILIZE YOUR ARMY TO FIT EACH SOLDIER'S STRENGTHS.
A
DARUI'S FIRST COMPANY
MIFUNÉ'S FIFTH COMPANY
KITSUCHI'S SECOND COMPANY
GAARA'S FOURTH COMPANY
B
WHEN YOU FACE AN ENEMY ON TWO FRONTS, YOU NEED TO OVERLOAD ONE FRONT FIRST AND WIN A DECISIVE VICTORY!
HERE, THEY'RE LABELED BATTLEFIELDS A AND B.
IN OUR CASE, START WITH A!
CONCENTRATE FORCES AROUND DARUI'S FIRST COMPANY!
A
DARUI'S FIRST COMPANY
KITSUCHI'S SECOND COMPANY
MIFUNÉ'S FIFTH COMPANY
GAARA'S FOURTH COMPANY
B
MIFUNÉ'S FIFTH COMPANY NEEDS TO JOIN UP WITH FIRST COMPANY TO REINFORCE THE RANKS WHILE MAINTAINING THE BELT FORMATION.
KITSUCHI'S SECOND COMPANY NEEDS TO FAN OUT LENGTHWISE. THEY MUST SURROUND THE ENEMY AND BOX THEM IN.
SECOND COMPANY WILL BE STRETCHED THIN, BUT FIFTH COMPANY WILL BUTTRESS THEM.
A
DARUI'S FIRST COMPANY
KITSUCHI'S SECOND COMPANY
MIFUNÉ'S FIFTH COMPANY
GAARA'S FOURTH COMPANY
B
GAARA'S FOURTH COMPANY NEEDS TO RETREAT INTO A REVERSE L-FORMATION. THIS WILL LURE THE ENEMY FORWARD.

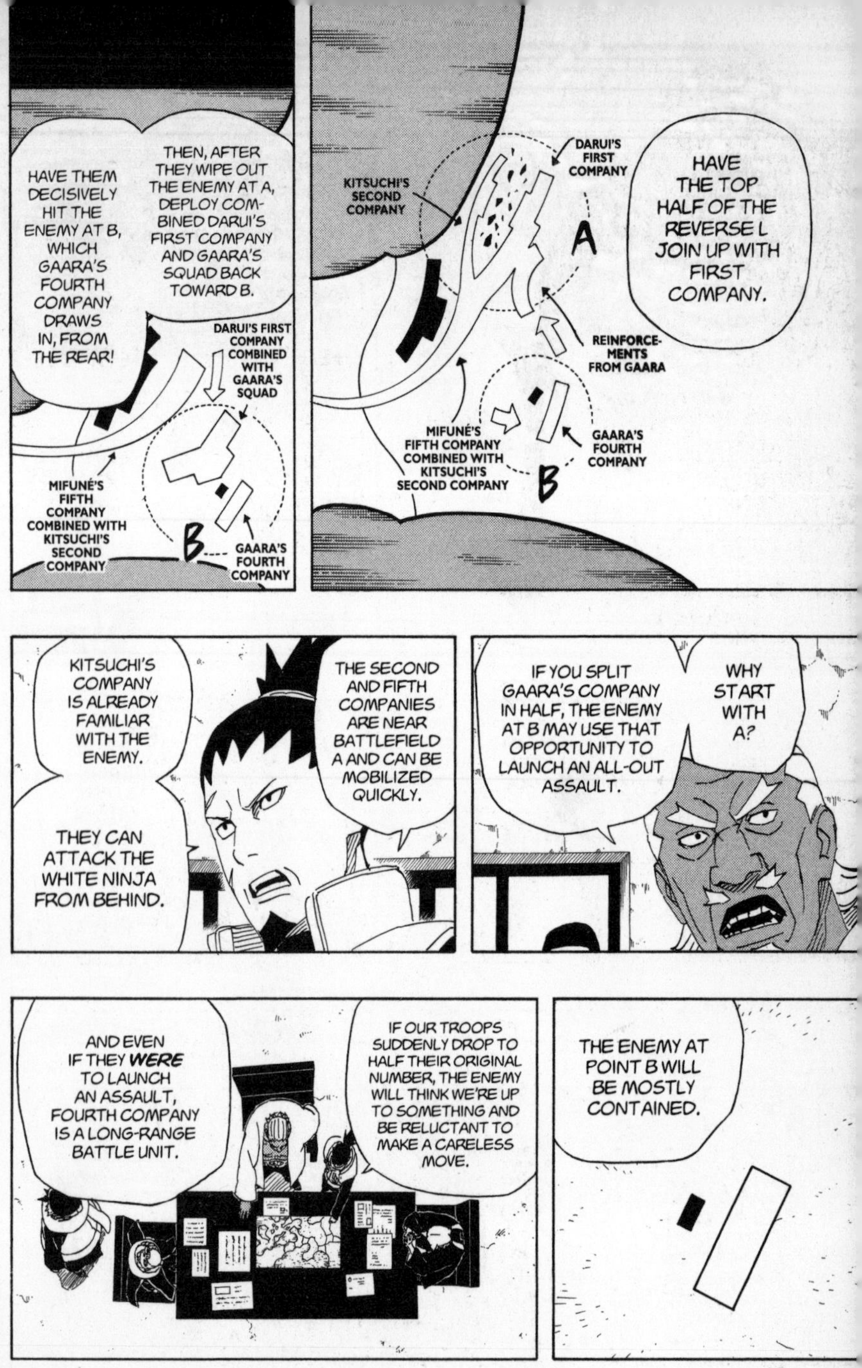
HAVE THE TOP HALF OF THE REVERSE L JOIN UP WITH FIRST COMPANY.
DARUI'S FIRST COMPANY
KITSUCHI'S SECOND COMPANY
A
REINFORCEMENTS FROM GAARA
GAARA'S FOURTH COMPANY
MIFUNÉ'S FIFTH COMPANY COMBINED WITH KITSUCHI'S SECOND COMPANY
B
THEN, AFTER THEY WIPE OUT THE ENEMY AT A, DEPLOY COMBINED DARUI'S FIRST COMPANY AND GAARA'S SQUAD BACK TOWARD B.
HAVE THEM DECISIVELY HIT THE ENEMY AT B, WHICH GAARA'S FOURTH COMPANY DRAWS IN, FROM THE REAR!
DARUI'S FIRST COMPANY COMBINED WITH GAARA'S SQUAD
MIFUNÉ'S FIFTH COMPANY COMBINED WITH KITSUCHI'S SECOND COMPANY
B
GAARA'S FOURTH COMPANY
WHY START WITH A?
IF YOU SPLIT GAARA'S COMPANY IN HALF, THE ENEMY AT B MAY USE THAT OPPORTUNITY TO LAUNCH AN ALL-OUT ASSAULT.
THE SECOND AND FIFTH COMPANIES ARE NEAR BATTLEFIELD A AND CAN BE MOBILIZED QUICKLY.
KITSUCHI'S COMPANY IS ALREADY FAMILIAR WITH THE ENEMY.
THEY CAN ATTACK THE WHITE NINJA FROM BEHIND.
THE ENEMY AT POINT B WILL BE MOSTLY CONTAINED.
IF OUR TROOPS SUDDENLY DROP TO HALF THEIR ORIGINAL NUMBER, THE ENEMY WILL THINK WE'RE UP TO SOMETHING AND BE RELUCTANT TO MAKE A CARELESS MOVE.
AND EVEN IF THEY *WERE* TO LAUNCH AN ASSAULT, FOURTH COMPANY IS A LONG-RANGE BATTLE UNIT.

READ THIS WAY

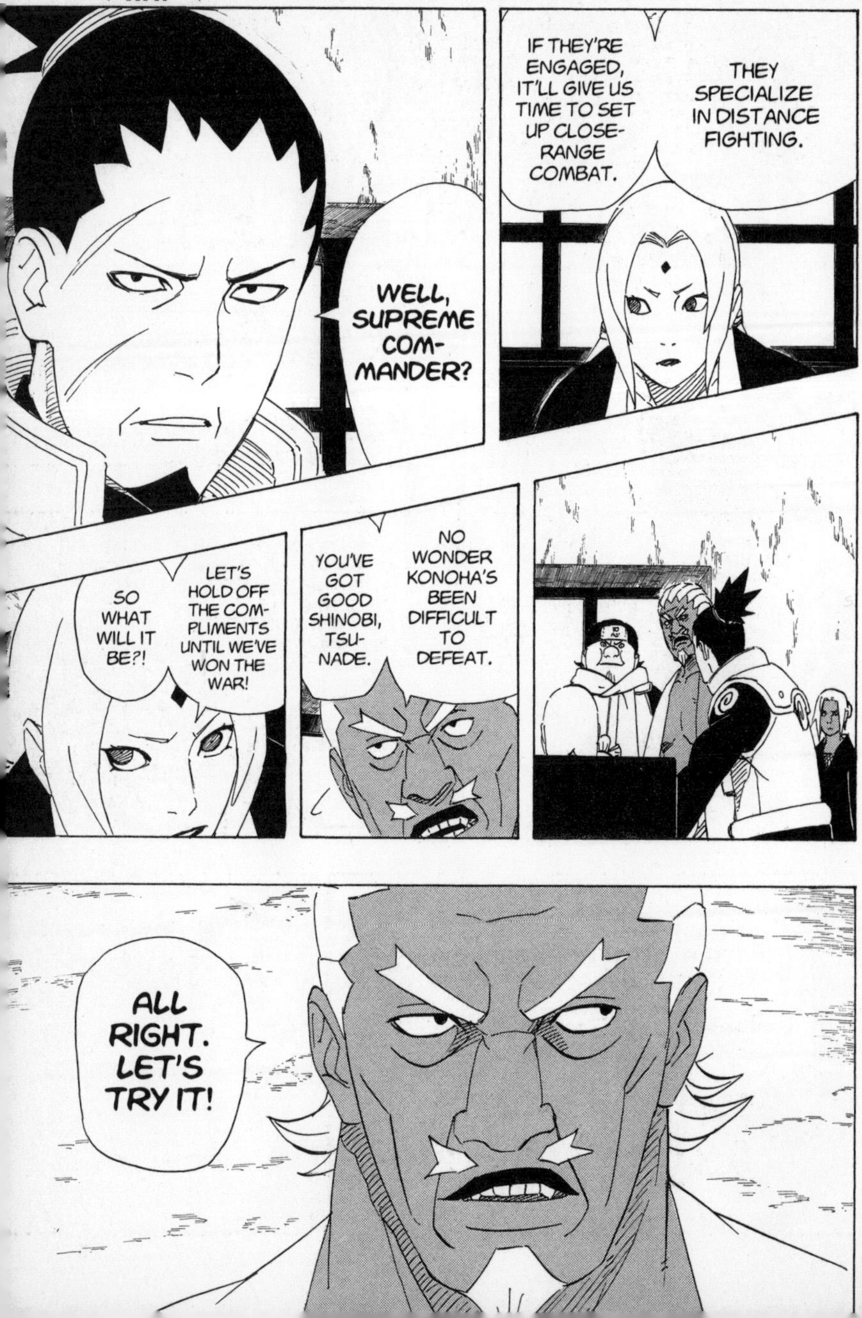
THEY SPECIALIZE IN DISTANCE FIGHTING.
IF THEY'RE ENGAGED, IT'LL GIVE US TIME TO SET UP CLOSE-RANGE COMBAT.
WELL, SUPREME COMMANDER?
NO WONDER KONOHA'S BEEN DIFFICULT TO DEFEAT.
YOU'VE GOT GOOD SHINOBI, TSUNADE.
LET'S HOLD OFF THE COMPLIMENTS UNTIL WE'VE WON THE WAR!
SO WHAT WILL IT BE?!
ALL RIGHT. LET'S TRY IT!

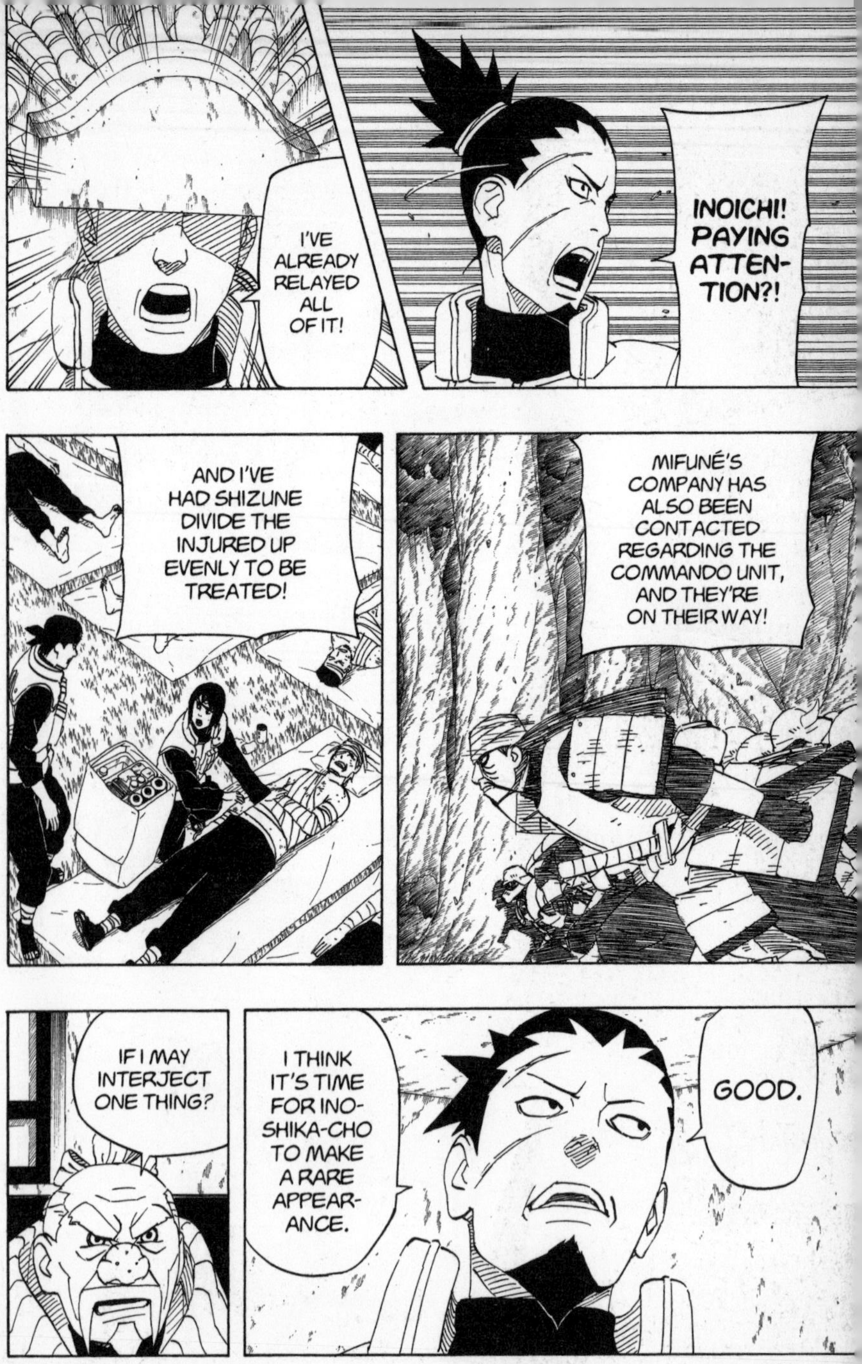
INOICHI! PAYING ATTENTION?!
I'VE ALREADY RELAYED ALL OF IT!
MIFUNÉ'S COMPANY HAS ALSO BEEN CONTACTED REGARDING THE COMMANDO UNIT, AND THEY'RE ON THEIR WAY!
AND I'VE HAD SHIZUNE DIVIDE THE INJURED UP EVENLY TO BE TREATED!
GOOD.
I THINK IT'S TIME FOR INO-SHIKA-CHO TO MAKE A RARE APPEARANCE.
IF I MAY INTERJECT ONE THING?

READ THIS WAY

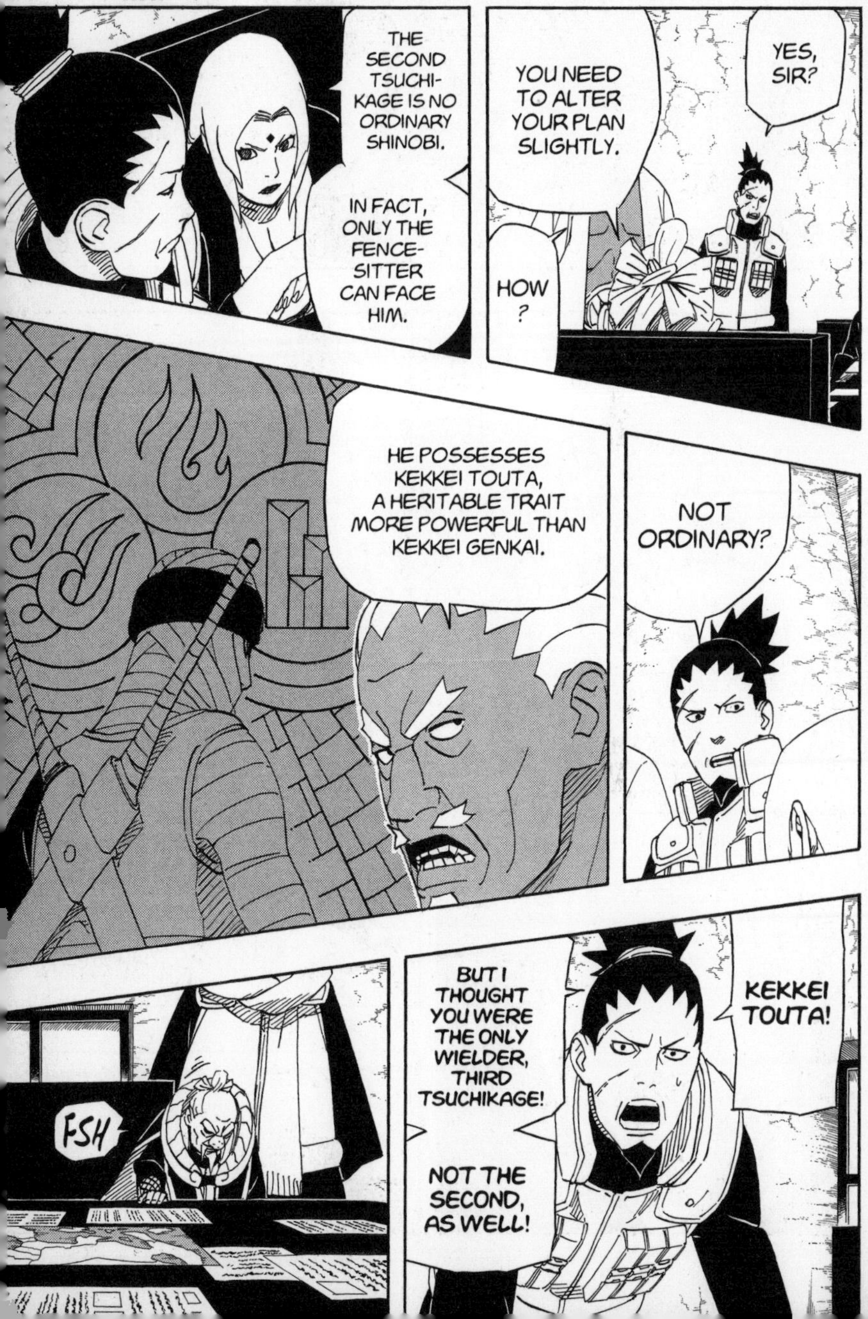
YES, SIR?
YOU NEED TO ALTER YOUR PLAN SLIGHTLY.
HOW?
THE SECOND TSUCHI-KAGE IS NO ORDINARY SHINOBI.
IN FACT, ONLY THE FENCE-SITTER CAN FACE HIM.
NOT ORDINARY?
HE POSSESSES KEKKEI TOUTA, A HERITABLE TRAIT MORE POWERFUL THAN KEKKEI GENKAI.
KEKKEI TOUTA!
BUT I THOUGHT YOU WERE THE ONLY WIELDER, THIRD TSUCHIKAGE!
NOT THE SECOND, AS WELL!
FSH

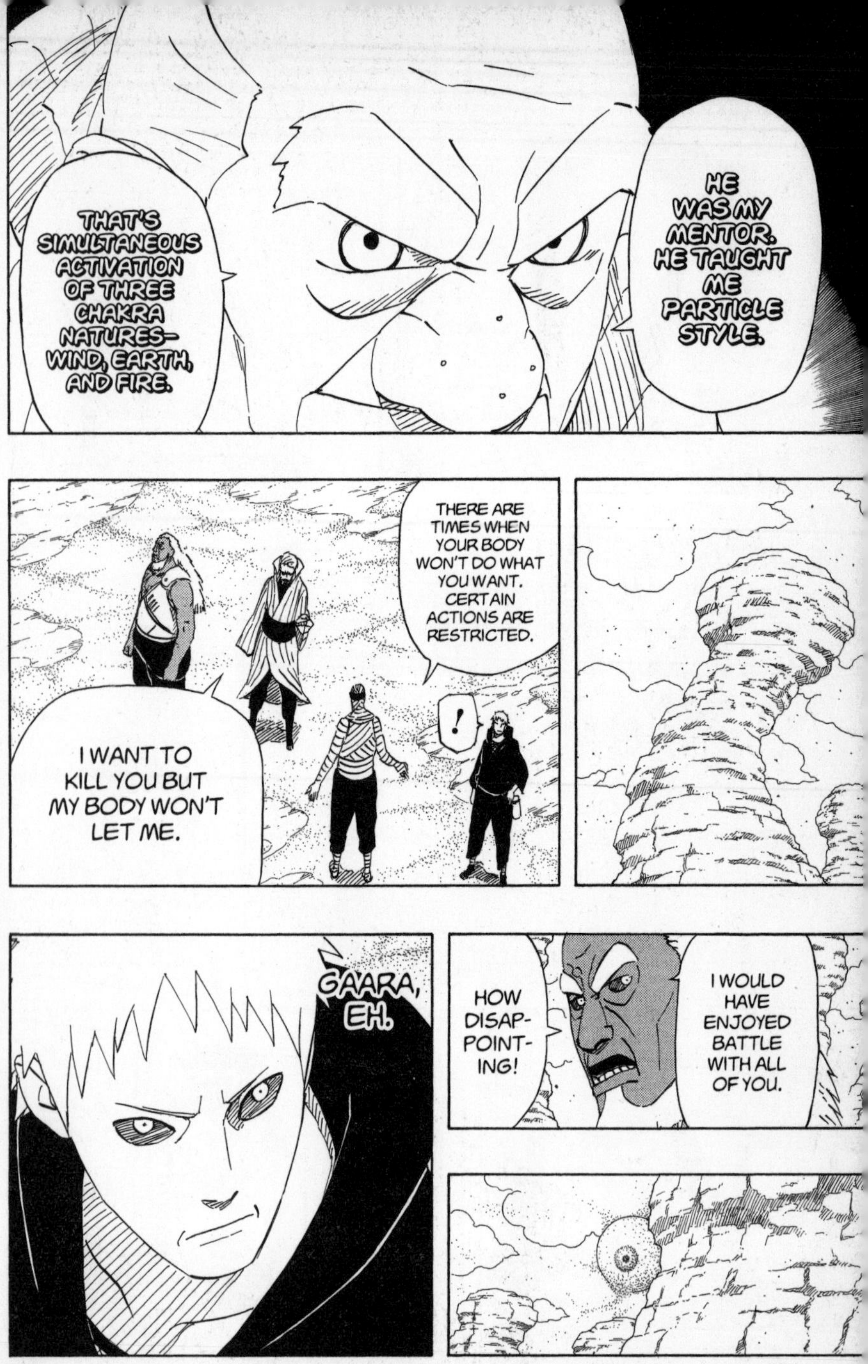
HE WAS MY MENTOR. HE TAUGHT ME PARTICLE STYLE.
THAT'S SIMULTANEOUS ACTIVATION OF THREE CHAKRA NATURES— WIND, EARTH, AND FIRE.
THERE ARE TIMES WHEN YOUR BODY WON'T DO WHAT YOU WANT. CERTAIN ACTIONS ARE RESTRICTED.
!
I WANT TO KILL YOU BUT MY BODY WON'T LET ME.
I WOULD HAVE ENJOYED BATTLE WITH ALL OF YOU.
HOW DISAP- POINT- ING!
GAARA, EH.

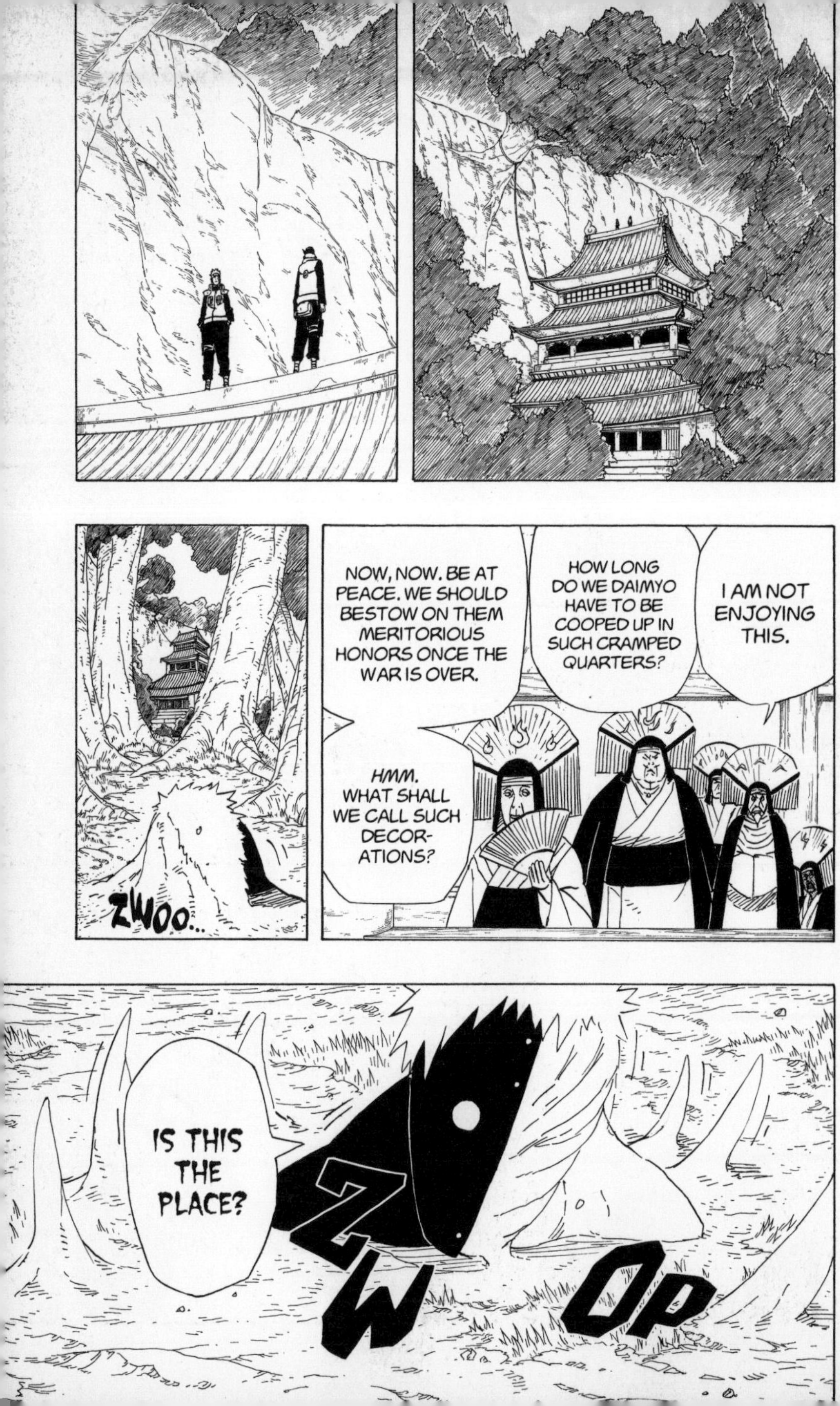
I AM NOT ENJOYING THIS.
HOW LONG DO WE DAIMYO HAVE TO BE COOPED UP IN SUCH CRAMPED QUARTERS?
NOW, NOW. BE AT PEACE. WE SHOULD BESTOW ON THEM MERITORIOUS HONORS ONCE THE WAR IS OVER.
HMM. WHAT SHALL WE CALL SUCH DECOR-ATIONS?
ZWOO...
IS THIS THE PLACE?
ZWOP

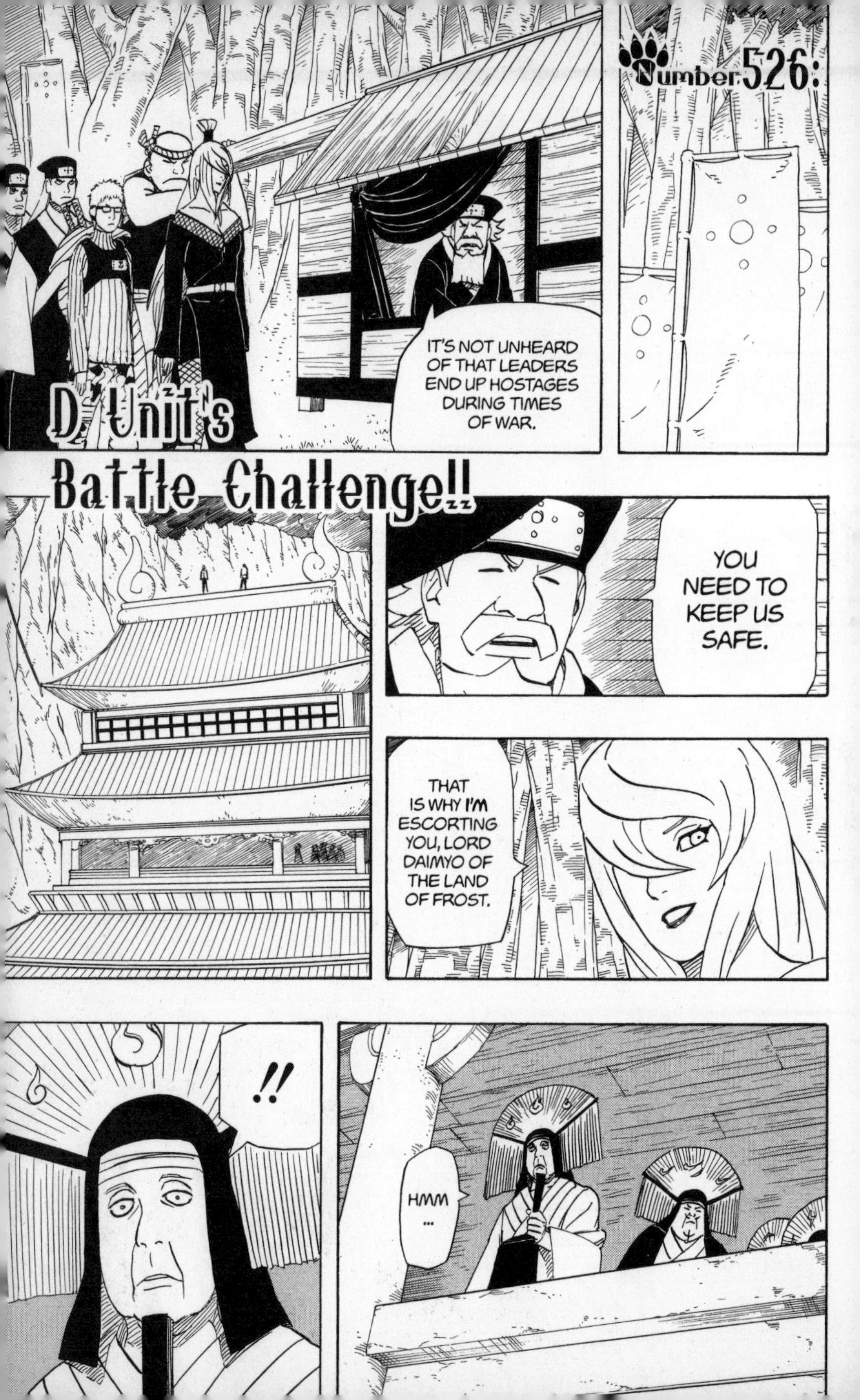
Number 526:
D Unit's Battle Challenge!!
IT'S NOT UNHEARD OF THAT LEADERS END UP HOSTAGES DURING TIMES OF WAR.
YOU NEED TO KEEP US SAFE.
THAT IS WHY I'M ESCORTING YOU, LORD DAIMYO OF THE LAND OF FROST.
HMM ...
!!

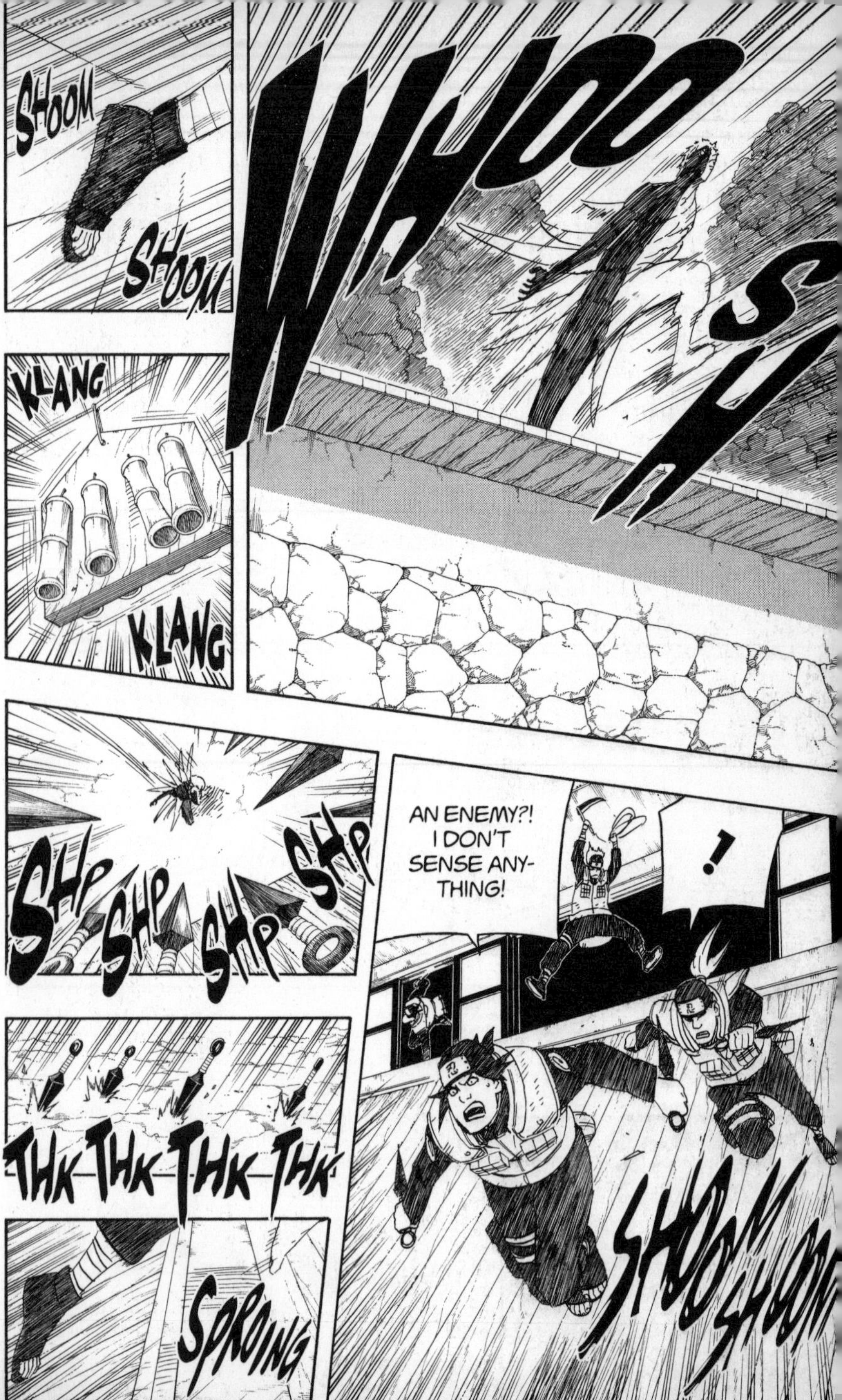
WHOOSH
SHOOM
SHOOM
KLANG
KLANG
!
AN ENEMY?! I DON'T SENSE ANY-THING!
SHOOM SHOOM
SHP SHP SHP SHP
THK THK THK THK
SPROING

READ THIS WAY

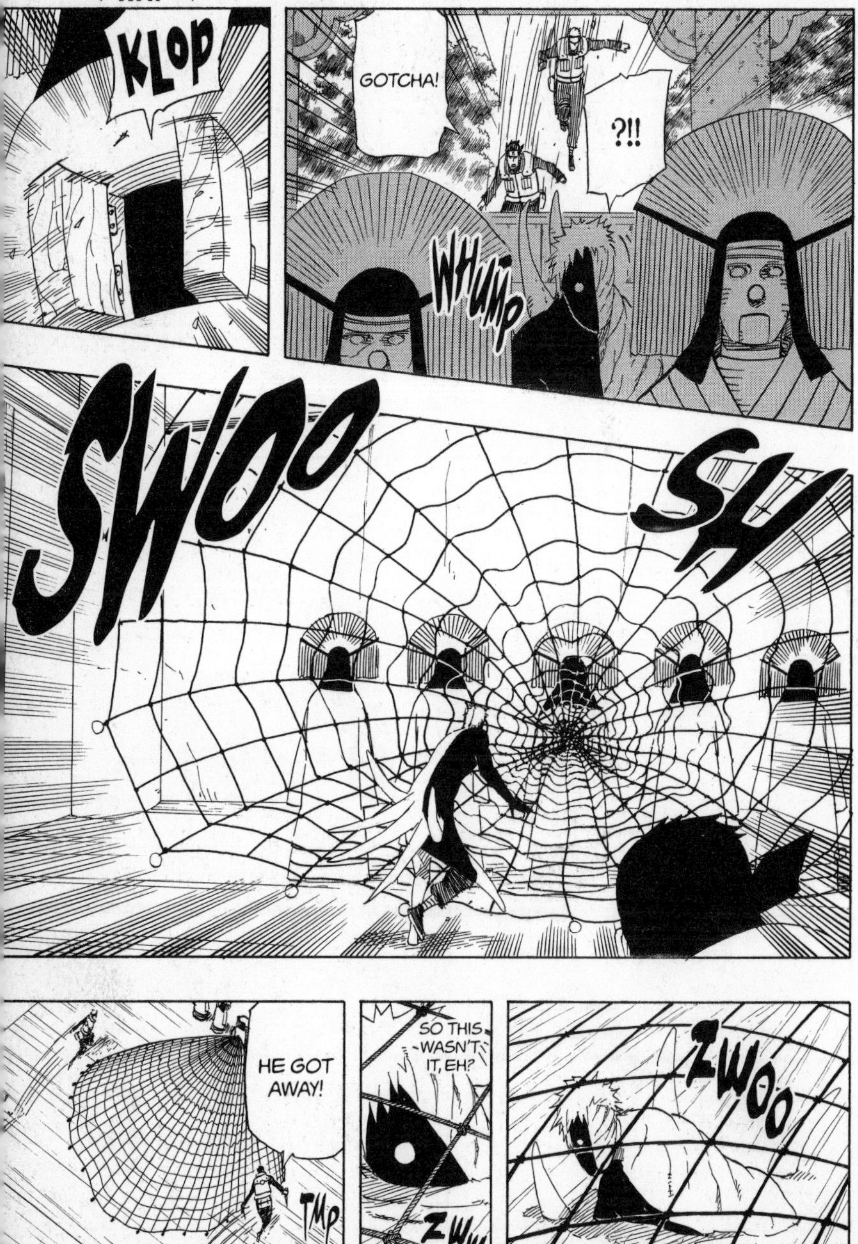
GOTCHA!
?!!
WHUMP
KLOP
SWOO
SH
ZWOO
SO THIS WASN'T IT, EH?
ZWW
HE GOT AWAY!
TMP

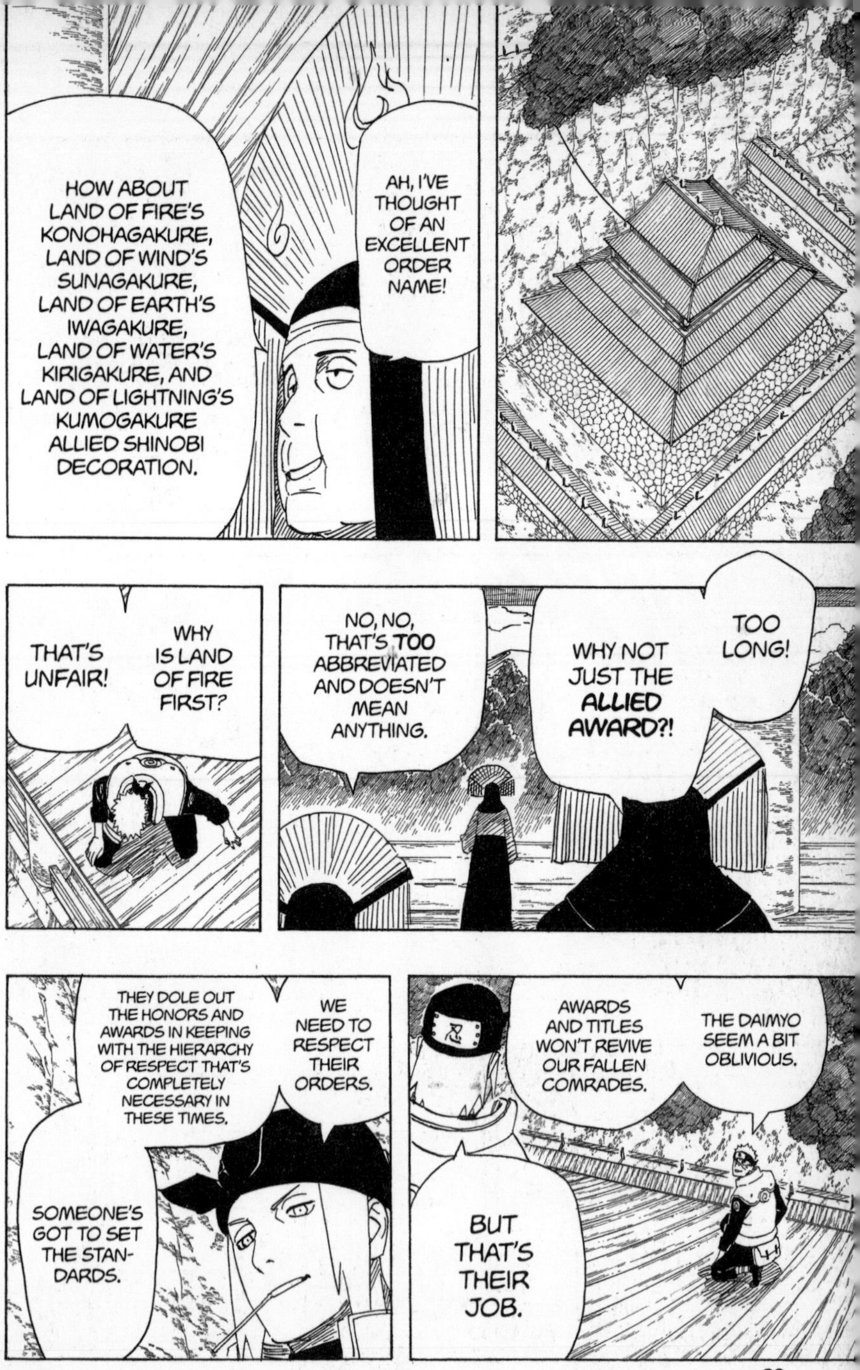
AH, I'VE THOUGHT OF AN EXCELLENT ORDER NAME!
HOW ABOUT LAND OF FIRE'S KONOHAGAKURE, LAND OF WIND'S SUNAGAKURE, LAND OF EARTH'S IWAGAKURE, LAND OF WATER'S KIRIGAKURE, AND LAND OF LIGHTNING'S KUMOGAKURE ALLIED SHINOBI DECORATION.
TOO LONG!
WHY NOT JUST THE ALLIED AWARD?!
NO, NO, THAT'S TOO ABBREVIATED AND DOESN'T MEAN ANYTHING.
WHY IS LAND OF FIRE FIRST?
THAT'S UNFAIR!
THE DAIMYO SEEM A BIT OBLIVIOUS.
AWARDS AND TITLES WON'T REVIVE OUR FALLEN COMRADES.
BUT THAT'S THEIR JOB.
WE NEED TO RESPECT THEIR ORDERS.
THEY DOLE OUT THE HONORS AND AWARDS IN KEEPING WITH THE HIERARCHY OF RESPECT THAT'S COMPLETELY NECESSARY IN THESE TIMES.
SOMEONE'S GOT TO SET THE STAN-DARDS.

READ THIS WAY

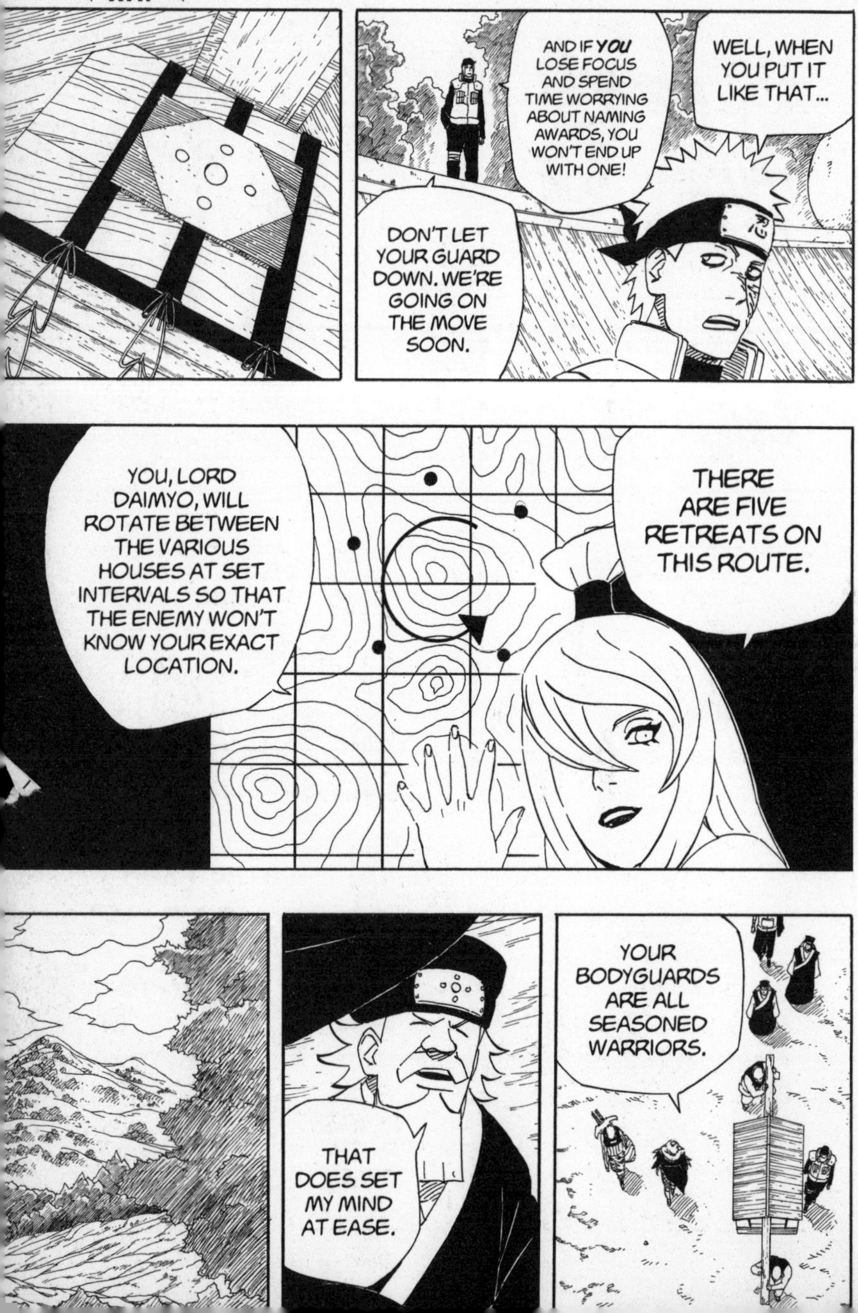
WELL, WHEN YOU PUT IT LIKE THAT...
AND IF *YOU* LOSE FOCUS AND SPEND TIME WORRYING ABOUT NAMING AWARDS, YOU WON'T END UP WITH ONE!
DON'T LET YOUR GUARD DOWN. WE'RE GOING ON THE MOVE SOON.
THERE ARE FIVE RETREATS ON THIS ROUTE.
YOU, LORD DAIMYO, WILL ROTATE BETWEEN THE VARIOUS HOUSES AT SET INTERVALS SO THAT THE ENEMY WON'T KNOW YOUR EXACT LOCATION.
YOUR BODYGUARDS ARE ALL SEASONED WARRIORS.
THAT DOES SET MY MIND AT EASE.

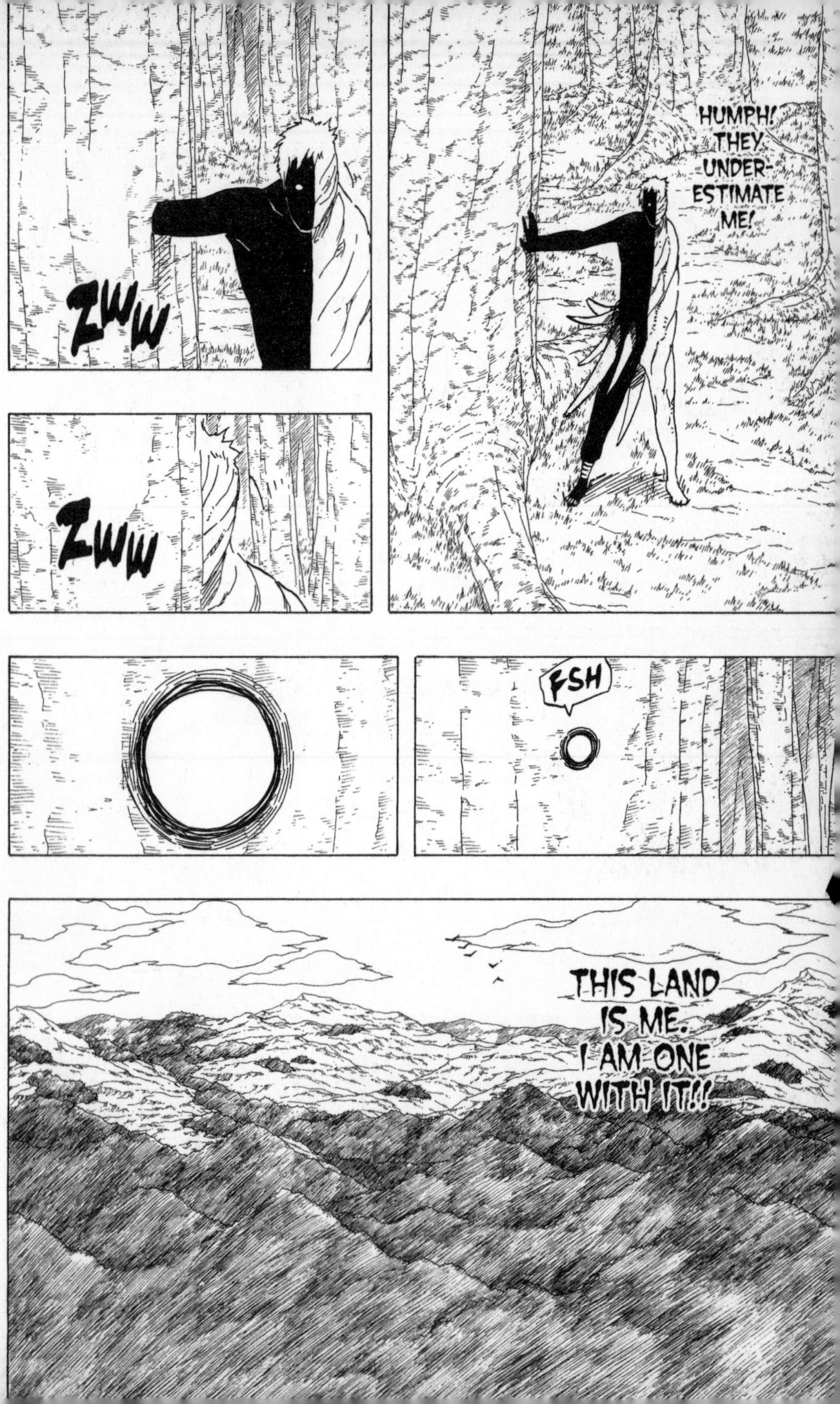
HUMPH! THEY UNDER-ESTIMATE ME!
ZWW
ZWW
FSH
THIS LAND IS ME. I AM ONE WITH IT!!

READ THIS WAY

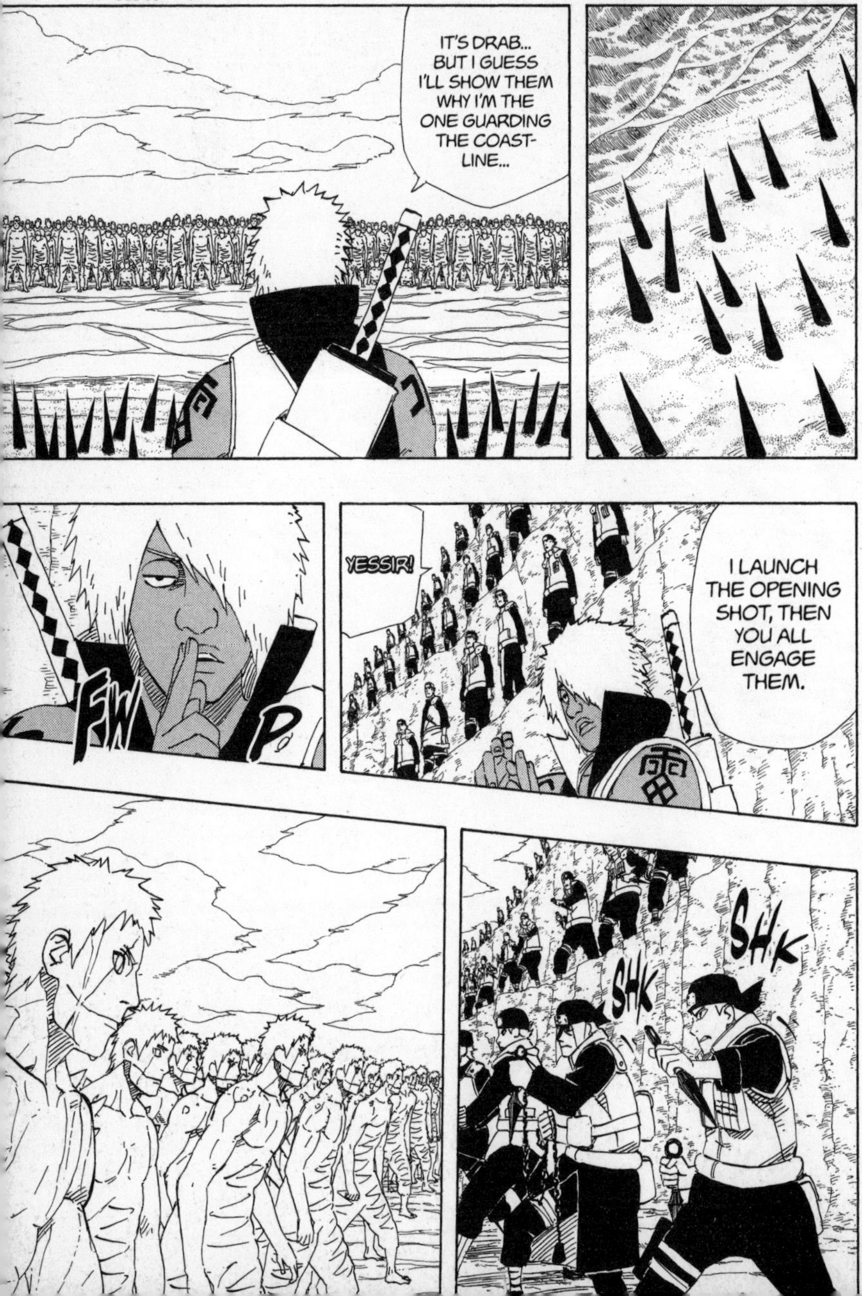
IT'S DRAB... BUT I GUESS I'LL SHOW THEM WHY I'M THE ONE GUARDING THE COAST-LINE...
I LAUNCH THE OPENING SHOT, THEN YOU ALL ENGAGE THEM.
YESSIR!
FWP
SHK
SHK

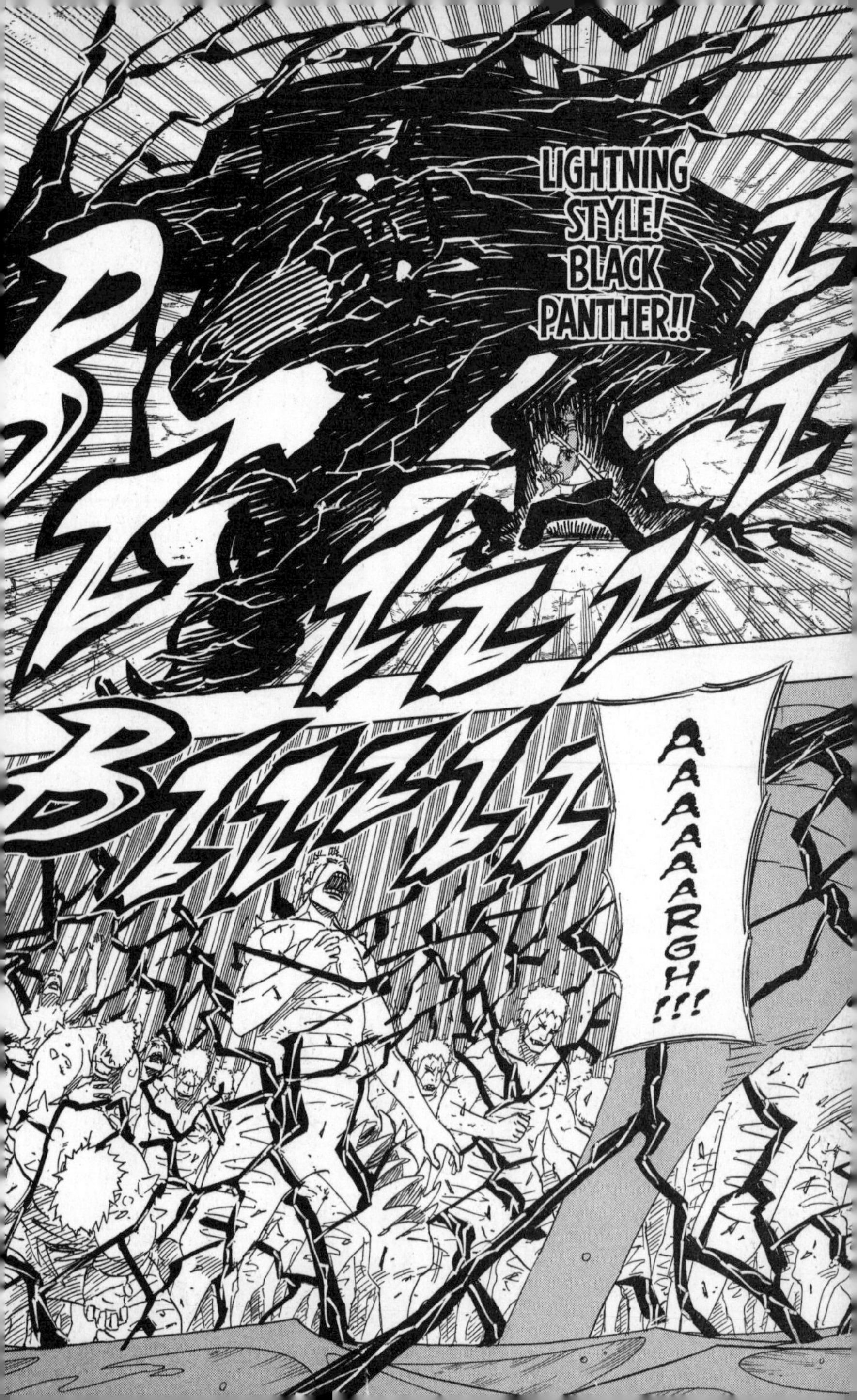
LIGHTNING STYLE! BLACK PANTHER!!
AAAAAARGH!!!

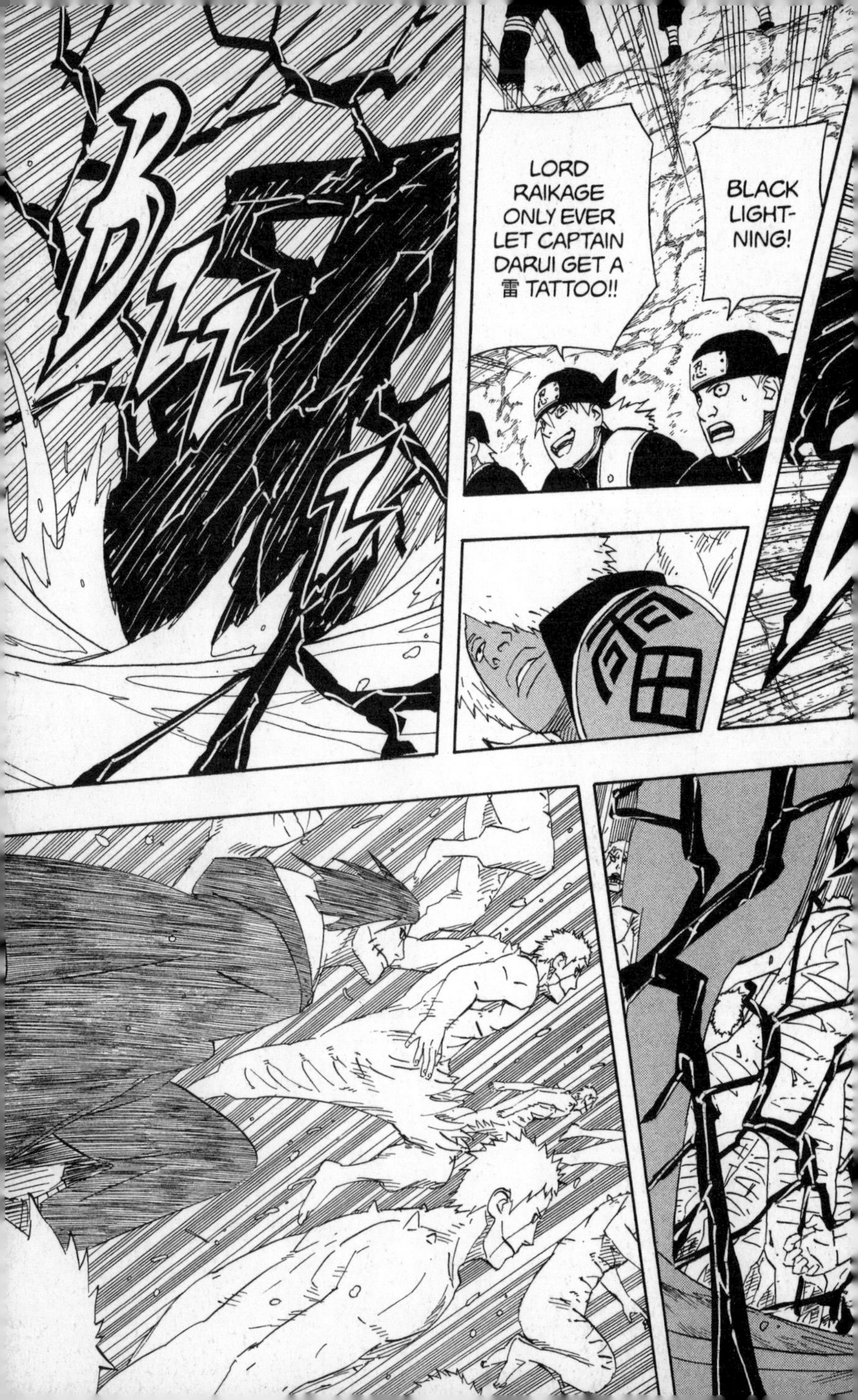
BLACK LIGHTNING!
LORD RAIKAGE ONLY EVER LET CAPTAIN DARUI GET A 雷 TATTOO!!

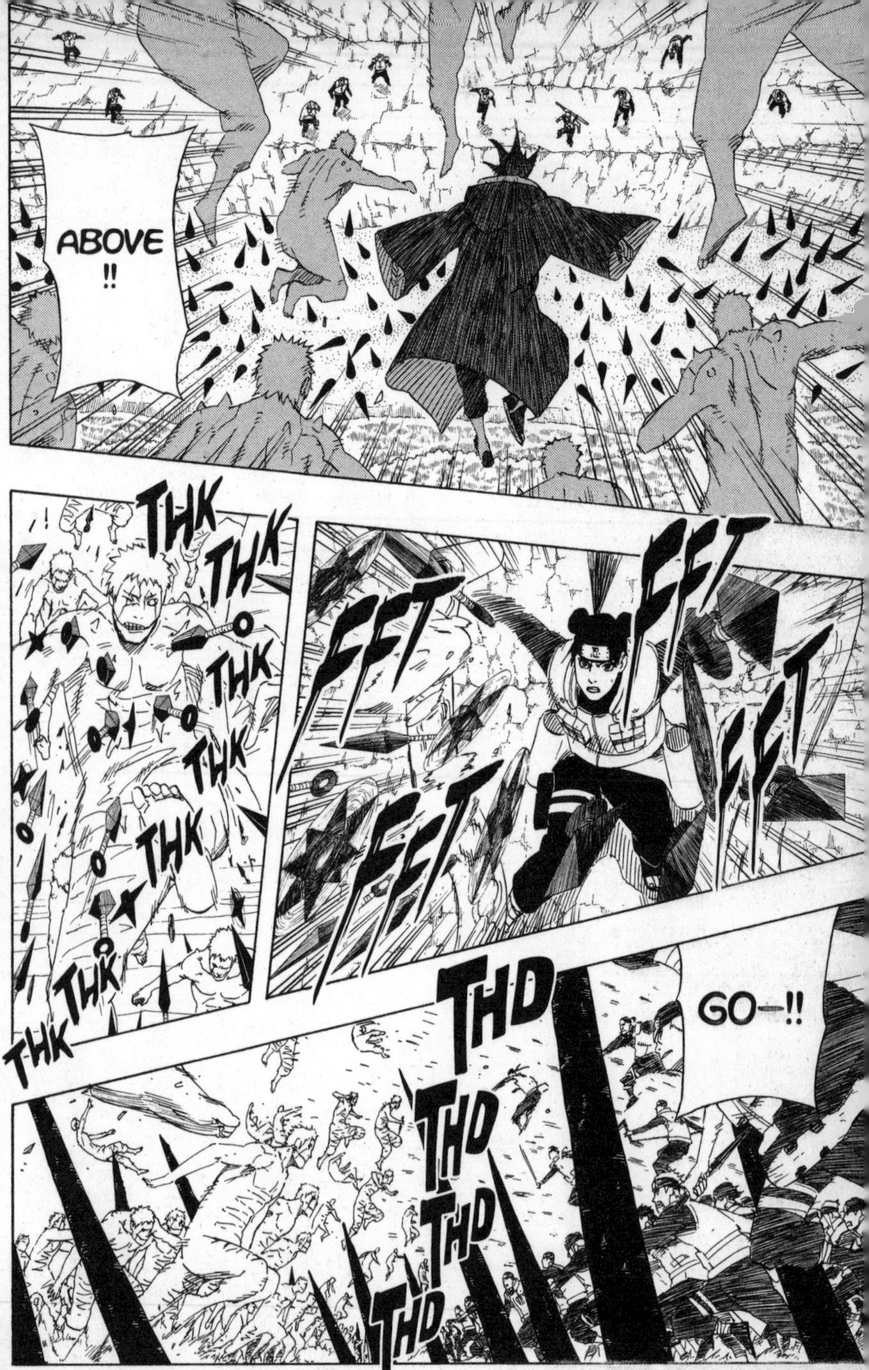
ABOVE !!
FFT
FFT
FFT
FFT
THK
THK
THK
THK
THK
THK
THK
GO—!!
THD
THD
THD
THD

READ THIS WAY

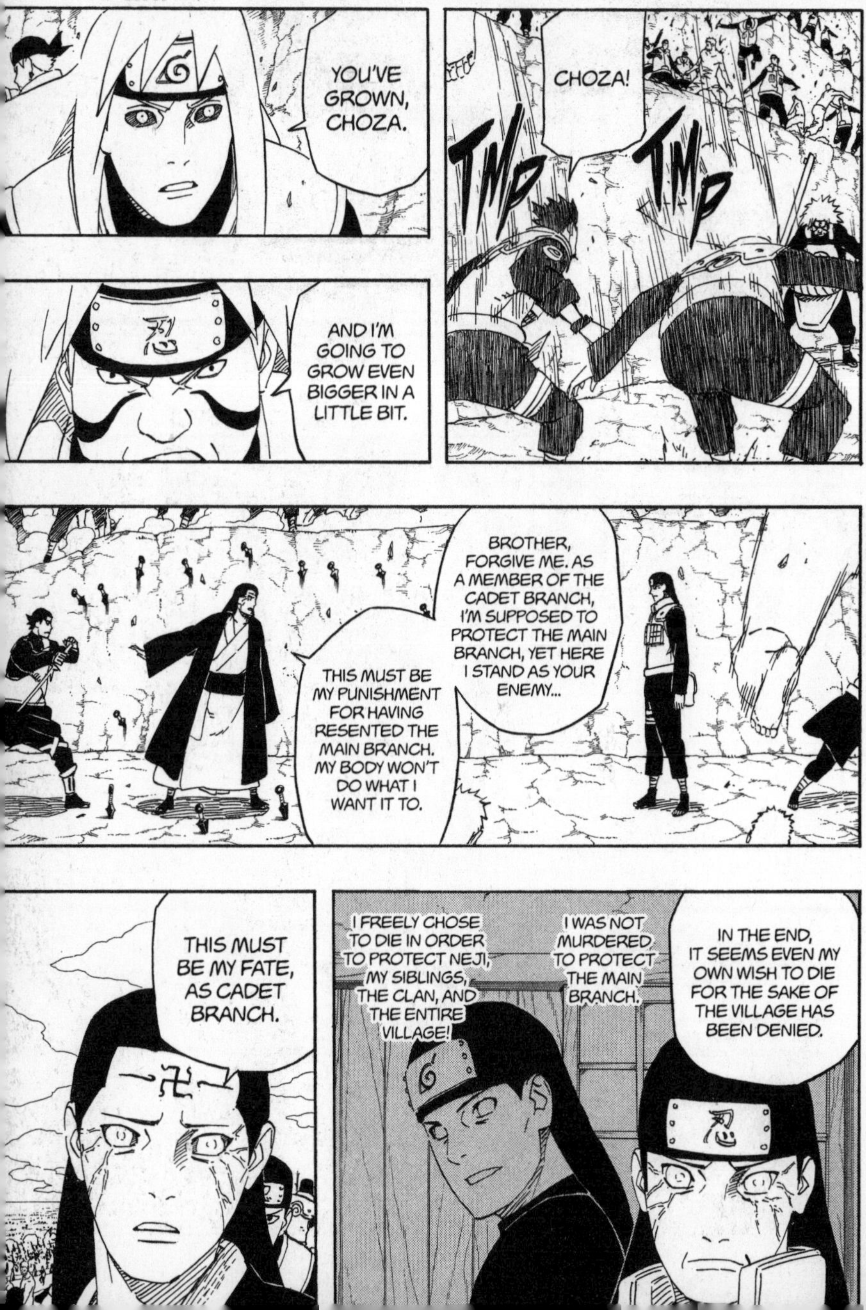
CHOZA!
TMP
TMP
YOU'VE GROWN, CHOZA.
AND I'M GOING TO GROW EVEN BIGGER IN A LITTLE BIT.
BROTHER, FORGIVE ME. AS A MEMBER OF THE CADET BRANCH, I'M SUPPOSED TO PROTECT THE MAIN BRANCH, YET HERE I STAND AS YOUR ENEMY...
THIS MUST BE MY PUNISHMENT FOR HAVING RESENTED THE MAIN BRANCH. MY BODY WON'T DO WHAT I WANT IT TO.
IN THE END, IT SEEMS EVEN MY OWN WISH TO DIE FOR THE SAKE OF THE VILLAGE HAS BEEN DENIED.
I WAS NOT MURDERED TO PROTECT THE MAIN BRANCH.
I FREELY CHOSE TO DIE IN ORDER TO PROTECT NEJI, MY SIBLINGS, THE CLAN, AND THE ENTIRE VILLAGE!
THIS MUST BE MY FATE, AS CADET BRANCH.

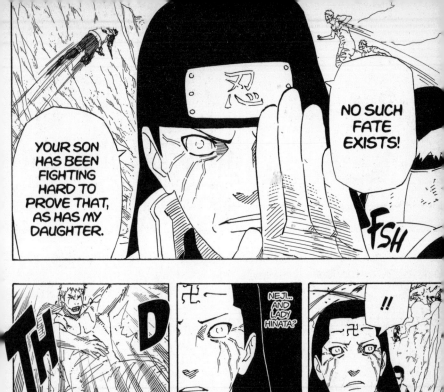

NO SUCH FATE EXISTS!
FSH
YOUR SON HAS BEEN FIGHTING HARD TO PROVE THAT, AS HAS MY DAUGHTER.
!!
NEJI... AND LADY HINATA?
THD
ARE YOU ALL RIGHT, COUSIN NEJI?!
YEAH... SORRY, HINATA!
HUF
HUF
G-G-
BAM
TODAY, THE CADET BRANCH DOES NOT LIVE TO SERVE AND PROTECT THE BLOOD OF THE MAIN BRANCH.
THEY STAND SIDE-BY-SIDE AS EQUALS AND PROTECT EACH OTHER!

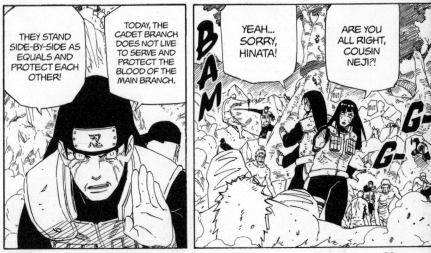

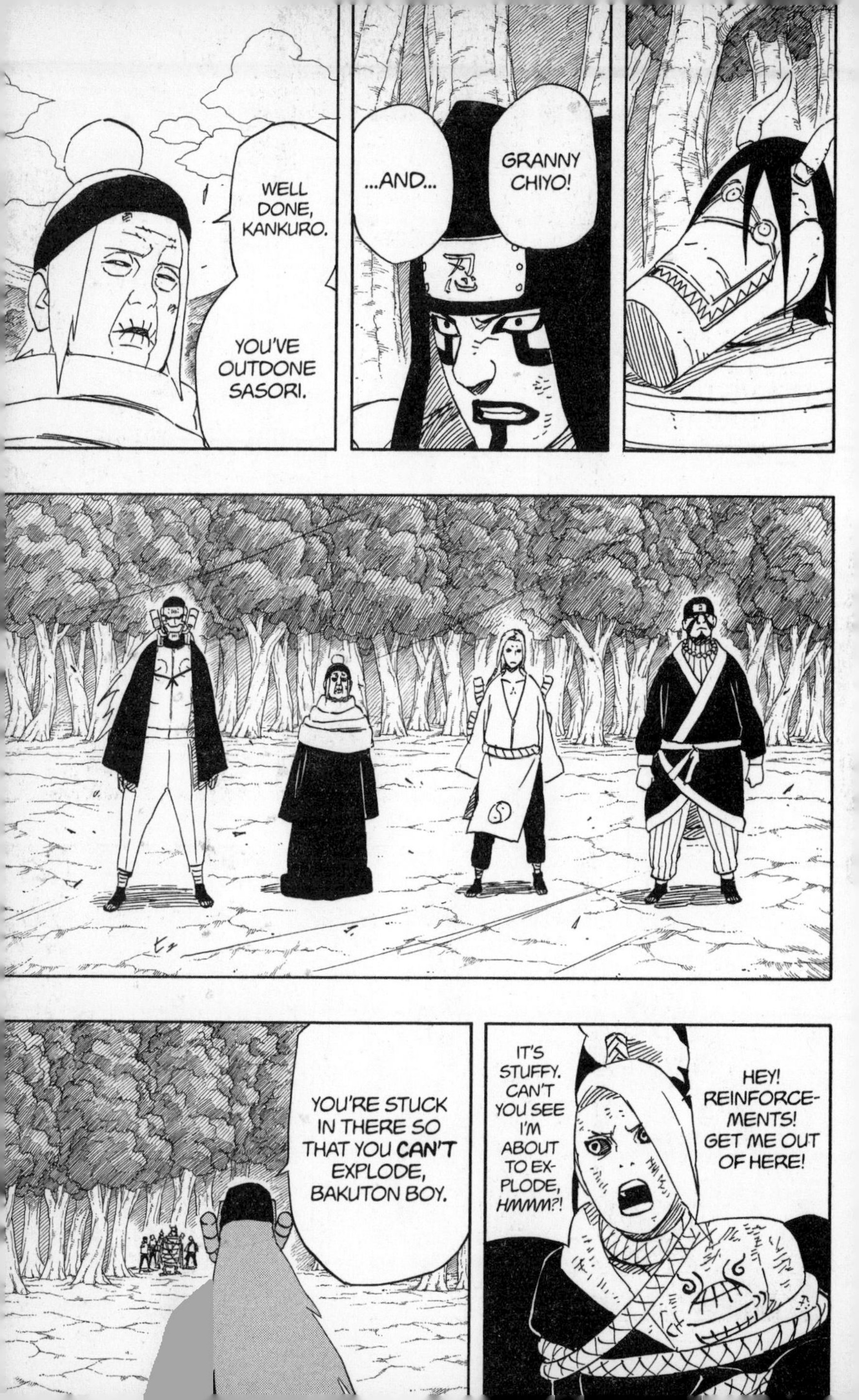
...AND...
GRANNY CHIYO!
WELL DONE, KANKURO.
YOU'VE OUTDONE SASORI.
HEY! REINFORCE-MENTS! GET ME OUT OF HERE!
IT'S STUFFY. CAN'T YOU SEE I'M ABOUT TO EX-PLODE, HMMM?!
YOU'RE STUCK IN THERE SO THAT YOU **CAN'T** EXPLODE, BAKUTON BOY.

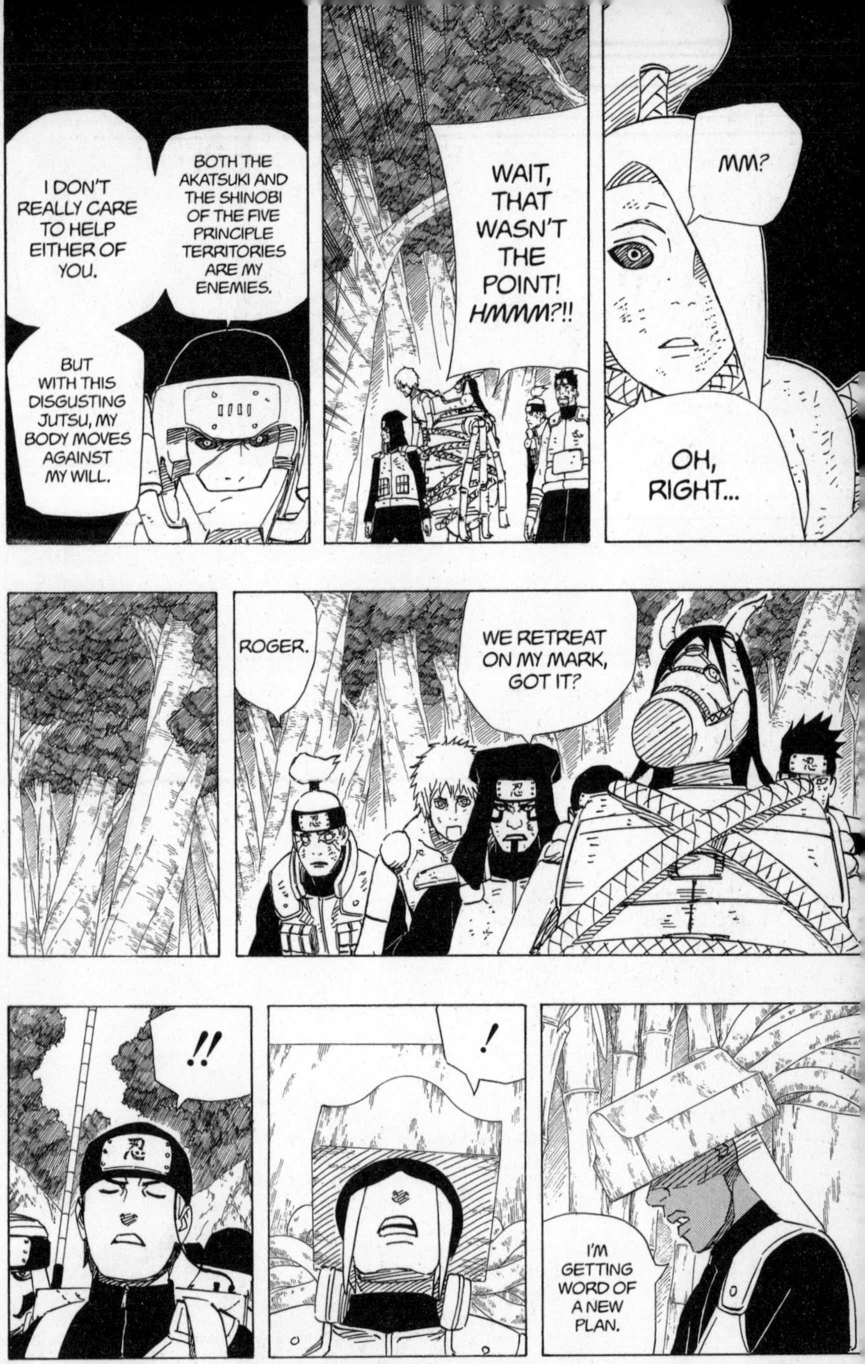
MM?
OH, RIGHT...
WAIT, THAT WASN'T THE POINT! HMMM?!!
BOTH THE AKATSUKI AND THE SHINOBI OF THE FIVE PRINCIPLE TERRITORIES ARE MY ENEMIES.
I DON'T REALLY CARE TO HELP EITHER OF YOU.
BUT WITH THIS DISGUSTING JUTSU, MY BODY MOVES AGAINST MY WILL.
WE RETREAT ON MY MARK, GOT IT?
ROGER.
I'M GETTING WORD OF A NEW PLAN.
!
!!

READ THIS WAY

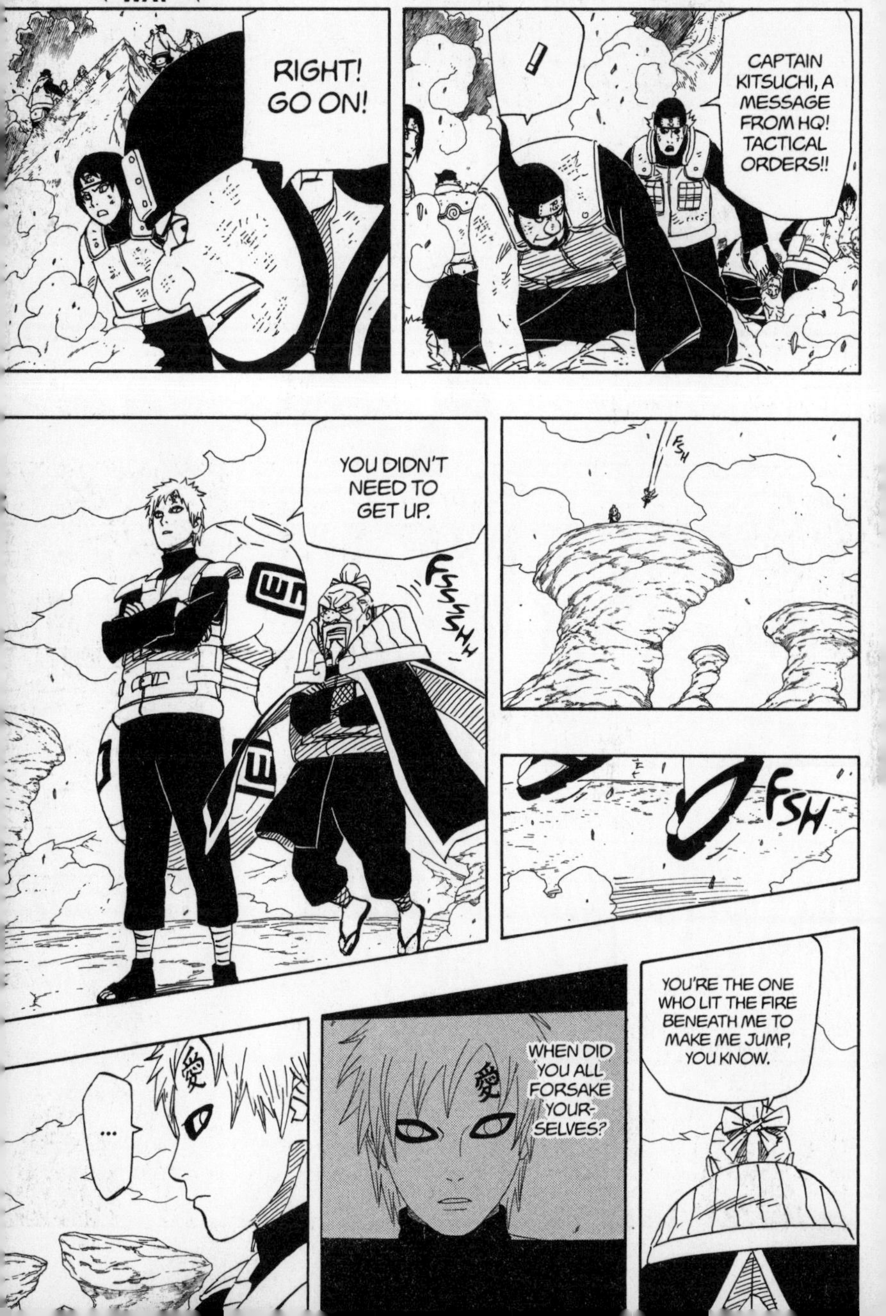
CAPTAIN KITSUCHI, A MESSAGE FROM HQ! TACTICAL ORDERS!!
!
RIGHT! GO ON!
FSH
FSH
YOU DIDN'T NEED TO GET UP.
FSSSHH
YOU'RE THE ONE WHO LIT THE FIRE BENEATH ME TO MAKE ME JUMP, YOU KNOW.
WHEN DID YOU ALL FORSAKE YOUR-SELVES?
...

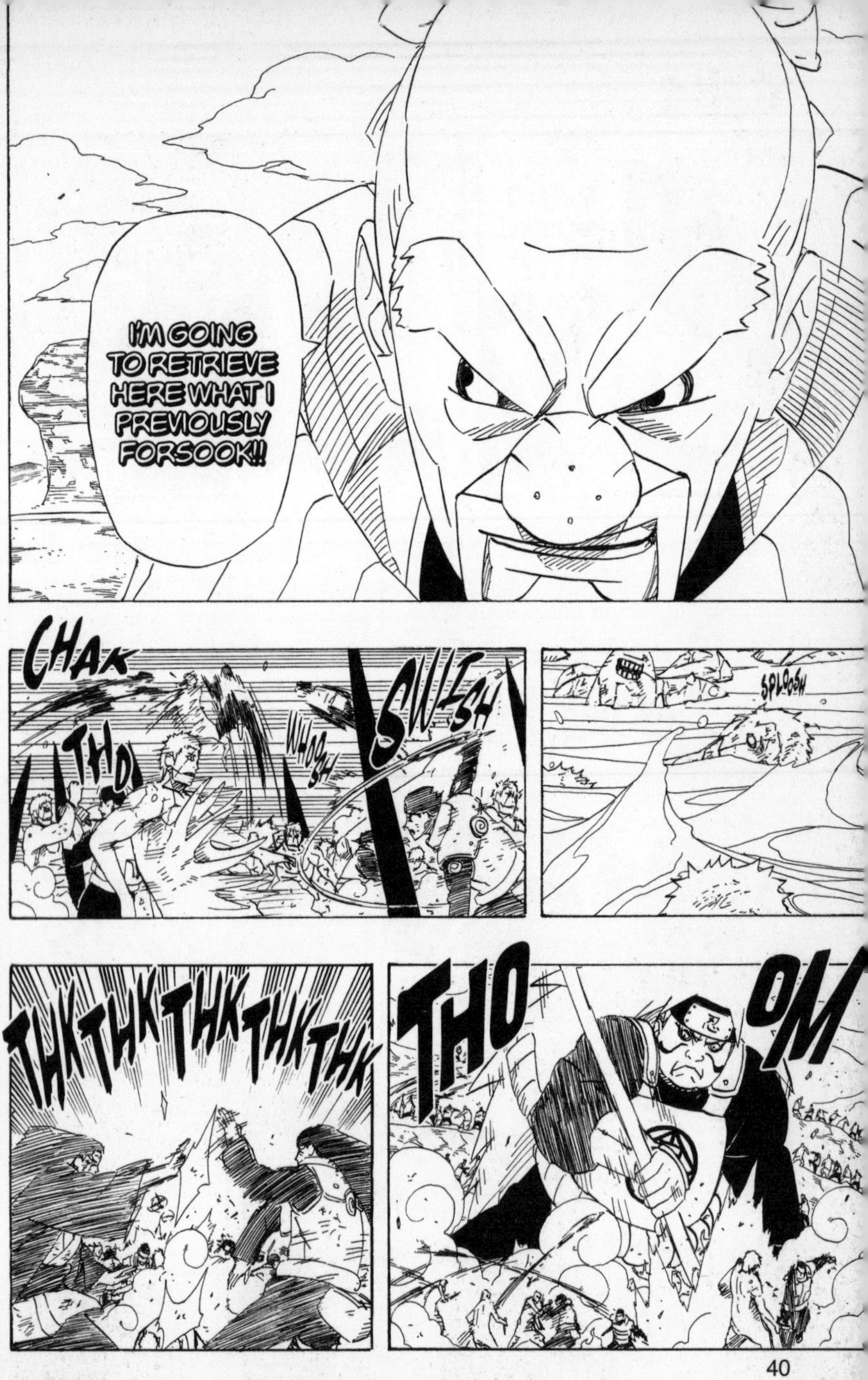
I'M GOING TO RETRIEVE HERE WHAT I PREVIOUSLY FORSOOK!!
SPLOOSH
SWISH
WHOOSH
CHAK
THD
THOOM
THKTHKTHKTHKTHK

READ THIS WAY

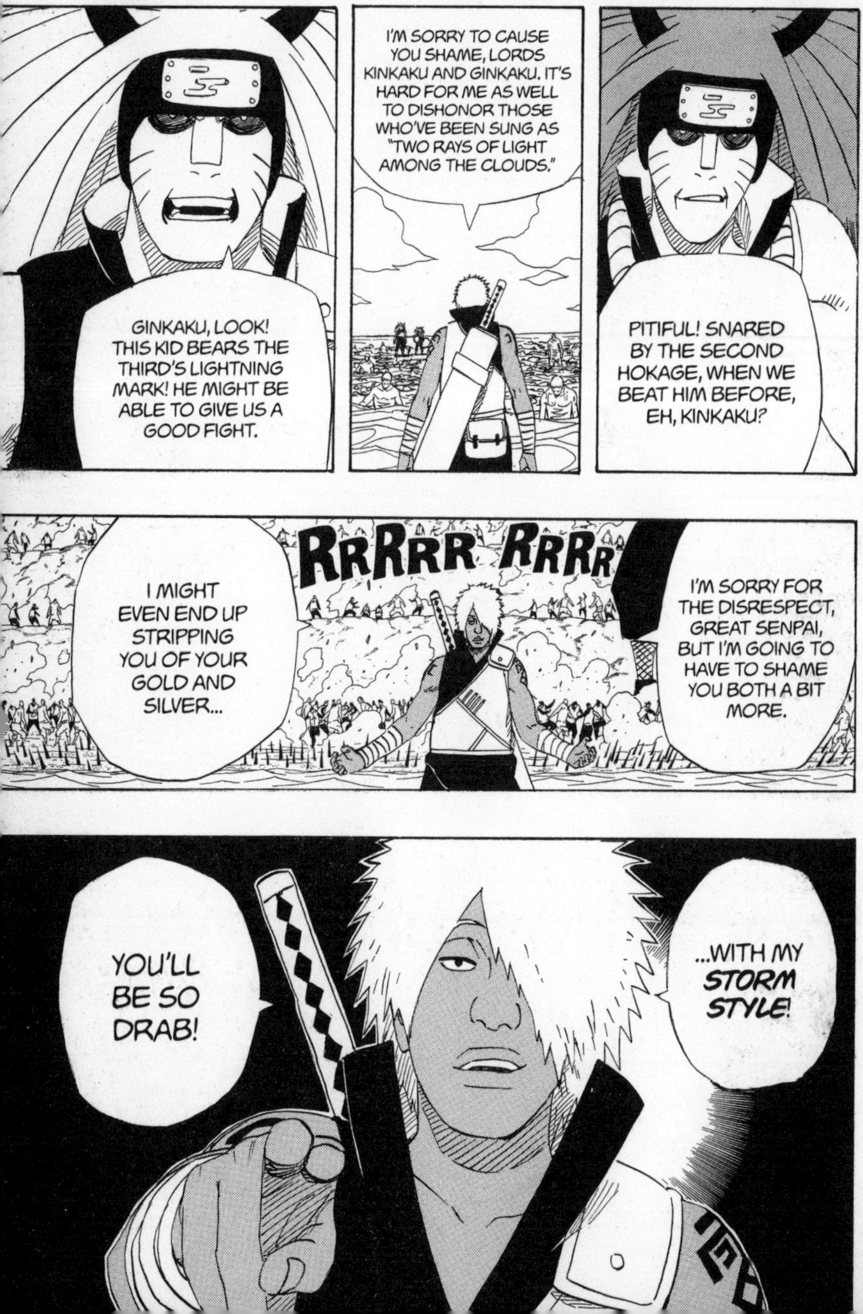
PITIFUL! SNARED BY THE SECOND HOKAGE, WHEN WE BEAT HIM BEFORE, EH, KINKAKU?
I'M SORRY TO CAUSE YOU SHAME, LORDS KINKAKU AND GINKAKU. IT'S HARD FOR ME AS WELL TO DISHONOR THOSE WHO'VE BEEN SUNG AS "TWO RAYS OF LIGHT AMONG THE CLOUDS."
GINKAKU, LOOK! THIS KID BEARS THE THIRD'S LIGHTNING MARK! HE MIGHT BE ABLE TO GIVE US A GOOD FIGHT.
I'M SORRY FOR THE DISRESPECT, GREAT SENPAI, BUT I'M GOING TO HAVE TO SHAME YOU BOTH A BIT MORE.
RRRRR RRRR
I MIGHT EVEN END UP STRIPPING YOU OF YOUR GOLD AND SILVER...
...WITH MY STORM STYLE!
YOU'LL BE SO DRAB!

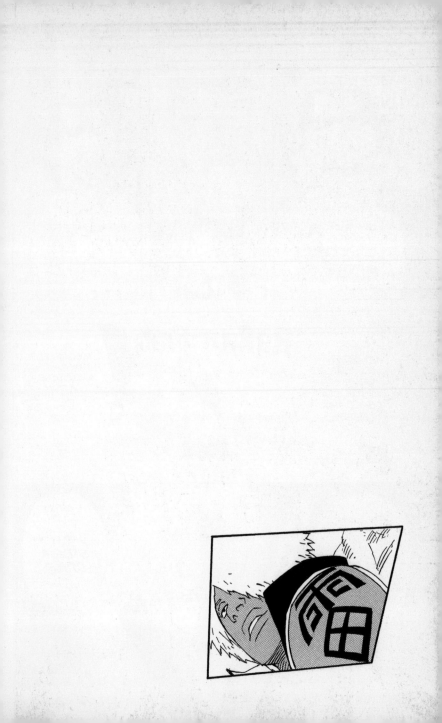

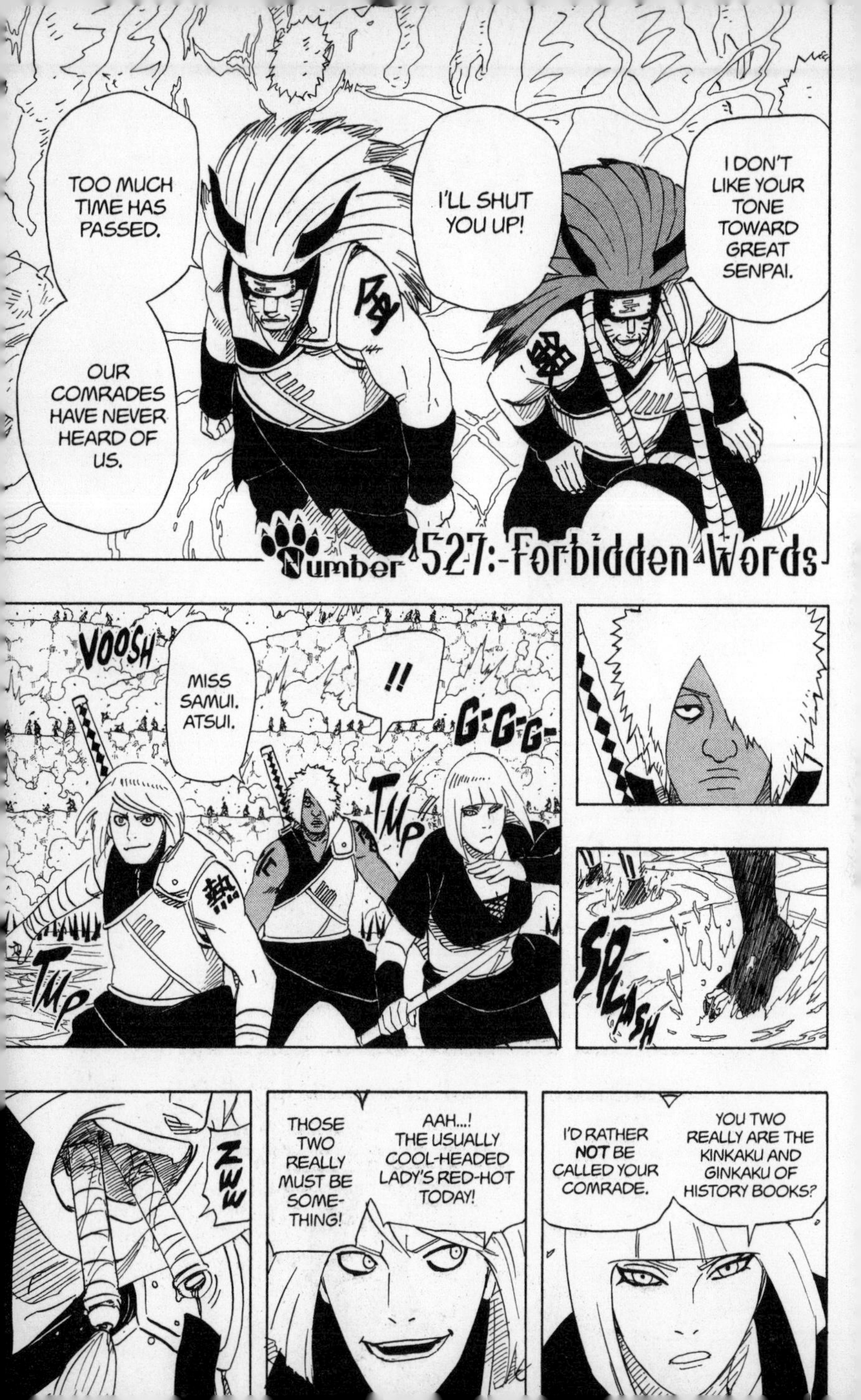
I DON'T LIKE YOUR TONE TOWARD GREAT SENPAI.
I'LL SHUT YOU UP!
TOO MUCH TIME HAS PASSED.
OUR COMRADES HAVE NEVER HEARD OF US.
Number 527: Forbidden Words
SPLASH
!!
G-G-G-
MISS SAMUI. ATSUI.
VOOSH
TMP
TMP
YOU TWO REALLY ARE THE KINKAKU AND GINKAKU OF HISTORY BOOKS?
I'D RATHER NOT BE CALLED YOUR COMRADE.
AAH...! THE USUALLY COOL-HEADED LADY'S RED-HOT TODAY!
THOSE TWO REALLY MUST BE SOME-THING!
ZWW

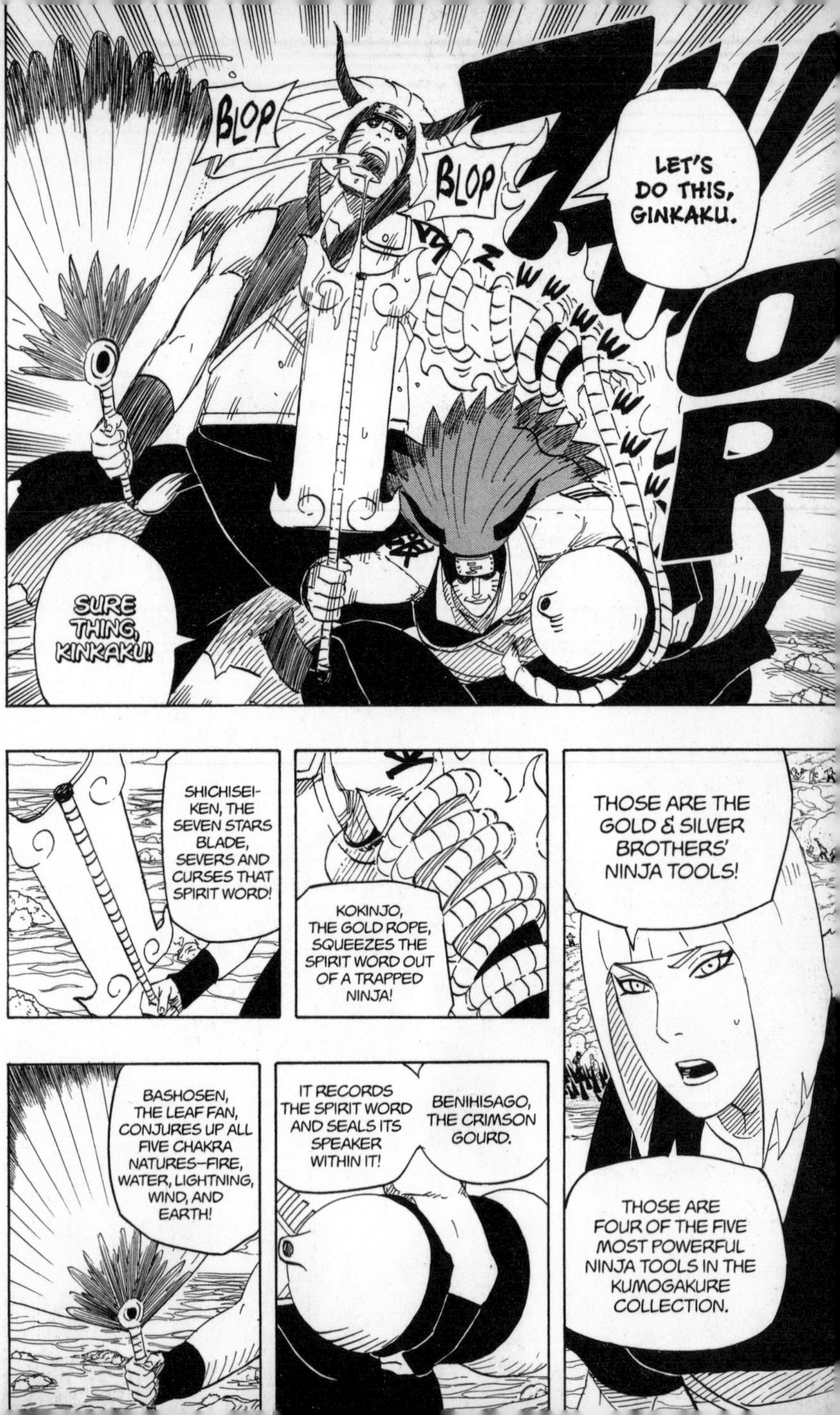

LET'S DO THIS, GINKAKU.
BLOP
BLOP
ZWWWWWWWWW
SURE THING, KINKAKU!
THOSE ARE THE GOLD & SILVER BROTHERS' NINJA TOOLS!
THOSE ARE FOUR OF THE FIVE MOST POWERFUL NINJA TOOLS IN THE KUMOGAKURE COLLECTION.
KOKINJO, THE GOLD ROPE, SQUEEZES THE SPIRIT WORD OUT OF A TRAPPED NINJA!
SHICHISEI-KEN, THE SEVEN STARS BLADE, SEVERS AND CURSES THAT SPIRIT WORD!
BENIHISAGO, THE CRIMSON GOURD.
IT RECORDS THE SPIRIT WORD AND SEALS ITS SPEAKER WITHIN IT!
BASHOSEN, THE LEAF FAN, CONJURES UP ALL FIVE CHAKRA NATURES–FIRE, WATER, LIGHTNING, WIND, AND EARTH!

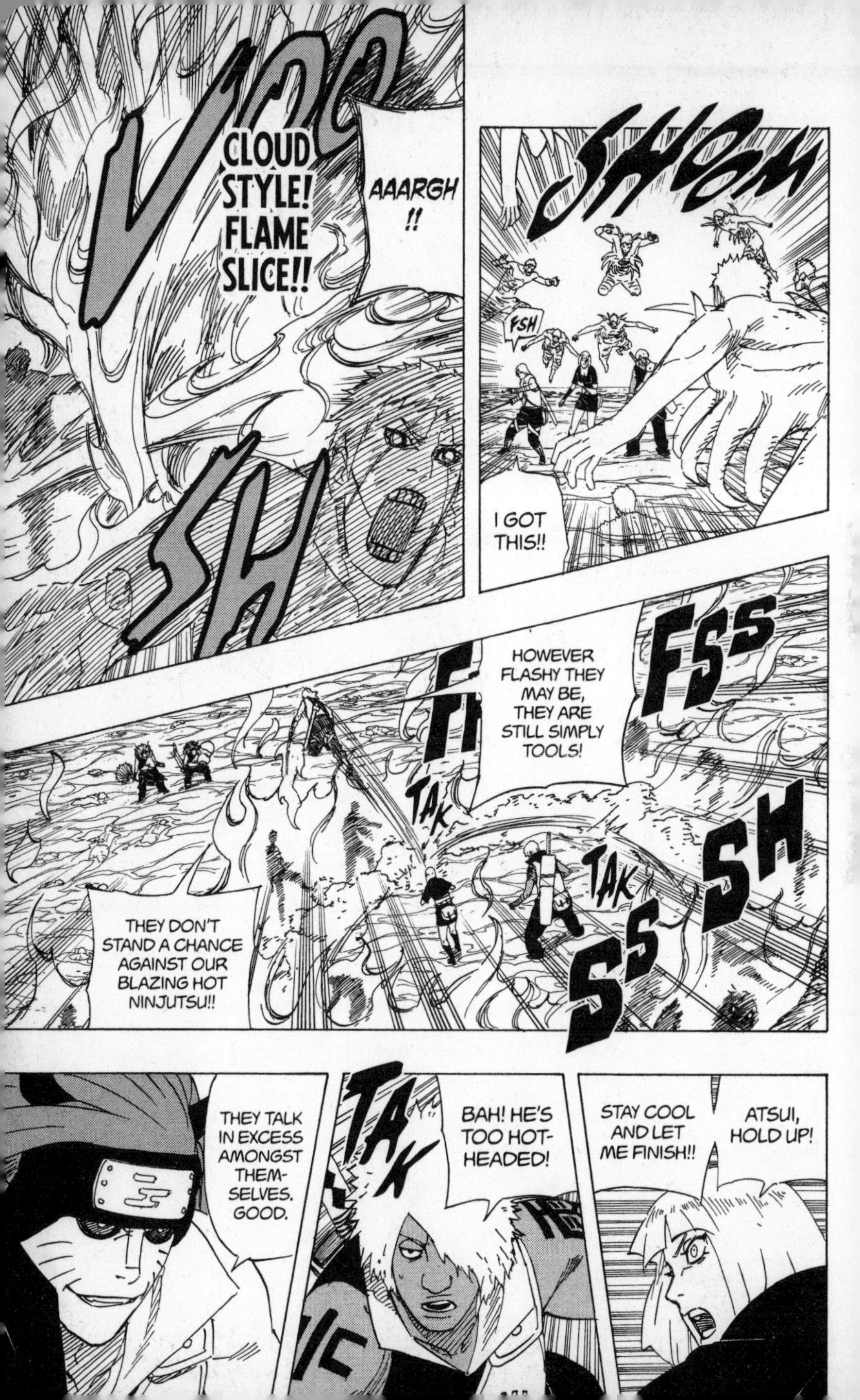
FSH
I GOT THIS!!
AAARGH!!
CLOUD STYLE! FLAME SLICE!!
SH
FSS
HOWEVER FLASHY THEY MAY BE, THEY ARE STILL SIMPLY TOOLS!
TAK
SH
TAK
SS
THEY DON'T STAND A CHANCE AGAINST OUR BLAZING HOT NINJUTSU!!
ATSUI, HOLD UP!
STAY COOL AND LET ME FINISH!!
BAH! HE'S TOO HOT-HEADED!
TAK
THEY TALK IN EXCESS AMONGST THEM-SELVES. GOOD.

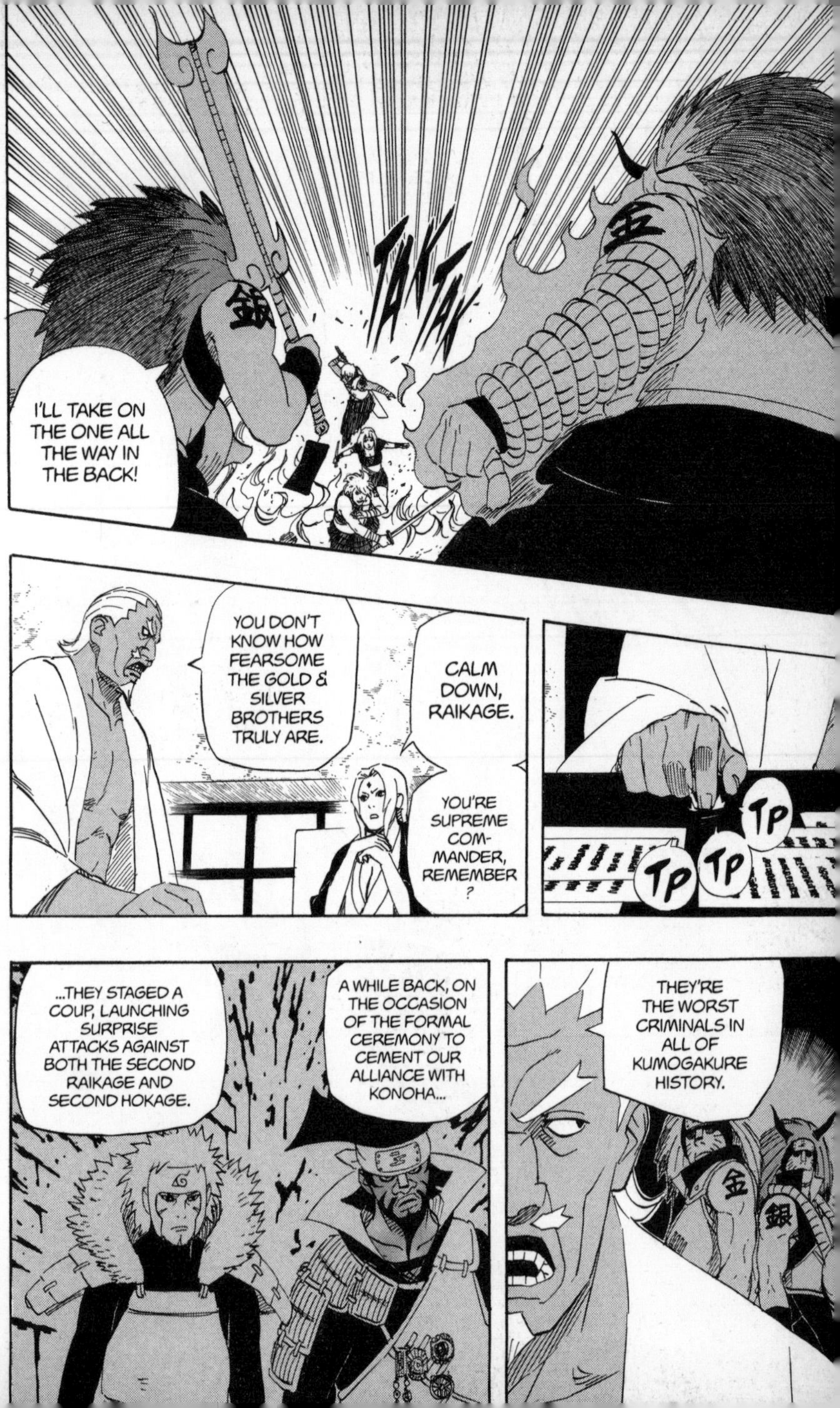
TAK TAK
I'LL TAKE ON THE ONE ALL THE WAY IN THE BACK!
Tp Tp Tp
CALM DOWN, RAIKAGE.
YOU'RE SUPREME COM-MANDER, REMEMBER?
YOU DON'T KNOW HOW FEARSOME THE GOLD & SILVER BROTHERS TRULY ARE.
THEY'RE THE WORST CRIMINALS IN ALL OF KUMOGAKURE HISTORY.
A WHILE BACK, ON THE OCCASION OF THE FORMAL CEREMONY TO CEMENT OUR ALLIANCE WITH KONOHA...
...THEY STAGED A COUP, LAUNCHING SURPRISE ATTACKS AGAINST BOTH THE SECOND RAIKAGE AND SECOND HOKAGE.

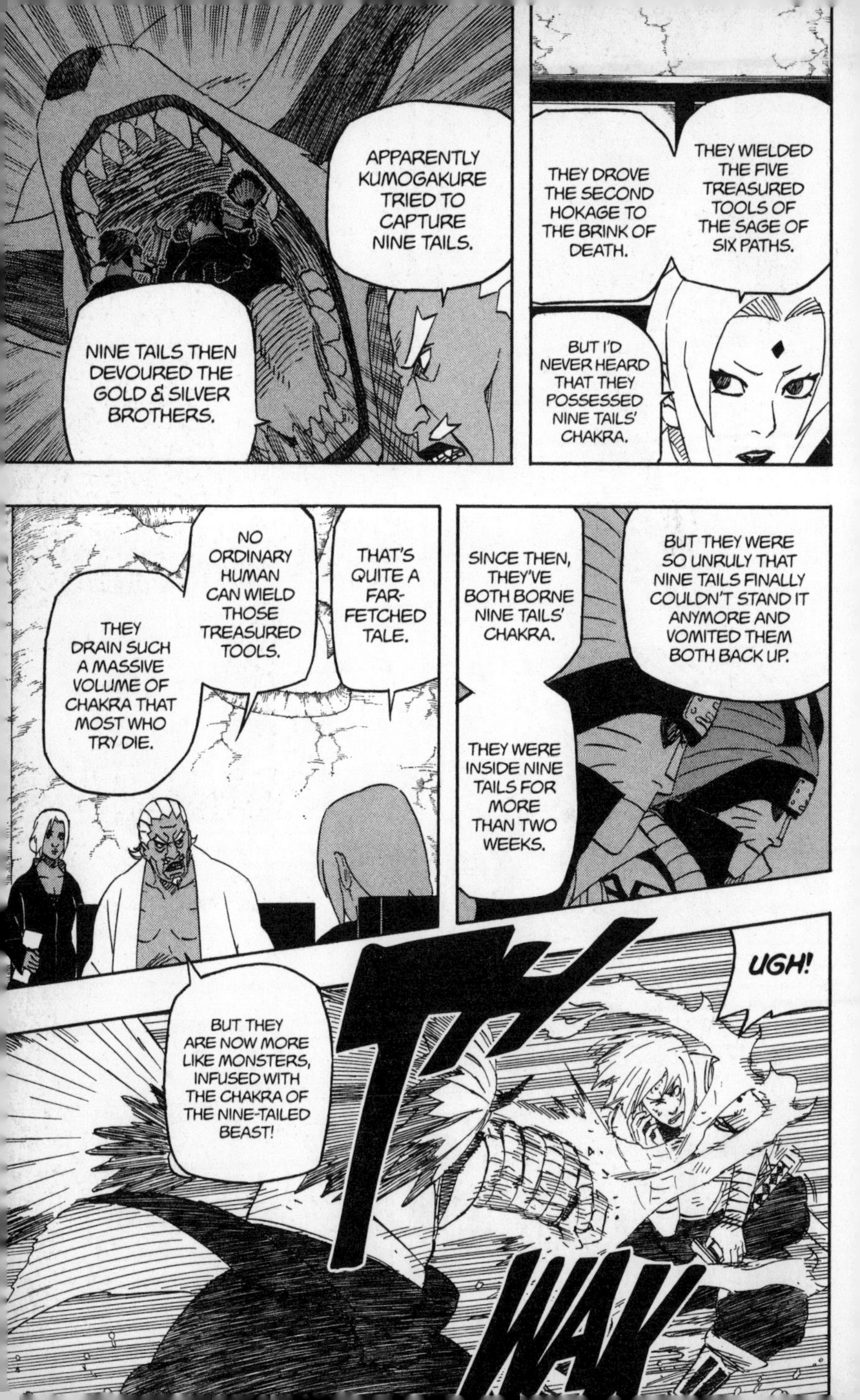
THEY WIELDED THE FIVE TREASURED TOOLS OF THE SAGE OF SIX PATHS.
THEY DROVE THE SECOND HOKAGE TO THE BRINK OF DEATH.
BUT I'D NEVER HEARD THAT THEY POSSESSED NINE TAILS' CHAKRA.
APPARENTLY KUMOGAKURE TRIED TO CAPTURE NINE TAILS.
NINE TAILS THEN DEVOURED THE GOLD & SILVER BROTHERS.
BUT THEY WERE SO UNRULY THAT NINE TAILS FINALLY COULDN'T STAND IT ANYMORE AND VOMITED THEM BOTH BACK UP.
SINCE THEN, THEY'VE BOTH BORNE NINE TAILS' CHAKRA.
THEY WERE INSIDE NINE TAILS FOR MORE THAN TWO WEEKS.
THAT'S QUITE A FAR-FETCHED TALE.
NO ORDINARY HUMAN CAN WIELD THOSE TREASURED TOOLS.
THEY DRAIN SUCH A MASSIVE VOLUME OF CHAKRA THAT MOST WHO TRY DIE.
UGH!
BUT THEY ARE NOW MORE LIKE MONSTERS, INFUSED WITH THE CHAKRA OF THE NINE-TAILED BEAST!
THWAK

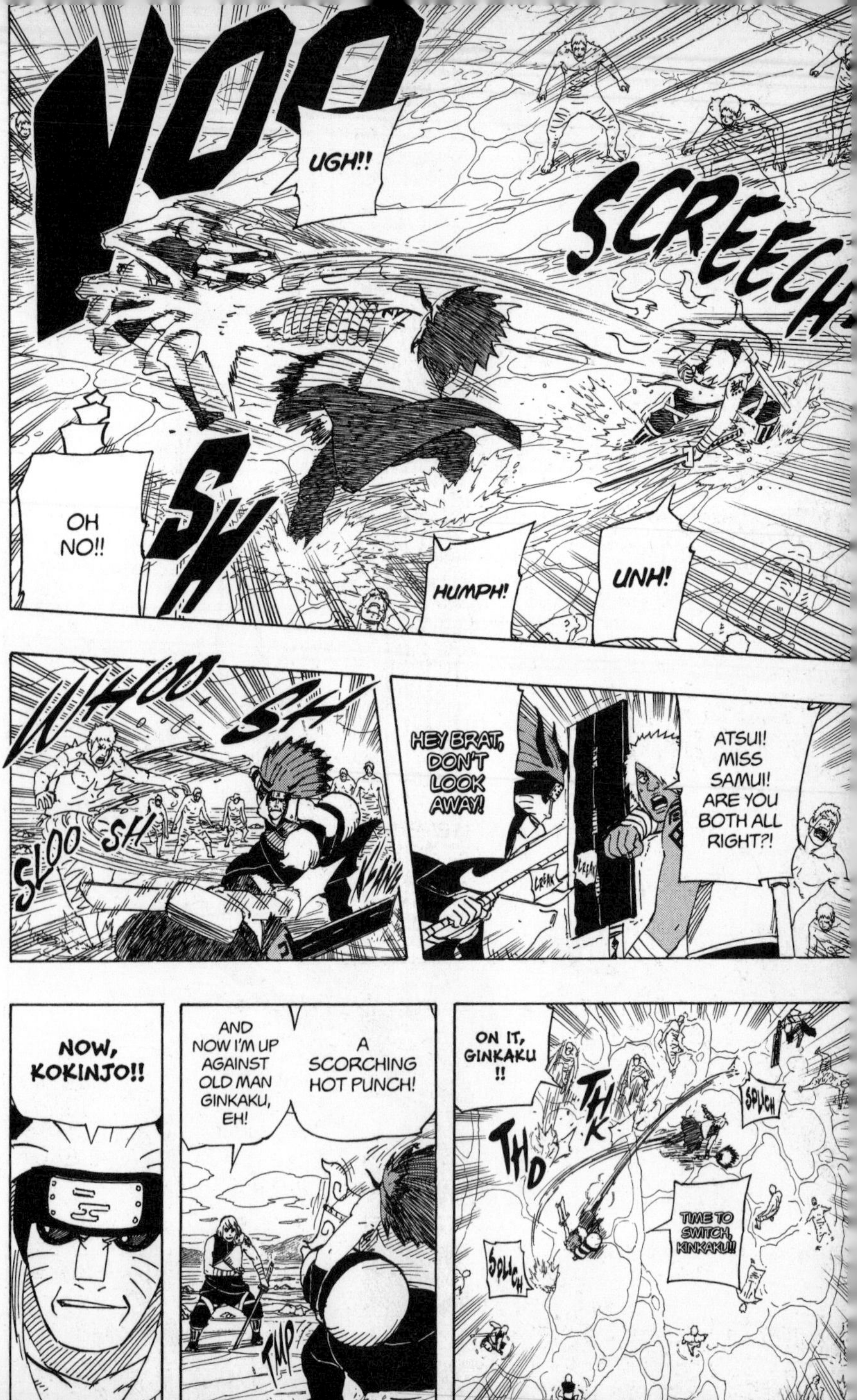
SCREECH
UGH!!
NOO
UNH!
HUMPH!
SH
OH NO!!
ATSUI! MISS SAMUI! ARE YOU BOTH ALL RIGHT?!
CREAK
CREAK
HEY BRAT, DON'T LOOK AWAY!
WHOOSH
SLOOSH
ON IT, GINKAKU!!
THK
SPLUCH
THD
TIME TO SWITCH, KINKAKU!!
SPLUCH
A SCORCHING HOT PUNCH!
AND NOW I'M UP AGAINST OLD MAN GINKAKU, EH!
TMP
NOW, KOKINJO!!

READ THIS WAY

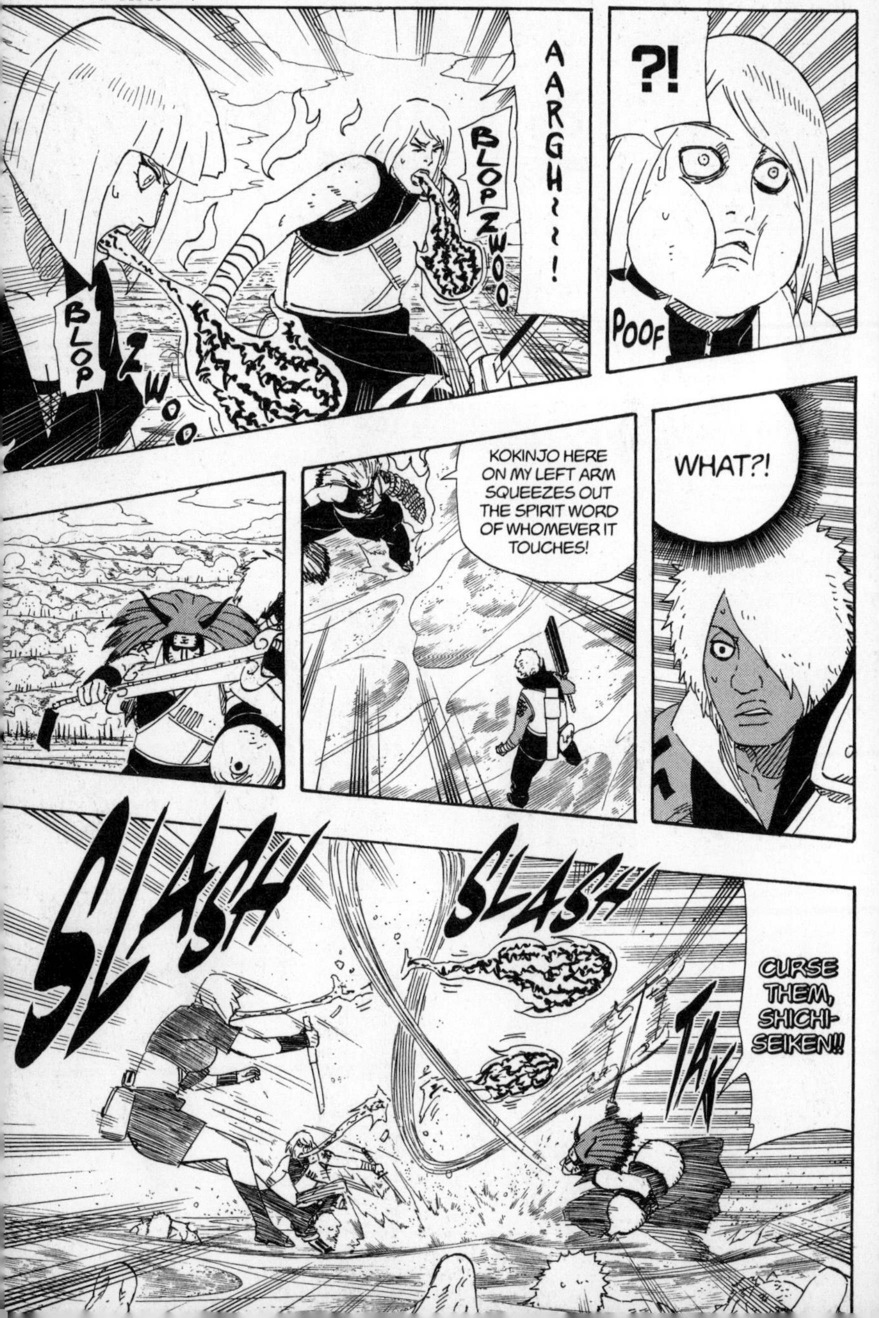
?!
POOF
AARGH~~!
BLOP ZWOO
BLOP ZWOO
WHAT?!
KOKINJO HERE ON MY LEFT ARM SQUEEZES OUT THE SPIRIT WORD OF WHOMEVER IT TOUCHES!
CURSE THEM, SHICHI-SEIKEN!!
TAK
SLASH
SLASH

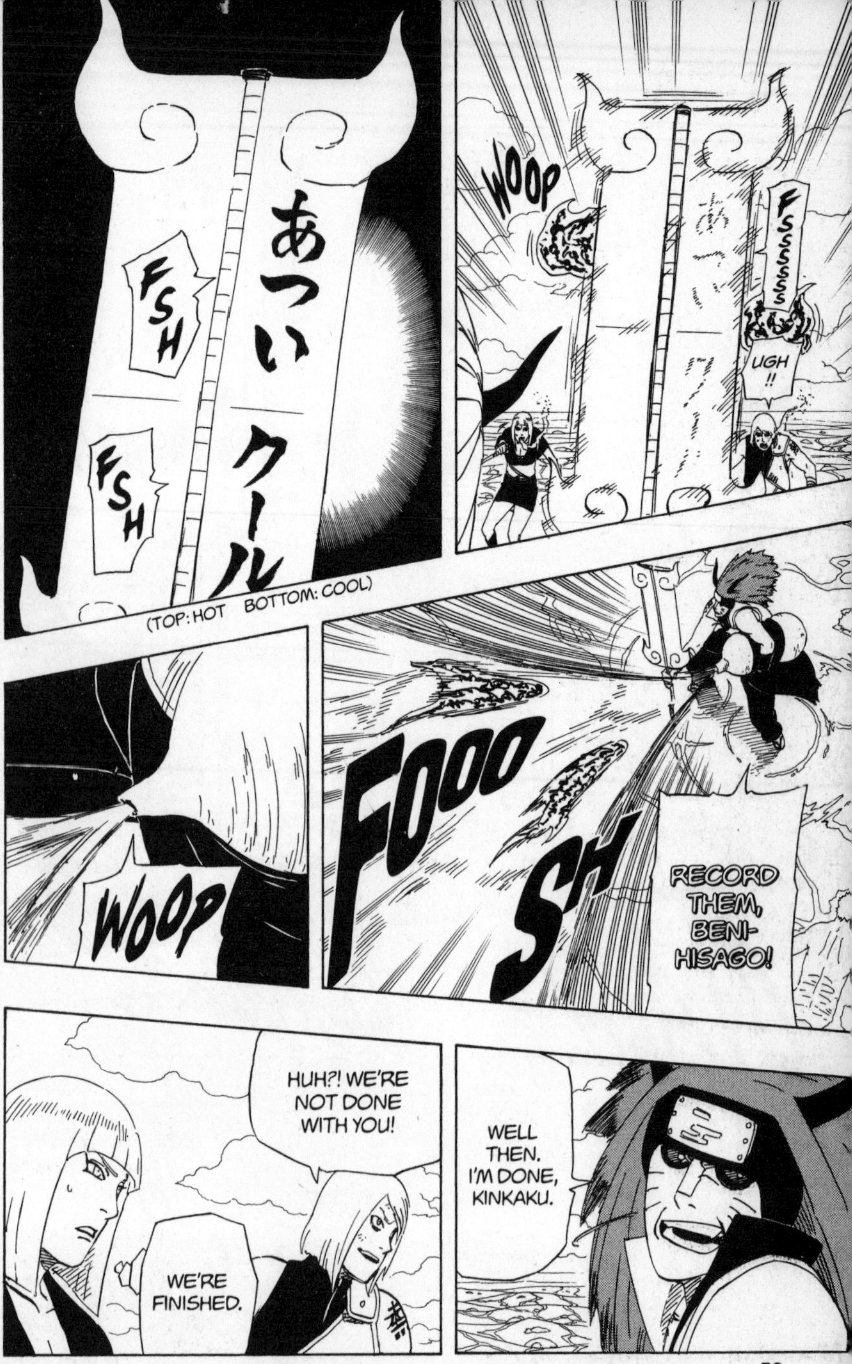
WOOP
FSSSSSS
UGH!!
FSH
FSH
あつい
クール
(TOP: HOT BOTTOM: COOL)
FOOOSH
RECORD THEM, BENI-HISAGO!
WOOP
WELL THEN. I'M DONE, KINKAKU.
HUH?! WE'RE NOT DONE WITH YOU!
WE'RE FINISHED.

READ THIS WAY

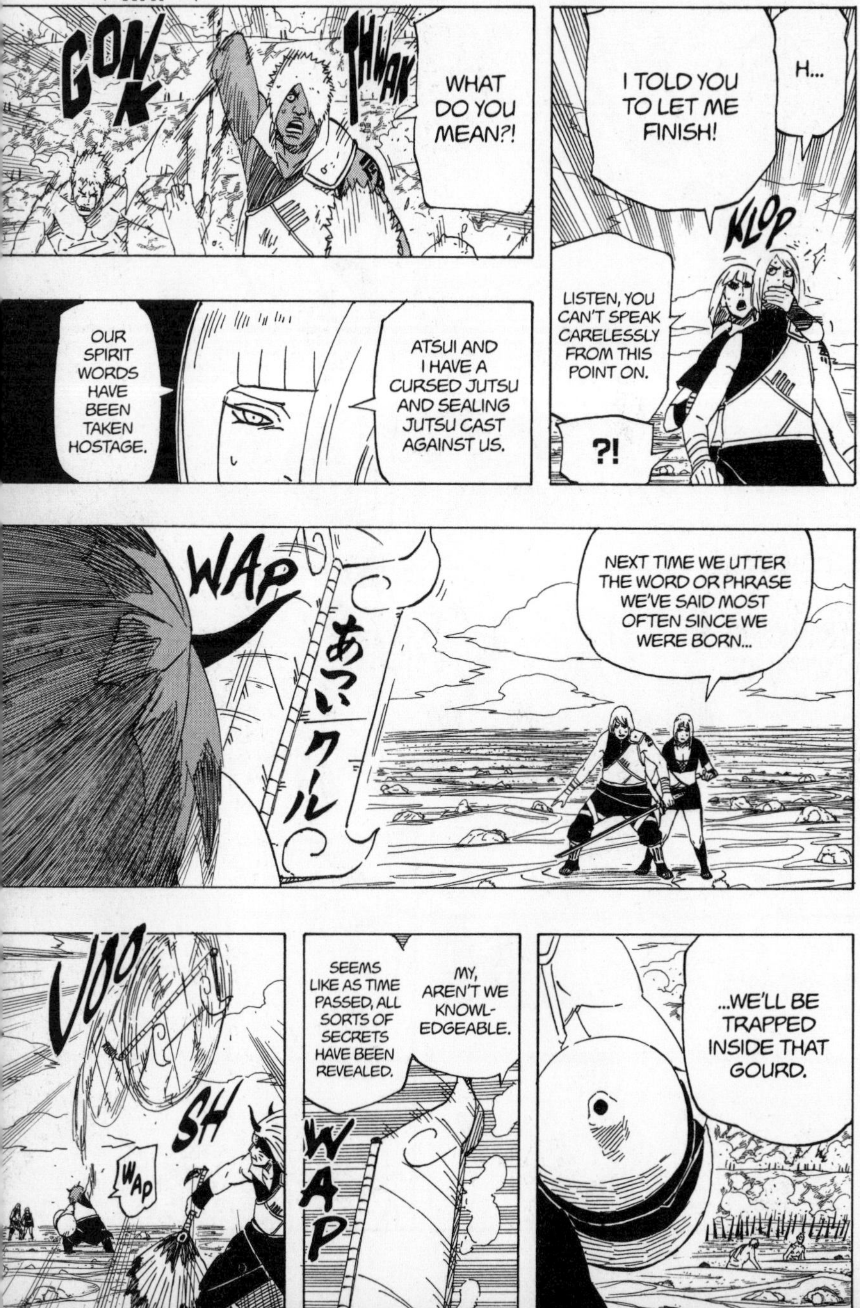
H...
I TOLD YOU TO LET ME FINISH!
KLOP
LISTEN, YOU CAN'T SPEAK CARELESSLY FROM THIS POINT ON.
?!
WHAT DO YOU MEAN?!
THWAK
GONK
ATSUI AND I HAVE A CURSED JUTSU AND SEALING JUTSU CAST AGAINST US.
OUR SPIRIT WORDS HAVE BEEN TAKEN HOSTAGE.
NEXT TIME WE UTTER THE WORD OR PHRASE WE'VE SAID MOST OFTEN SINCE WE WERE BORN...
あついクル
WAP
...WE'LL BE TRAPPED INSIDE THAT GOURD.
MY, AREN'T WE KNOWL-EDGEABLE.
SEEMS LIKE AS TIME PASSED, ALL SORTS OF SECRETS HAVE BEEN REVEALED.
WAP
JOO
SH
WAP

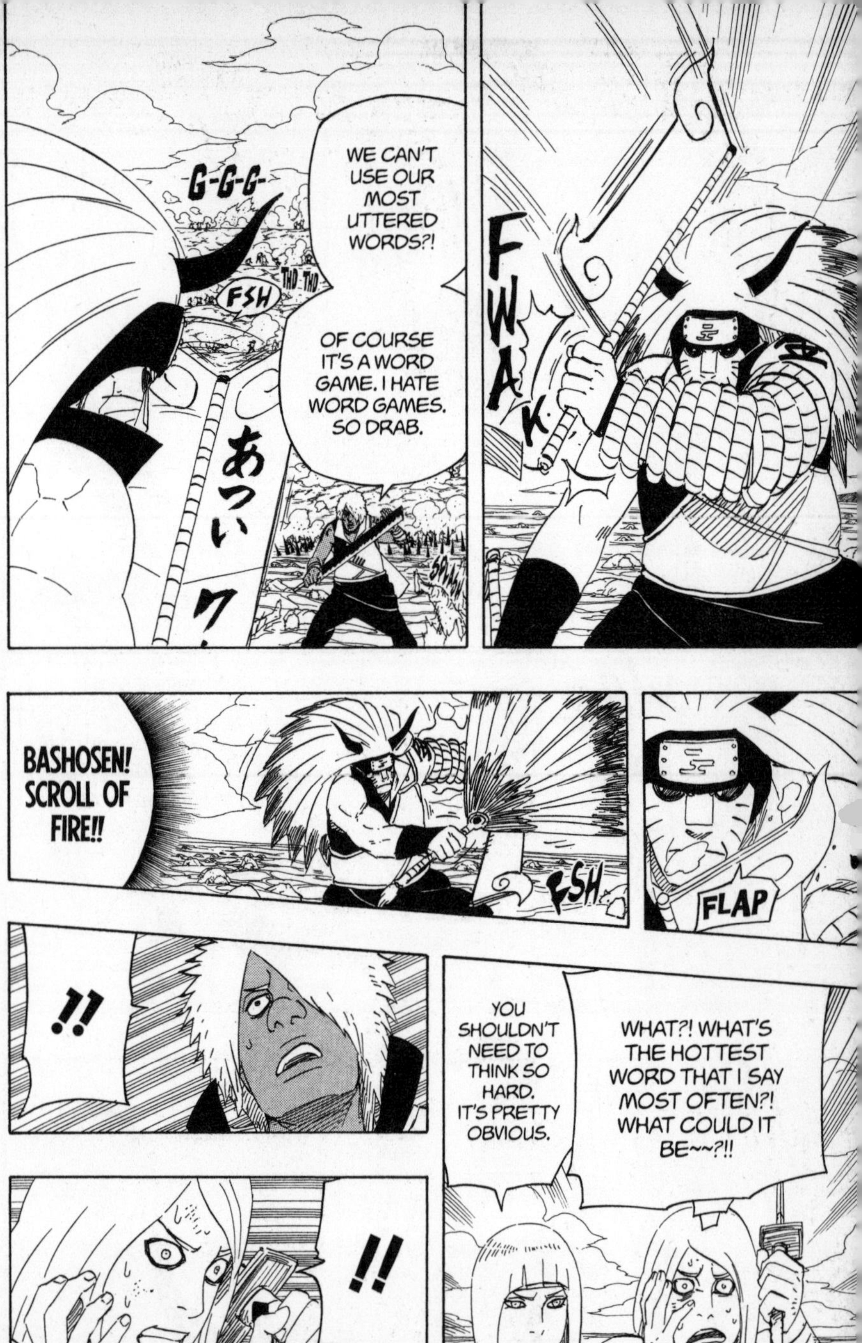
FWAK
-G-G-G-
FSH
THD THD
WE CAN'T USE OUR MOST UTTERED WORDS?!
OF COURSE IT'S A WORD GAME. I HATE WORD GAMES. SO DRAB.
あつい
SPLASH
FLAP
BASHOSEN! SCROLL OF FIRE!!
FSH
WHAT?! WHAT'S THE HOTTEST WORD THAT I SAY MOST OFTEN?! WHAT COULD IT BE~~?!!
YOU SHOULDN'T NEED TO THINK SO HARD. IT'S PRETTY OBVIOUS.
!!
!!

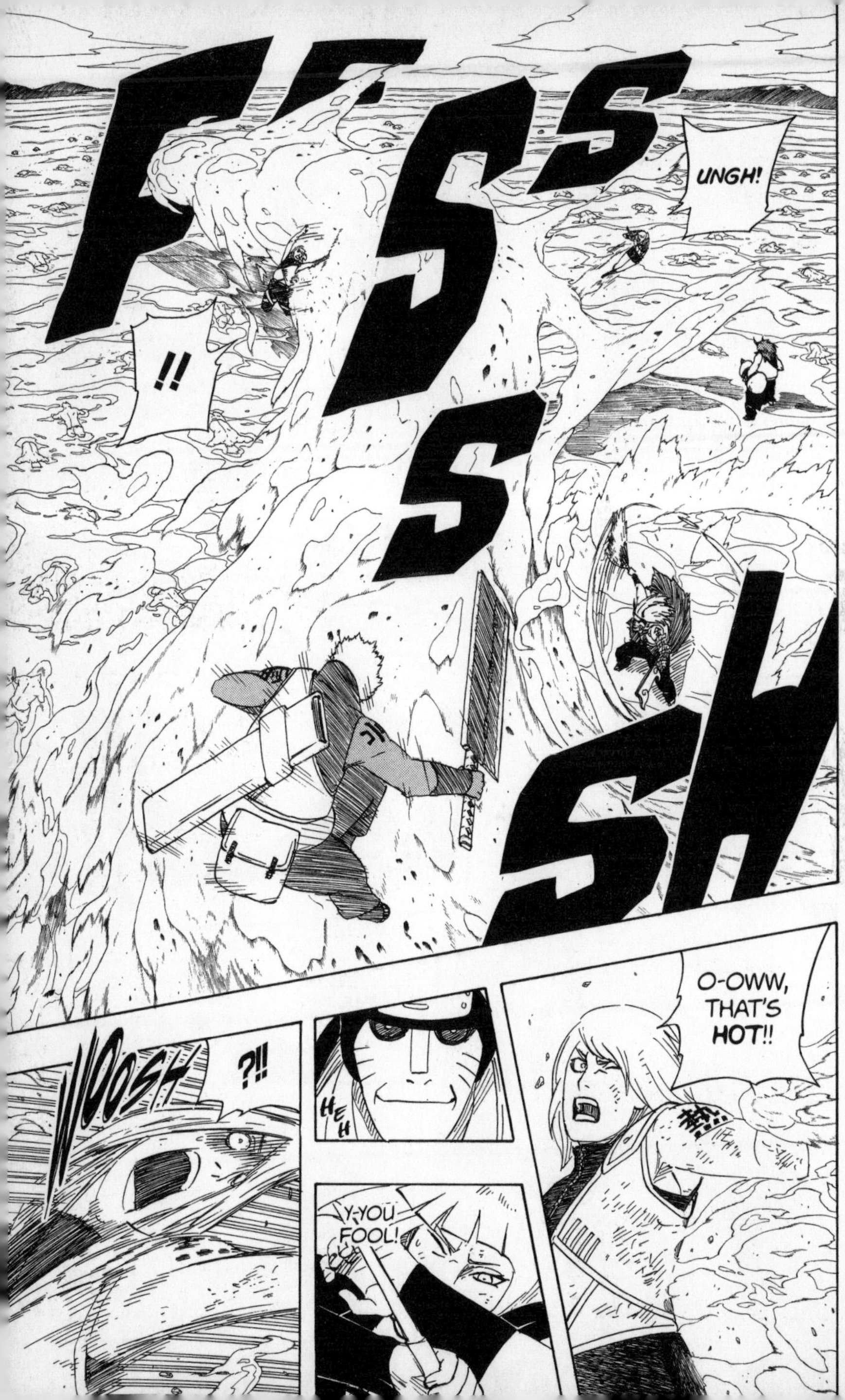
FSSSSSH
UNGH!
!!
O-OWW, THAT'S HOT!!
HEH
?!!
WOOSH
Y-YOU FOOL!

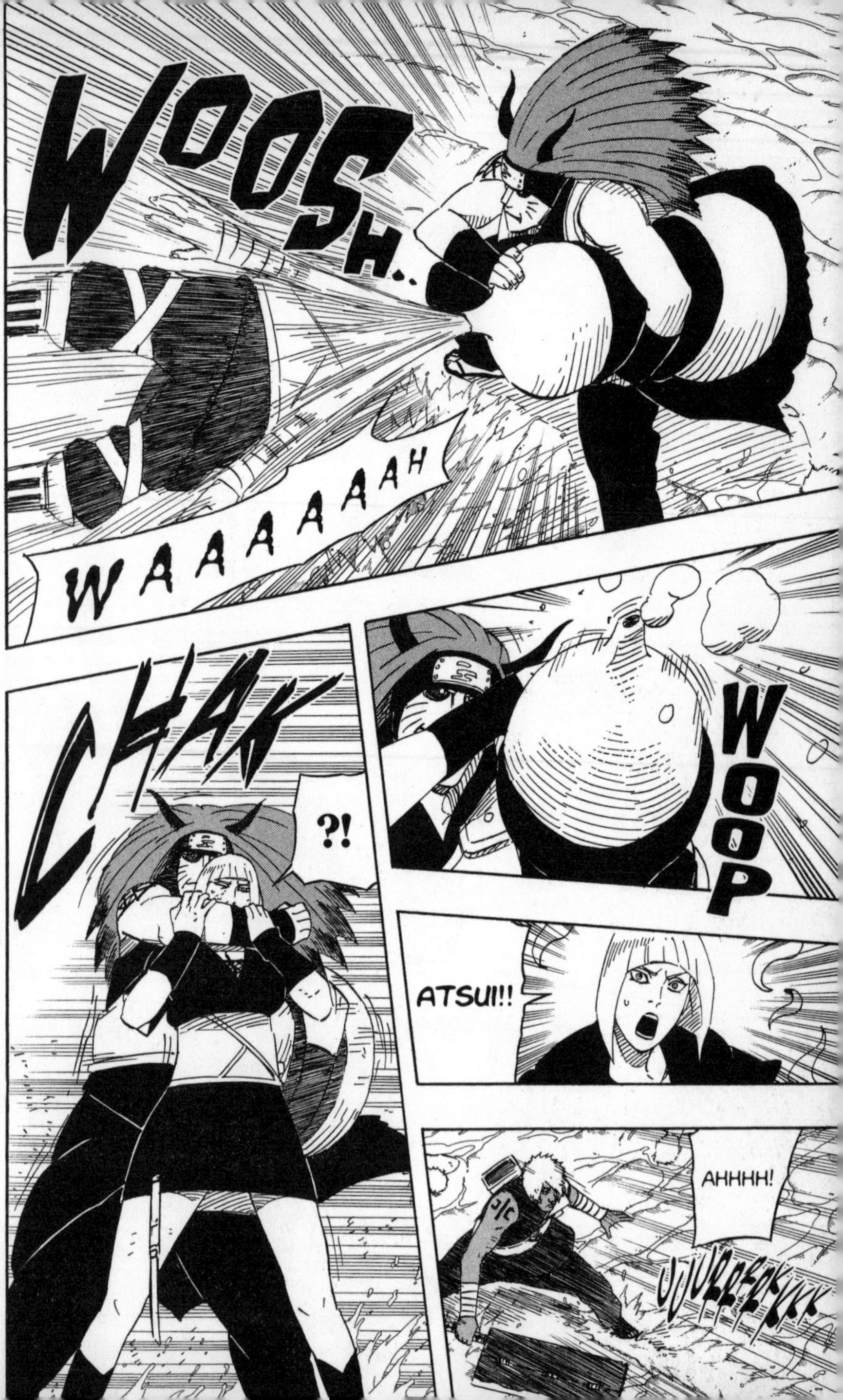
WOOSH..
WAAAAAAAH
WOOP
ATSUI!!!
AHHHH!
UURRRKKK
CHAK
?!

READ THIS WAY

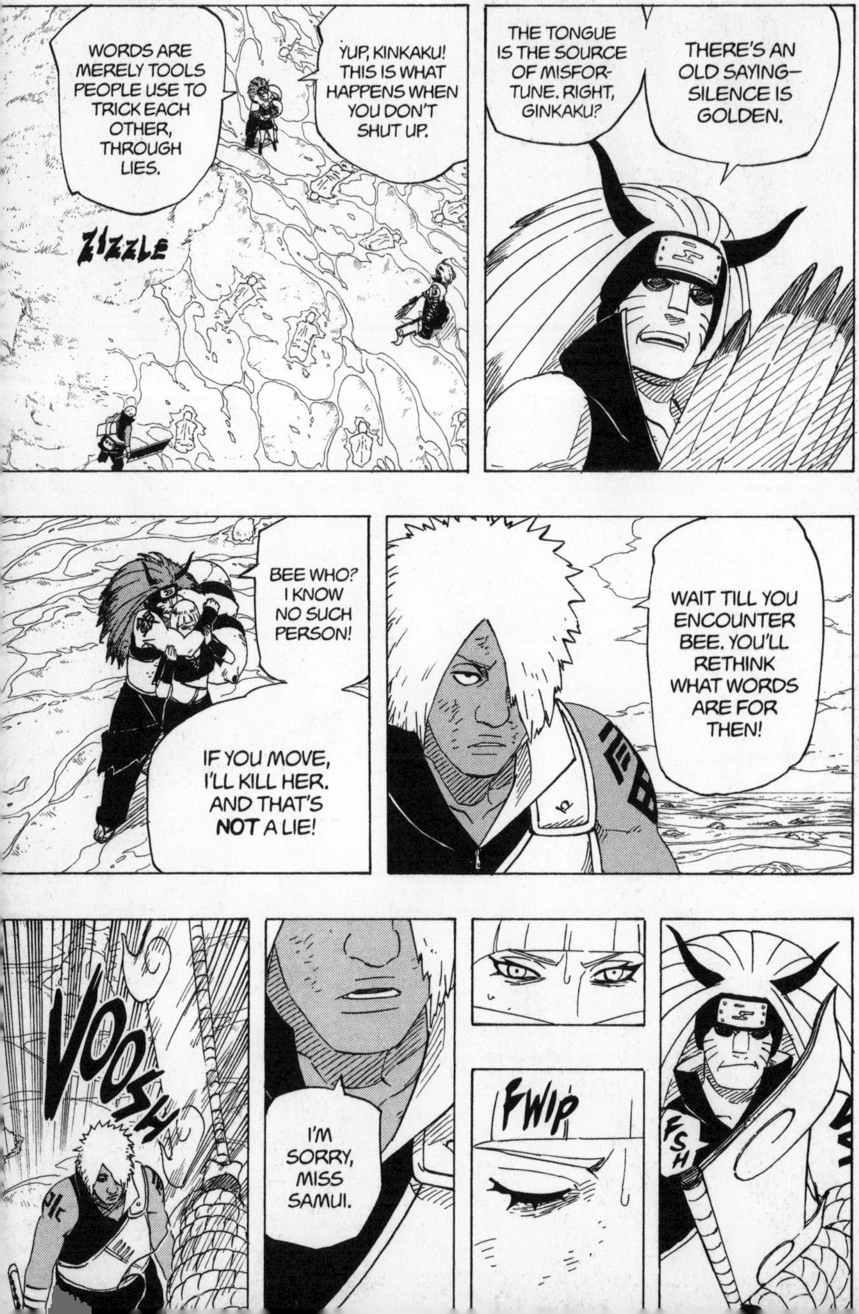
THERE'S AN OLD SAYING— SILENCE IS GOLDEN.
THE TONGUE IS THE SOURCE OF MISFORTUNE. RIGHT, GINKAKU?
YUP, KINKAKU! THIS IS WHAT HAPPENS WHEN YOU DON'T SHUT UP.
WORDS ARE MERELY TOOLS PEOPLE USE TO TRICK EACH OTHER, THROUGH LIES.
ZIZZLE
WAIT TILL YOU ENCOUNTER BEE. YOU'LL RETHINK WHAT WORDS ARE FOR THEN!
BEE WHO? I KNOW NO SUCH PERSON!
IF YOU MOVE, I'LL KILL HER. AND THAT'S **NOT** A LIE!
FSH
FWIP
I'M SORRY, MISS SAMUI.
VOOSH

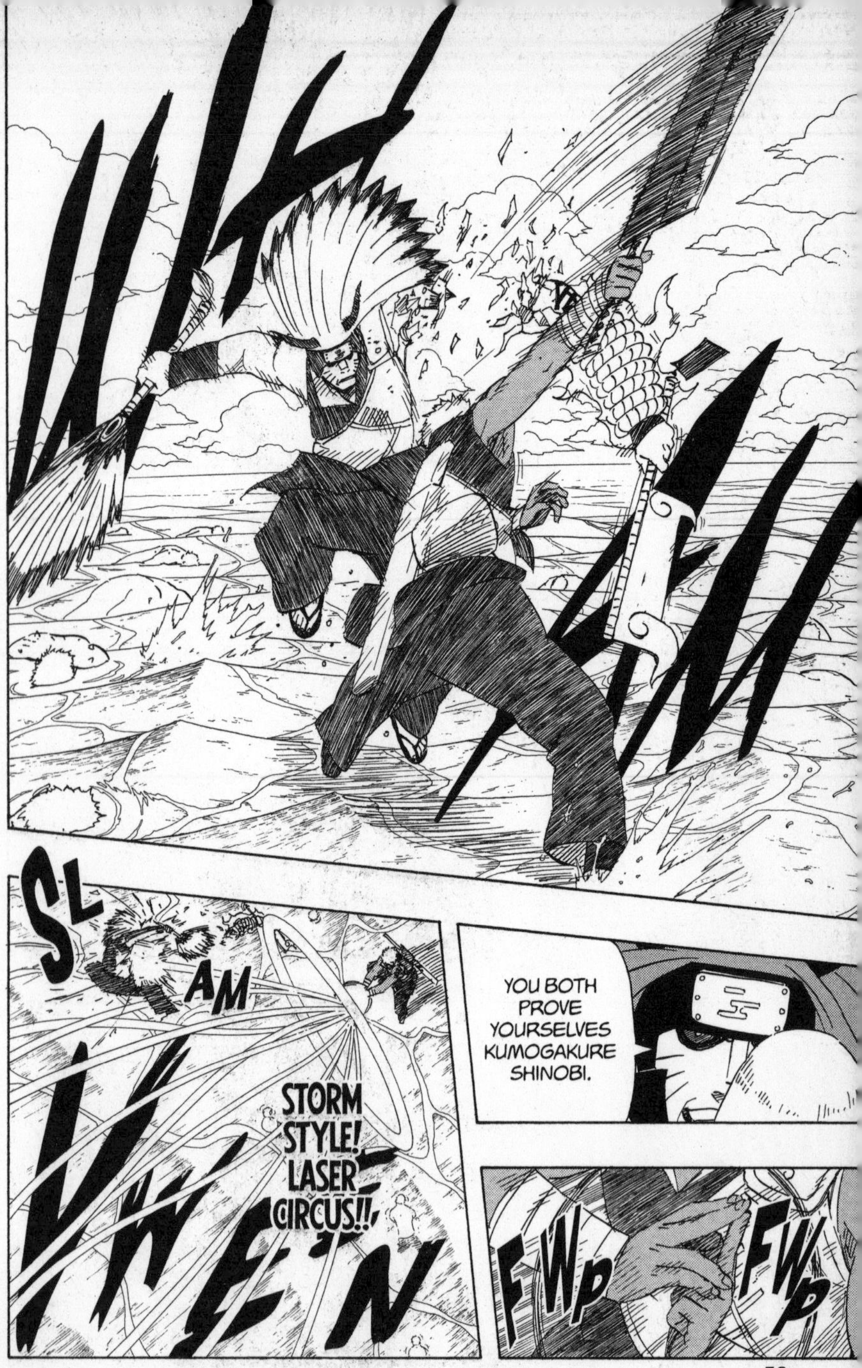
YOU BOTH PROVE YOURSELVES KUMOGAKURE SHINOBI.
FWP
FWP
SLAM
STORM STYLE! LASER CIRCUS!!

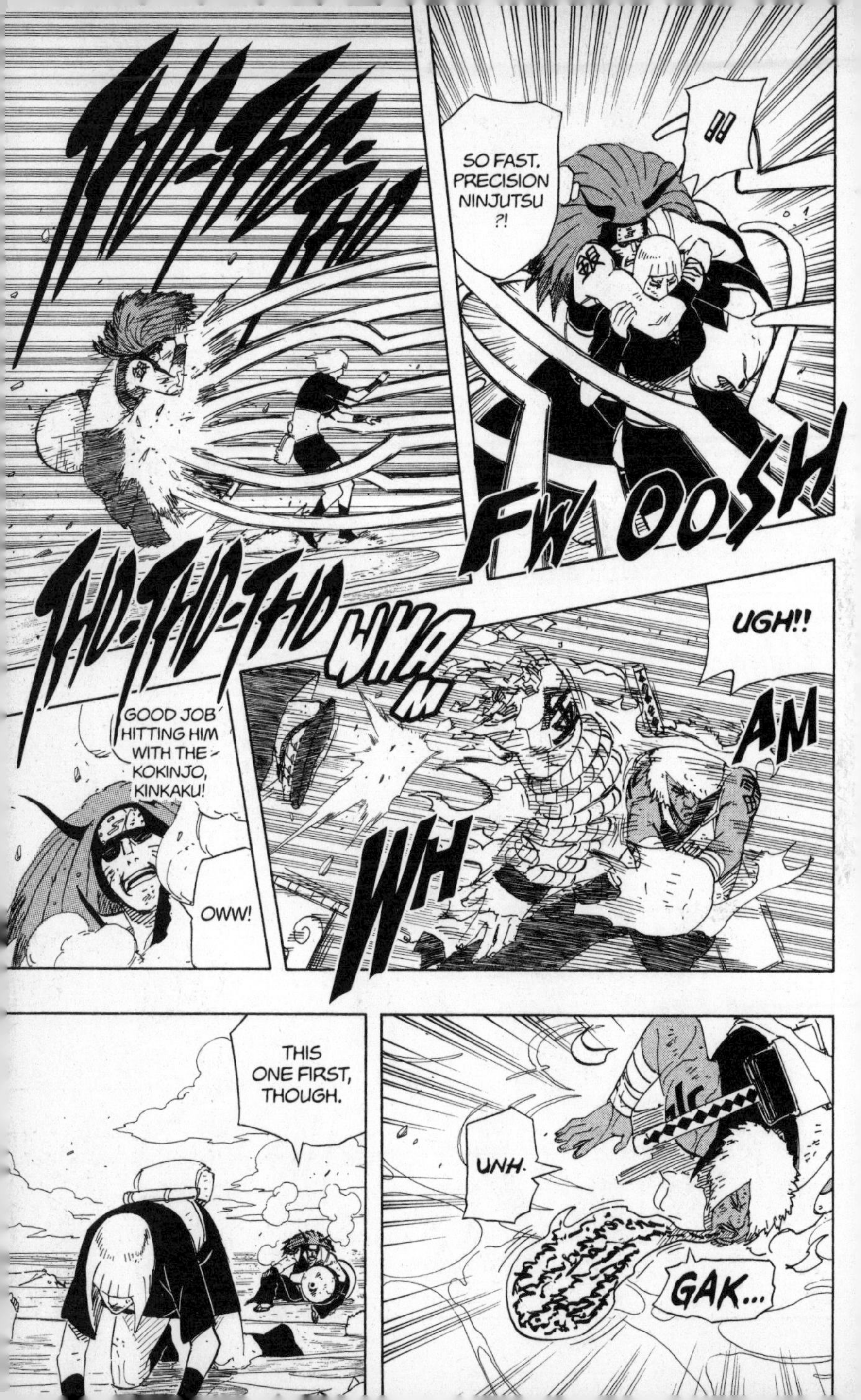
!!
SO FAST. PRECISION NINJUTSU ?!
FWOOSH
THO-THO-THO
UGH!!
WHAM
WHAM
GOOD JOB HITTING HIM WITH THE KOKINJO, KINKAKU!
OWW!
UNH.
GAK...
THIS ONE FIRST, THOUGH.

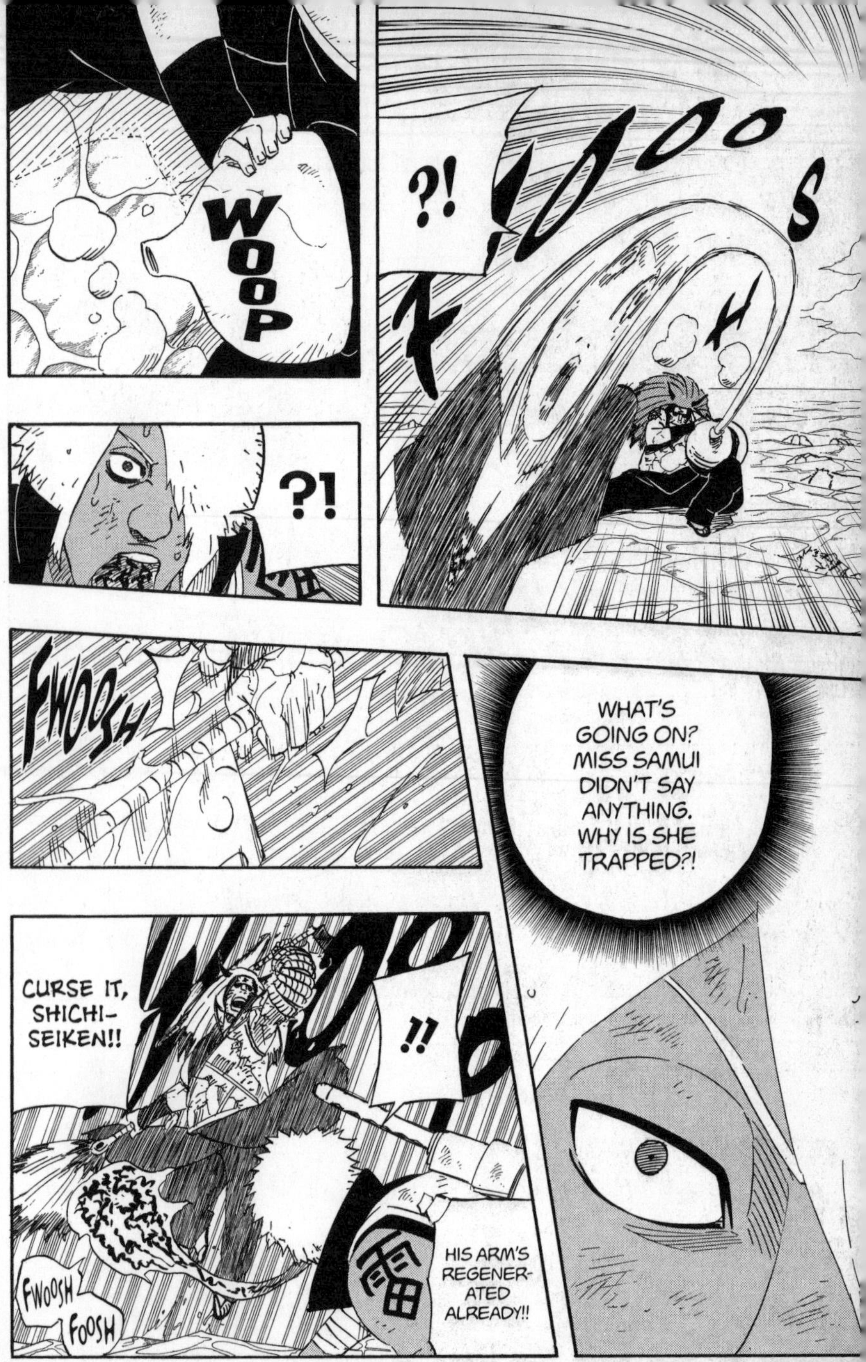
?!
WOOP
?!
WHAT'S GOING ON? MISS SAMUI DIDN'T SAY ANYTHING. WHY IS SHE TRAPPED?!
FWOOSH
!!
HIS ARM'S REGENER-ATED ALREADY!!
CURSE IT, SHICHI-SEIKEN!!
FWOOSH
FOOSH

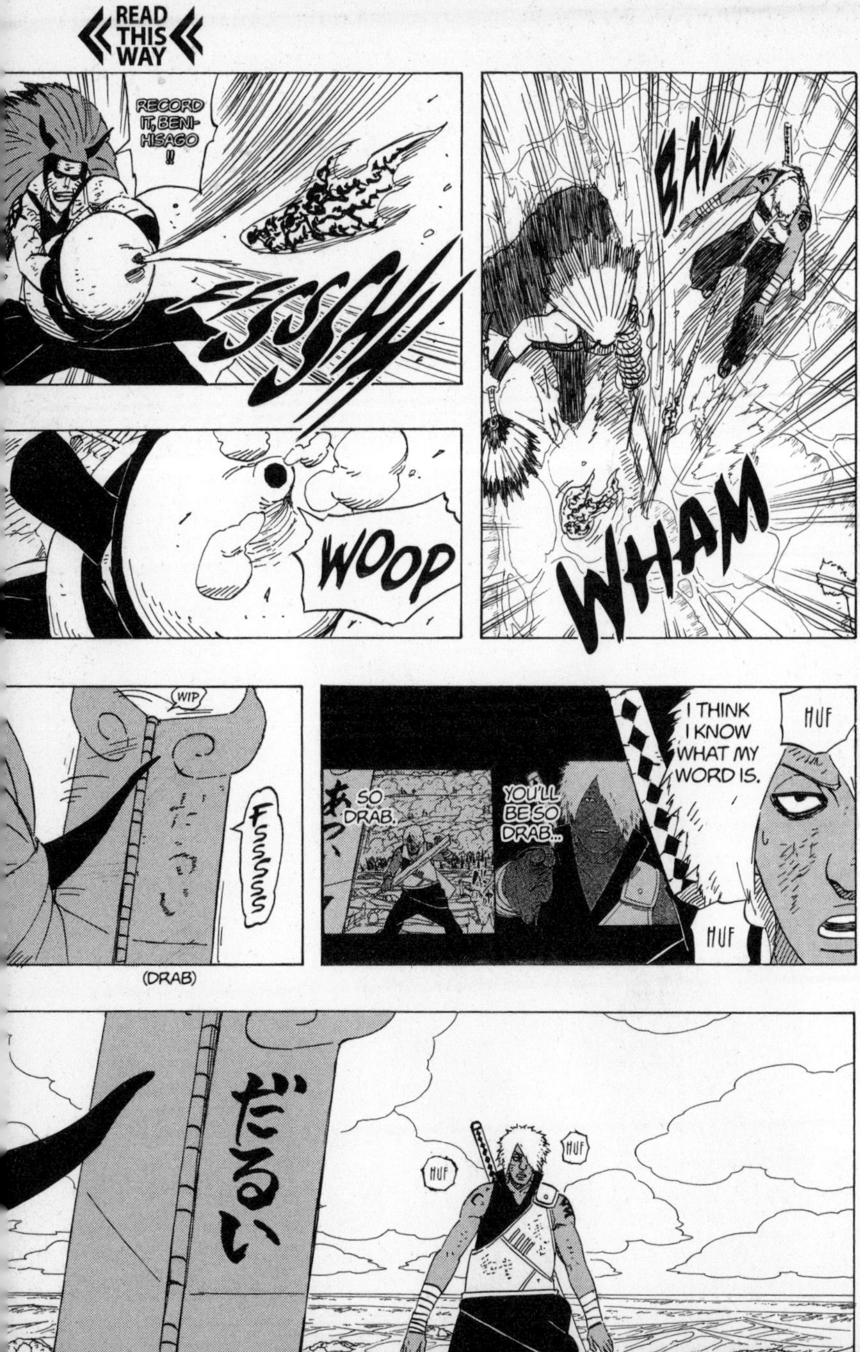
READ THIS WAY
BAM
WHAM
RECORD IT, BENI-HISAGO!!
FSSSHH
WOOP
HUF
I THINK I KNOW WHAT MY WORD IS.
HUF
YOU'LL BE SO DRAB...
SO DRAB.
あっ、
WIP
Fssssss
だるい
(DRAB)
HUF
HUF
だるい

NARUTO

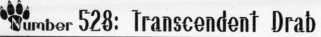

Number 528: Transcendent Drab

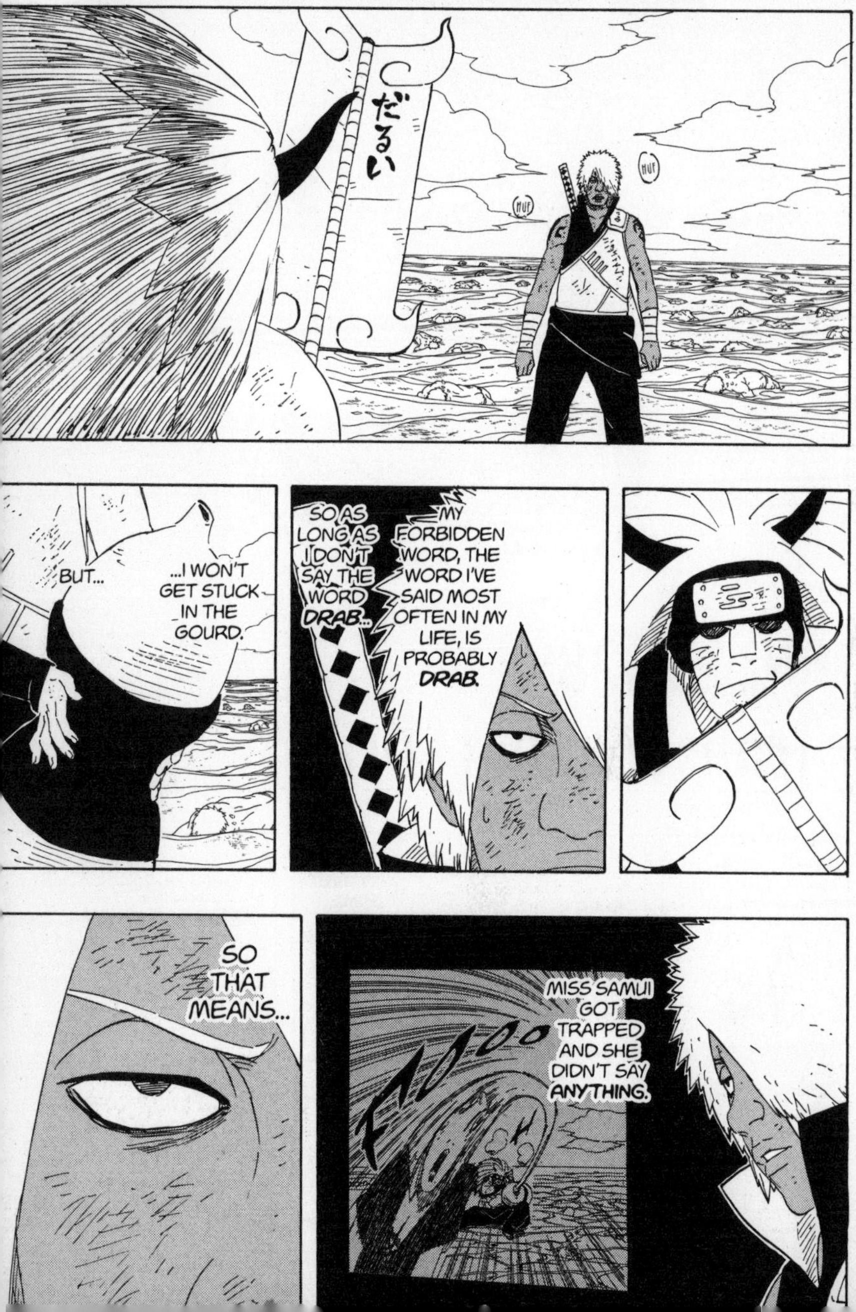

だるい
HUF
HUF
MY FORBIDDEN WORD, THE WORD I'VE SAID MOST OFTEN IN MY LIFE, IS PROBABLY DRAB.
SO AS LONG AS I DON'T SAY THE WORD DRAB...
...I WON'T GET STUCK IN THE GOURD.
BUT...
MISS SAMUI GOT TRAPPED AND SHE DIDN'T SAY ANYTHING.
SO THAT MEANS...

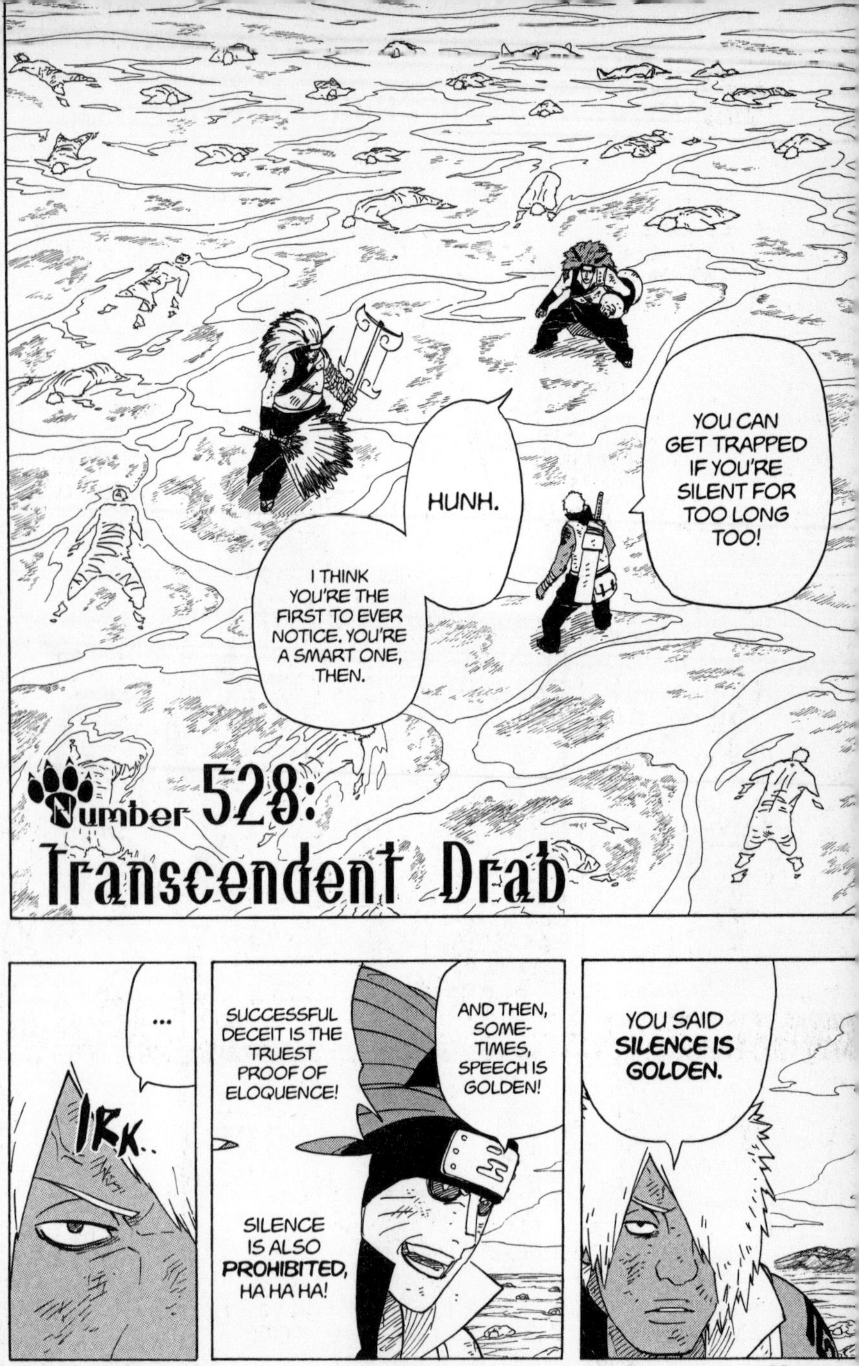
YOU CAN GET TRAPPED IF YOU'RE SILENT FOR TOO LONG TOO!
HUNH.
I THINK YOU'RE THE FIRST TO EVER NOTICE. YOU'RE A SMART ONE, THEN.
Number 528: Transcendent Drab
YOU SAID SILENCE IS GOLDEN.
AND THEN, SOME-TIMES, SPEECH IS GOLDEN!
SUCCESSFUL DECEIT IS THE TRUEST PROOF OF ELOQUENCE!
SILENCE IS ALSO PROHIBITED, HA HA HA!
...
IRK..

READ THIS WAY

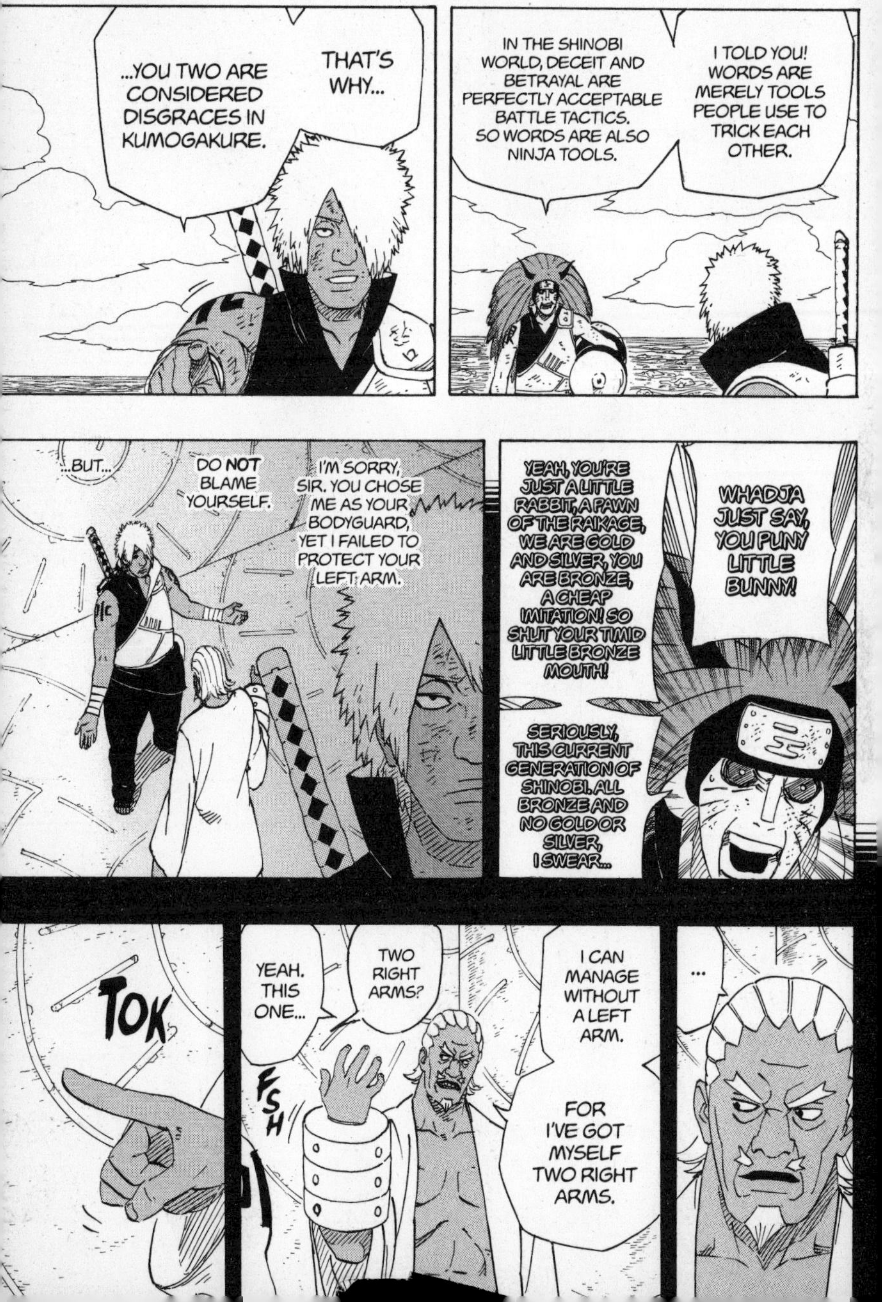
I TOLD YOU! WORDS ARE MERELY TOOLS PEOPLE USE TO TRICK EACH OTHER.
IN THE SHINOBI WORLD, DECEIT AND BETRAYAL ARE PERFECTLY ACCEPTABLE BATTLE TACTICS. SO WORDS ARE ALSO NINJA TOOLS.
THAT'S WHY...
...YOU TWO ARE CONSIDERED DISGRACES IN KUMOGAKURE.
WHADJA JUST SAY, YOU PUNY LITTLE BUNNY!
YEAH, YOU'RE JUST A LITTLE RABBIT, A PAWN OF THE RAIKAGE. WE ARE GOLD AND SILVER, YOU ARE BRONZE, A CHEAP IMITATION! SO SHUT YOUR TIMID LITTLE BRONZE MOUTH!
SERIOUSLY, THIS CURRENT GENERATION OF SHINOBI. ALL BRONZE AND NO GOLD OR SILVER, I SWEAR...
I'M SORRY, SIR. YOU CHOSE ME AS YOUR BODYGUARD, YET I FAILED TO PROTECT YOUR LEFT ARM.
DO NOT BLAME YOURSELF.
...BUT...
...
I CAN MANAGE WITHOUT A LEFT ARM.
FOR I'VE GOT MYSELF TWO RIGHT ARMS.
TWO RIGHT ARMS?
YEAH. THIS ONE...
FSH
TOK

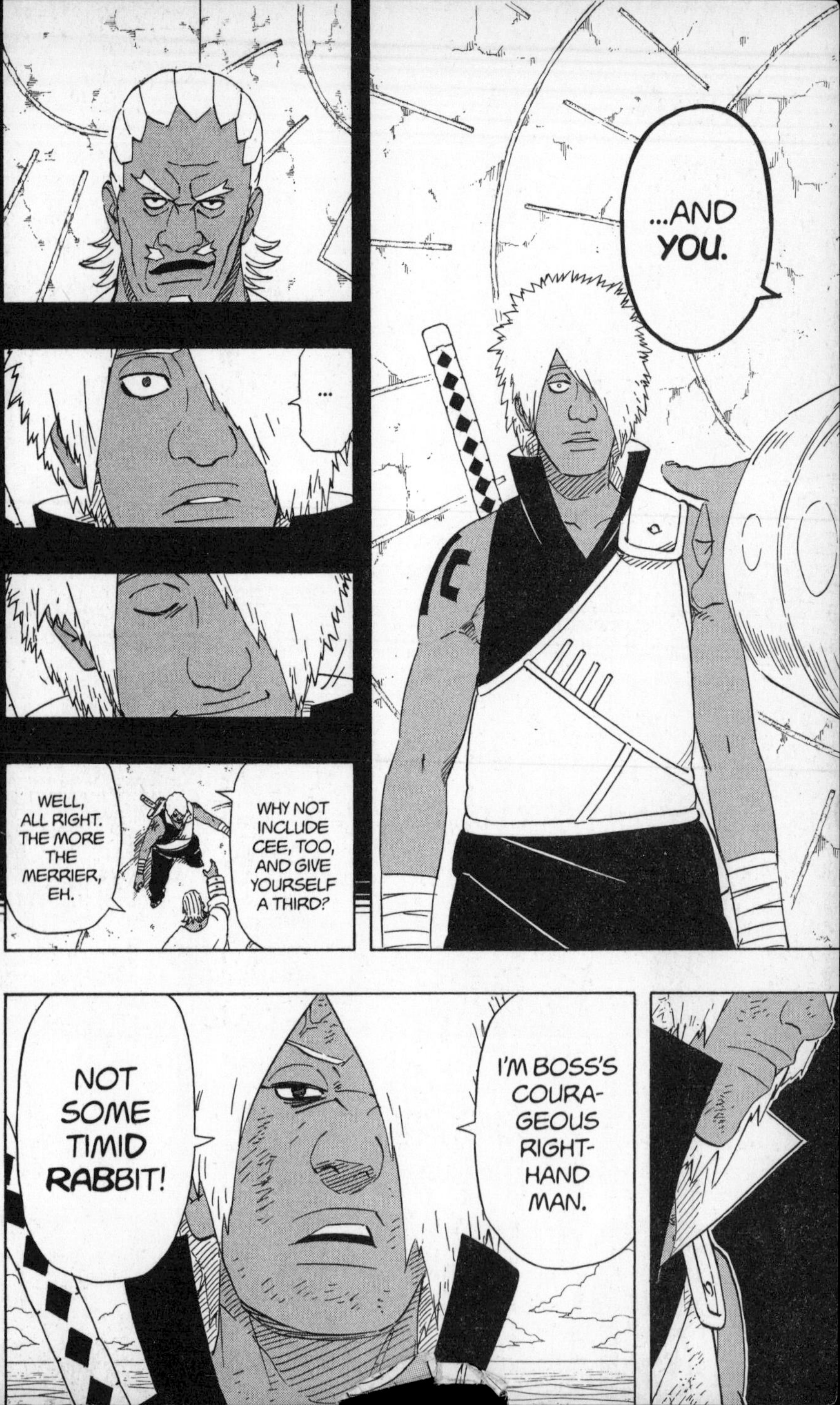
...AND YOU.
...
WHY NOT INCLUDE CEE, TOO, AND GIVE YOURSELF A THIRD?
WELL, ALL RIGHT. THE MORE THE MERRIER, EH.
I'M BOSS'S COURAGEOUS RIGHT-HAND MAN.
NOT SOME TIMID RABBIT!

READ THIS WAY

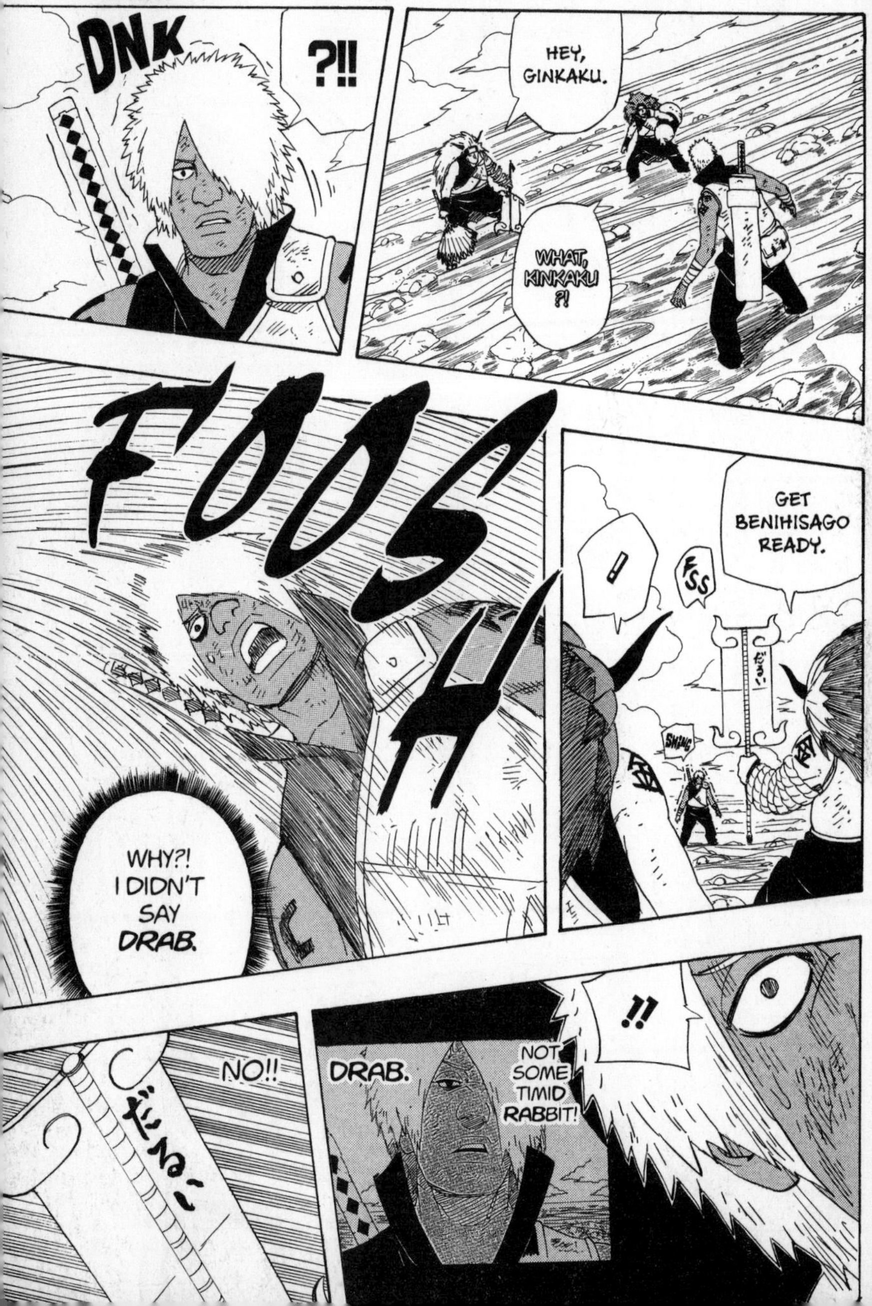
HEY, GINKAKU.
WHAT, KINKAKU?!
DNK
?!!
GET BENIHISAGO READY.
!
FSS
SHING
FOOSH
WHY?! I DIDN'T SAY DRAB.
!!
NOT SOME TIMID RABBIT!
DRAB.
NO!!
だるい

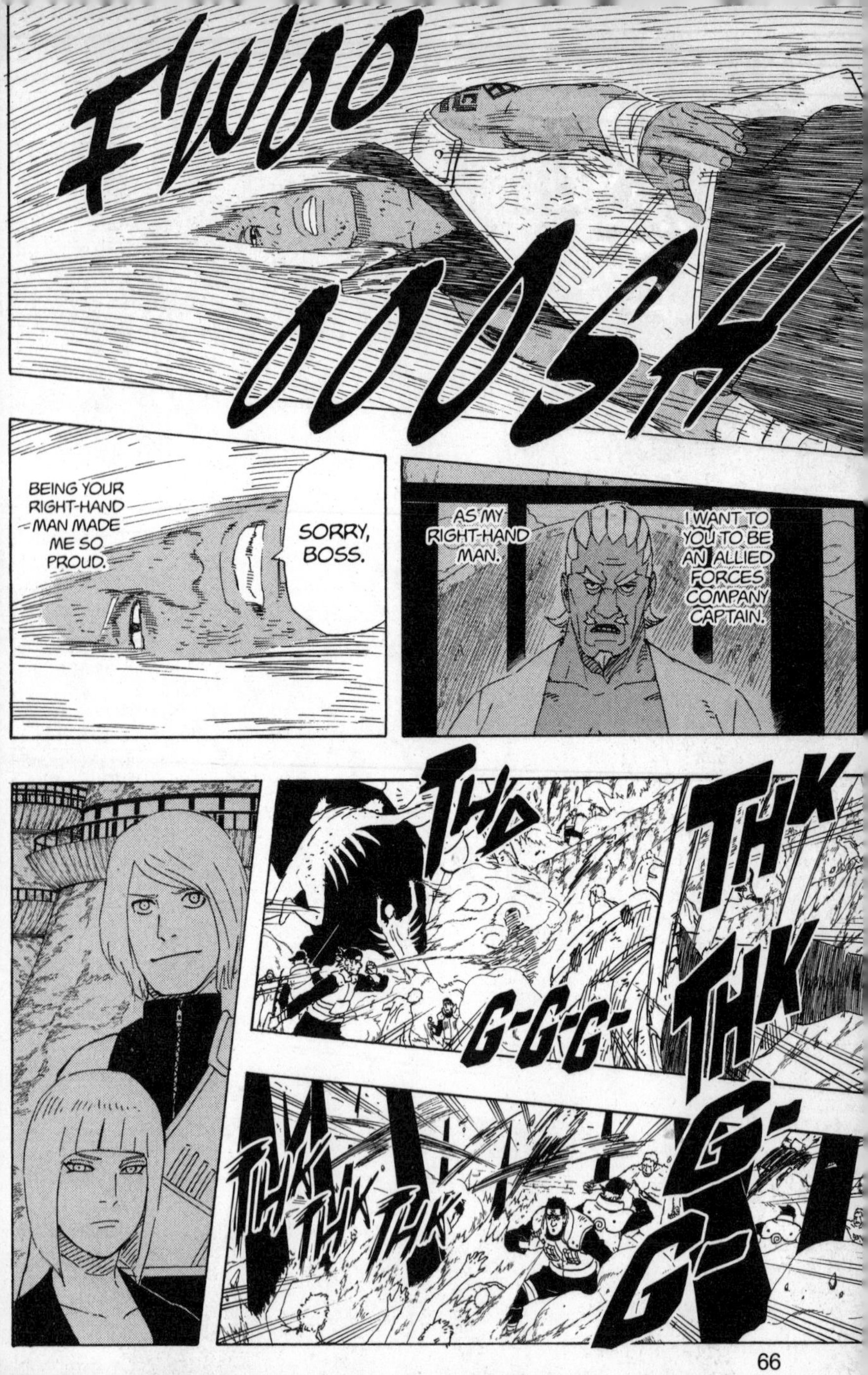
FWOO
OOOSH
I WANT TO YOU TO BE AN ALLIED FORCES COMPANY CAPTAIN.
AS MY RIGHT-HAND MAN.
SORRY, BOSS.
BEING YOUR RIGHT-HAND MAN MADE ME SO PROUD.
THD
THK THK
G-G-G-
THK THK THK
G-G-G-

READ THIS WAY

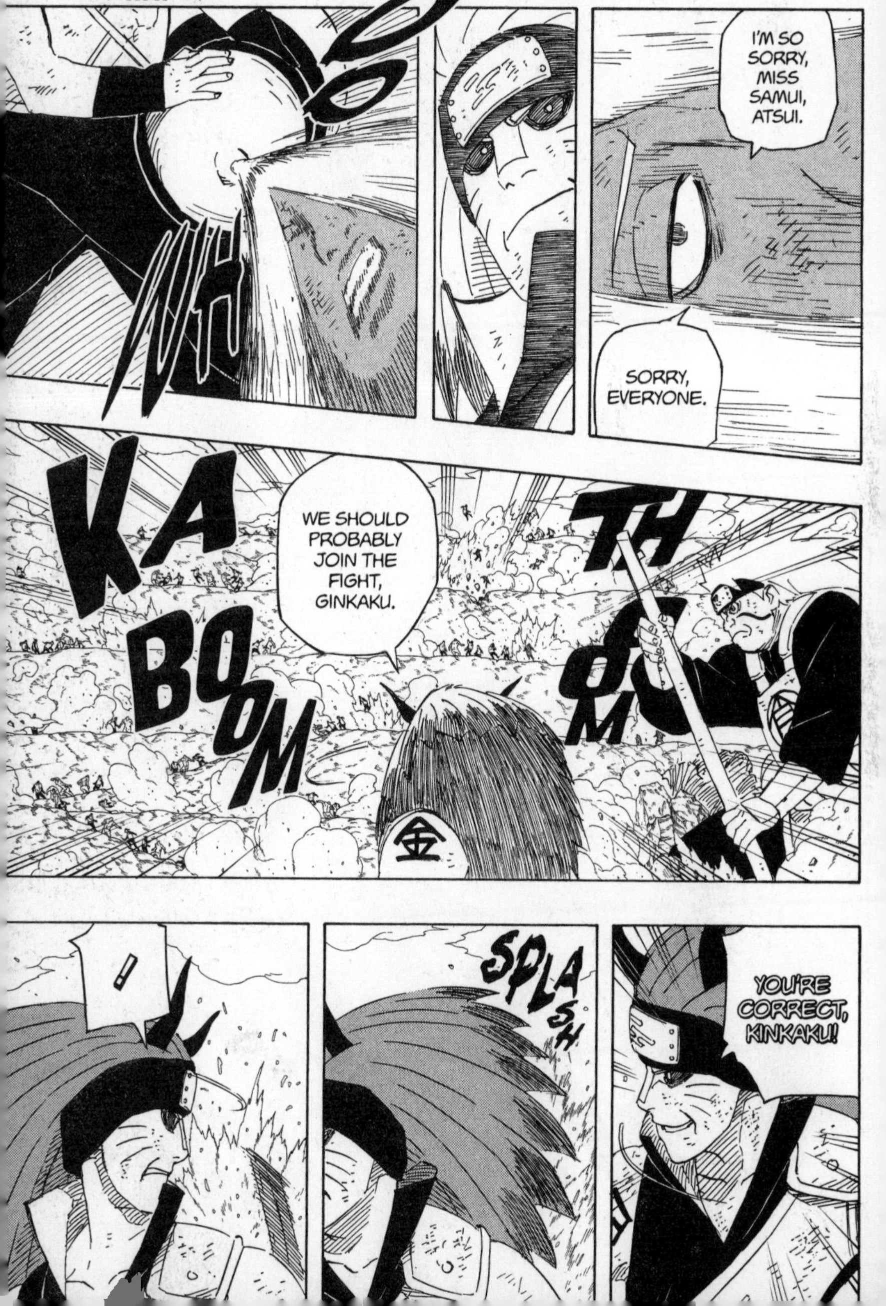
I'M SO SORRY, MISS SAMUI, ATSUI.
SORRY, EVERYONE.
WE SHOULD PROBABLY JOIN THE FIGHT, GINKAKU.
KABOOM
YOU'RE CORRECT, KINKAKU!
SPLASH
!

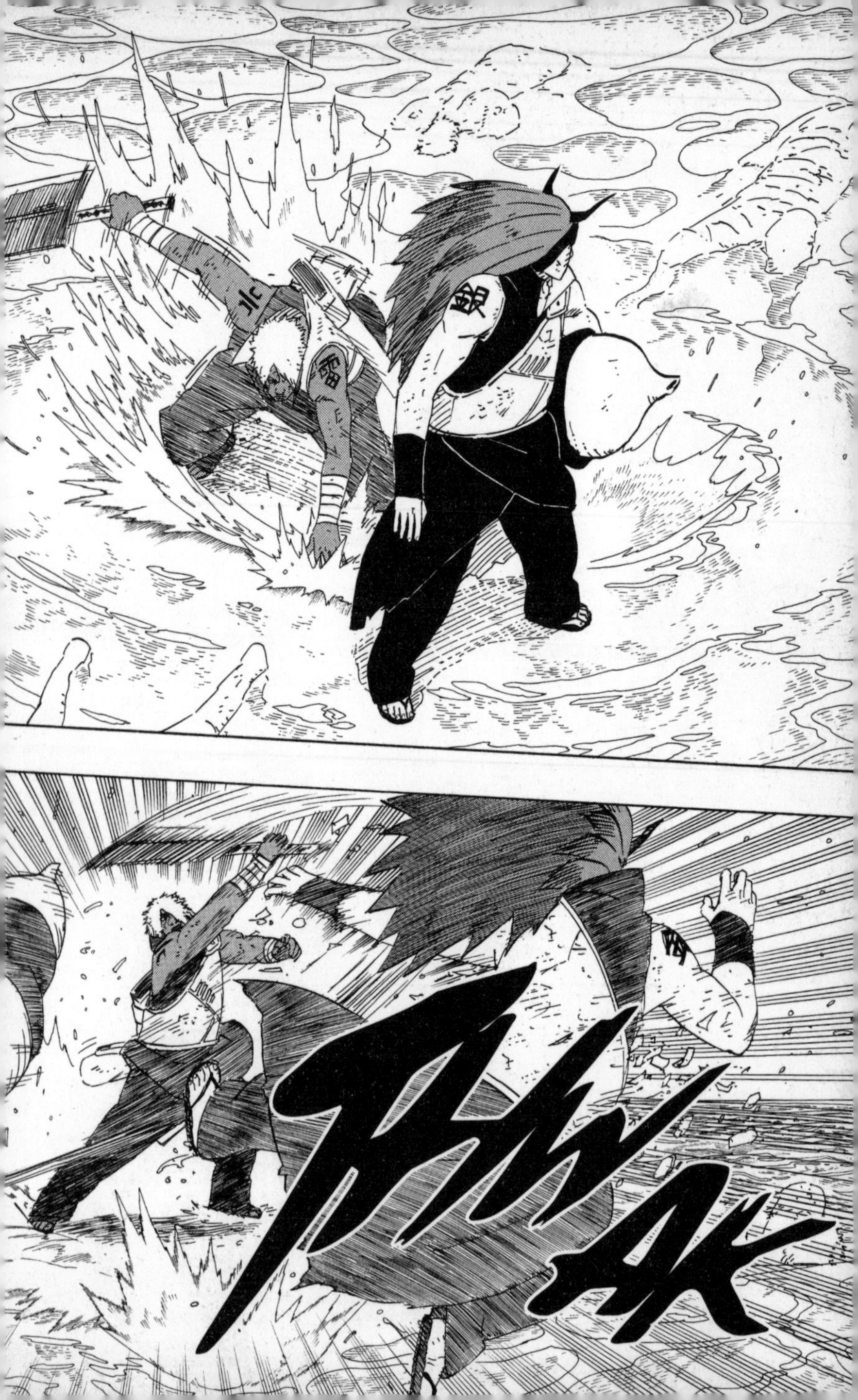
THWAK

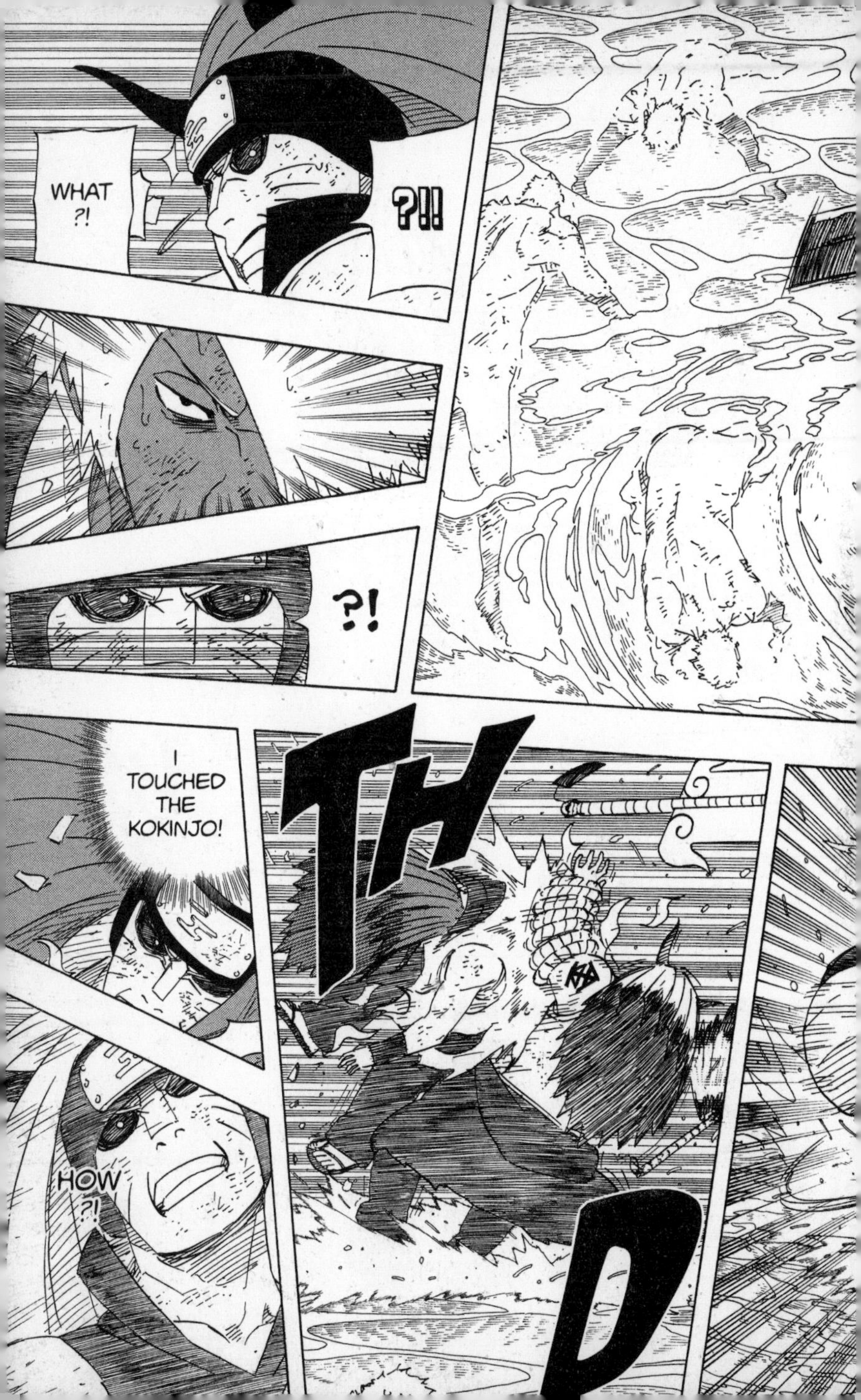
?!!
WHAT ?!
?!
THD
I TOUCHED THE KOKINJO!
HOW ?!

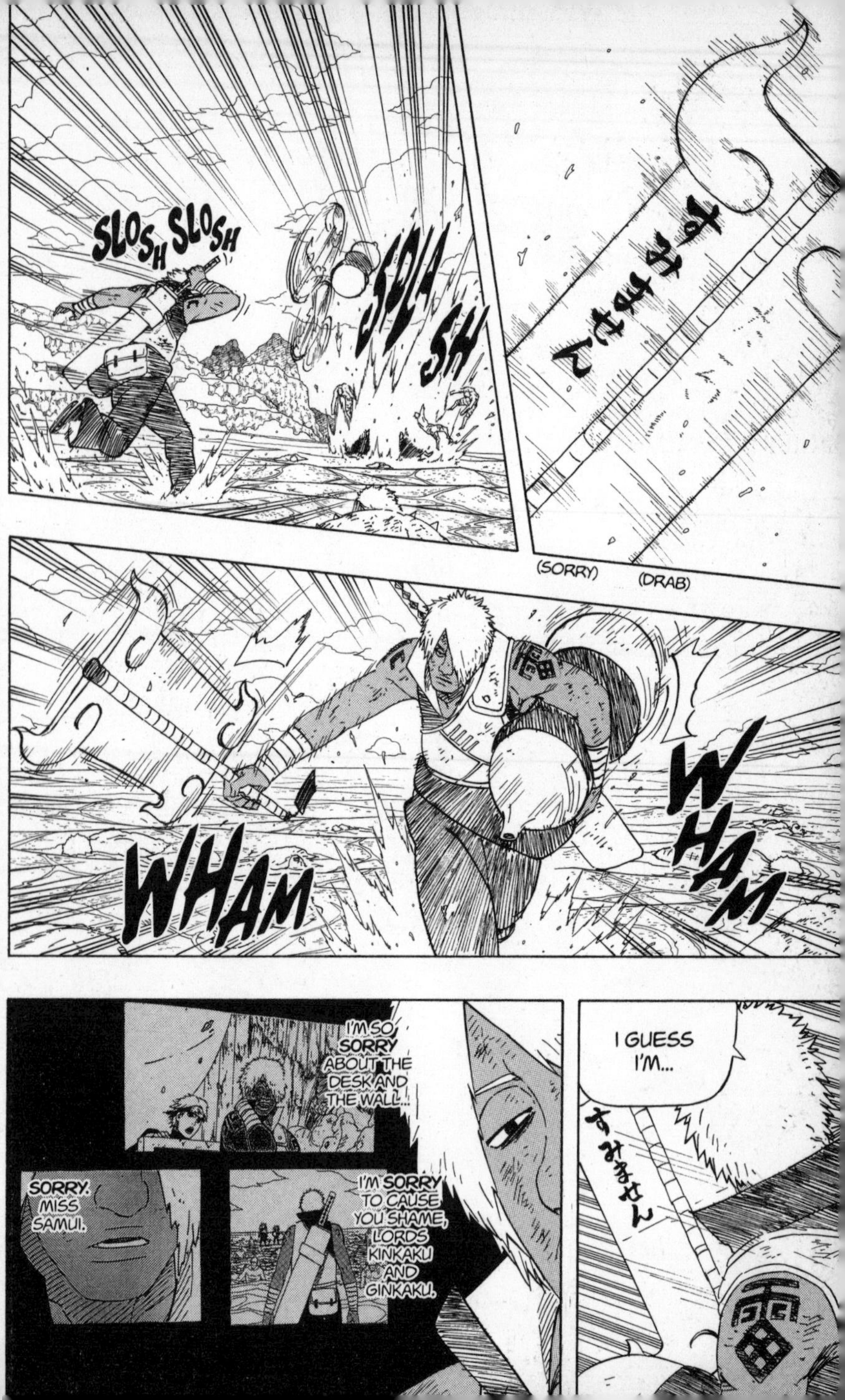
すみません
(SORRY)
(DRAB)
SLOSH SLOSH
SPLASH
WHAM
WHAM
I GUESS I'M...
すみません
I'M SO SORRY ABOUT THE DESK AND THE WALL...
I'M SORRY TO CAUSE YOU SHAME, LORDS KINKAKU AND GINKAKU.
SORRY. MISS SAMUI.

« READ THIS WAY «

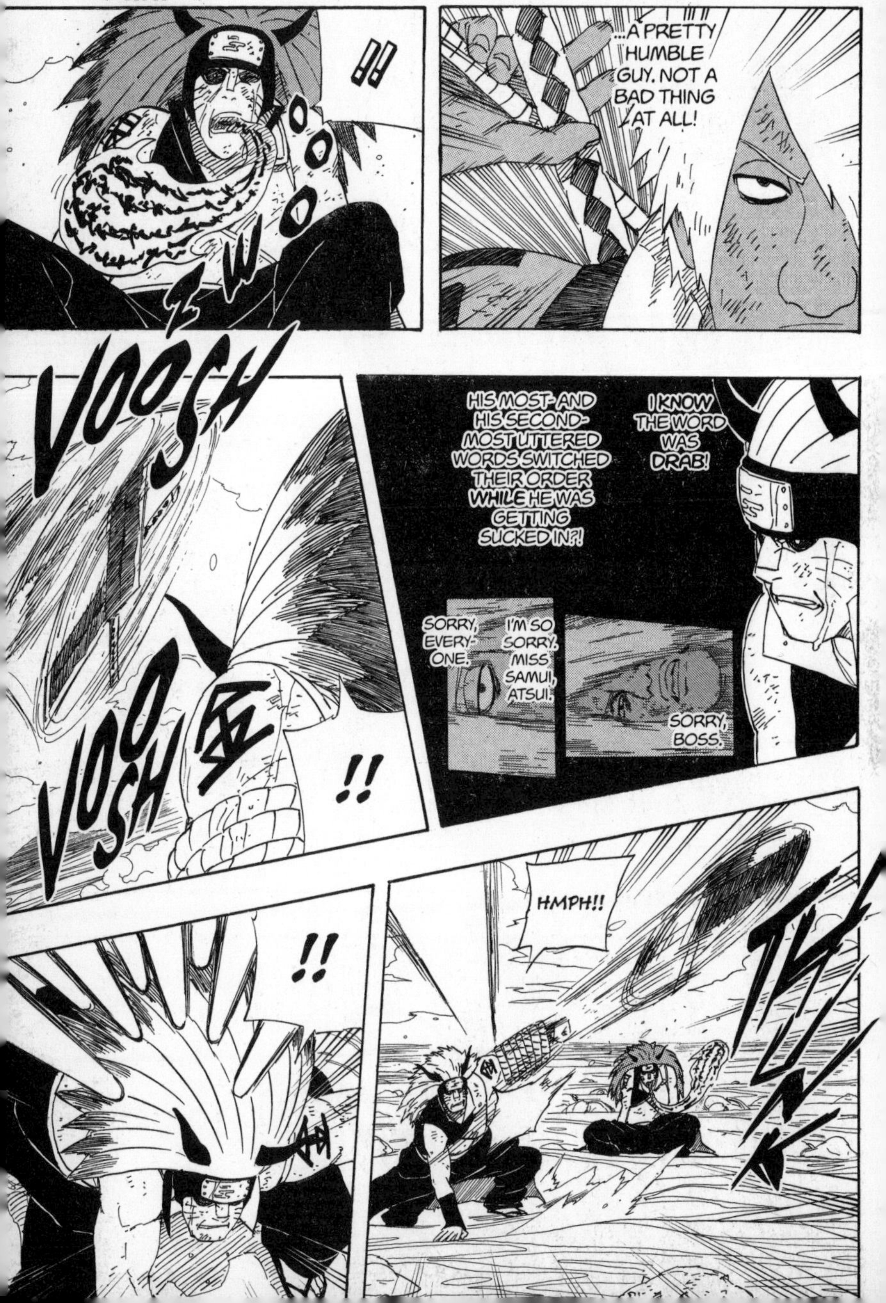
...A PRETTY HUMBLE GUY. NOT A BAD THING AT ALL!
!!
ZWOOO
I KNOW THE WORD WAS DRAB!
HIS MOST- AND HIS SECOND-MOST UTTERED WORDS SWITCHED THEIR ORDER WHILE HE WAS GETTING SUCKED IN?!
SORRY, BOSS.
I'M SO SORRY. MISS SAMUI, ATSUI.
SORRY, EVERY-ONE.
VOOSH
VOOSH
!!
HMPH!!
THUNK
!!

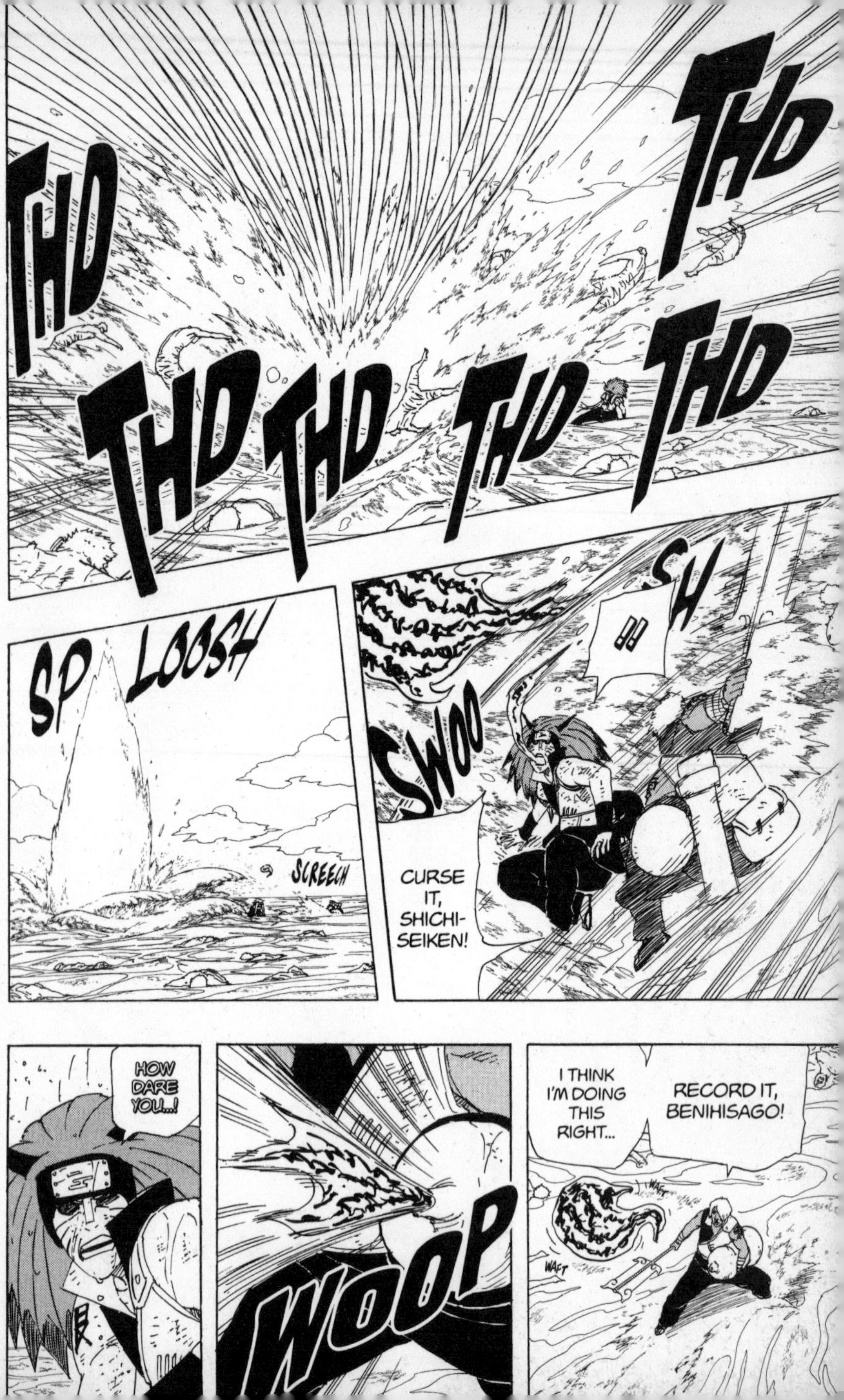
THD
THD
THD
THD
THD
THD
SH
!!
SWOO
CURSE IT, SHICHISEIKEN!
SPLOOSH
SCREECH
RECORD IT, BENIHISAGO!
I THINK I'M DOING THIS RIGHT...
WAFT
WAFT
WOOP
HOW DARE YOU...!

READ THIS WAY

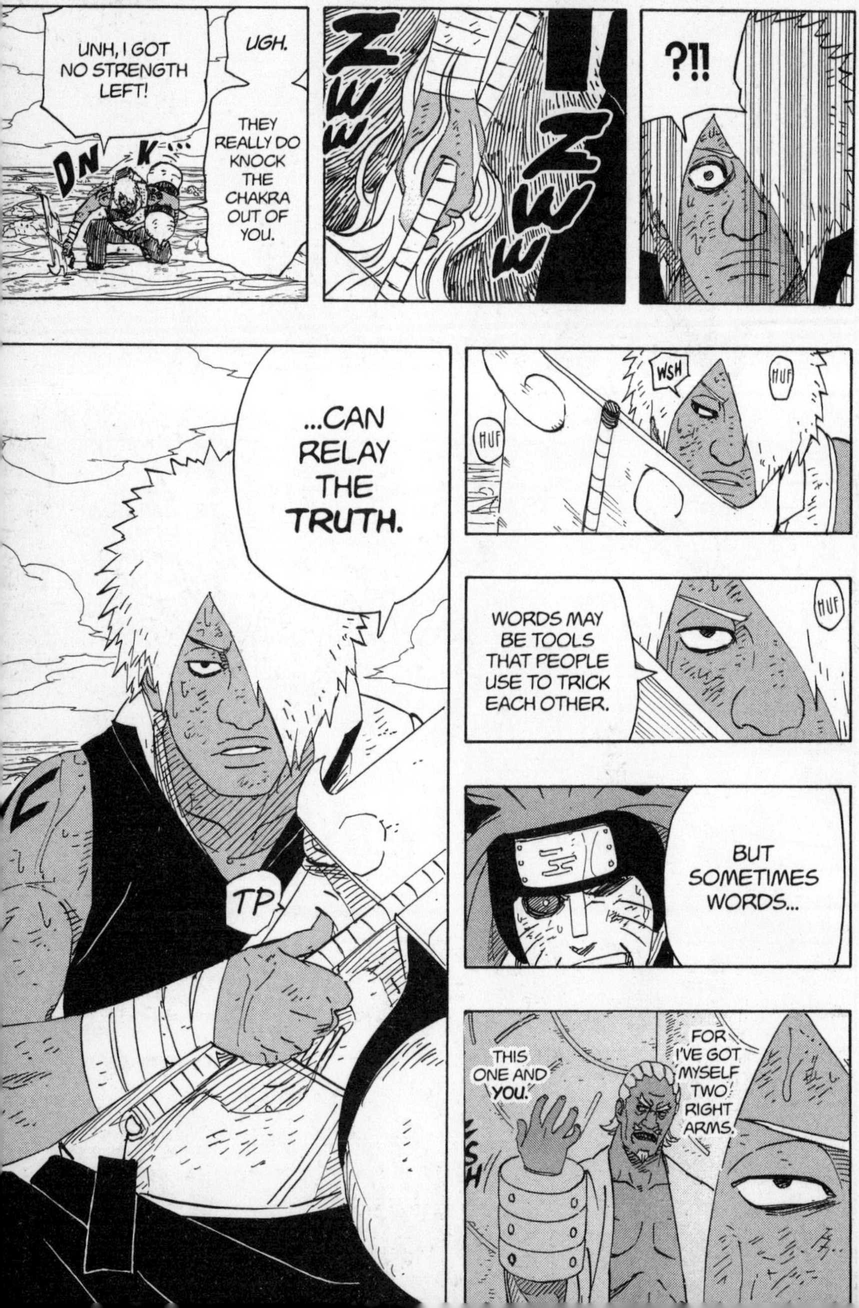
?!!
UGH.
THEY REALLY DO KNOCK THE CHAKRA OUT OF YOU.
UNH, I GOT NO STRENGTH LEFT!
DNK...
WSH
HUF
HUF
HUF
WORDS MAY BE TOOLS THAT PEOPLE USE TO TRICK EACH OTHER.
BUT SOMETIMES WORDS...
FOR I'VE GOT MYSELF TWO RIGHT ARMS.
THIS ONE AND YOU.
...CAN RELAY THE TRUTH.
TP

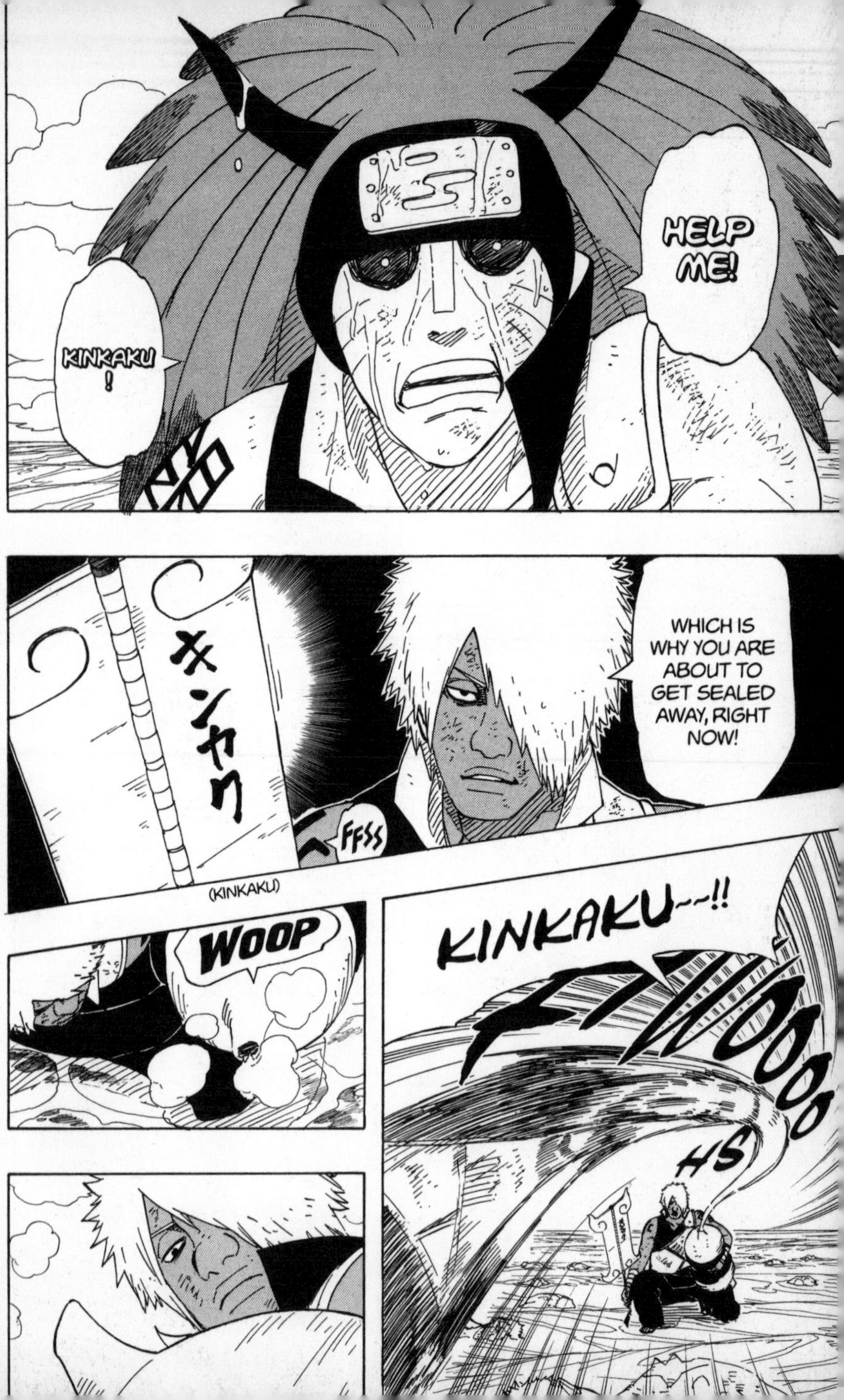
HELP ME!
KINKAKU!
WHICH IS WHY YOU ARE ABOUT TO GET SEALED AWAY, RIGHT NOW!
キンカク
FFSS
(KINKAKU)
KINKAKU~~!!
FWOOOOOSH
WOOP

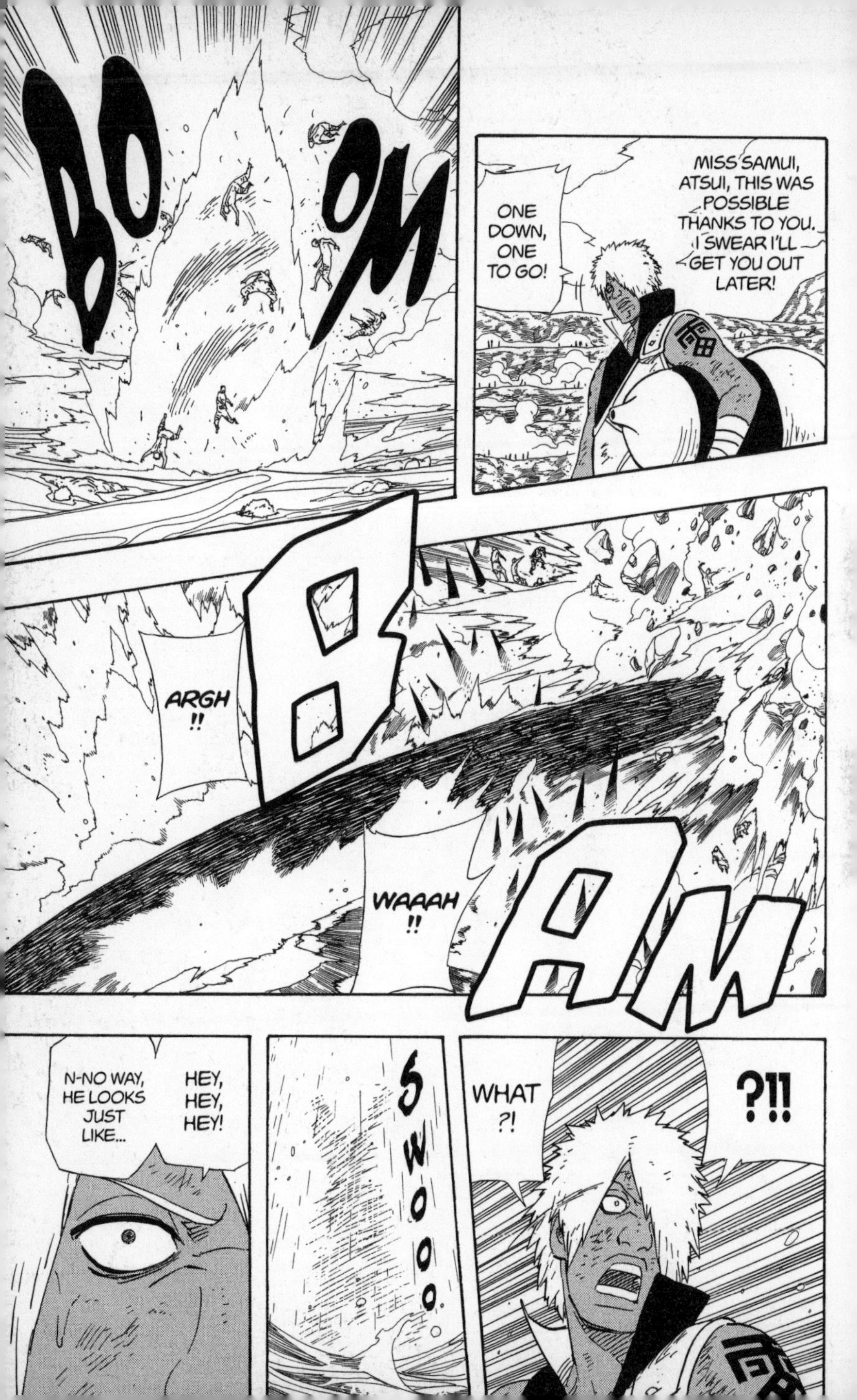
MISS SAMUI, ATSUI, THIS WAS POSSIBLE THANKS TO YOU. I SWEAR I'LL GET YOU OUT LATER!
ONE DOWN, ONE TO GO!
BOOM
BAM
ARGH !!
WAAAH !!
?!!
WHAT ?!
SWOOO
HEY, HEY, HEY!
N-NO WAY, HE LOOKS JUST LIKE...

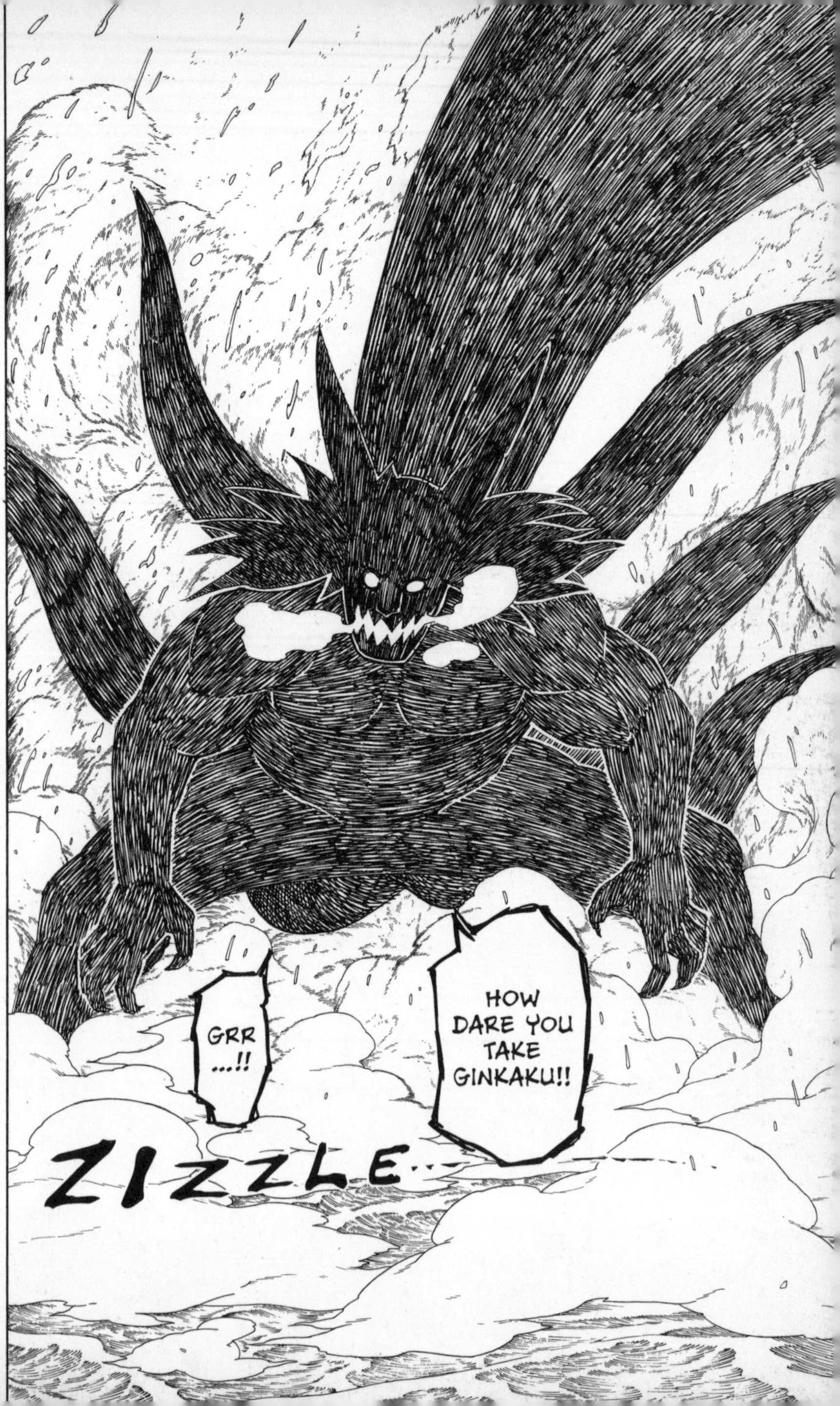
HOW DARE YOU TAKE GINKAKU!!
GRR ...!!
ZIZZLE...

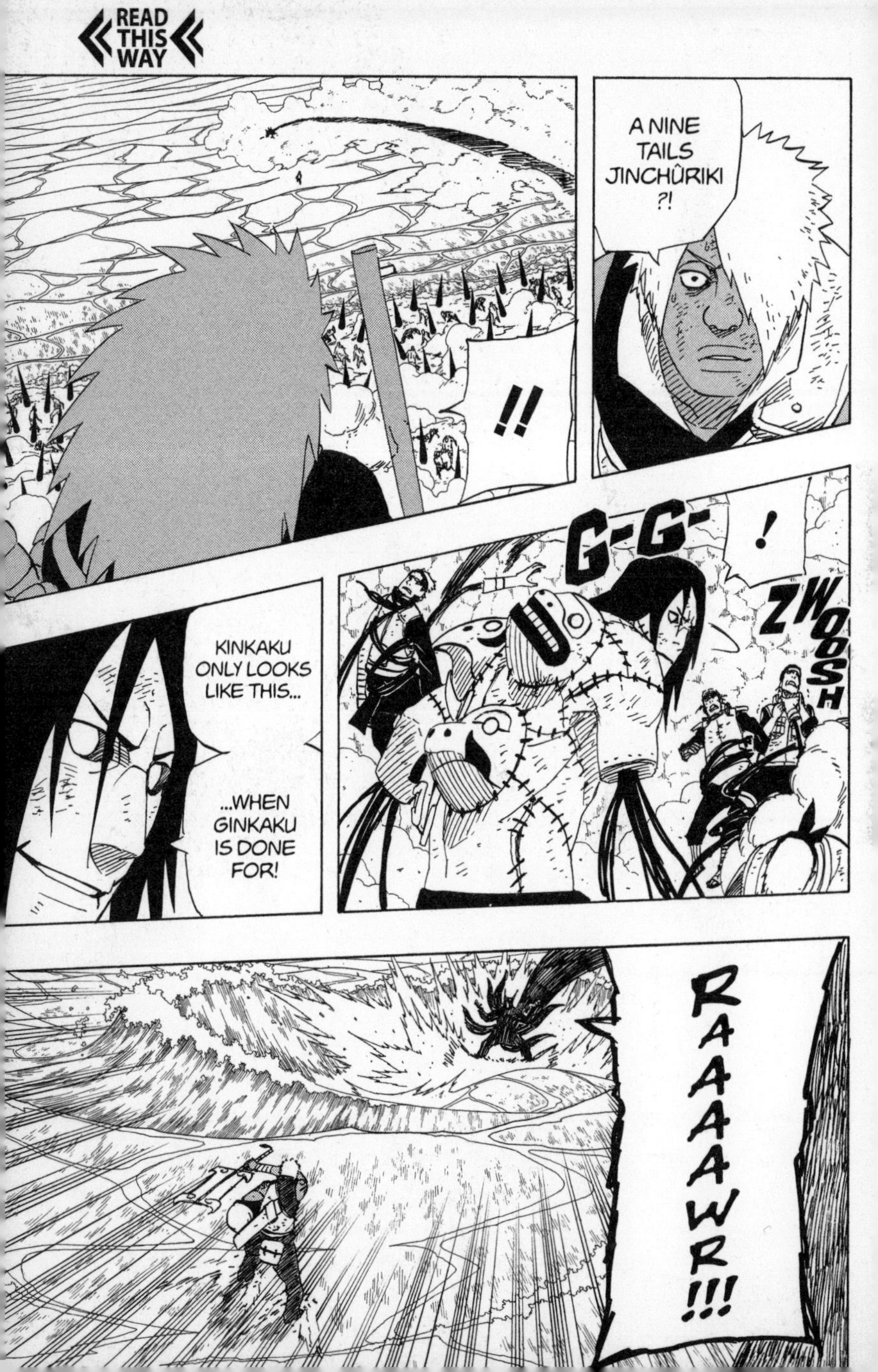
READ THIS WAY
A NINE TAILS JINCHÛRIKI ?!
!!
G-G-
!
ZWOOSH
KINKAKU ONLY LOOKS LIKE THIS...
...WHEN GINKAKU IS DONE FOR!
RAAAAWR!!!

NARUTO

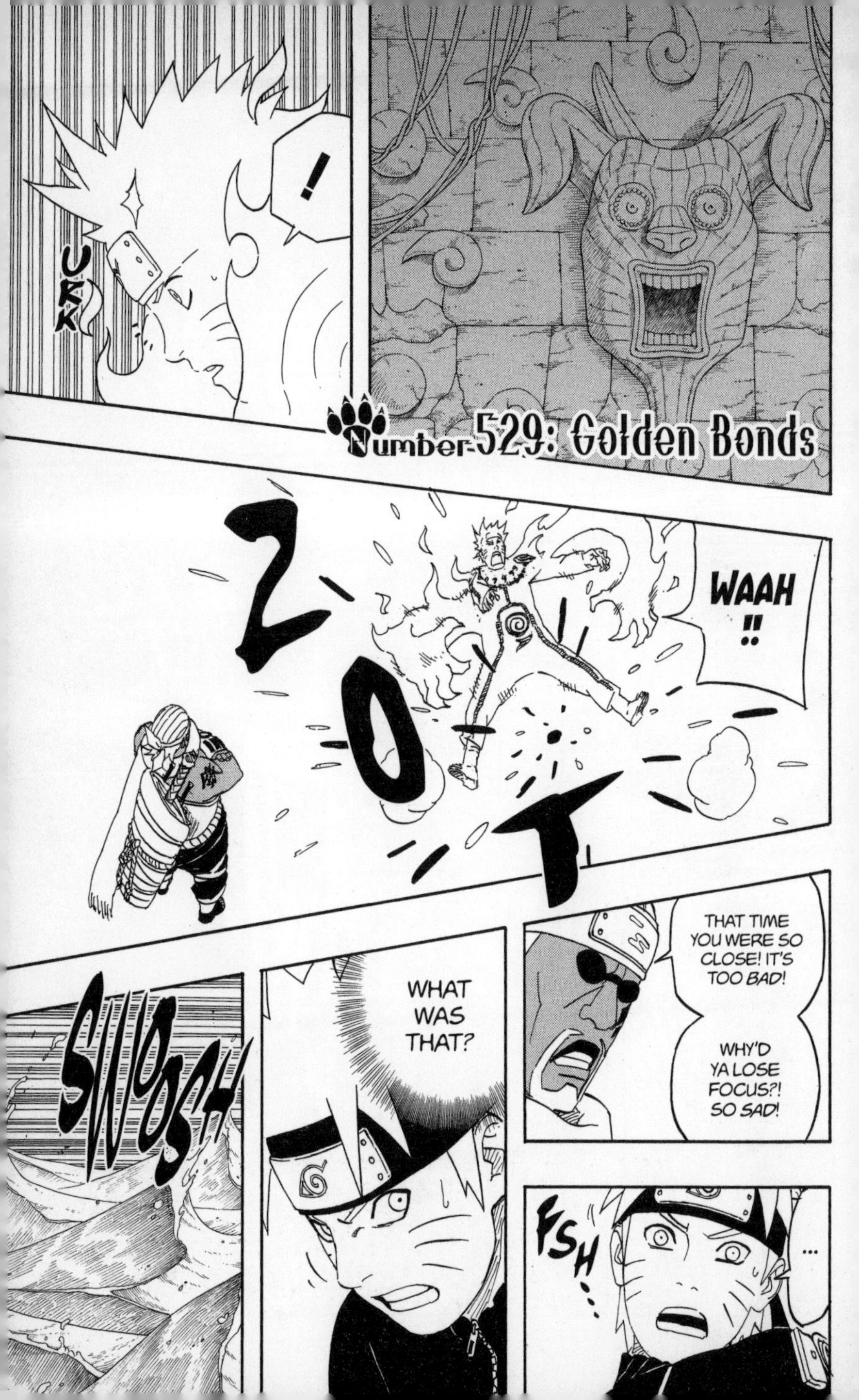
Number 529: Golden Bonds
!
URK
WAAH!!
ZOT
THAT TIME YOU WERE SO CLOSE! IT'S TOO BAD!
WHY'D YA LOSE FOCUS?! SO SAD!
FSH...
...
WHAT WAS THAT?
SWOSH

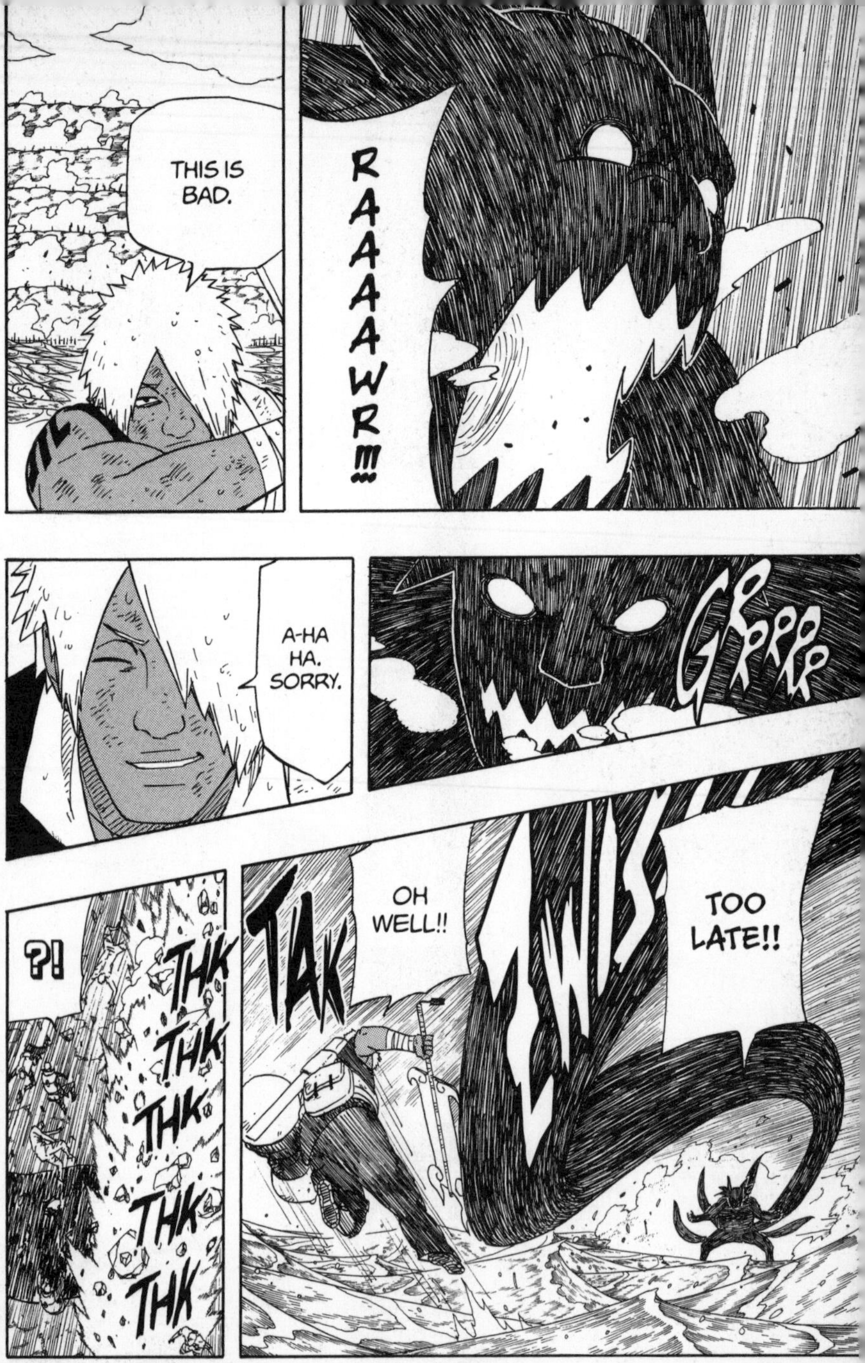
RAAAAAWR!!!
THIS IS BAD.
GRRRR
A-HA HA. SORRY.
TOO LATE!!
OH WELL!!
TAK
?!
THK THK THK THK THK

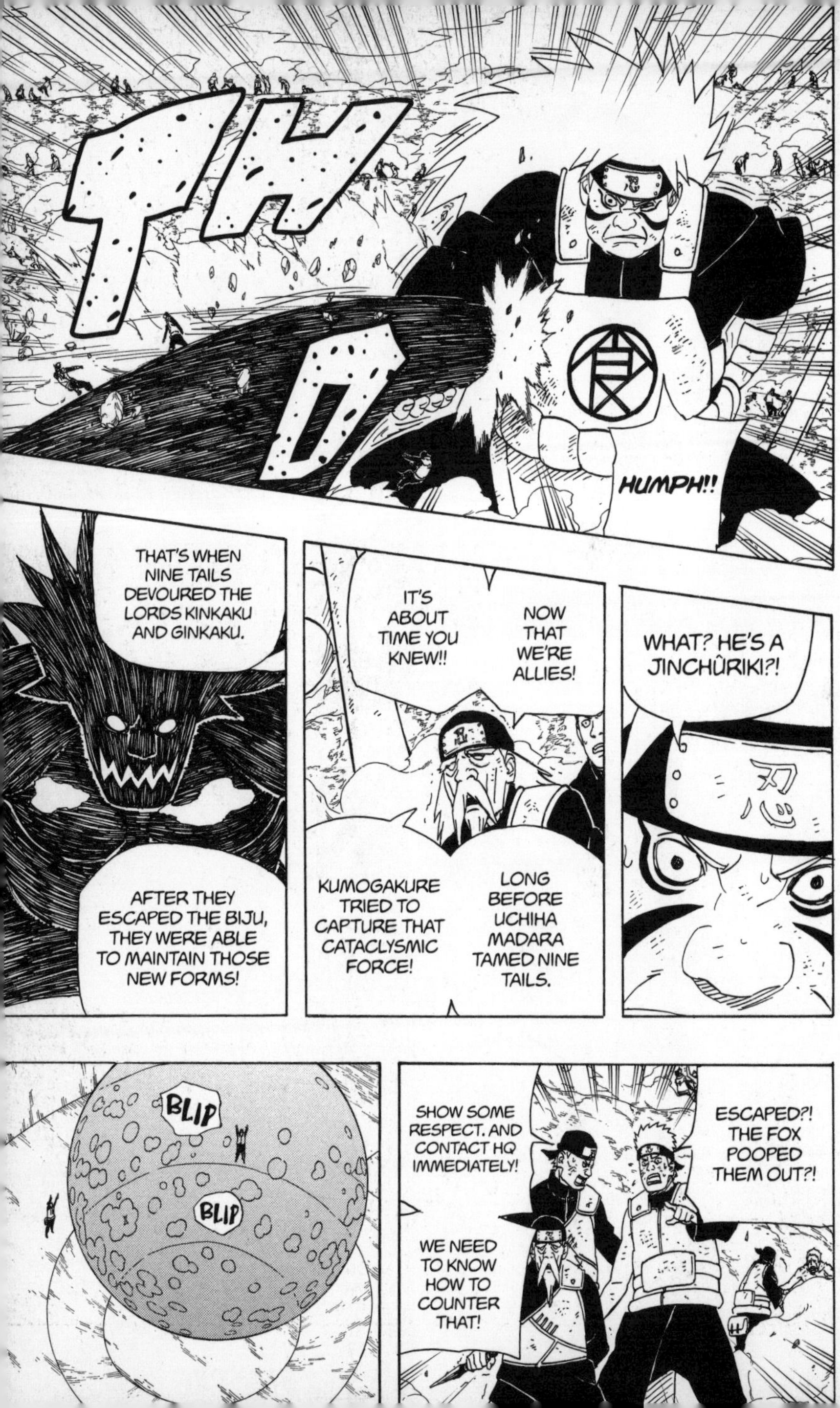

HUMPH!!
WHAT? HE'S A JINCHÛRIKI?!
NOW THAT WE'RE ALLIES!
IT'S ABOUT TIME YOU KNEW!!
LONG BEFORE UCHIHA MADARA TAMED NINE TAILS.
KUMOGAKURE TRIED TO CAPTURE THAT CATACLYSMIC FORCE!
THAT'S WHEN NINE TAILS DEVOURED THE LORDS KINKAKU AND GINKAKU.
AFTER THEY ESCAPED THE BIJU, THEY WERE ABLE TO MAINTAIN THOSE NEW FORMS!
ESCAPED?! THE FOX POOPED THEM OUT?!
SHOW SOME RESPECT. AND CONTACT HQ IMMEDIATELY!
WE NEED TO KNOW HOW TO COUNTER THAT!
BLIP
BLIP

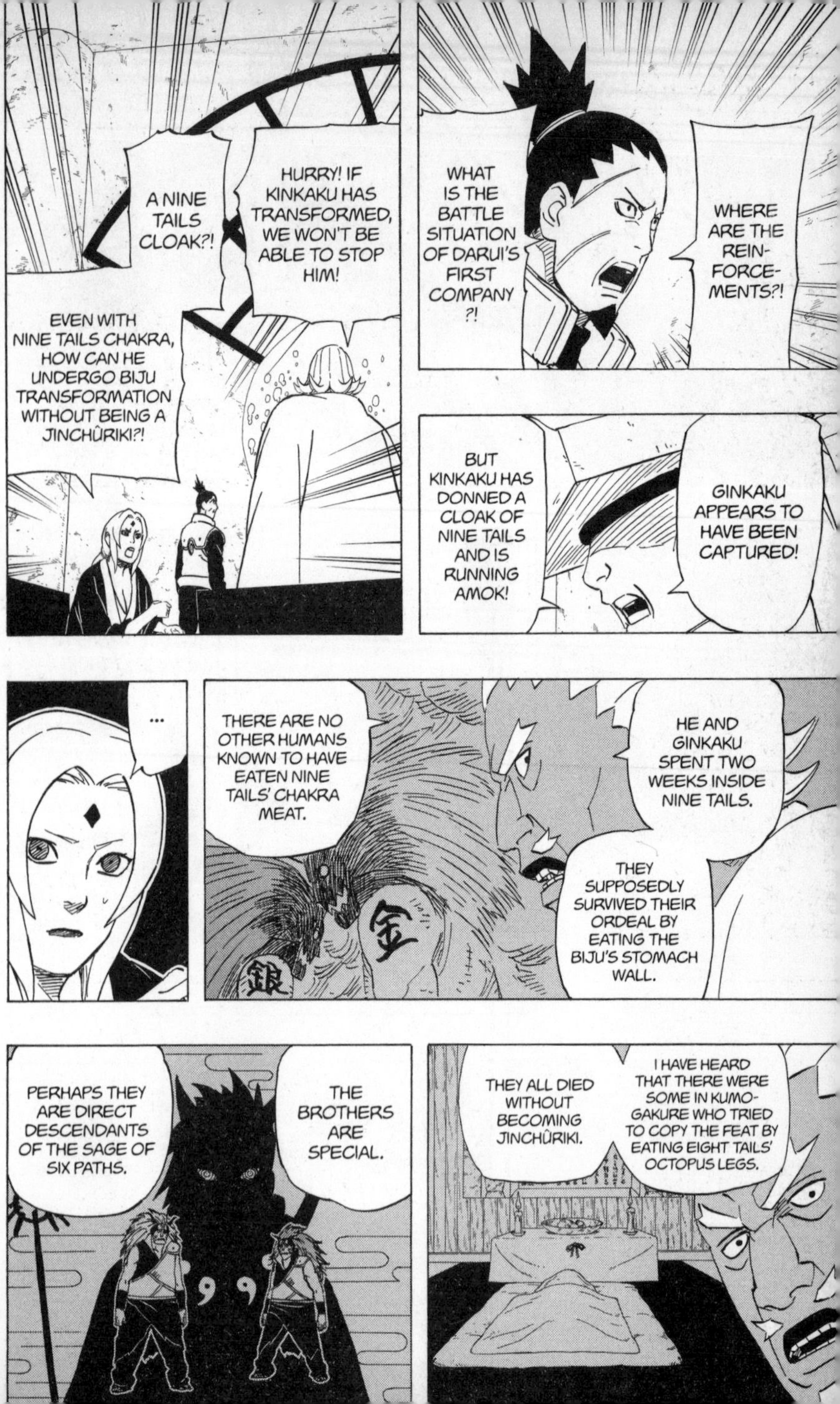

WHERE ARE THE REIN-FORCEMENTS?!
WHAT IS THE BATTLE SITUATION OF DARUI'S FIRST COMPANY ?!
GINKAKU APPEARS TO HAVE BEEN CAPTURED!
BUT KINKAKU HAS DONNED A CLOAK OF NINE TAILS AND IS RUNNING AMOK!
HURRY! IF KINKAKU HAS TRANSFORMED, WE WON'T BE ABLE TO STOP HIM!
A NINE TAILS CLOAK?!
EVEN WITH NINE TAILS CHAKRA, HOW CAN HE UNDERGO BIJU TRANSFORMATION WITHOUT BEING A JINCHÛRIKI?!
HE AND GINKAKU SPENT TWO WEEKS INSIDE NINE TAILS.
THEY SUPPOSEDLY SURVIVED THEIR ORDEAL BY EATING THE BIJU'S STOMACH WALL.
THERE ARE NO OTHER HUMANS KNOWN TO HAVE EATEN NINE TAILS' CHAKRA MEAT.
...
I HAVE HEARD THAT THERE WERE SOME IN KUMO-GAKURE WHO TRIED TO COPY THE FEAT BY EATING EIGHT TAILS' OCTOPUS LEGS.
THEY ALL DIED WITHOUT BECOMING JINCHÛRIKI.
THE BROTHERS ARE SPECIAL.
PERHAPS THEY ARE DIRECT DESCENDANTS OF THE SAGE OF SIX PATHS.

READ THIS WAY

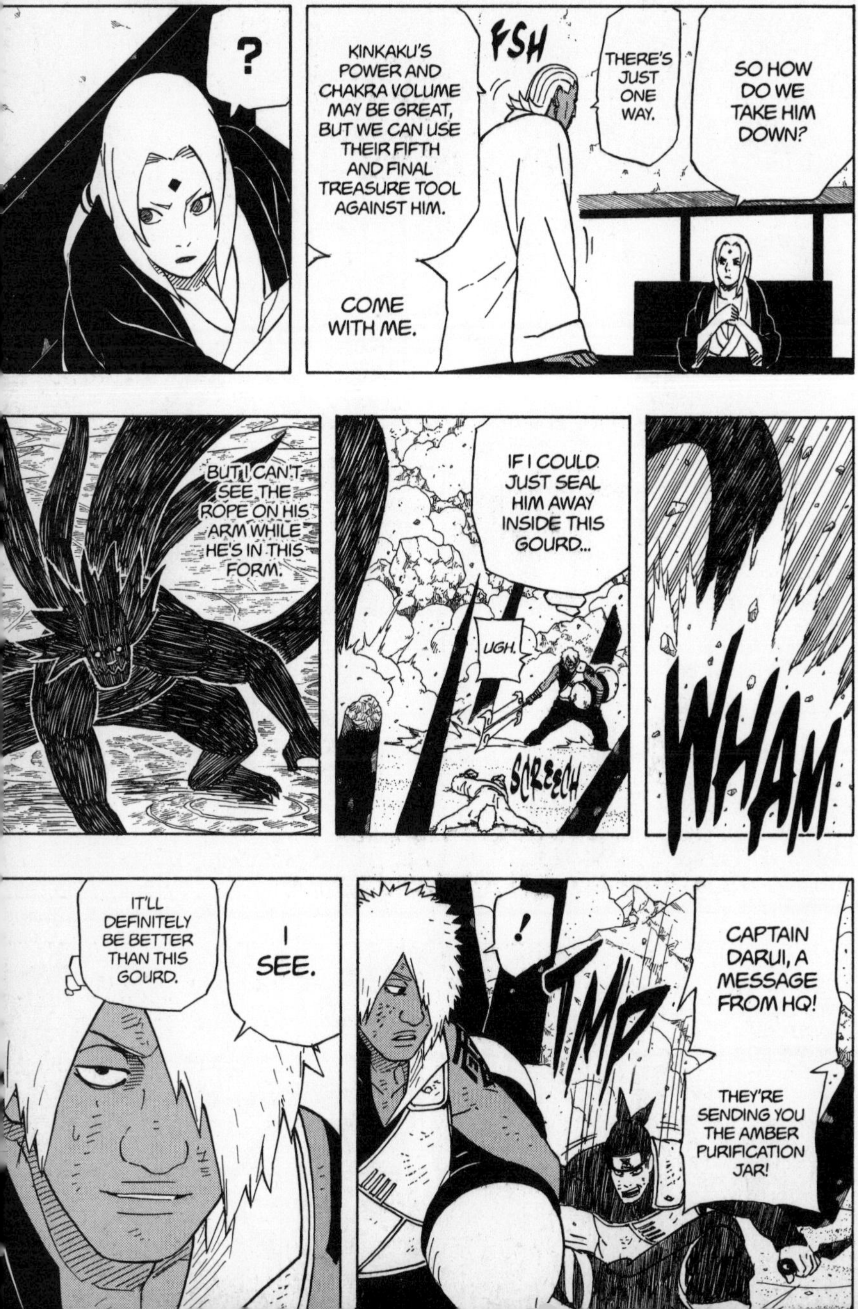
SO HOW DO WE TAKE HIM DOWN?
THERE'S JUST ONE WAY.
FSH
KINKAKU'S POWER AND CHAKRA VOLUME MAY BE GREAT, BUT WE CAN USE THEIR FIFTH AND FINAL TREASURE TOOL AGAINST HIM.
COME WITH ME.
?
WHAM
IF I COULD JUST SEAL HIM AWAY INSIDE THIS GOURD...
UGH.
SCREECH
BUT I CAN'T SEE THE ROPE ON HIS ARM WHILE HE'S IN THIS FORM.
CAPTAIN DARUI, A MESSAGE FROM HQ!
!
TMP
THEY'RE SENDING YOU THE AMBER PURIFICATION JAR!
I SEE.
IT'LL DEFINITELY BE BETTER THAN THIS GOURD.

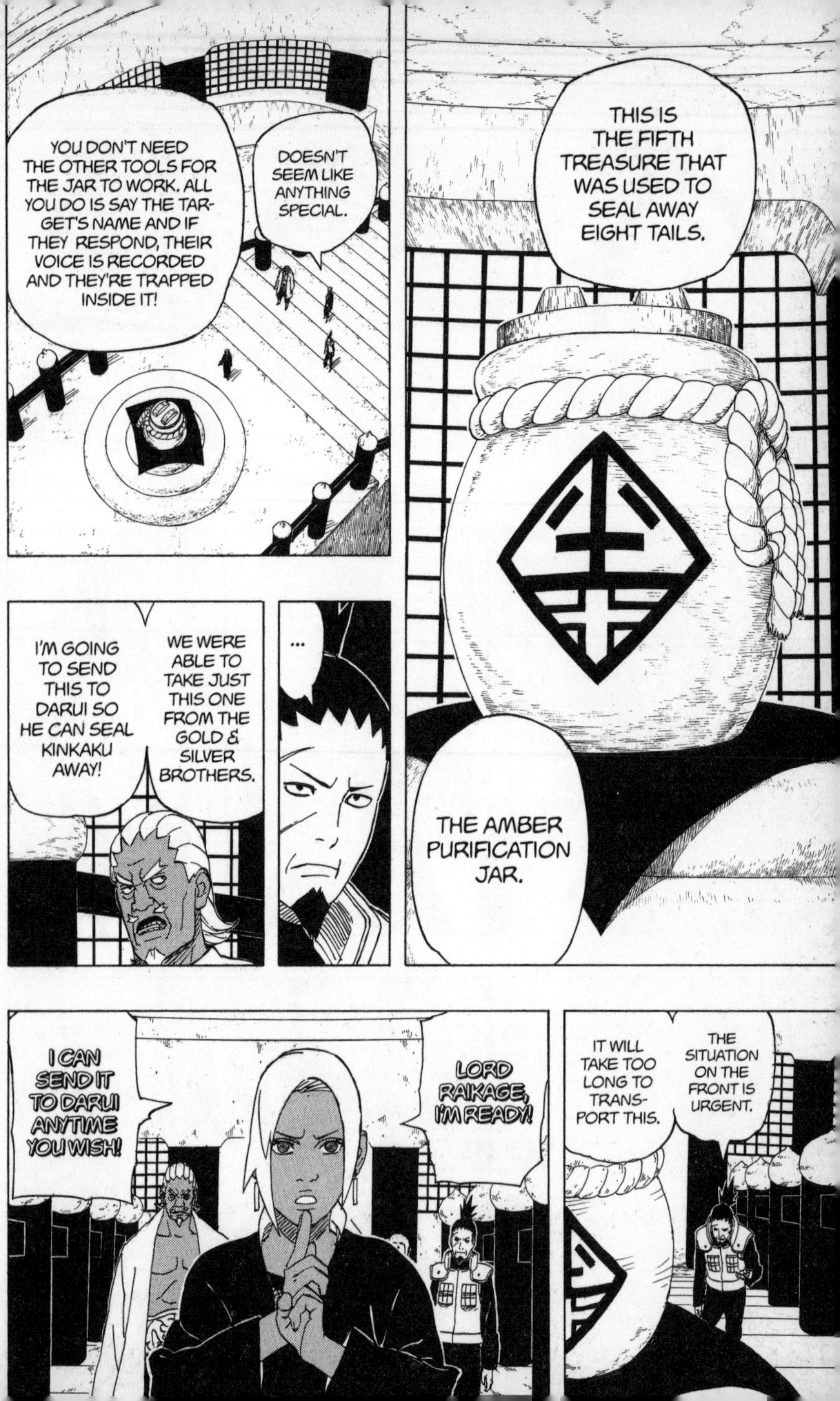
THIS IS THE FIFTH TREASURE THAT WAS USED TO SEAL AWAY EIGHT TAILS.
THE AMBER PURIFICATION JAR.
DOESN'T SEEM LIKE ANYTHING SPECIAL.
YOU DON'T NEED THE OTHER TOOLS FOR THE JAR TO WORK. ALL YOU DO IS SAY THE TAR-GET'S NAME AND IF THEY RESPOND, THEIR VOICE IS RECORDED AND THEY'RE TRAPPED INSIDE IT!
...
WE WERE ABLE TO TAKE JUST THIS ONE FROM THE GOLD & SILVER BROTHERS.
I'M GOING TO SEND THIS TO DARUI SO HE CAN SEAL KINKAKU AWAY!
THE SITUATION ON THE FRONT IS URGENT.
IT WILL TAKE TOO LONG TO TRANS-PORT THIS.
LORD RAIKAGE, I'M READY!
I CAN SEND IT TO DARUI ANYTIME YOU WISH!

READ THIS WAY

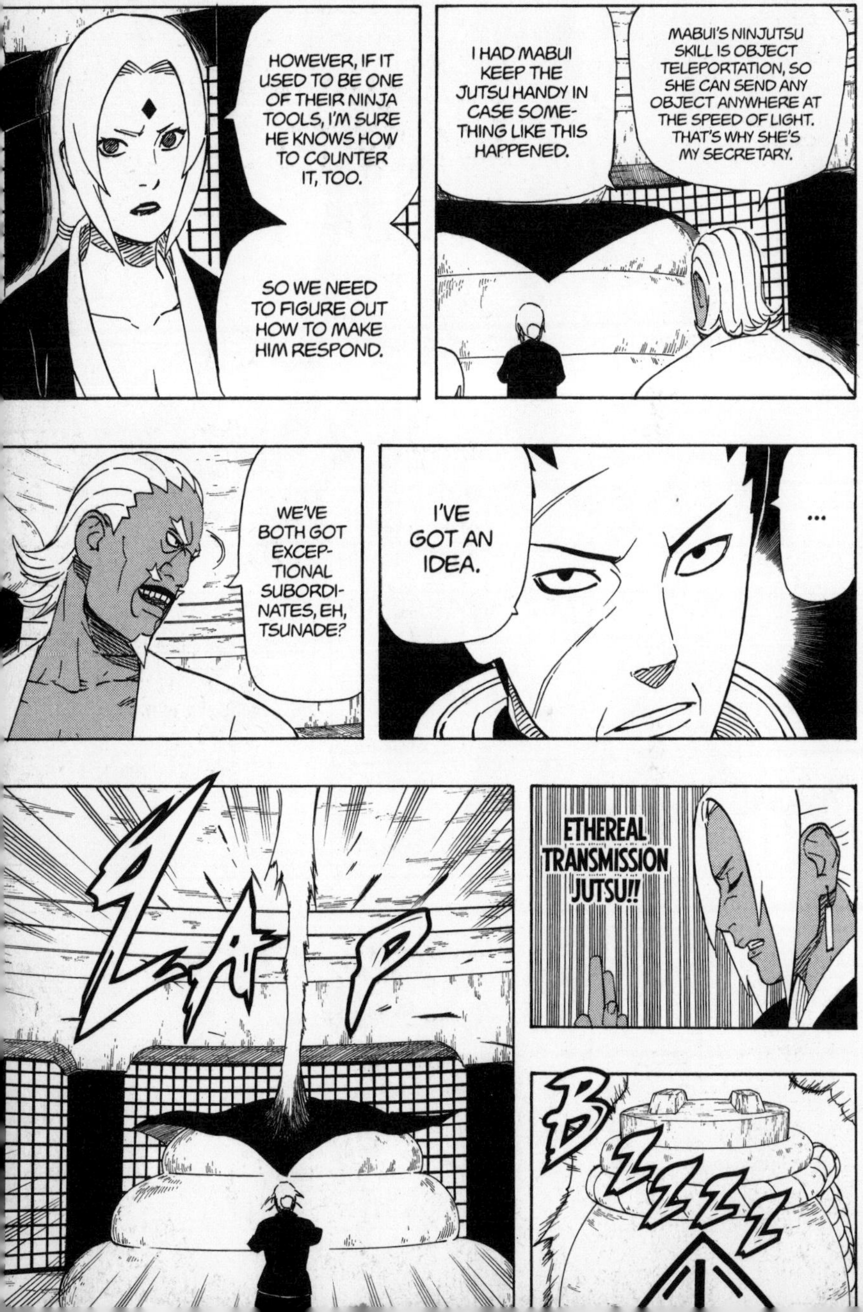
MABUI'S NINJUTSU SKILL IS OBJECT TELEPORTATION, SO SHE CAN SEND ANY OBJECT ANYWHERE AT THE SPEED OF LIGHT. THAT'S WHY SHE'S MY SECRETARY.
I HAD MABUI KEEP THE JUTSU HANDY IN CASE SOME-THING LIKE THIS HAPPENED.
HOWEVER, IF IT USED TO BE ONE OF THEIR NINJA TOOLS, I'M SURE HE KNOWS HOW TO COUNTER IT, TOO.
SO WE NEED TO FIGURE OUT HOW TO MAKE HIM RESPOND.
...
I'VE GOT AN IDEA.
WE'VE BOTH GOT EXCEP-TIONAL SUBORDI-NATES, EH, TSUNADE?
ETHEREAL TRANSMISSION JUTSU!!
BZZZZZ
ZAP

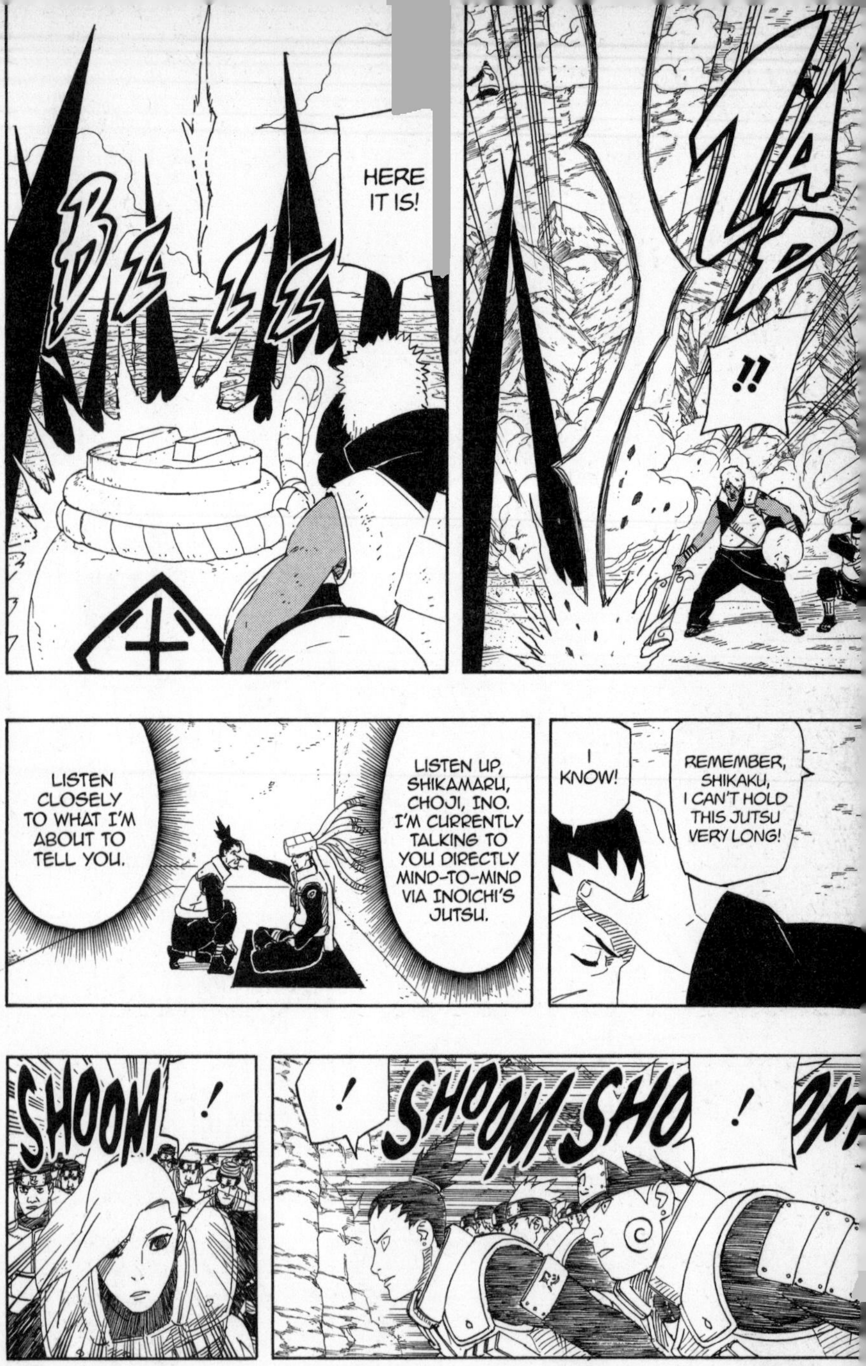
ZAP
!!
BZZZ
HERE IT IS!
REMEMBER, SHIKAKU, I CAN'T HOLD THIS JUTSU VERY LONG!
I KNOW!
LISTEN UP, SHIKAMARU, CHOJI, INO. I'M CURRENTLY TALKING TO YOU DIRECTLY MIND-TO-MIND VIA INOICHI'S JUTSU.
LISTEN CLOSELY TO WHAT I'M ABOUT TO TELL YOU.
!
SHOOM SHO
!
SHOOM
!

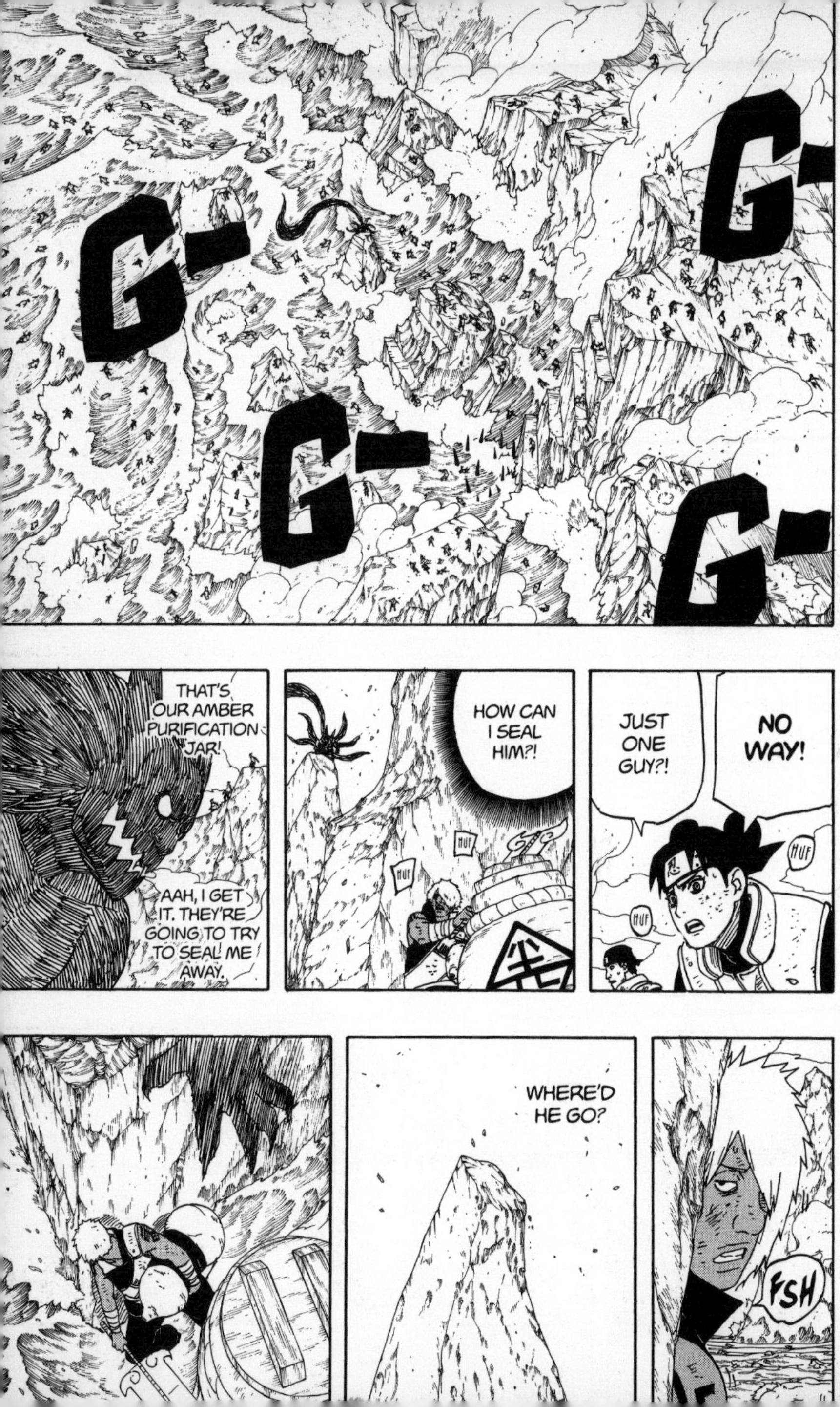
G-
G-
G-
G-
NO WAY!
JUST ONE GUY?!
HUF
HUF
HOW CAN I SEAL HIM?!
HUF
HUF
THAT'S OUR AMBER PURIFICATION JAR!
AAH, I GET IT. THEY'RE GOING TO TRY TO SEAL ME AWAY.
FSH
WHERE'D HE GO?

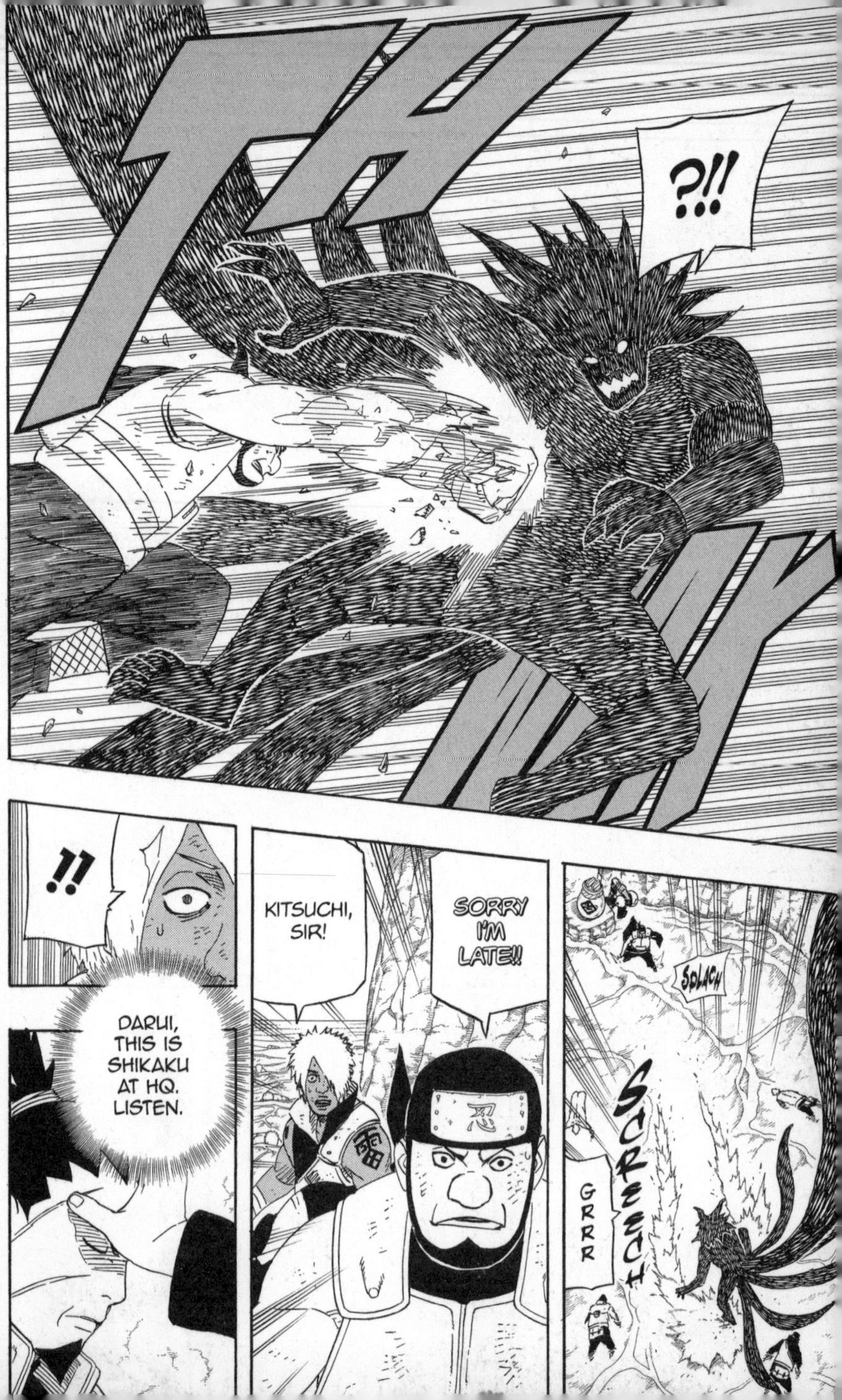
?!!
SPLACH
SCREECH
GRRR
SORRY I'M LATE!!
KITSUCHI, SIR!
!!
DARUI, THIS IS SHIKAKU AT HQ. LISTEN.

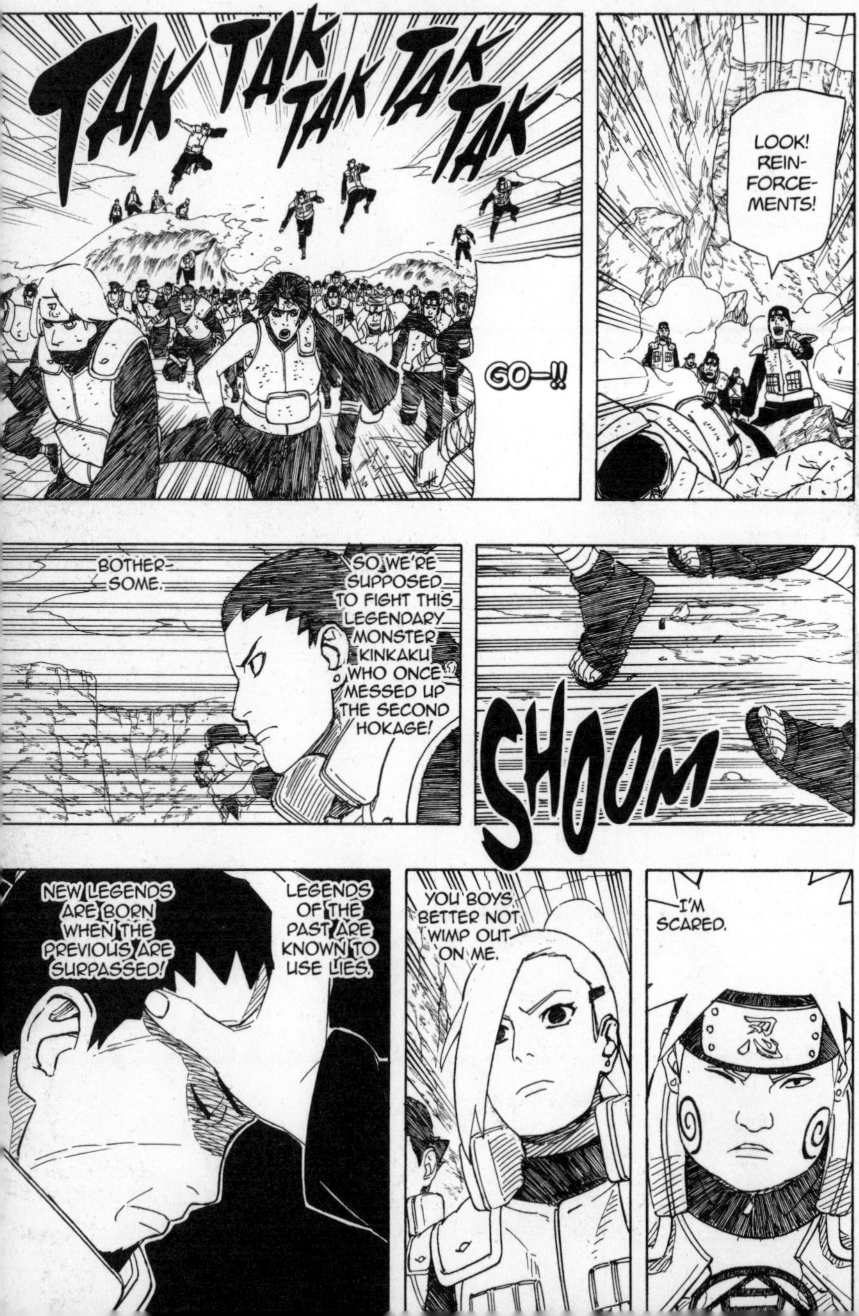
LOOK! REINFORCEMENTS!
TAK TAK TAK TAK TAK TAK
GO—!!
SHOOM
SO WE'RE SUPPOSED TO FIGHT THIS LEGENDARY MONSTER KINKAKU WHO ONCE MESSED UP THE SECOND HOKAGE!
BOTHERSOME.
I'M SCARED.
YOU BOYS BETTER NOT WIMP OUT ON ME.
LEGENDS OF THE PAST ARE KNOWN TO USE LIES.
NEW LEGENDS ARE BORN WHEN THE PREVIOUS ARE SURPASSED!

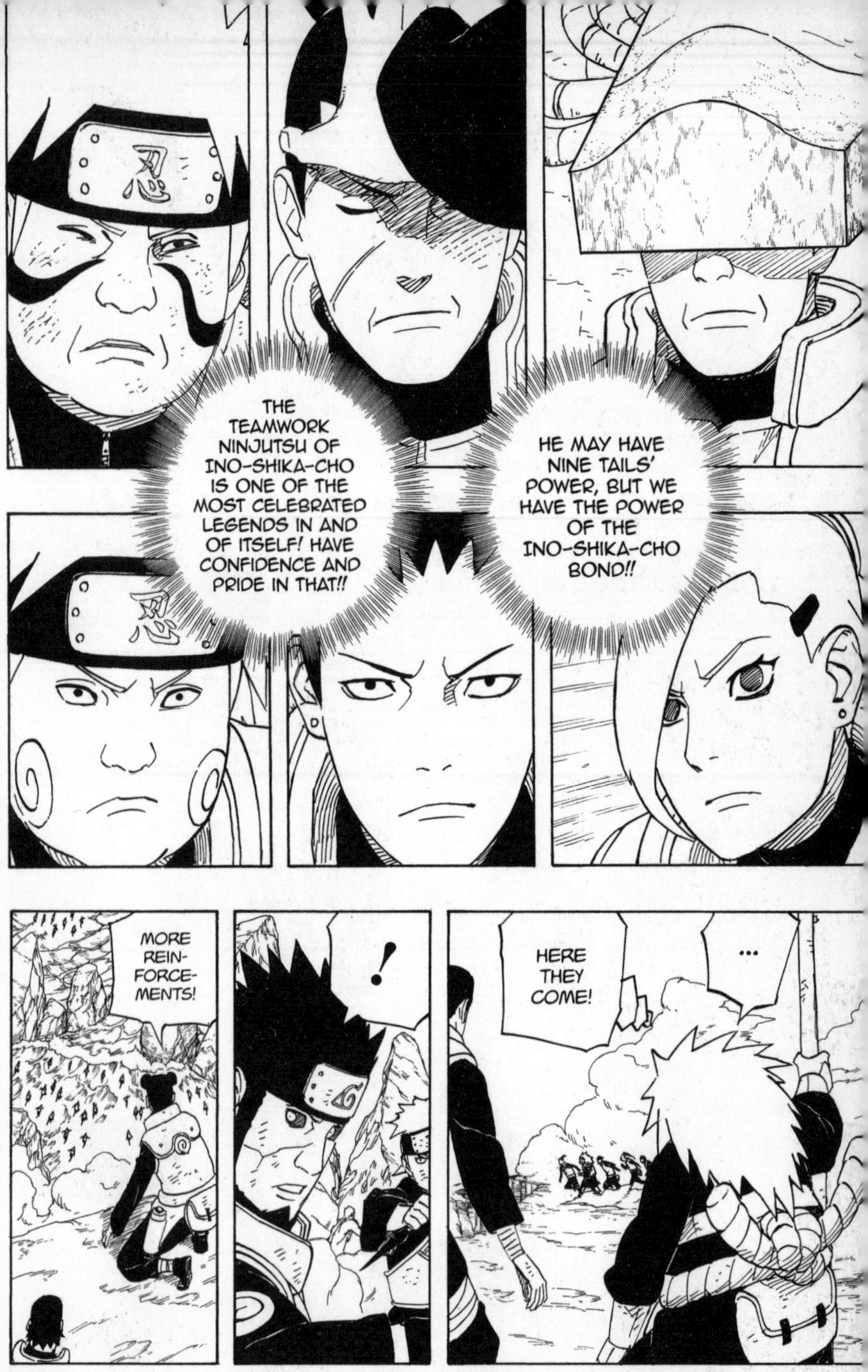
HE MAY HAVE NINE TAILS' POWER, BUT WE HAVE THE POWER OF THE INO-SHIKA-CHO BOND!!
THE TEAMWORK NINJUTSU OF INO-SHIKA-CHO IS ONE OF THE MOST CELEBRATED LEGENDS IN AND OF ITSELF! HAVE CONFIDENCE AND PRIDE IN THAT!!
...
HERE THEY COME!
!
MORE REIN-FORCE-MENTS!

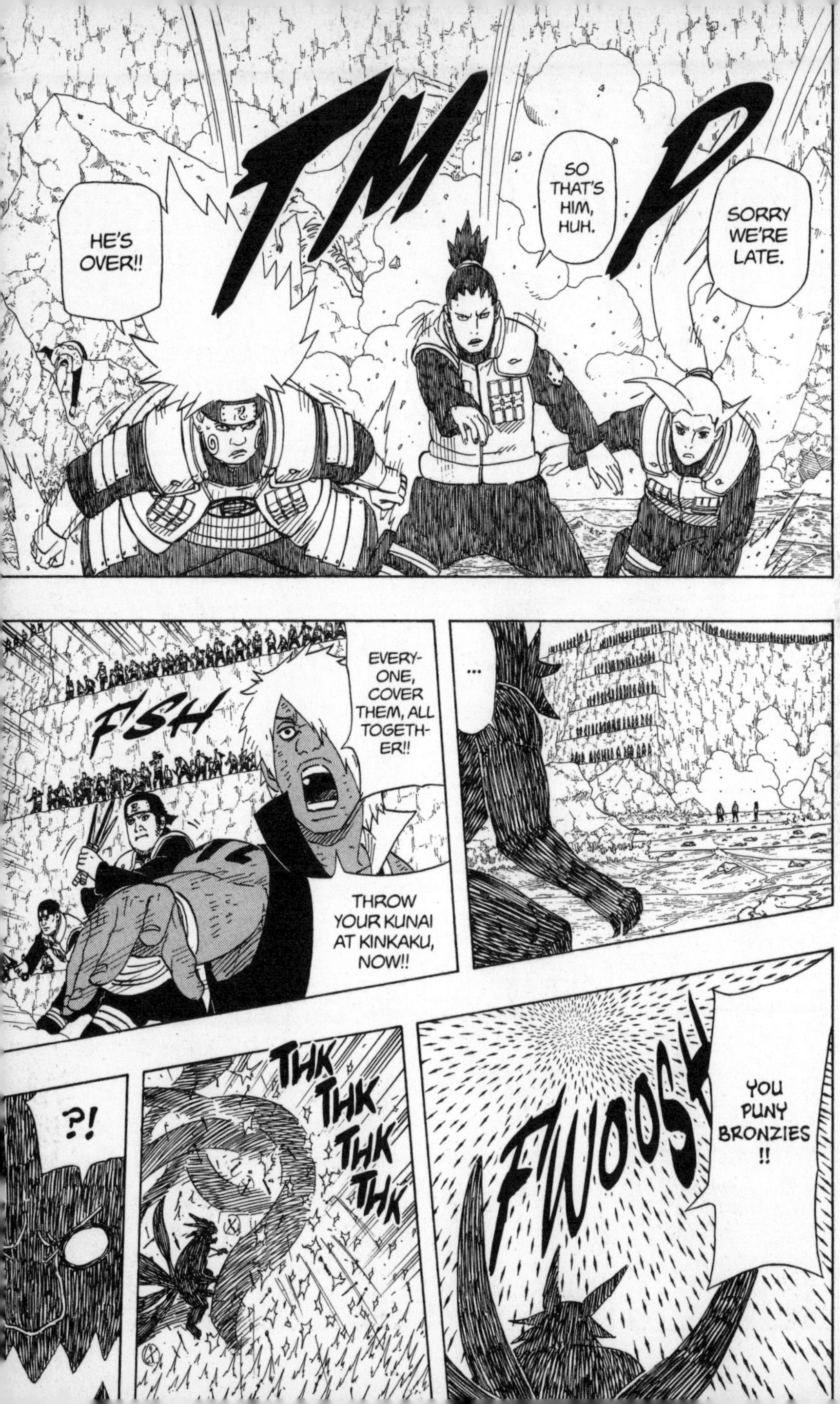
SORRY WE'RE LATE.
SO THAT'S HIM, HUH.
TMP
HE'S OVER!!
...
EVERYONE, COVER THEM, ALL TOGETHER!!
FISH
THROW YOUR KUNAI AT KINKAKU, NOW!!
YOU PUNY BRONZIES!!
FWOOSH
THK THK THK THK
?!

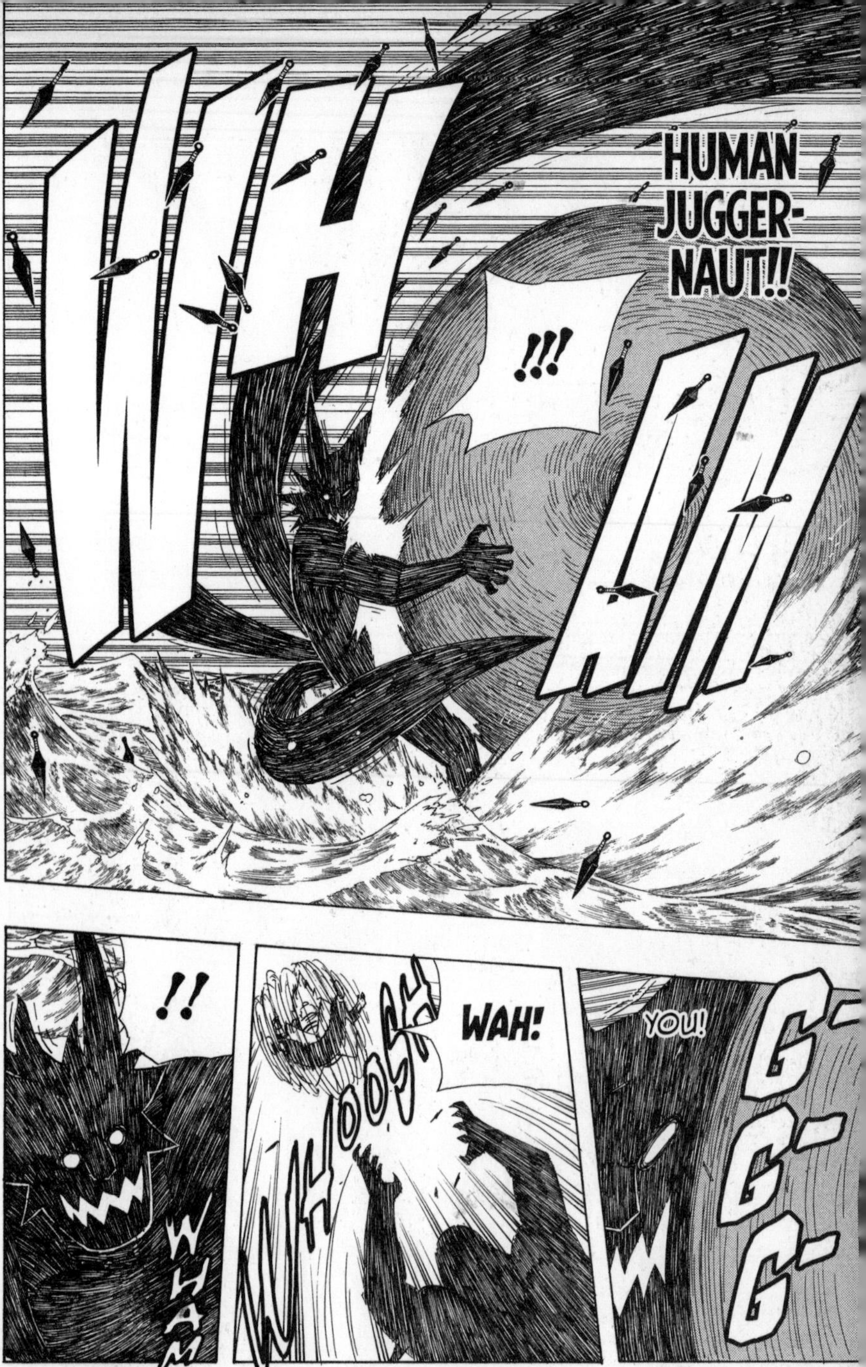
HUMAN JUGGER-NAUT!!
!!!
WHAAM
YOU!
G-G-G-
WAH!
WHOOSH
!!
WHAM

READ THIS WAY

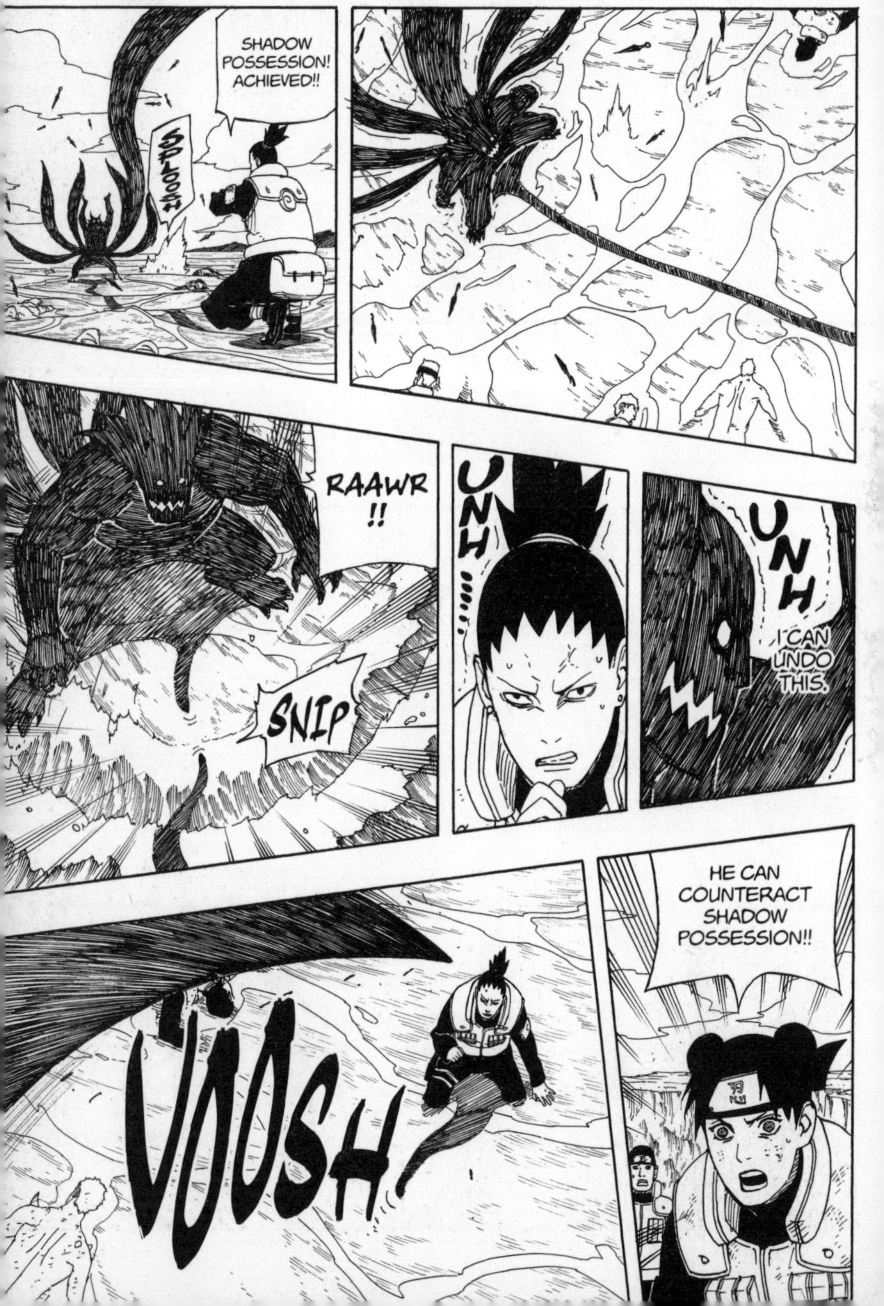
SHADOW POSSESSION! ACHIEVED!!
SPLOOSH
UNH
I CAN UNDO THIS.
UNH......
RAAWR !!
SNIP
HE CAN COUNTERACT SHADOW POSSESSION!!
VOOSH

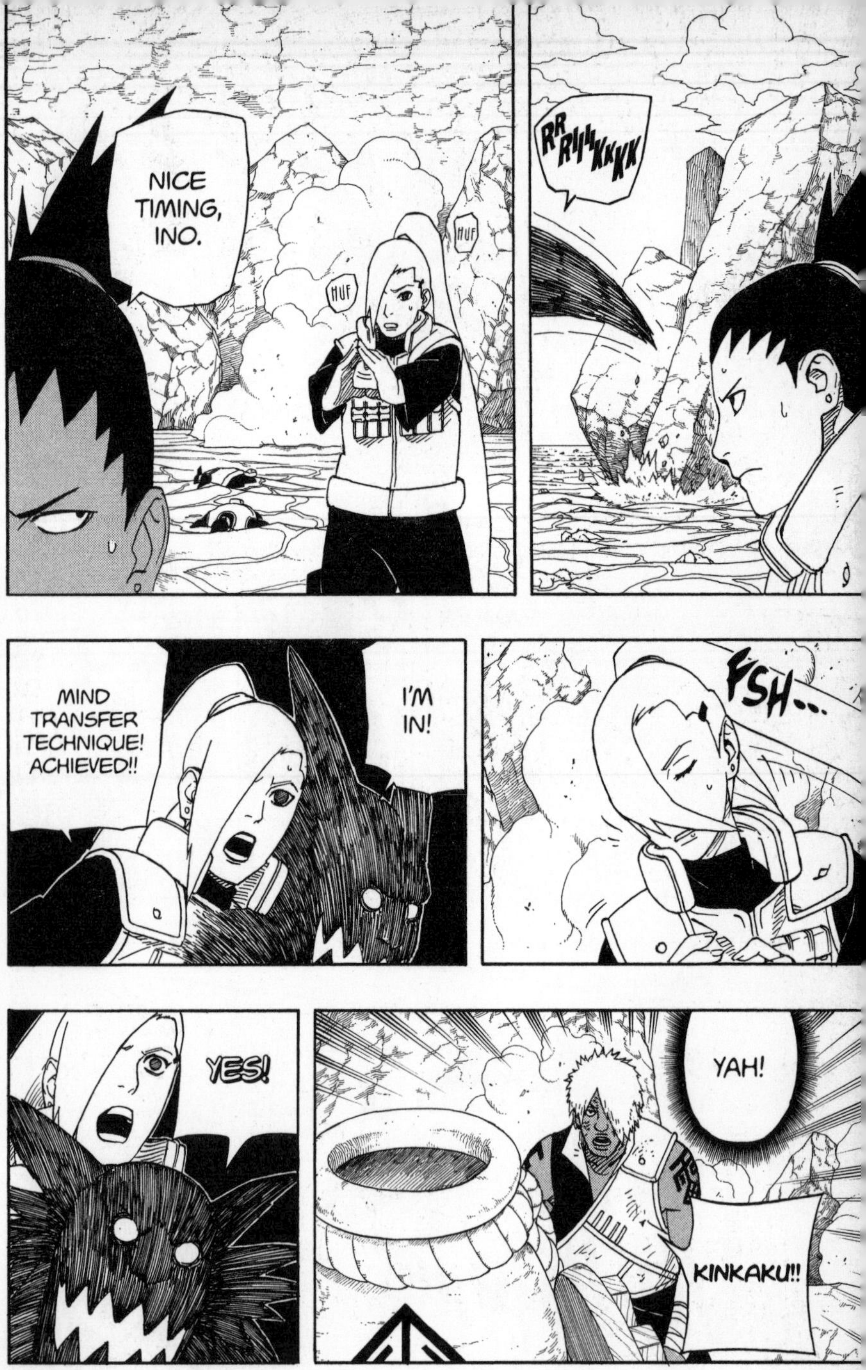
RRRIIIKKKK
HUF
NICE TIMING, INO.
HUF
FSH...
I'M IN!
MIND TRANSFER TECHNIQUE! ACHIEVED!!
YAH!
KINKAKU!!
YES!

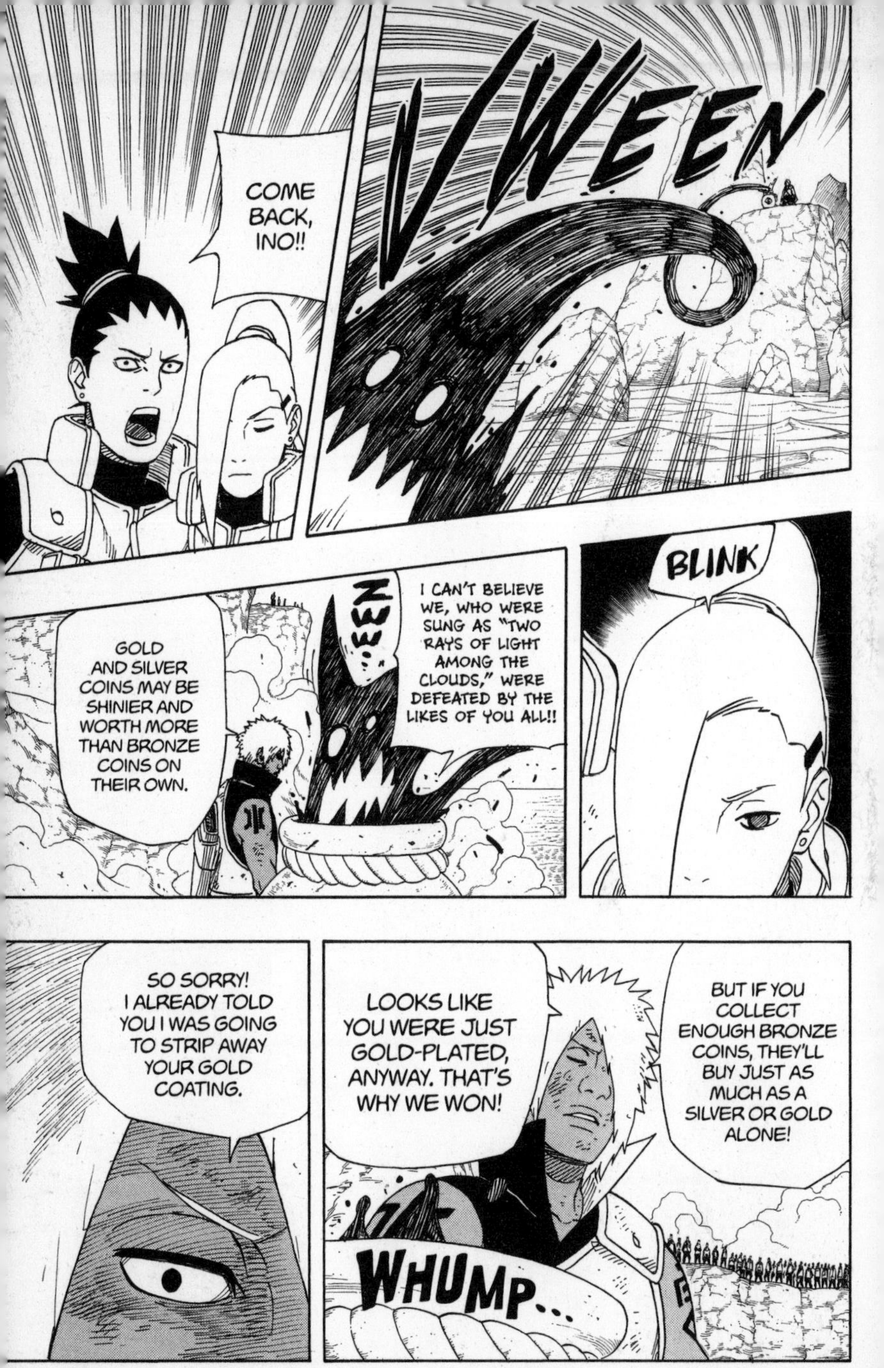
VWEEN
COME BACK, INO!!
BLINK
I CAN'T BELIEVE WE, WHO WERE SUNG AS "TWO RAYS OF LIGHT AMONG THE CLOUDS," WERE DEFEATED BY THE LIKES OF YOU ALL!!
ZWEEN...
GOLD AND SILVER COINS MAY BE SHINIER AND WORTH MORE THAN BRONZE COINS ON THEIR OWN.
BUT IF YOU COLLECT ENOUGH BRONZE COINS, THEY'LL BUY JUST AS MUCH AS A SILVER OR GOLD ALONE!
LOOKS LIKE YOU WERE JUST GOLD-PLATED, ANYWAY. THAT'S WHY WE WON!
WHUMP...
SO SORRY! I ALREADY TOLD YOU I WAS GOING TO STRIP AWAY YOUR GOLD COATING.

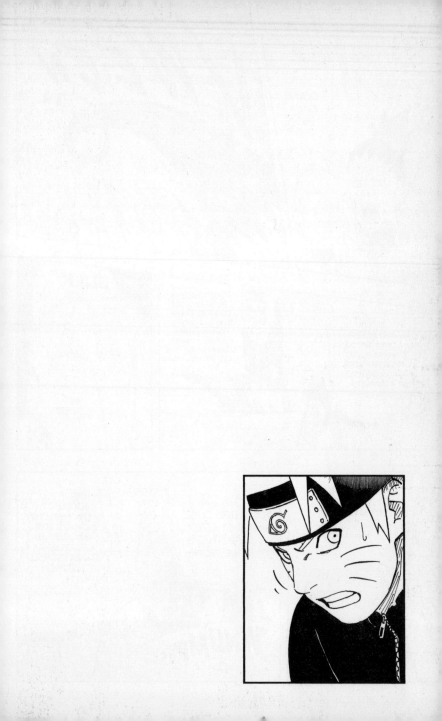

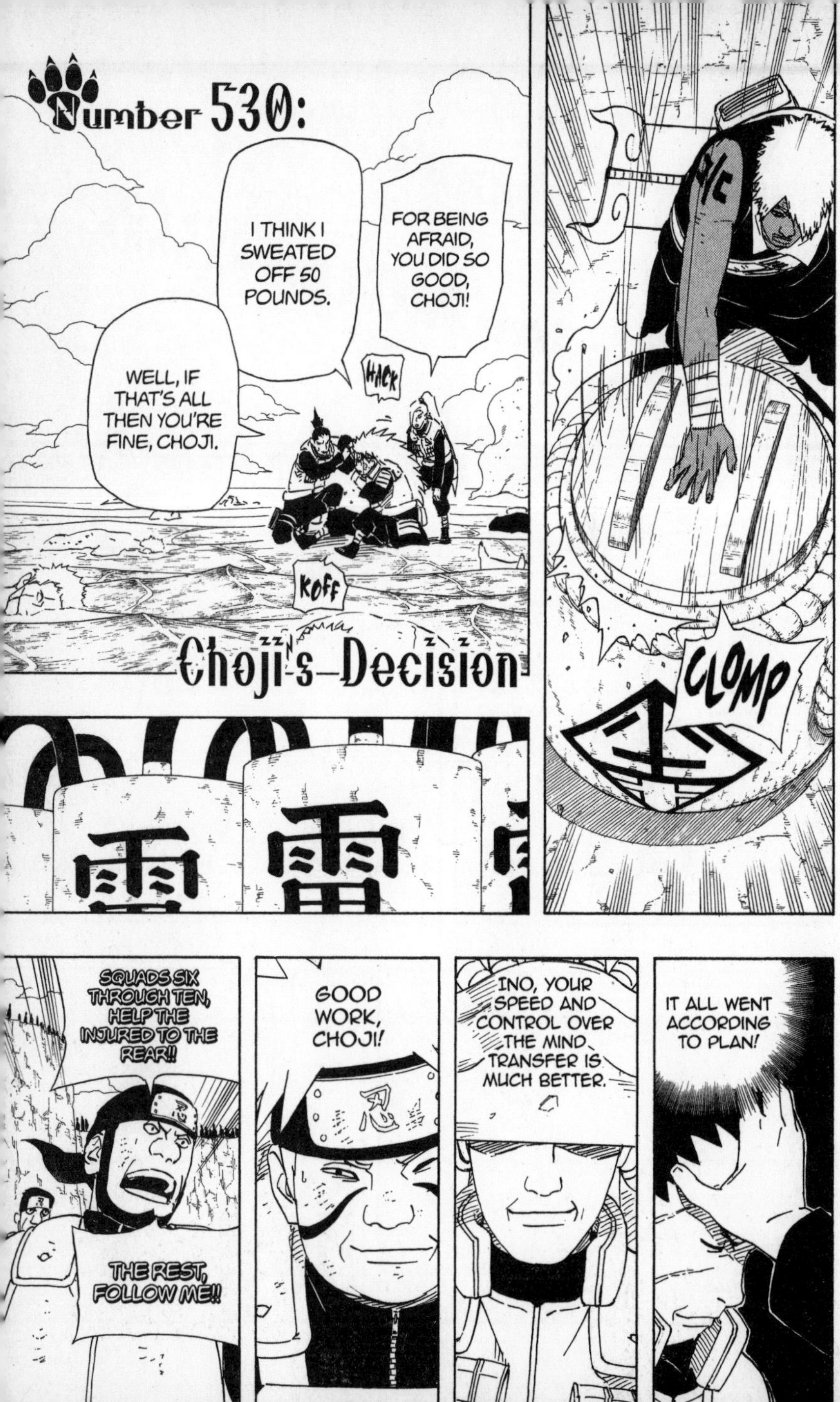
CLOMP
Number 530:
FOR BEING AFRAID, YOU DID SO GOOD, CHOJI!
I THINK I SWEATED OFF 50 POUNDS.
HACK
WELL, IF THAT'S ALL THEN YOU'RE FINE, CHOJI.
KOFF
Choji's Decision
雷
雷
IT ALL WENT ACCORDING TO PLAN!
INO, YOUR SPEED AND CONTROL OVER THE MIND TRANSFER IS MUCH BETTER.
GOOD WORK, CHOJI!
SQUADS SIX THROUGH TEN, HELP THE INJURED TO THE REAR!!
THE REST, FOLLOW ME!!

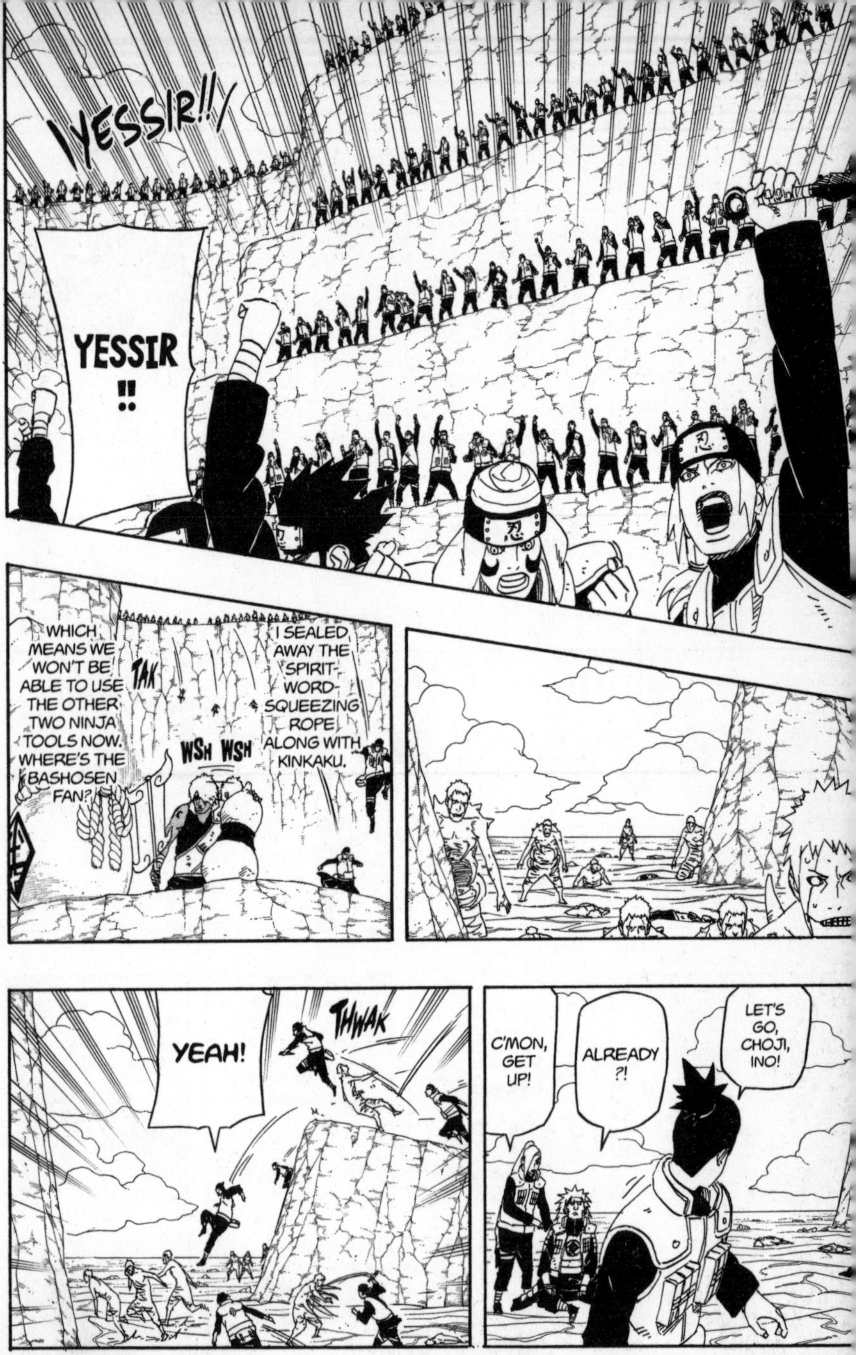
YESSIR!!
YESSIR!!
I SEALED AWAY THE SPIRIT-WORD-SQUEEZING ROPE ALONG WITH KINKAKU.
WHICH MEANS WE WON'T BE ABLE TO USE THE OTHER TWO NINJA TOOLS NOW. WHERE'S THE BASHOSEN FAN?!
TAK
WSH WSH
LET'S GO, CHOJI, INO!
ALREADY?!
C'MON, GET UP!
THWAK
YEAH!

READ THIS WAY

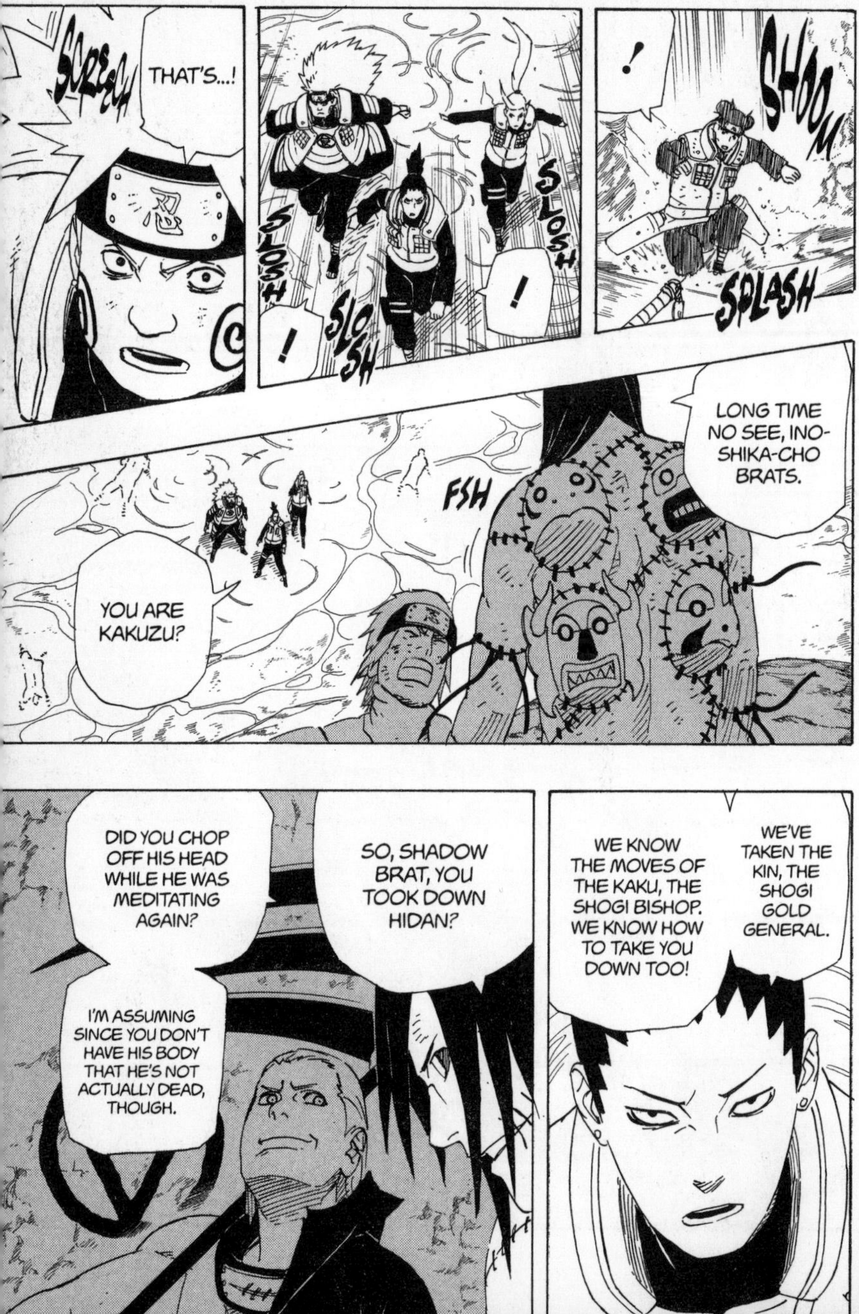
!
SHOOM
SPLASH
SLOSH
SLOSH
SLOSH
!
!
SCREECH
THAT'S...!
LONG TIME NO SEE, INO-SHIKA-CHO BRATS.
FSH
YOU ARE KAKUZU?
WE'VE TAKEN THE KIN, THE SHOGI GOLD GENERAL.
WE KNOW THE MOVES OF THE KAKU, THE SHOGI BISHOP. WE KNOW HOW TO TAKE YOU DOWN TOO!
SO, SHADOW BRAT, YOU TOOK DOWN HIDAN?
DID YOU CHOP OFF HIS HEAD WHILE HE WAS MEDITATING AGAIN?
I'M ASSUMING SINCE YOU DON'T HAVE HIS BODY THAT HE'S NOT ACTUALLY DEAD, THOUGH.

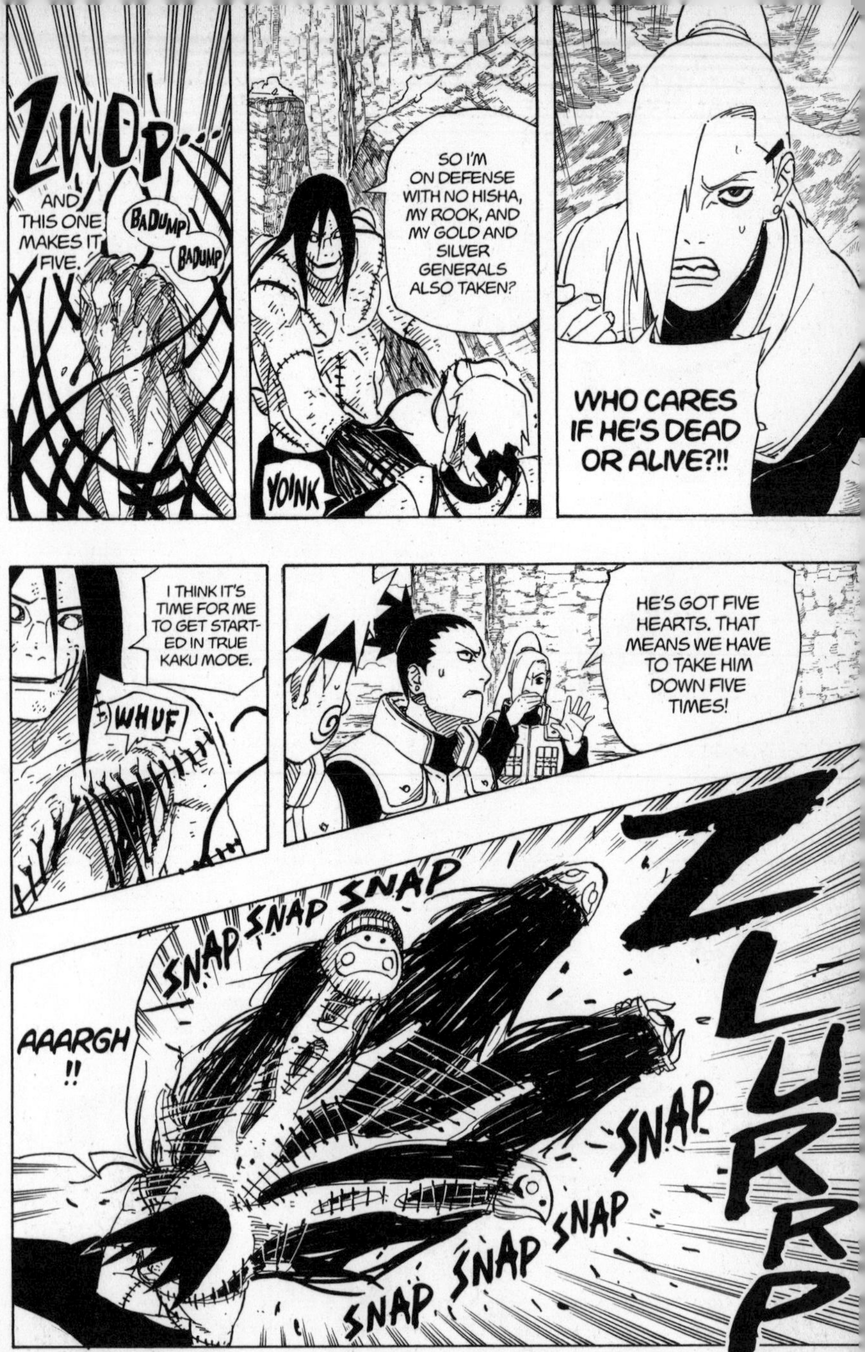
WHO CARES IF HE'S DEAD OR ALIVE?!!
SO I'M ON DEFENSE WITH NO HISHA, MY ROOK, AND MY GOLD AND SILVER GENERALS ALSO TAKEN?
YOINK
ZWOP...
AND THIS ONE MAKES IT FIVE.
BADUMP
BADUMP
HE'S GOT FIVE HEARTS. THAT MEANS WE HAVE TO TAKE HIM DOWN FIVE TIMES!
I THINK IT'S TIME FOR ME TO GET STARTED IN TRUE KAKU MODE.
WHUF
ZLURP
SNAP SNAP SNAP SNAP
SNAP
SNAP SNAP SNAP
AAARGH !!

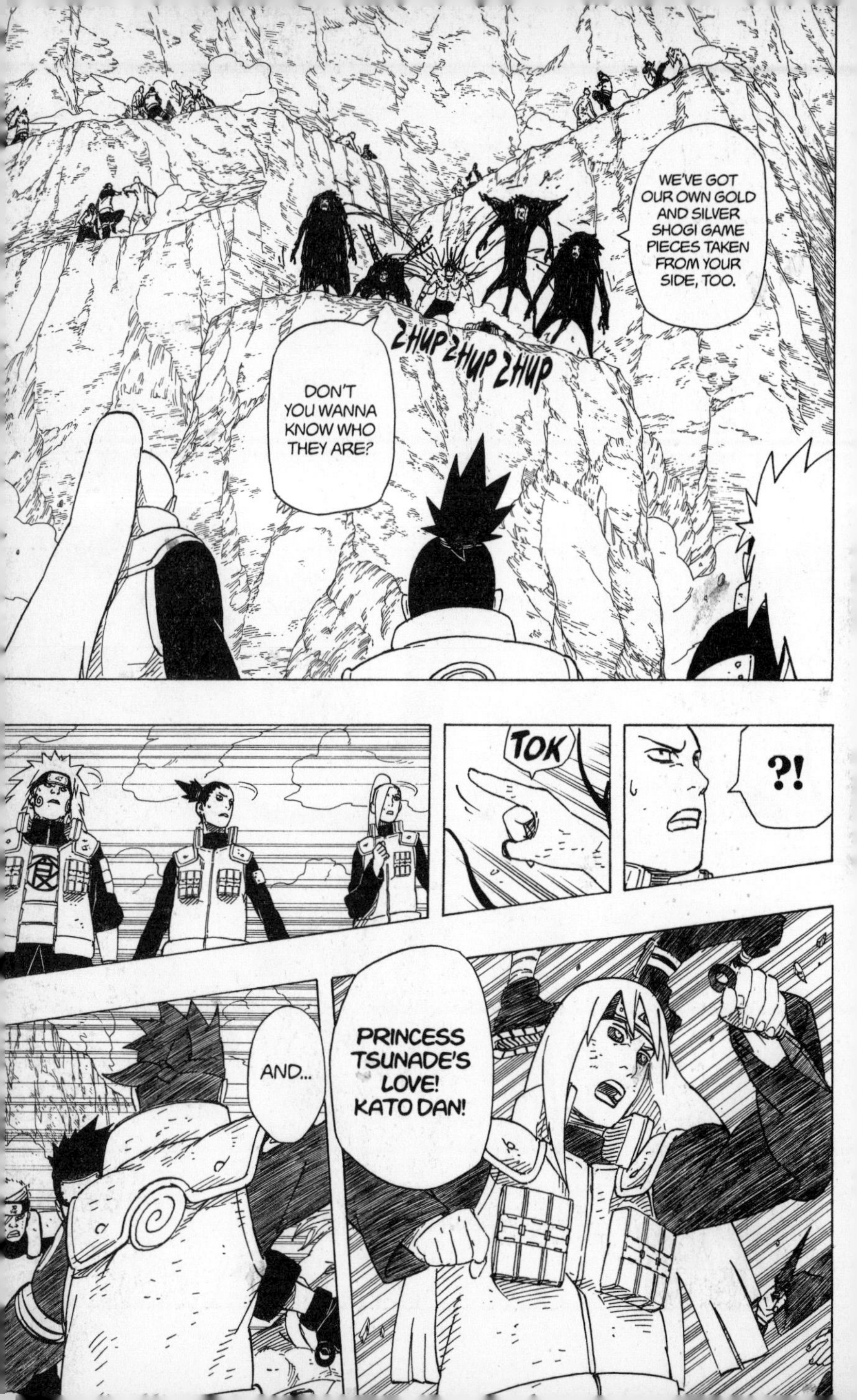
WE'VE GOT OUR OWN GOLD AND SILVER SHOGI GAME PIECES TAKEN FROM YOUR SIDE, TOO.
ZHUP ZHUP ZHUP
DON'T YOU WANNA KNOW WHO THEY ARE?
?!
TOK
PRINCESS TSUNADE'S LOVE! KATO DAN!
AND...

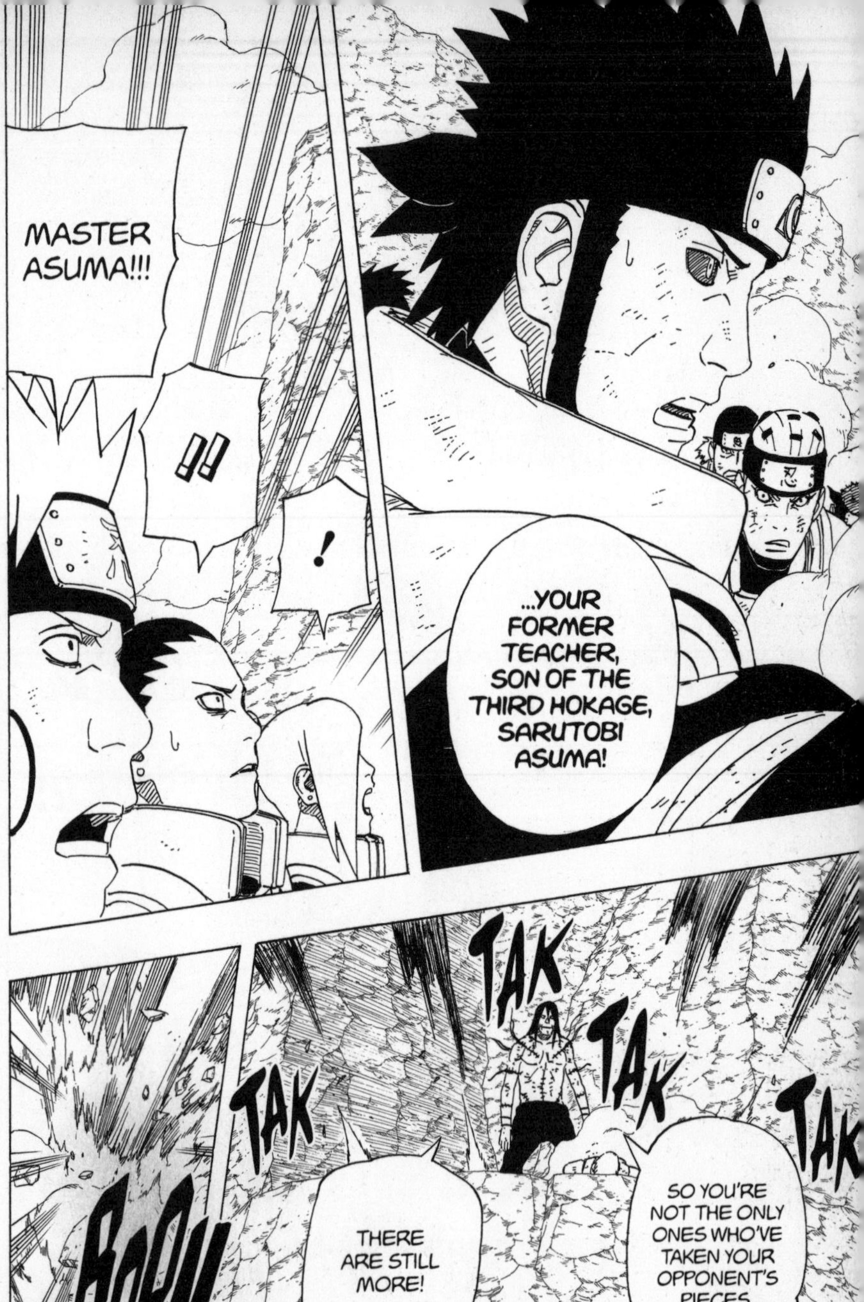

...YOUR FORMER TEACHER, SON OF THE THIRD HOKAGE, SARUTOBI ASUMA!
!
!!
MASTER ASUMA!!!
TAK
TAK
TAK
SO YOU'RE NOT THE ONLY ONES WHO'VE TAKEN YOUR OPPONENT'S PIECES.
TAK
THERE ARE STILL MORE!
BOOM

READ THIS WAY

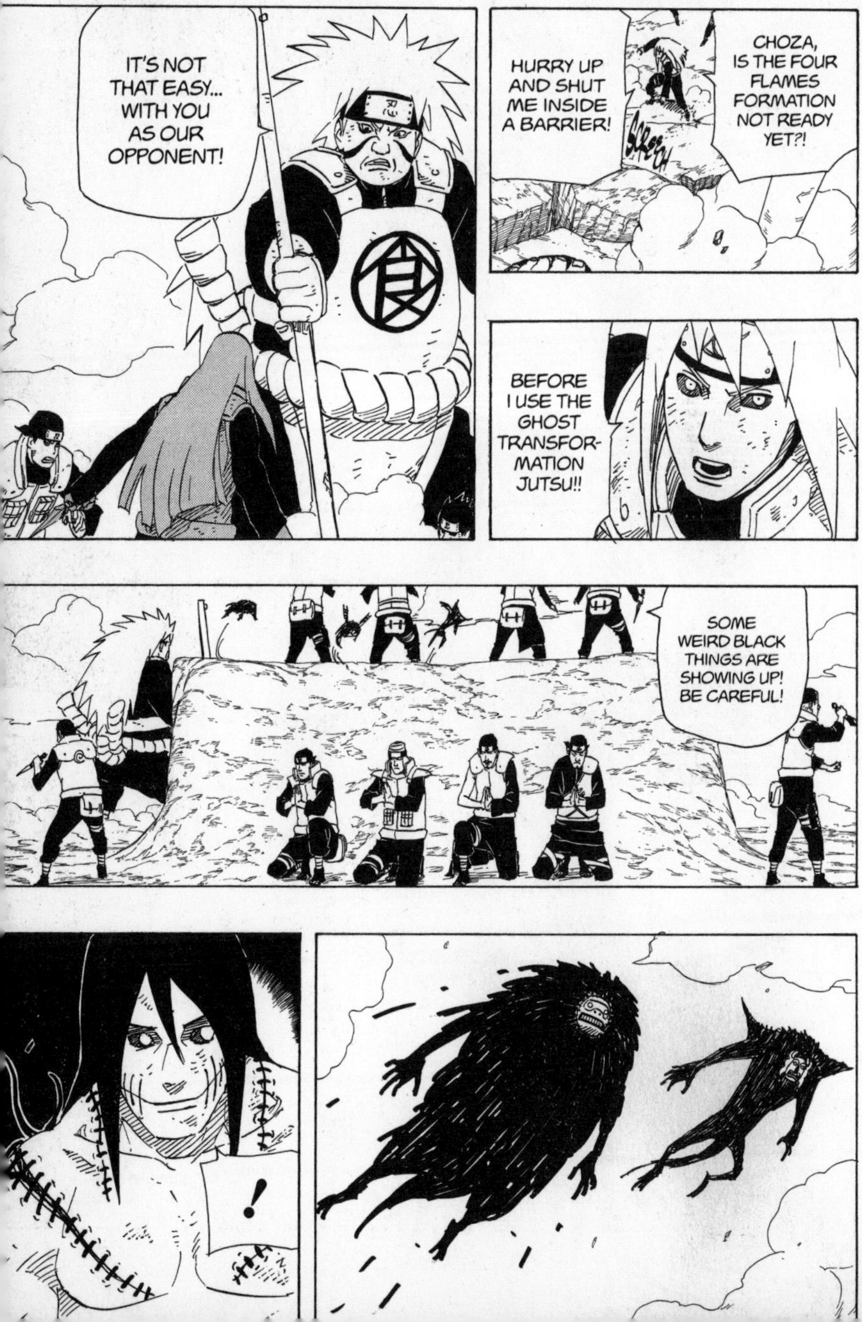
CHOZA, IS THE FOUR FLAMES FORMATION NOT READY YET?!
HURRY UP AND SHUT ME INSIDE A BARRIER!
SCREECH
BEFORE I USE THE GHOST TRANSFORMATION JUTSU!!
IT'S NOT THAT EASY... WITH YOU AS OUR OPPONENT!
SOME WEIRD BLACK THINGS ARE SHOWING UP! BE CAREFUL!
!

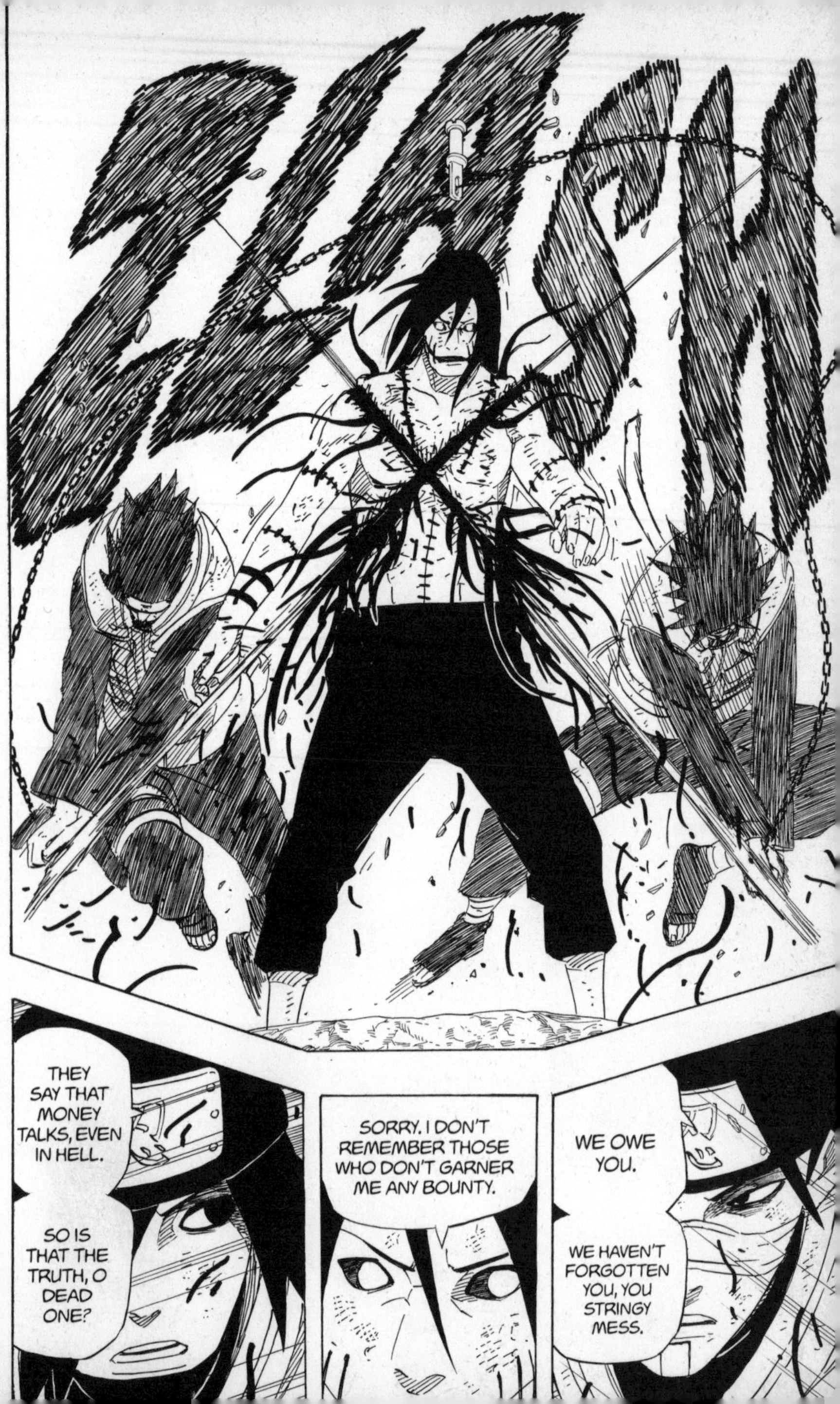
WE OWE YOU.
WE HAVEN'T FORGOTTEN YOU, YOU STRINGY MESS.
SORRY. I DON'T REMEMBER THOSE WHO DON'T GARNER ME ANY BOUNTY.
THEY SAY THAT MONEY TALKS, EVEN IN HELL.
SO IS THAT THE TRUTH, O DEAD ONE?

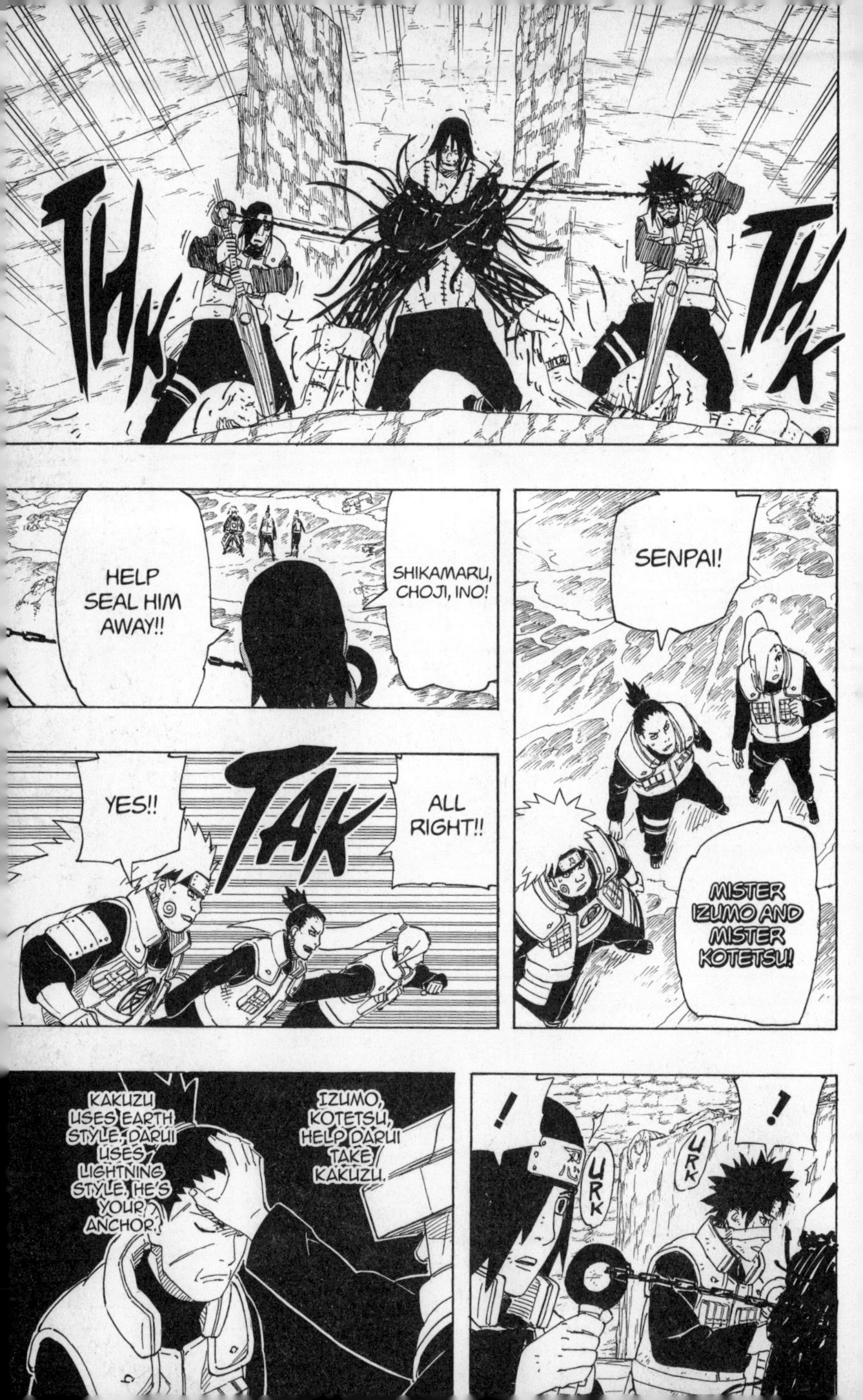
THK
THK
SENPAI!
MISTER IZUMO AND MISTER KOTETSU!
SHIKAMARU, CHOJI, INO!
HELP SEAL HIM AWAY!!
ALL RIGHT!!
TAK
YES!!
!
!
URK
URK
IZUMO, KOTETSU, HELP DARUI TAKE KAKUZU.
KAKUZU USES EARTH STYLE, DARUI USES LIGHTNING STYLE. HE'S YOUR ANCHOR.

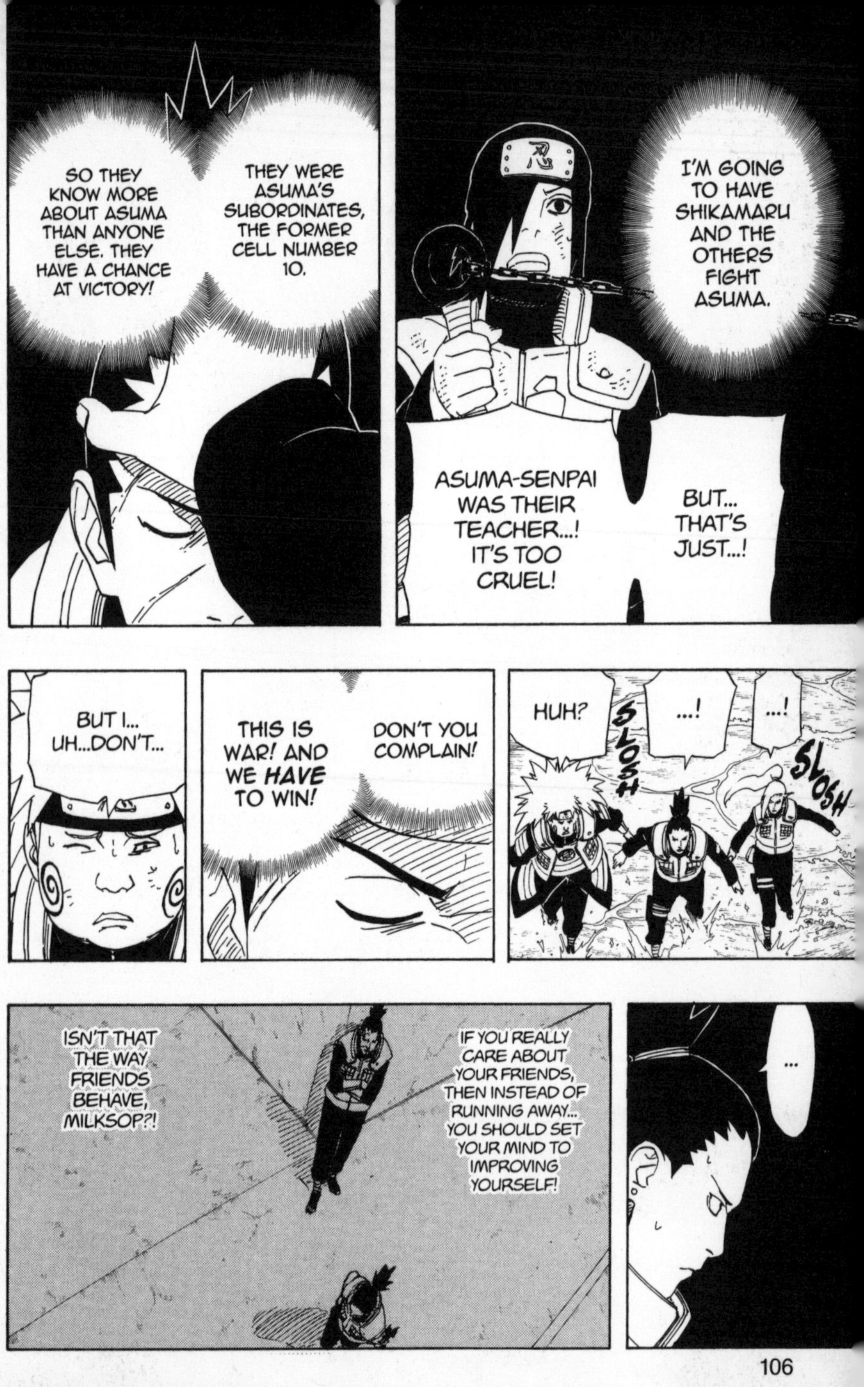

I'M GOING TO HAVE SHIKAMARU AND THE OTHERS FIGHT ASUMA.
BUT... THAT'S JUST...!
ASUMA-SENPAI WAS THEIR TEACHER...! IT'S TOO CRUEL!
THEY WERE ASUMA'S SUBORDINATES, THE FORMER CELL NUMBER 10.
SO THEY KNOW MORE ABOUT ASUMA THAN ANYONE ELSE. THEY HAVE A CHANCE AT VICTORY!
...!
...!
SLOSH
HUH?
SLOSH
DON'T YOU COMPLAIN!
THIS IS WAR! AND WE *HAVE* TO WIN!
BUT I... UH...DON'T...
...
IF YOU REALLY CARE ABOUT YOUR FRIENDS, THEN INSTEAD OF RUNNING AWAY... YOU SHOULD SET YOUR MIND TO IMPROVING YOURSELF!
ISN'T THAT THE WAY FRIENDS BEHAVE, MILKSOP?!

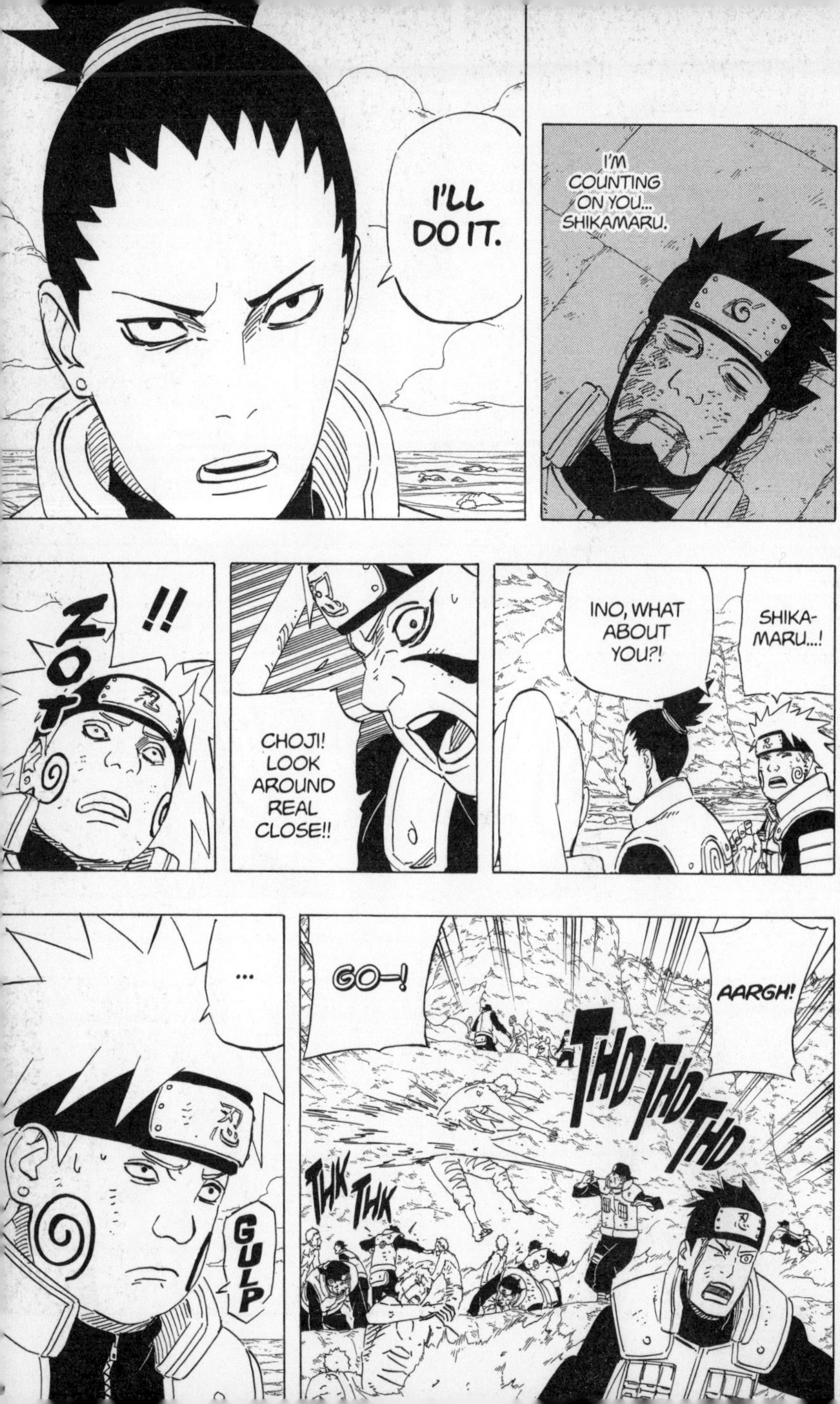
I'M COUNTING ON YOU... SHIKAMARU.
I'LL DO IT.
SHIKA-MARU...!
INO, WHAT ABOUT YOU?!
CHOJI! LOOK AROUND REAL CLOSE!!
!!
ZOT
AARGH!
GO—!
THD THD THD
THK THK
...
GULP

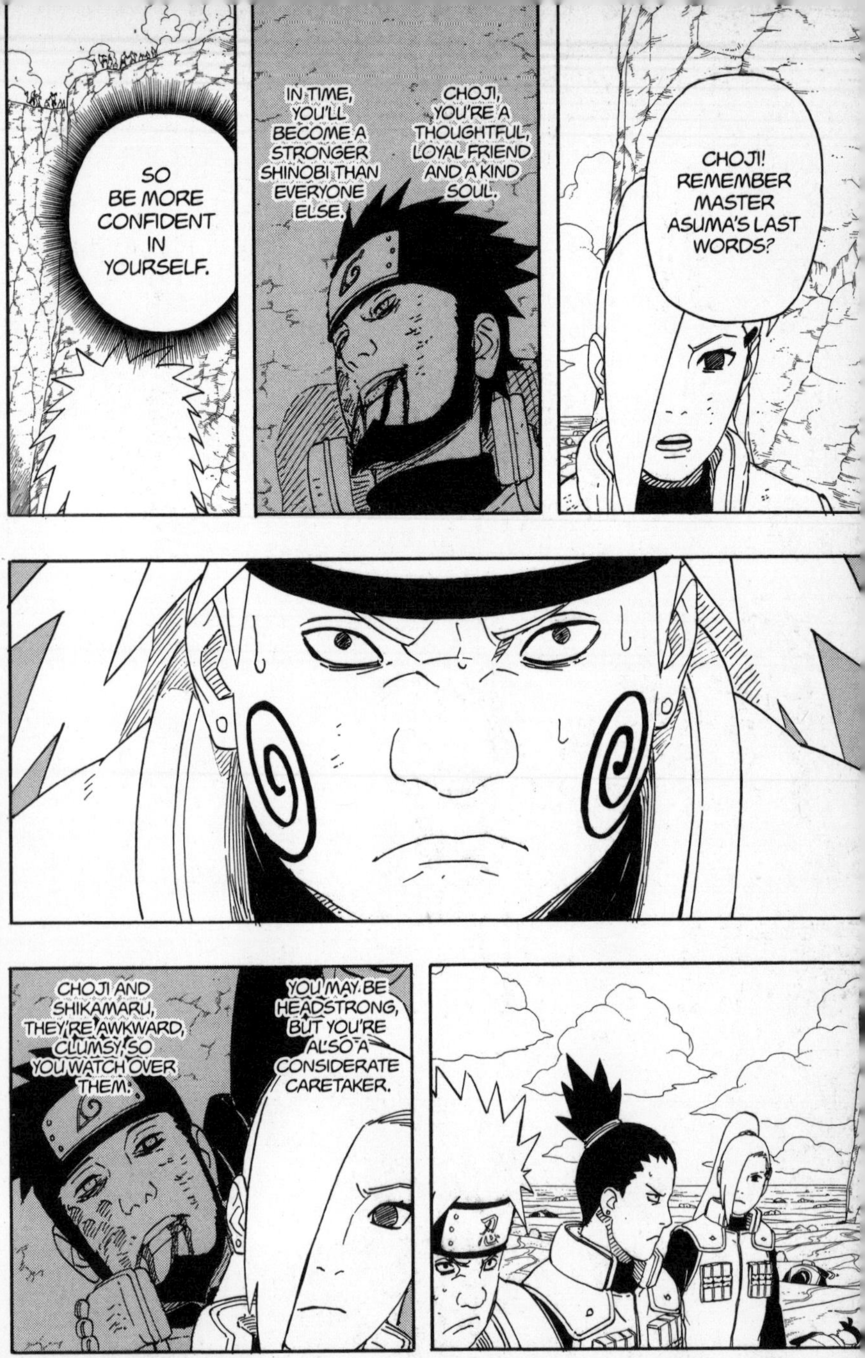
CHOJI! REMEMBER MASTER ASUMA'S LAST WORDS?
CHOJI, YOU'RE A THOUGHTFUL, LOYAL FRIEND AND A KIND SOUL.
IN TIME, YOU'LL BECOME A STRONGER SHINOBI THAN EVERYONE ELSE.
SO BE MORE CONFIDENT IN YOURSELF.
YOU MAY BE HEADSTRONG, BUT YOU'RE ALSO A CONSIDERATE CARETAKER.
CHOJI AND SHIKAMARU, THEY'RE AWKWARD, CLUMSY, SO YOU WATCH OVER THEM.

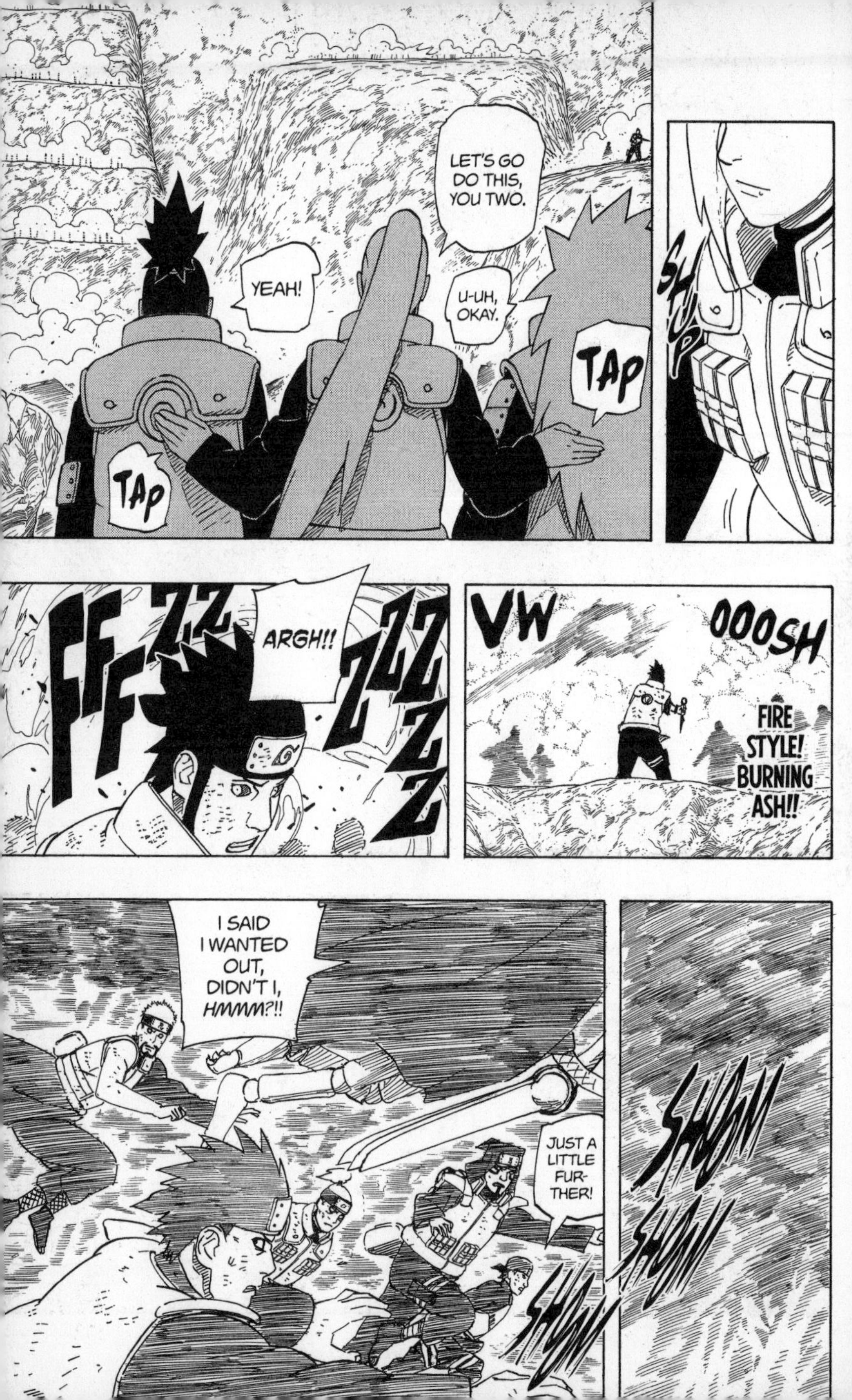
SHUP
LET'S GO DO THIS, YOU TWO.
U-UH, OKAY.
YEAH!
TAP
TAP
VW OOOSH
FIRE STYLE! BURNING ASH!!
ZZZZZ
ARGH!!
FFF ZZ
SHUN
I SAID I WANTED OUT, DIDN'T I, *HMMM?!!*
JUST A LITTLE FUR-THER!
SHUN SHUN

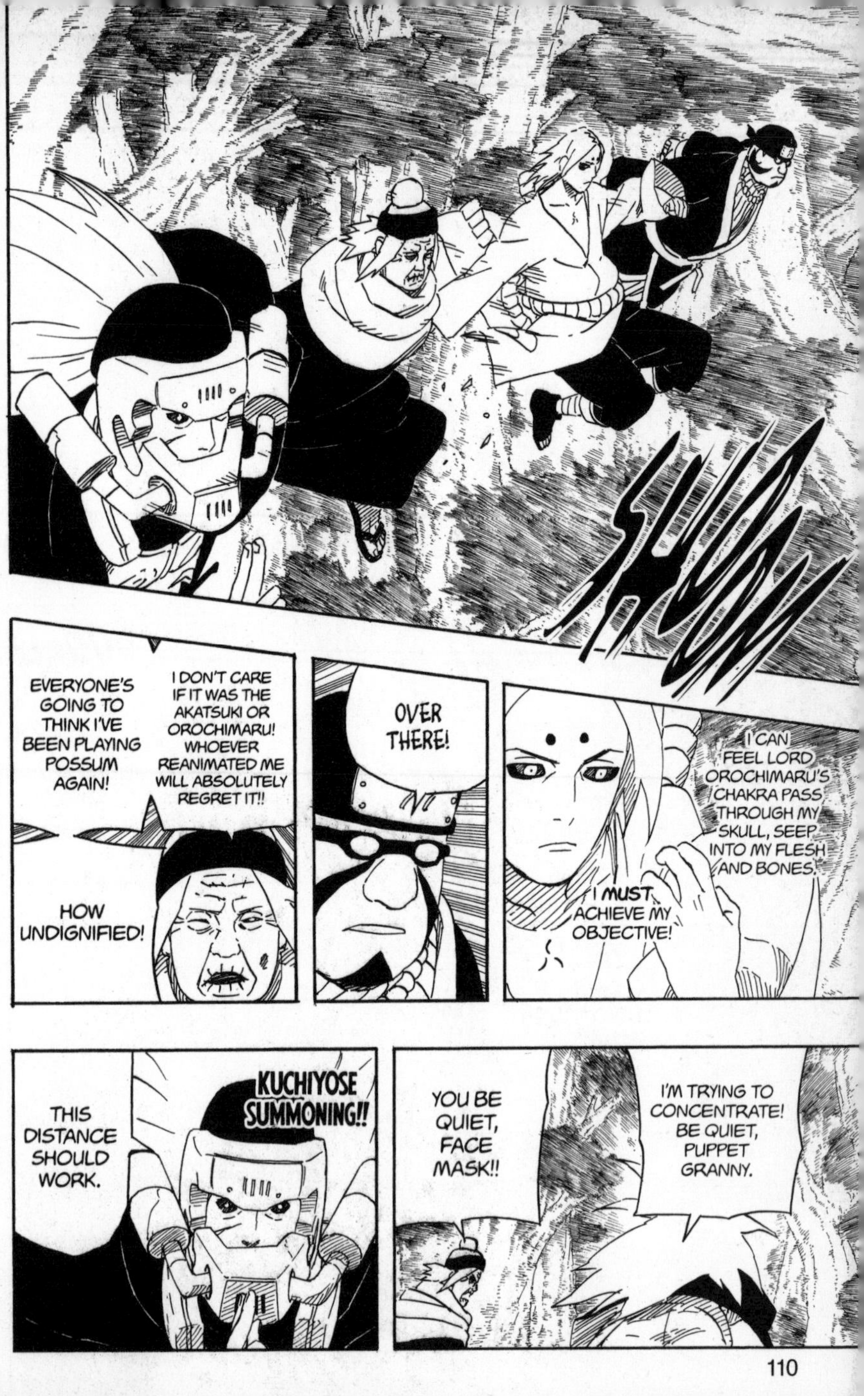
I CAN FEEL LORD OROCHIMARU'S CHAKRA PASS THROUGH MY SKULL, SEEP INTO MY FLESH AND BONES.
I MUST ACHIEVE MY OBJECTIVE!
OVER THERE!
I DON'T CARE IF IT WAS THE AKATSUKI OR OROCHIMARU! WHOEVER REANIMATED ME WILL ABSOLUTELY REGRET IT!!
EVERYONE'S GOING TO THINK I'VE BEEN PLAYING POSSUM AGAIN!
HOW UNDIGNIFIED!
I'M TRYING TO CONCENTRATE! BE QUIET, PUPPET GRANNY.
YOU BE QUIET, FACE MASK!!
KUCHIYOSE SUMMONING!!
THIS DISTANCE SHOULD WORK.

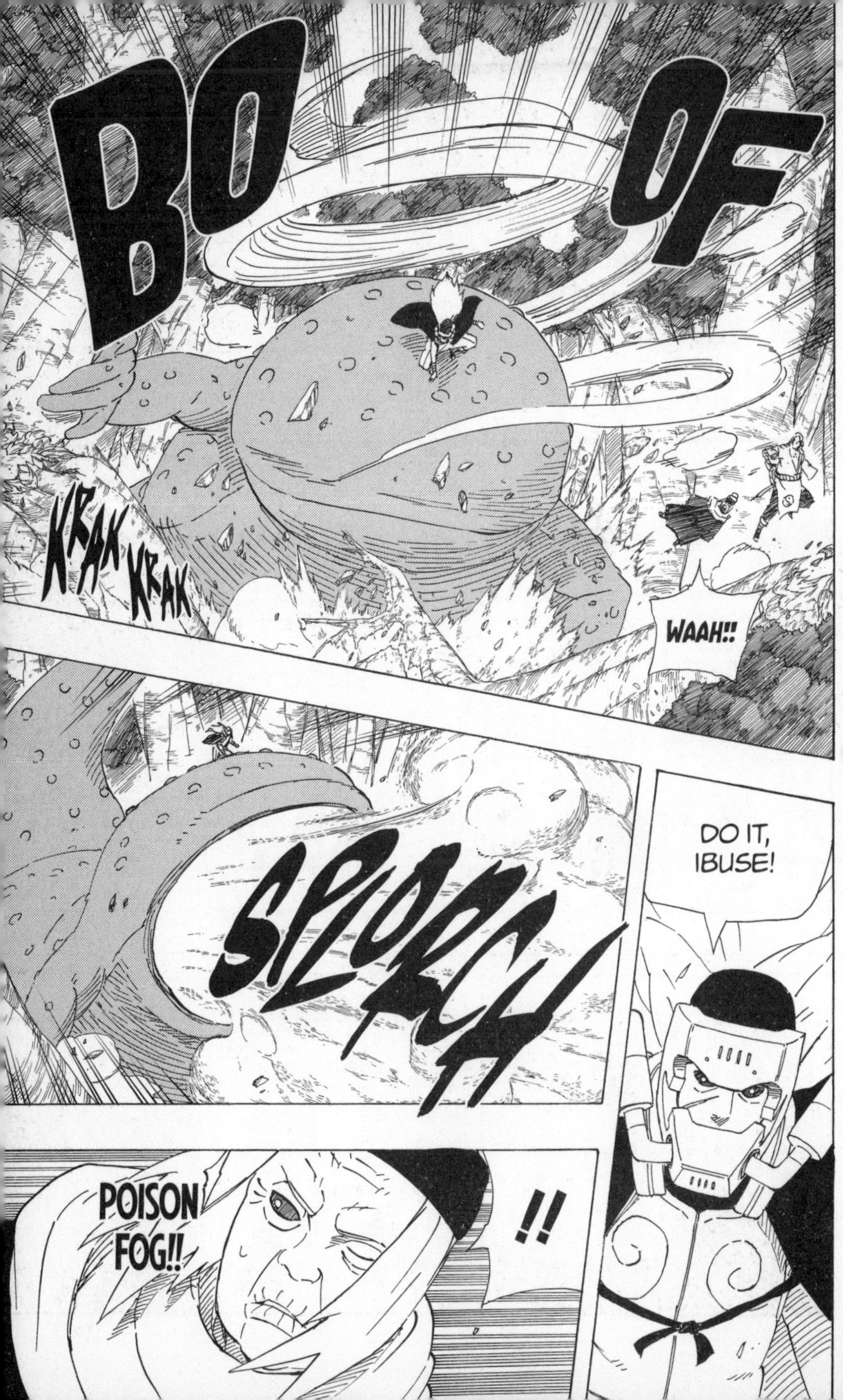
BOOF
WAAH!!
KRAK KRAK
DO IT, IBUSE!
SPLORCH
!!
POISON FOG!!

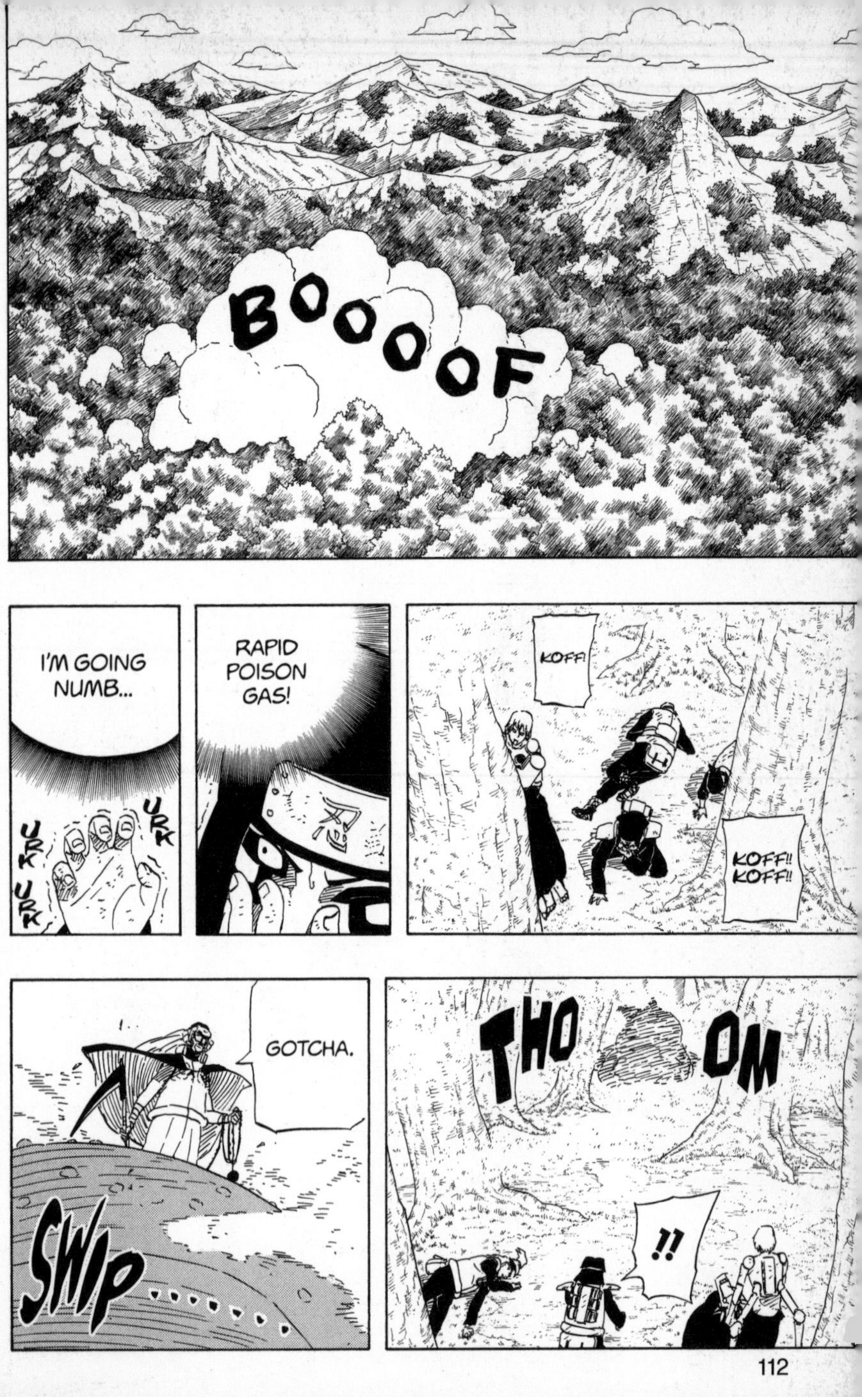
BOOOOF
KOFF!
KOFF!! KOFF!!
RAPID POISON GAS!
I'M GOING NUMB...
URK
URK
URK
URK
THOOM
!!
GOTCHA.
SWIP

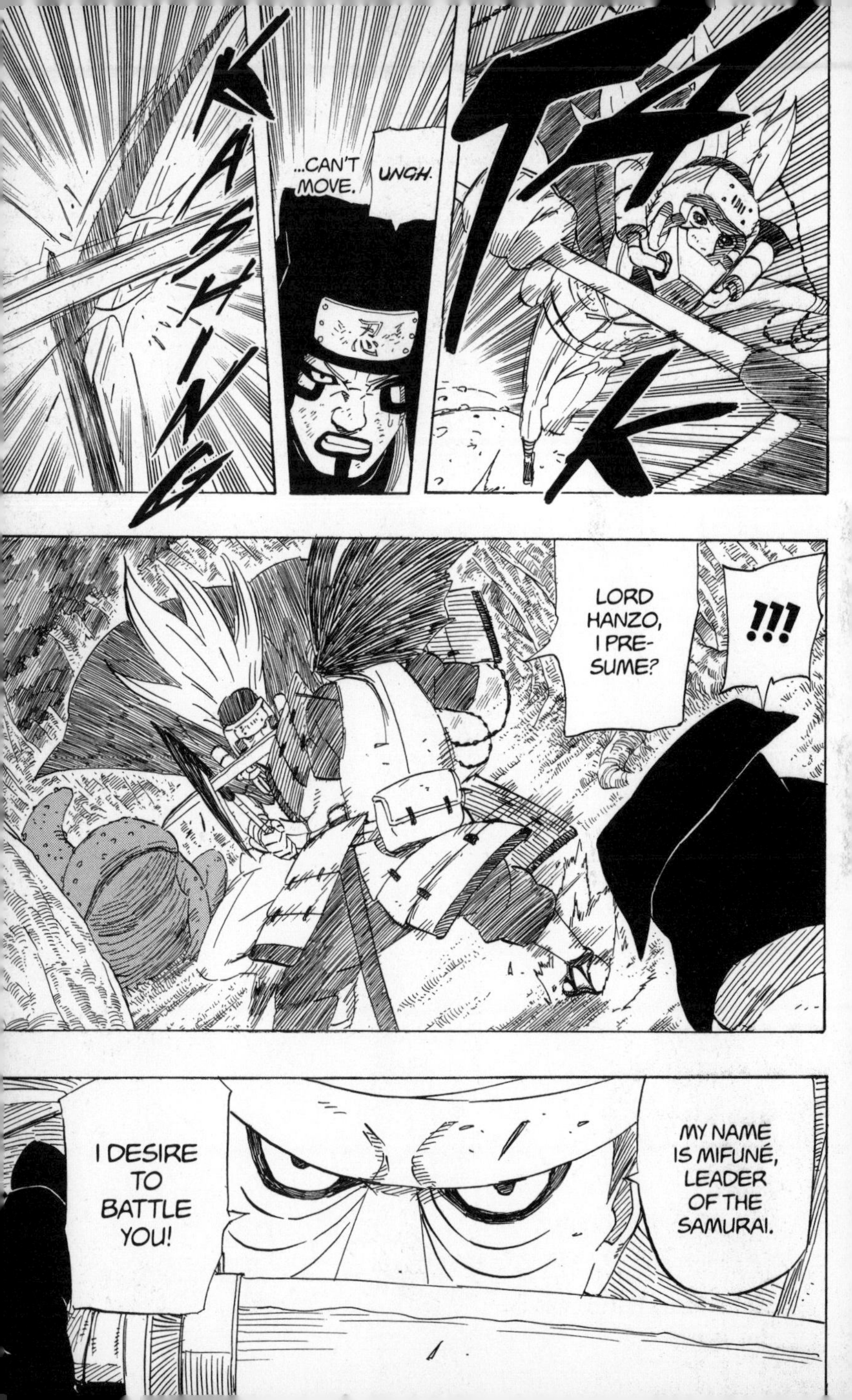
TAK
UNGH.
...CAN'T MOVE.
KASHING
!!!
LORD HANZO, I PRE-SUME?
MY NAME IS MIFUNÉ, LEADER OF THE SAMURAI.
I DESIRE TO BATTLE YOU!

NARUTO

Number 531: Team Asuma, Reunited!

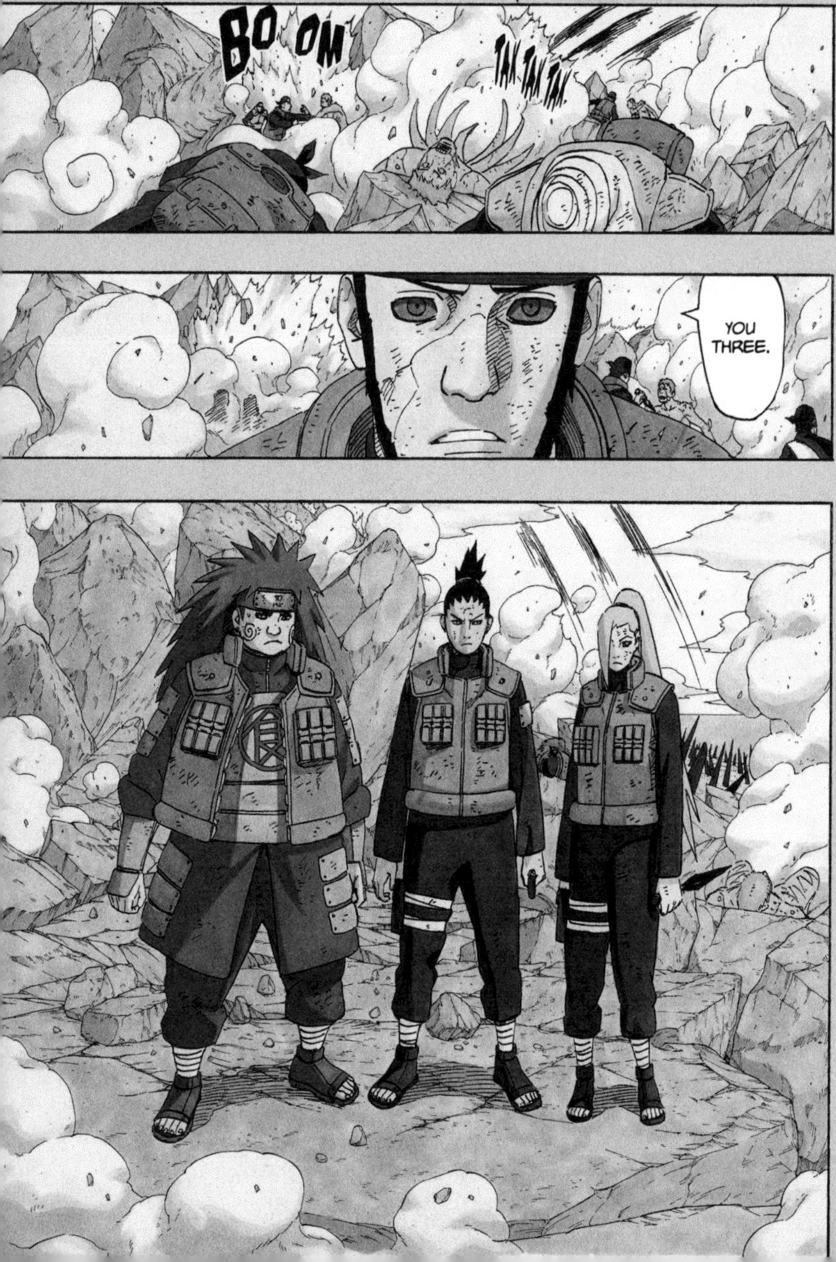
BOOM
TAK TAK TAK
YOU THREE.

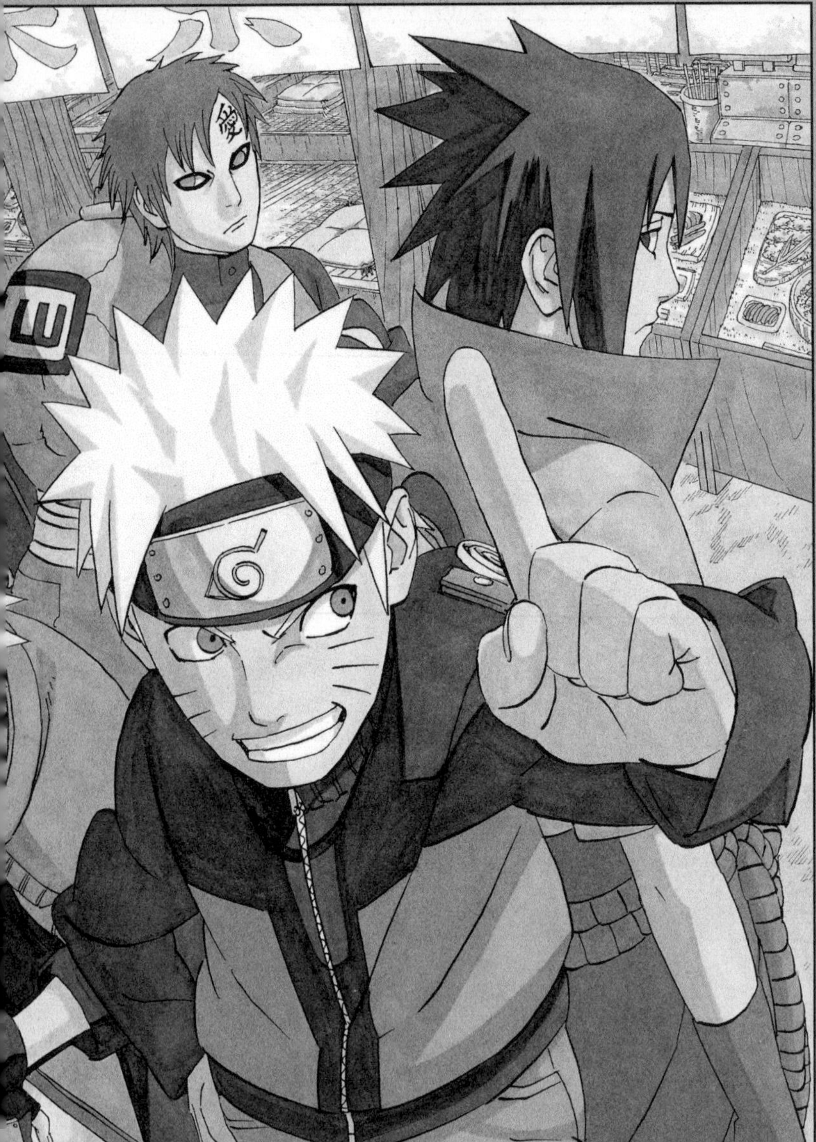

Number 531: Team Asuma, Reunited!

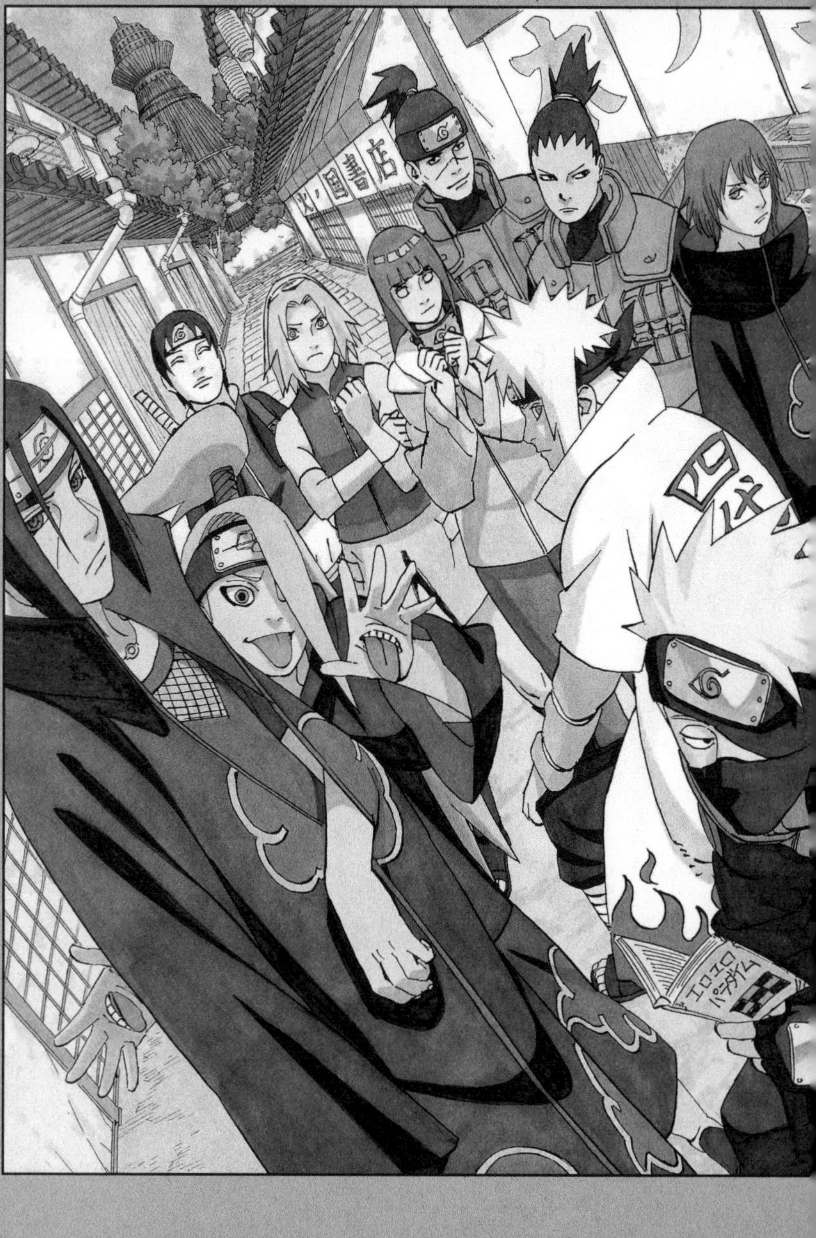
火ノ国書店

NARUTO

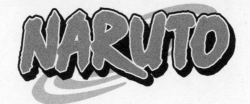

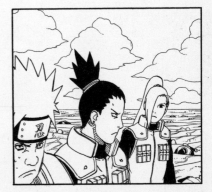

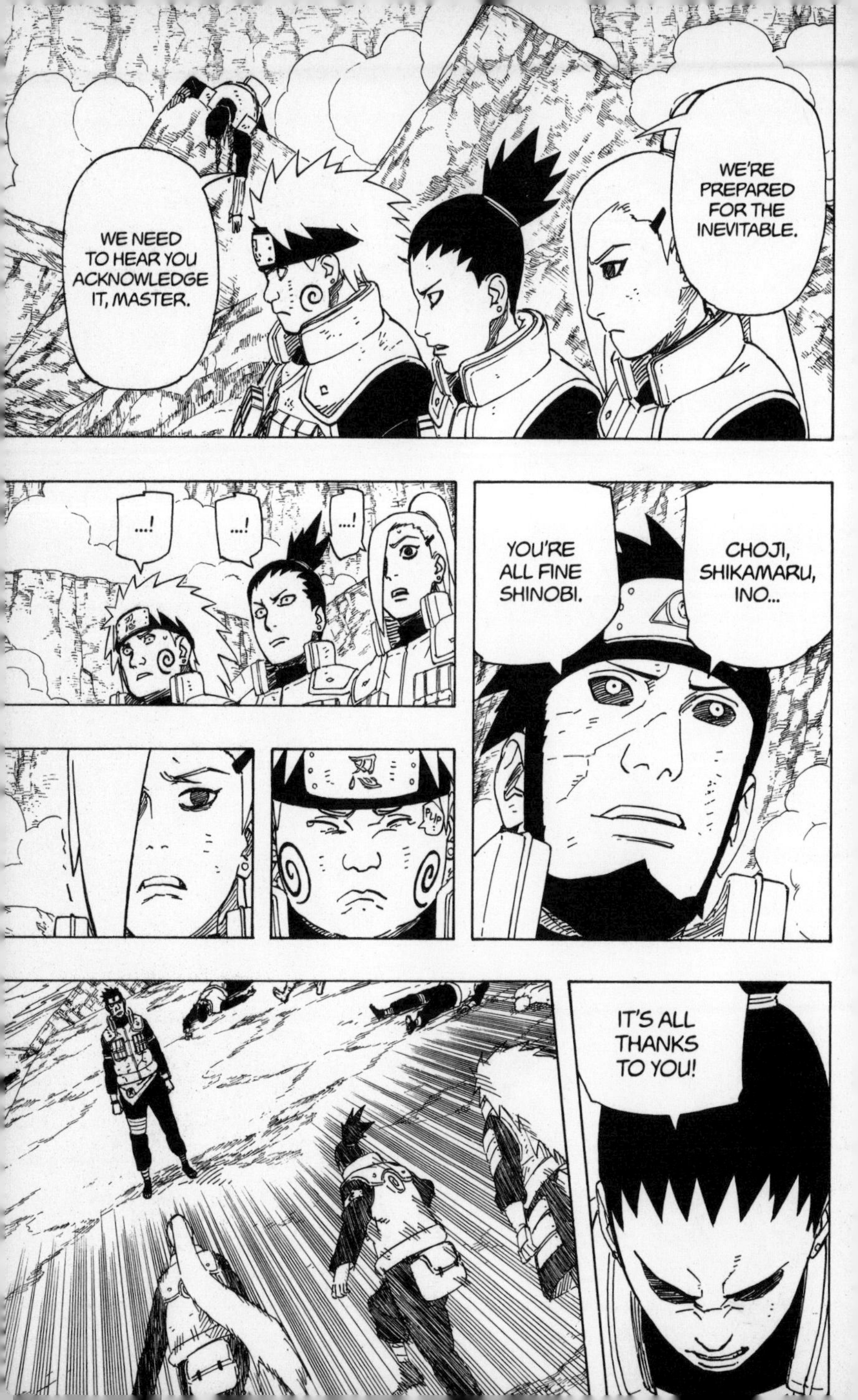
WE'RE PREPARED FOR THE INEVITABLE.
WE NEED TO HEAR YOU ACKNOWLEDGE IT, MASTER.
CHOJI, SHIKAMARU, INO...
YOU'RE ALL FINE SHINOBI.
...!
...!
...!
PLIP
IT'S ALL THANKS TO YOU!

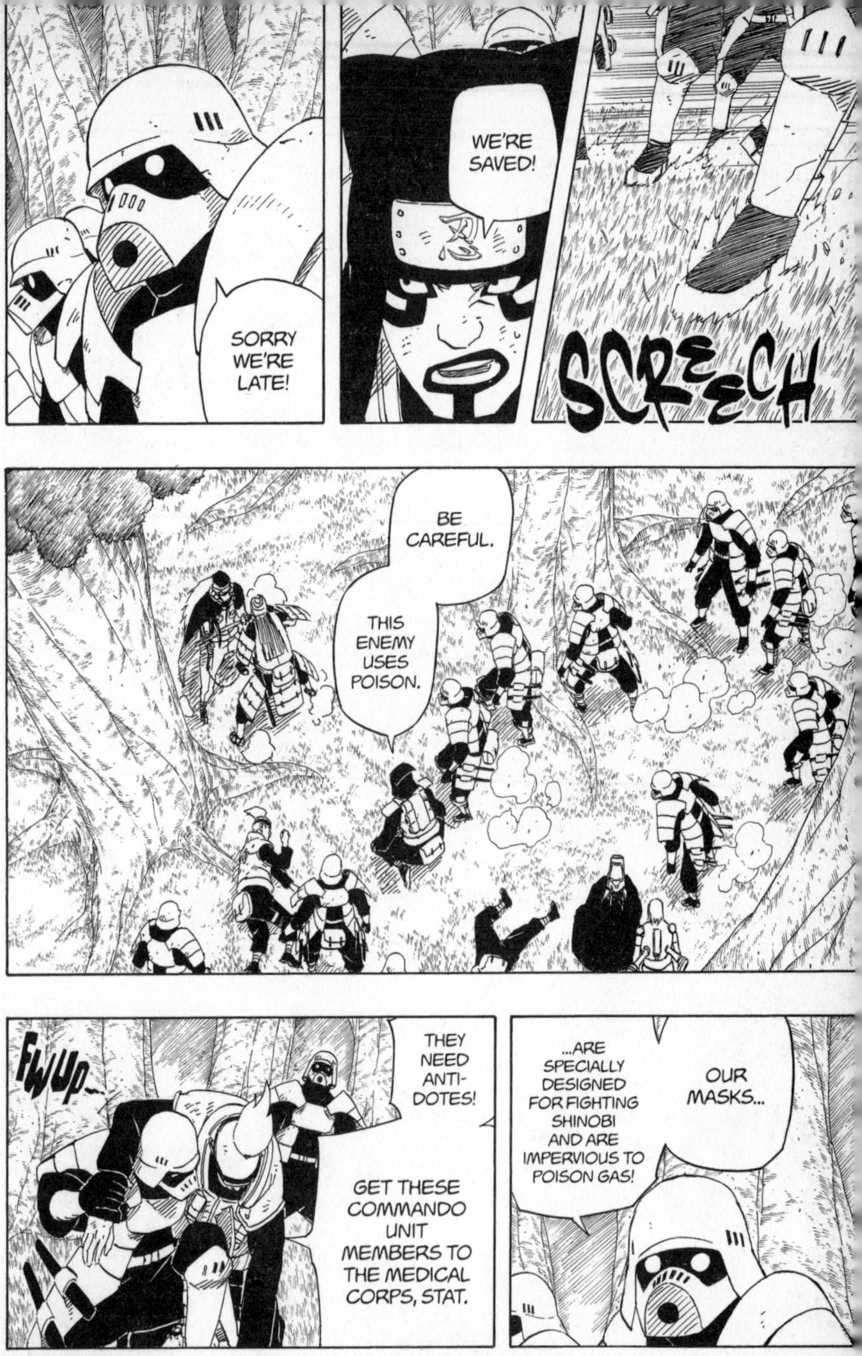
SCREECH
WE'RE SAVED!
SORRY WE'RE LATE!
BE CAREFUL.
THIS ENEMY USES POISON.
OUR MASKS...
...ARE SPECIALLY DESIGNED FOR FIGHTING SHINOBI AND ARE IMPERVIOUS TO POISON GAS!
THEY NEED ANTI-DOTES!
GET THESE COMMANDO UNIT MEMBERS TO THE MEDICAL CORPS, STAT.
FWUP

READ THIS WAY

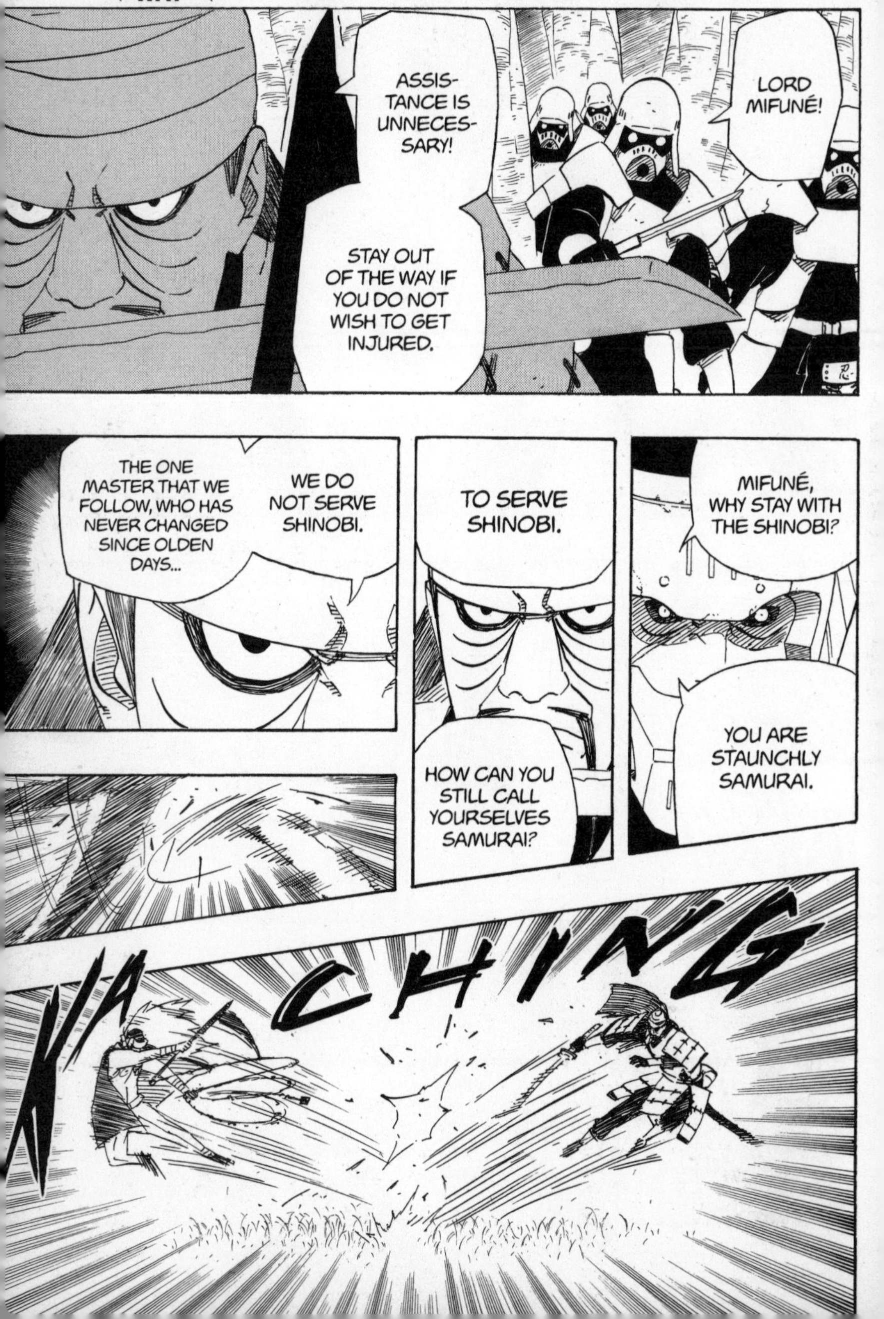
LORD MIFUNÉ!
ASSIS-TANCE IS UNNECES-SARY!
STAY OUT OF THE WAY IF YOU DO NOT WISH TO GET INJURED.
MIFUNÉ, WHY STAY WITH THE SHINOBI?
YOU ARE STAUNCHLY SAMURAI.
TO SERVE SHINOBI.
HOW CAN YOU STILL CALL YOURSELVES SAMURAI?
WE DO NOT SERVE SHINOBI.
THE ONE MASTER THAT WE FOLLOW, WHO HAS NEVER CHANGED SINCE OLDEN DAYS...
KA CHING

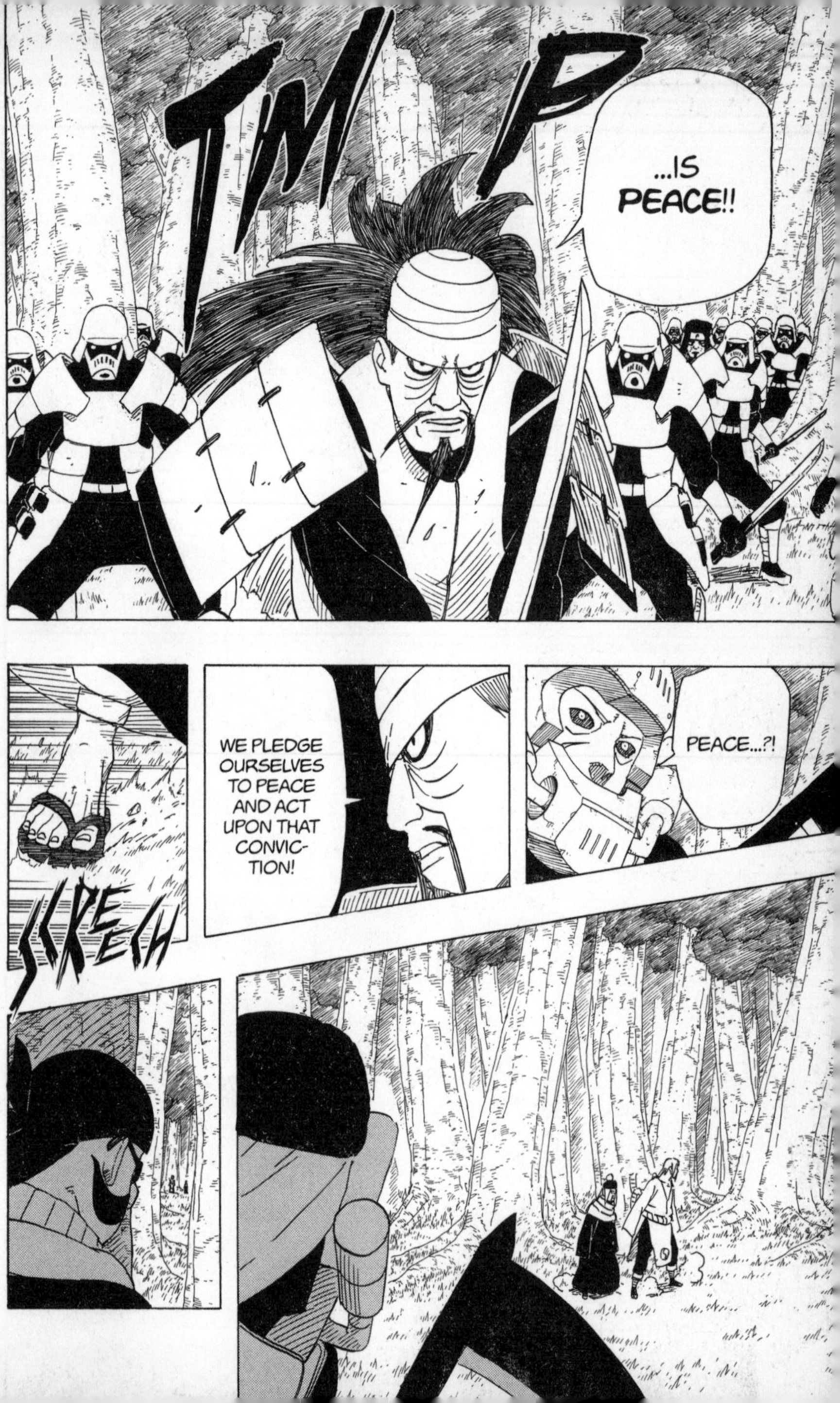
...IS PEACE!!
TMP
PEACE...?!
WE PLEDGE OURSELVES TO PEACE AND ACT UPON THAT CONVIC-TION!
SCREECH

READ THIS WAY

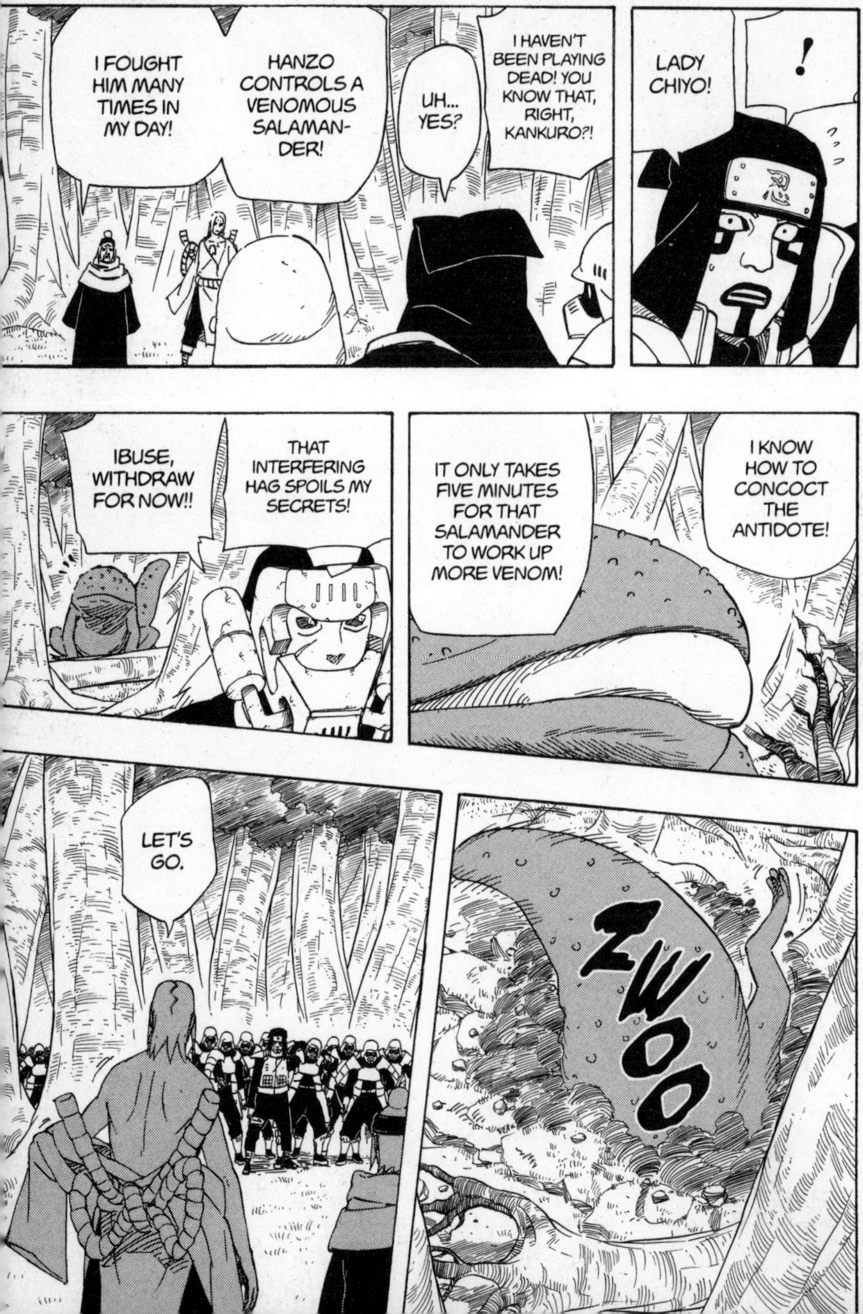
!
LADY CHIYO!
I HAVEN'T BEEN PLAYING DEAD! YOU KNOW THAT, RIGHT, KANKURO?!
UH... YES?
HANZO CONTROLS A VENOMOUS SALAMAN-DER!
I FOUGHT HIM MANY TIMES IN MY DAY!
I KNOW HOW TO CONCOCT THE ANTIDOTE!
IT ONLY TAKES FIVE MINUTES FOR THAT SALAMANDER TO WORK UP MORE VENOM!
THAT INTERFERING HAG SPOILS MY SECRETS!
IBUSE, WITHDRAW FOR NOW!!
ZWOO
LET'S GO.

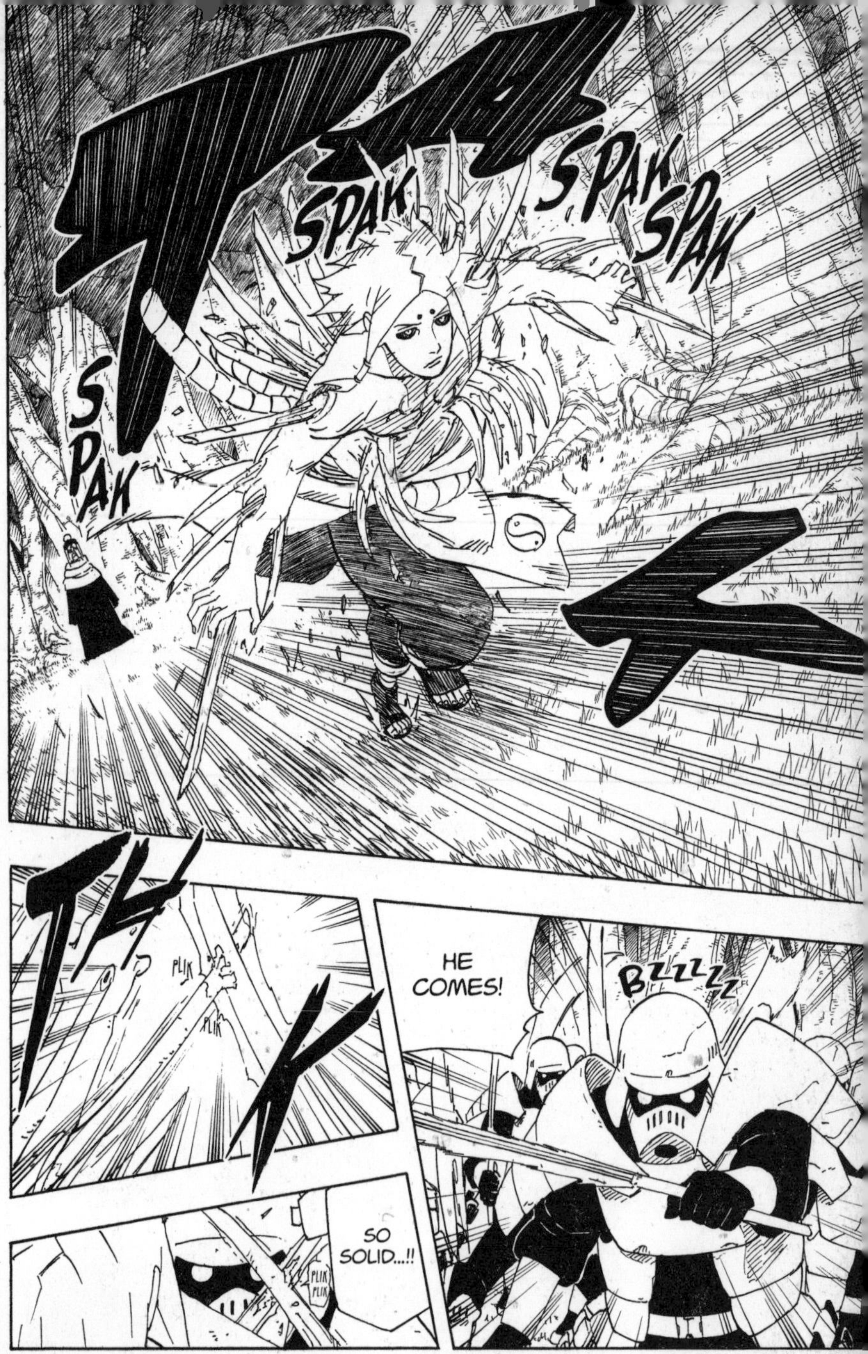
SPAK
SPAK
SPAK
SPAK
HE COMES!
BZZZZZ
PLIK
PLIK
SO SOLID...!!
PLIK
PLIK

READ THIS WAY

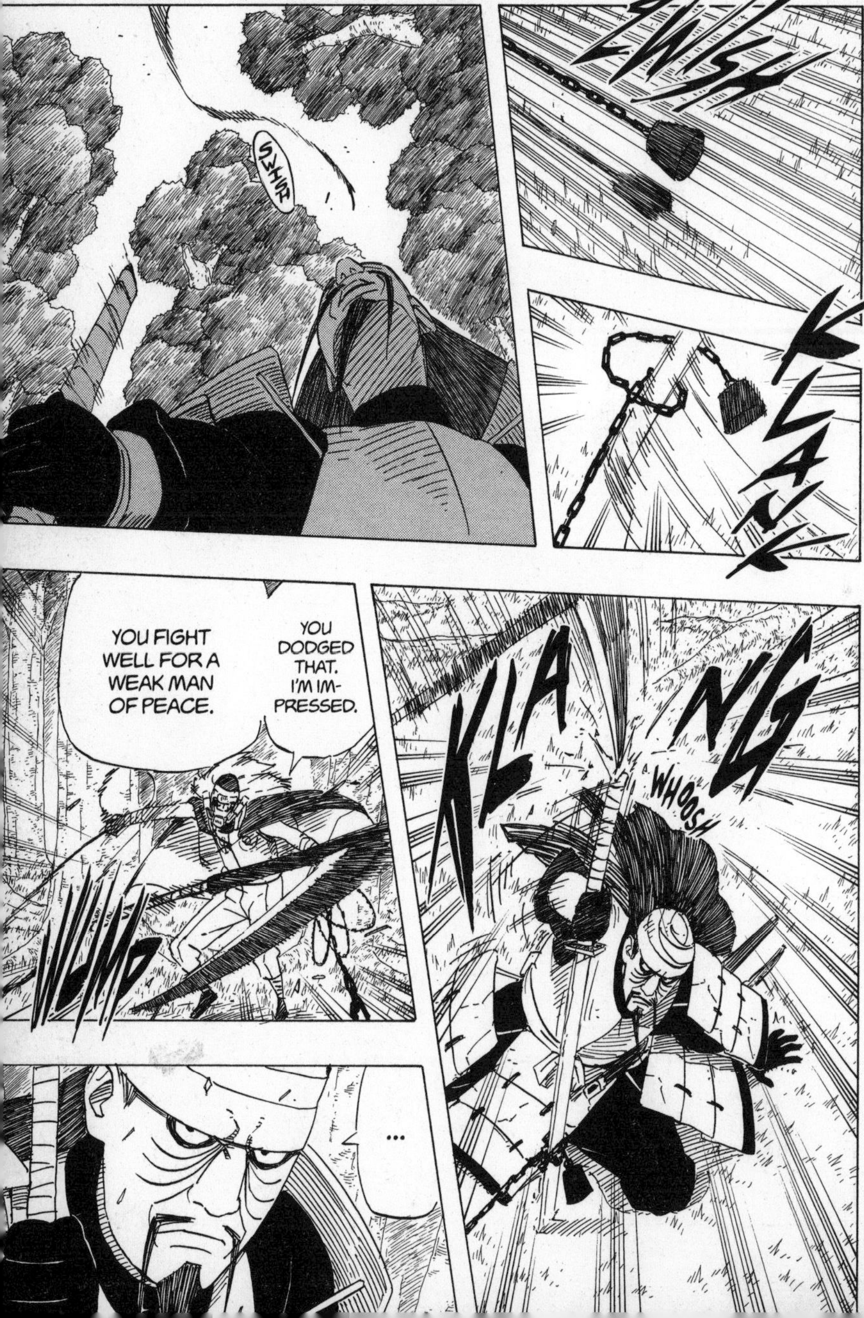
SWISH
KLANK
SWISH
KLANG
WHOOSH
YOU DODGED THAT. I'M IM-PRESSED.
YOU FIGHT WELL FOR A WEAK MAN OF PEACE.
WUMP
...

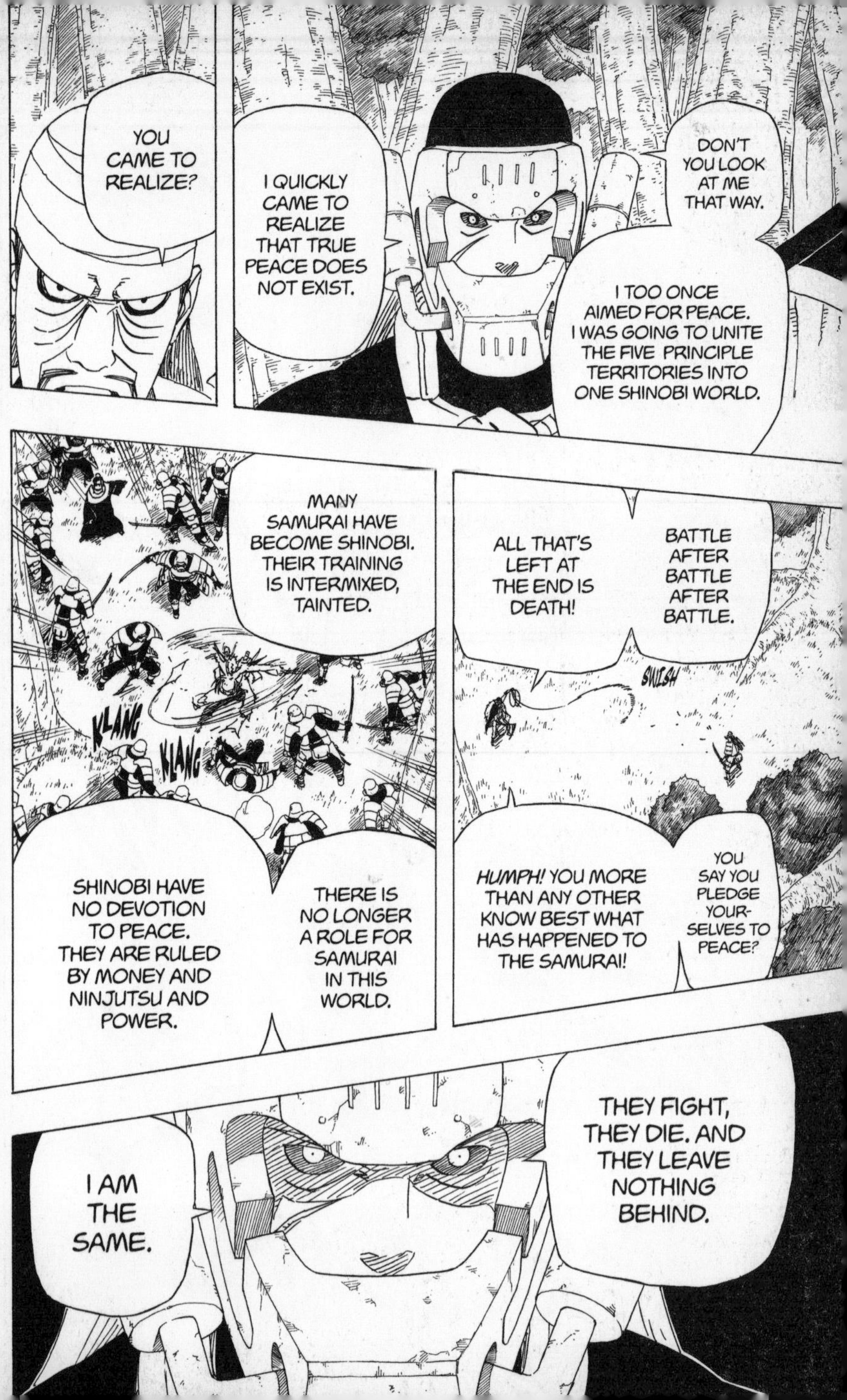
DON'T YOU LOOK AT ME THAT WAY.
I TOO ONCE AIMED FOR PEACE. I WAS GOING TO UNITE THE FIVE PRINCIPLE TERRITORIES INTO ONE SHINOBI WORLD.
I QUICKLY CAME TO REALIZE THAT TRUE PEACE DOES NOT EXIST.
YOU CAME TO REALIZE?
BATTLE AFTER BATTLE AFTER BATTLE.
ALL THAT'S LEFT AT THE END IS DEATH!
SWISH
YOU SAY YOU PLEDGE YOURSELVES TO PEACE?
HUMPH! YOU MORE THAN ANY OTHER KNOW BEST WHAT HAS HAPPENED TO THE SAMURAI!
MANY SAMURAI HAVE BECOME SHINOBI. THEIR TRAINING IS INTERMIXED, TAINTED.
KLANG
KLANG
THERE IS NO LONGER A ROLE FOR SAMURAI IN THIS WORLD.
SHINOBI HAVE NO DEVOTION TO PEACE. THEY ARE RULED BY MONEY AND NINJUTSU AND POWER.
THEY FIGHT, THEY DIE. AND THEY LEAVE NOTHING BEHIND.
I AM THE SAME.

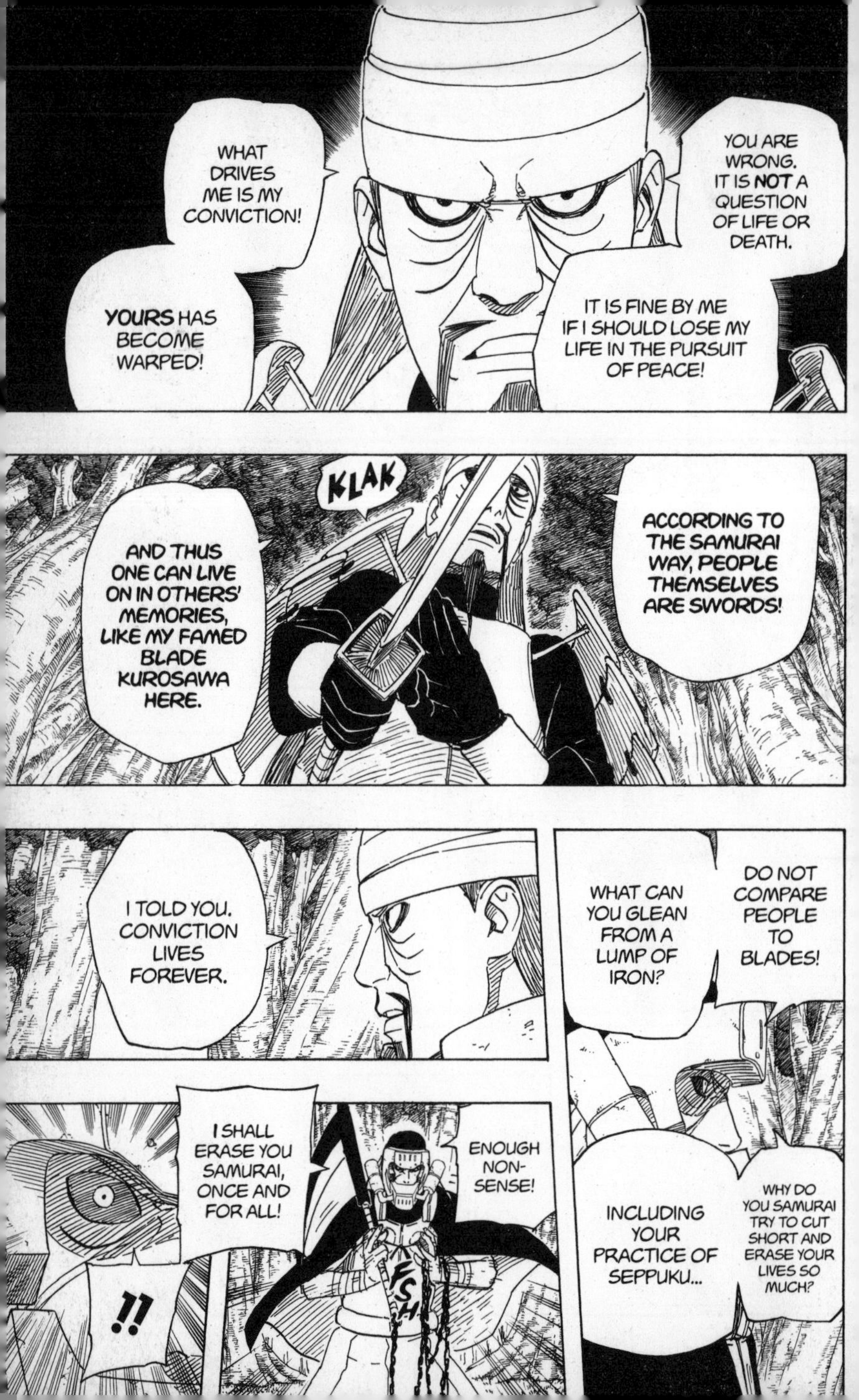

YOU ARE WRONG. IT IS **NOT** A QUESTION OF LIFE OR DEATH.
IT IS FINE BY ME IF I SHOULD LOSE MY LIFE IN THE PURSUIT OF PEACE!
WHAT DRIVES ME IS MY CONVICTION!
YOURS HAS BECOME WARPED!
ACCORDING TO THE SAMURAI WAY, PEOPLE THEMSELVES ARE SWORDS!
KLAK
AND THUS ONE CAN LIVE ON IN OTHERS' MEMORIES, LIKE MY FAMED BLADE KUROSAWA HERE.
DO NOT COMPARE PEOPLE TO BLADES!
WHAT CAN YOU GLEAN FROM A LUMP OF IRON?
WHY DO YOU SAMURAI TRY TO CUT SHORT AND ERASE YOUR LIVES SO MUCH?
INCLUDING YOUR PRACTICE OF SEPPUKU...
I TOLD YOU. CONVICTION LIVES FOREVER.
ENOUGH NON-SENSE!
I SHALL ERASE YOU SAMURAI, ONCE AND FOR ALL!
FSH
!!

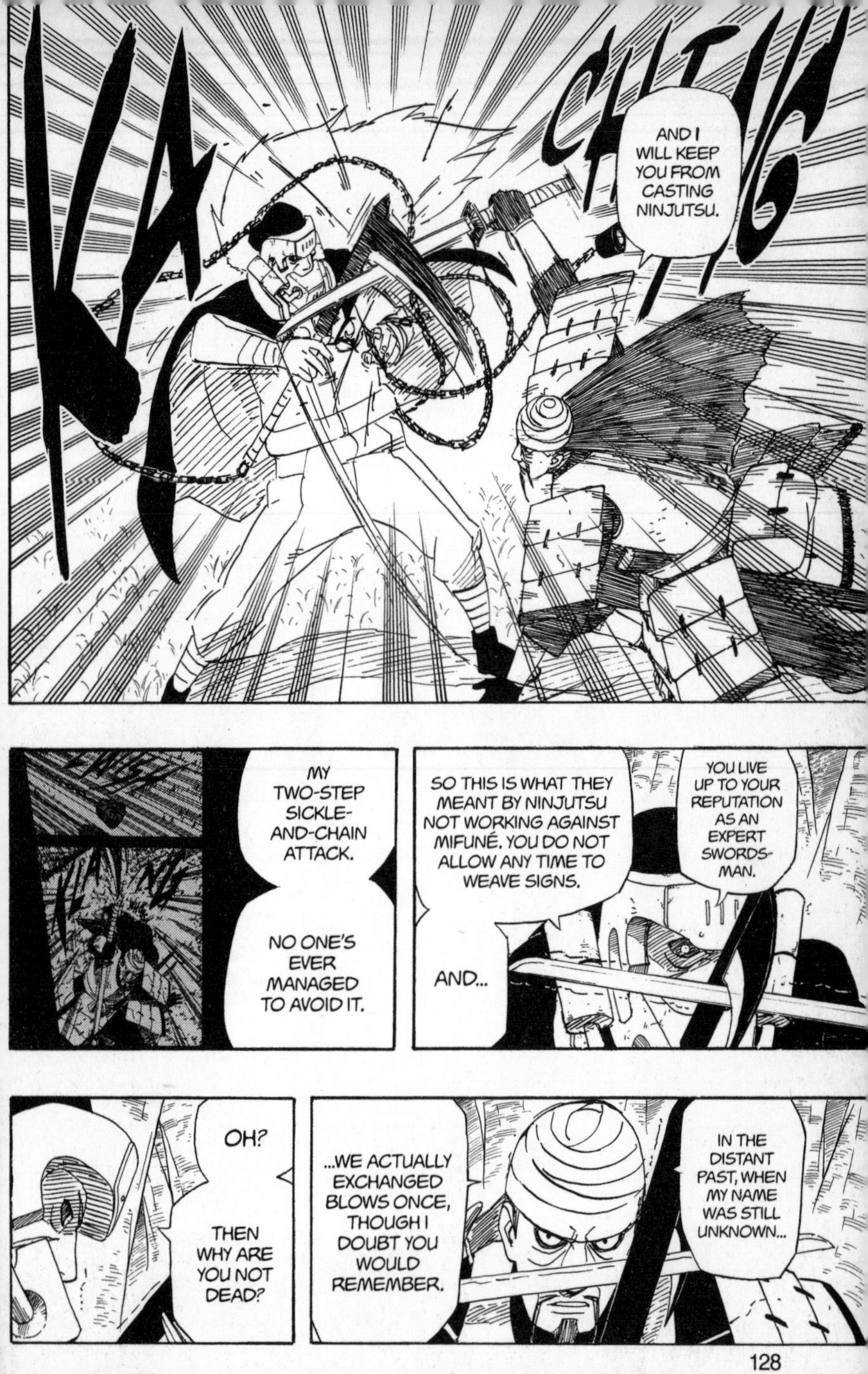
KA
AND I WILL KEEP YOU FROM CASTING NINJUTSU.
YOU LIVE UP TO YOUR REPUTATION AS AN EXPERT SWORDS-MAN.
SO THIS IS WHAT THEY MEANT BY NINJUTSU NOT WORKING AGAINST MIFUNÉ. YOU DO NOT ALLOW ANY TIME TO WEAVE SIGNS.
AND...
MY TWO-STEP SICKLE-AND-CHAIN ATTACK.
NO ONE'S EVER MANAGED TO AVOID IT.
IN THE DISTANT PAST, WHEN MY NAME WAS STILL UNKNOWN...
...WE ACTUALLY EXCHANGED BLOWS ONCE, THOUGH I DOUBT YOU WOULD REMEMBER.
OH?
THEN WHY ARE YOU NOT DEAD?

READ THIS WAY

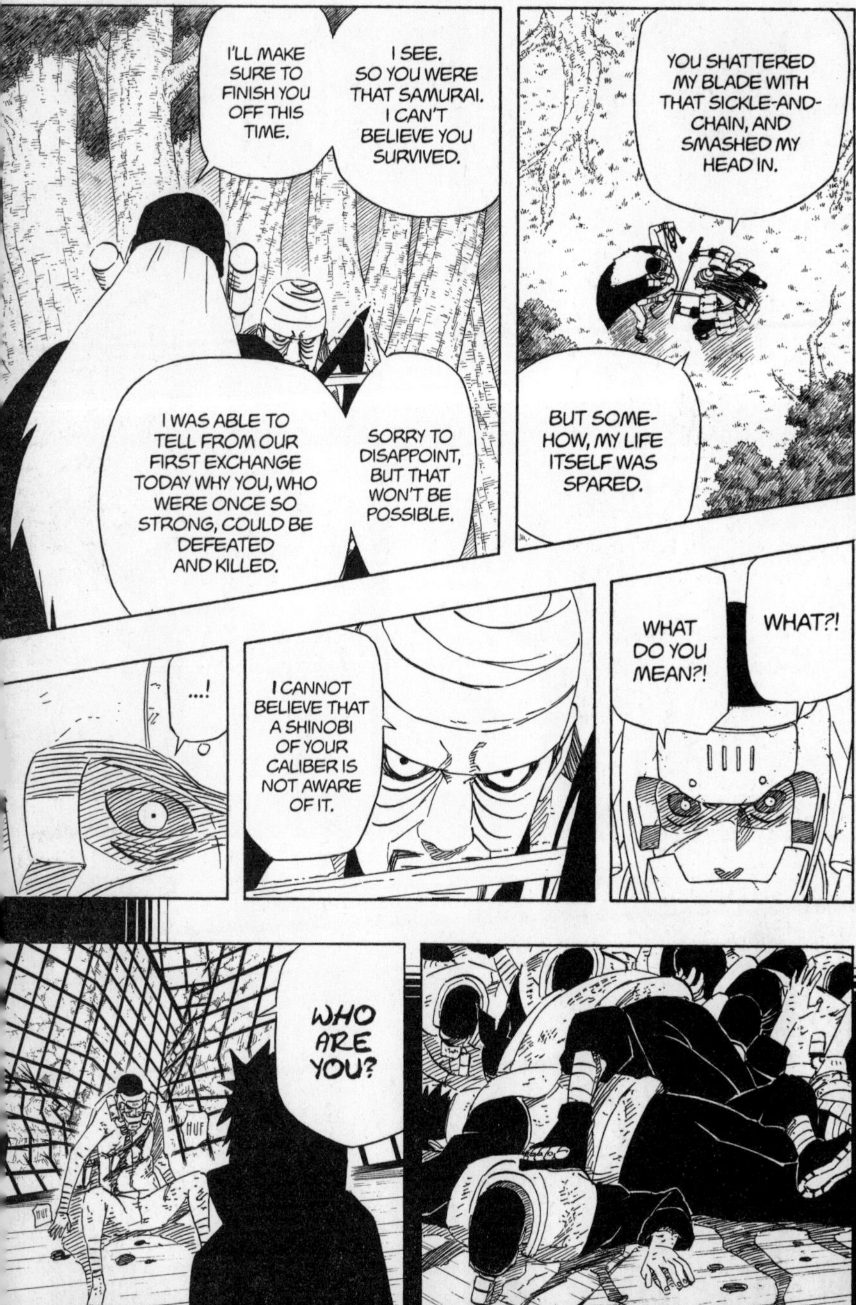
YOU SHATTERED MY BLADE WITH THAT SICKLE-AND-CHAIN, AND SMASHED MY HEAD IN.
BUT SOME-HOW, MY LIFE ITSELF WAS SPARED.
I SEE. SO YOU WERE THAT SAMURAI. I CAN'T BELIEVE YOU SURVIVED.
I'LL MAKE SURE TO FINISH YOU OFF THIS TIME.
SORRY TO DISAPPOINT, BUT THAT WON'T BE POSSIBLE.
I WAS ABLE TO TELL FROM OUR FIRST EXCHANGE TODAY WHY YOU, WHO WERE ONCE SO STRONG, COULD BE DEFEATED AND KILLED.
WHAT?!
WHAT DO YOU MEAN?!
I CANNOT BELIEVE THAT A SHINOBI OF YOUR CALIBER IS NOT AWARE OF IT.
...!
WHO ARE YOU?
HUF
HUF

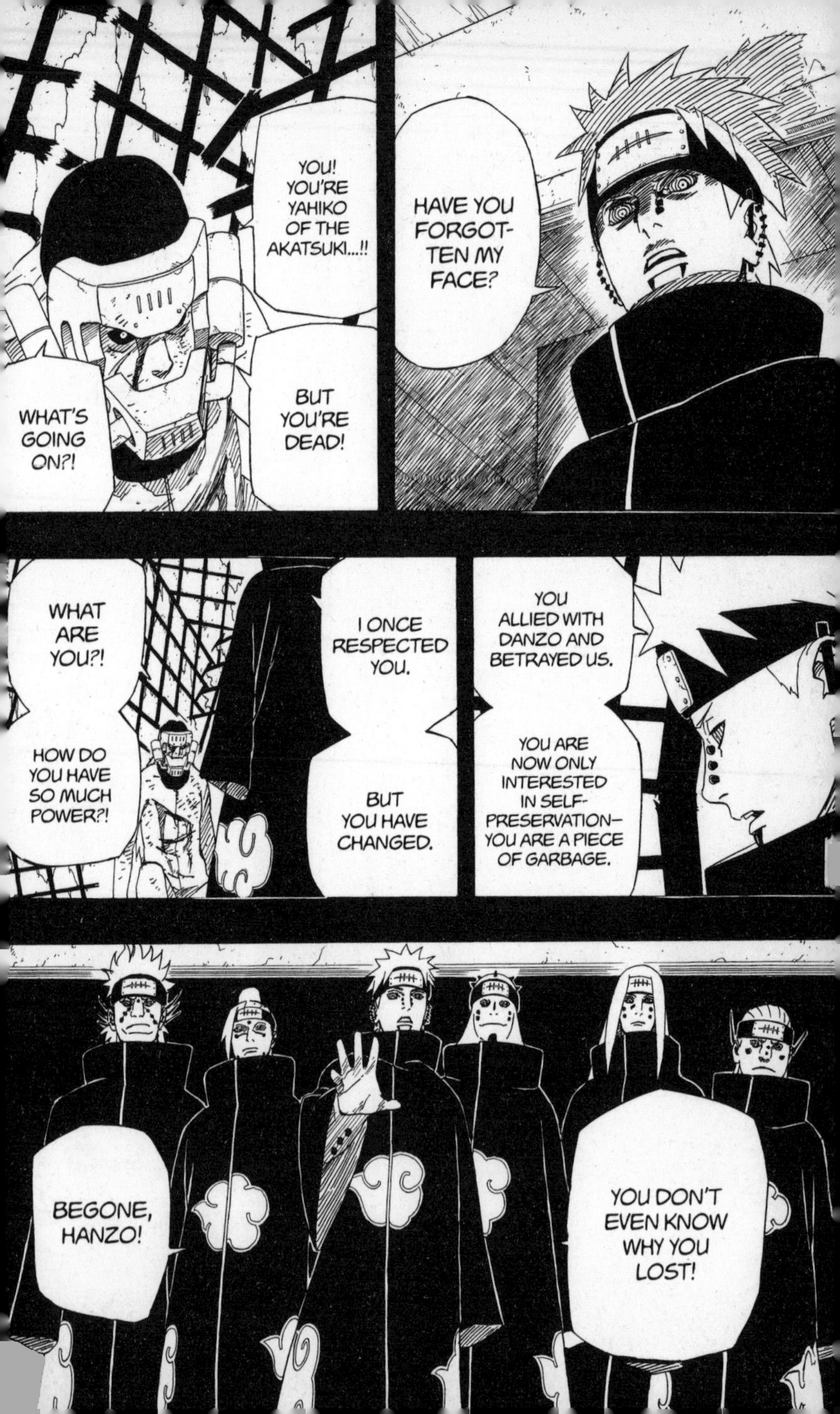
HAVE YOU FORGOTTEN MY FACE?
YOU! YOU'RE YAHIKO OF THE AKATSUKI...!!
BUT YOU'RE DEAD!
WHAT'S GOING ON?!
YOU ALLIED WITH DANZO AND BETRAYED US.
YOU ARE NOW ONLY INTERESTED IN SELF-PRESERVATION— YOU ARE A PIECE OF GARBAGE.
I ONCE RESPECTED YOU.
BUT YOU HAVE CHANGED.
WHAT ARE YOU?!
HOW DO YOU HAVE SO MUCH POWER?!
YOU DON'T EVEN KNOW WHY YOU LOST!
BEGONE, HANZO!

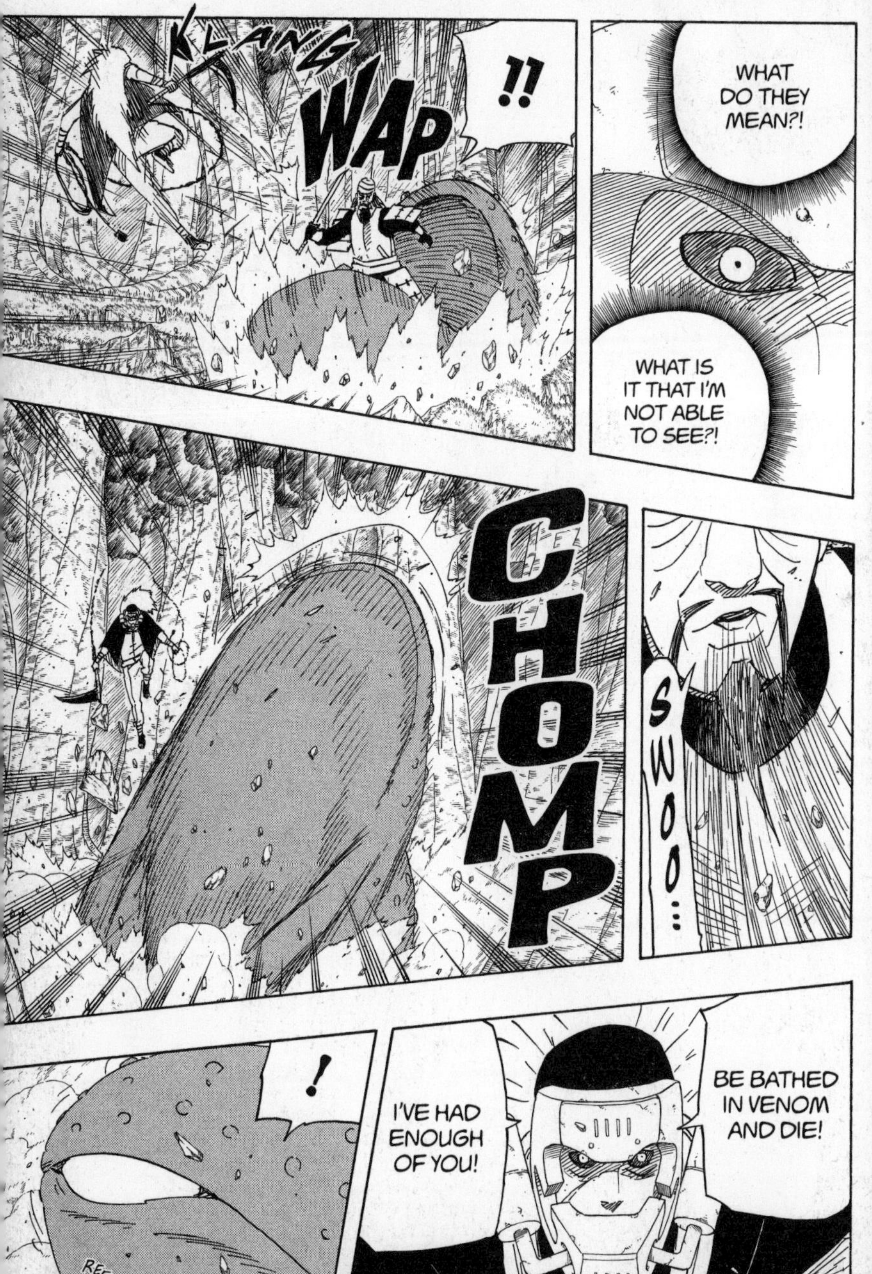
WHAT DO THEY MEAN?!
WHAT IS IT THAT I'M NOT ABLE TO SEE?!
KLANG
WAP
!!
SWOO...
CHOMP
BE BATHED IN VENOM AND DIE!
I'VE HAD ENOUGH OF YOU!
!
REEEEEK

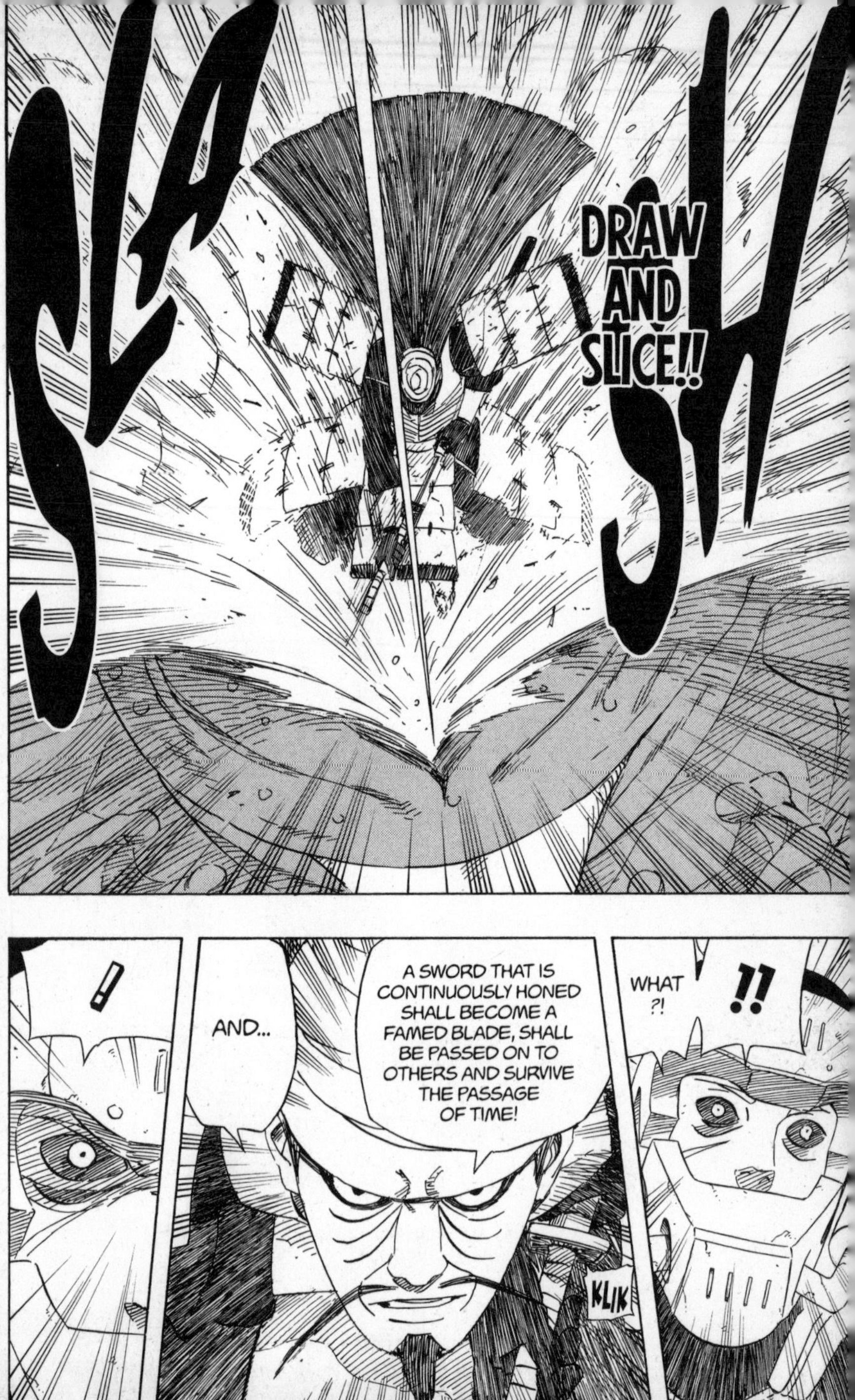
SLASH
DRAW AND SLICE!!
WHAT ?!
!!
A SWORD THAT IS CONTINUOUSLY HONED SHALL BECOME A FAMED BLADE, SHALL BE PASSED ON TO OTHERS AND SURVIVE THE PASSAGE OF TIME!
AND...
KLIK
!

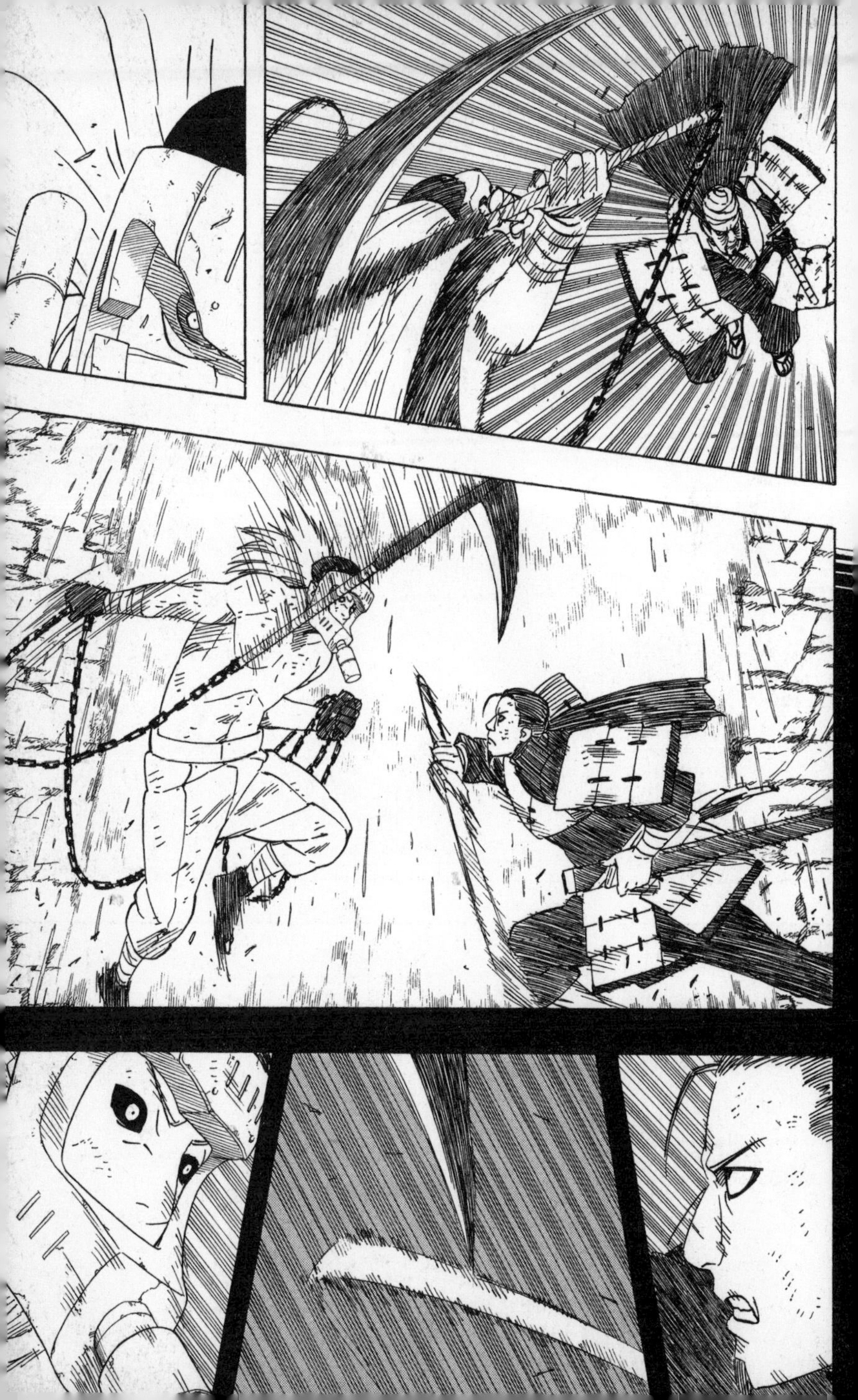

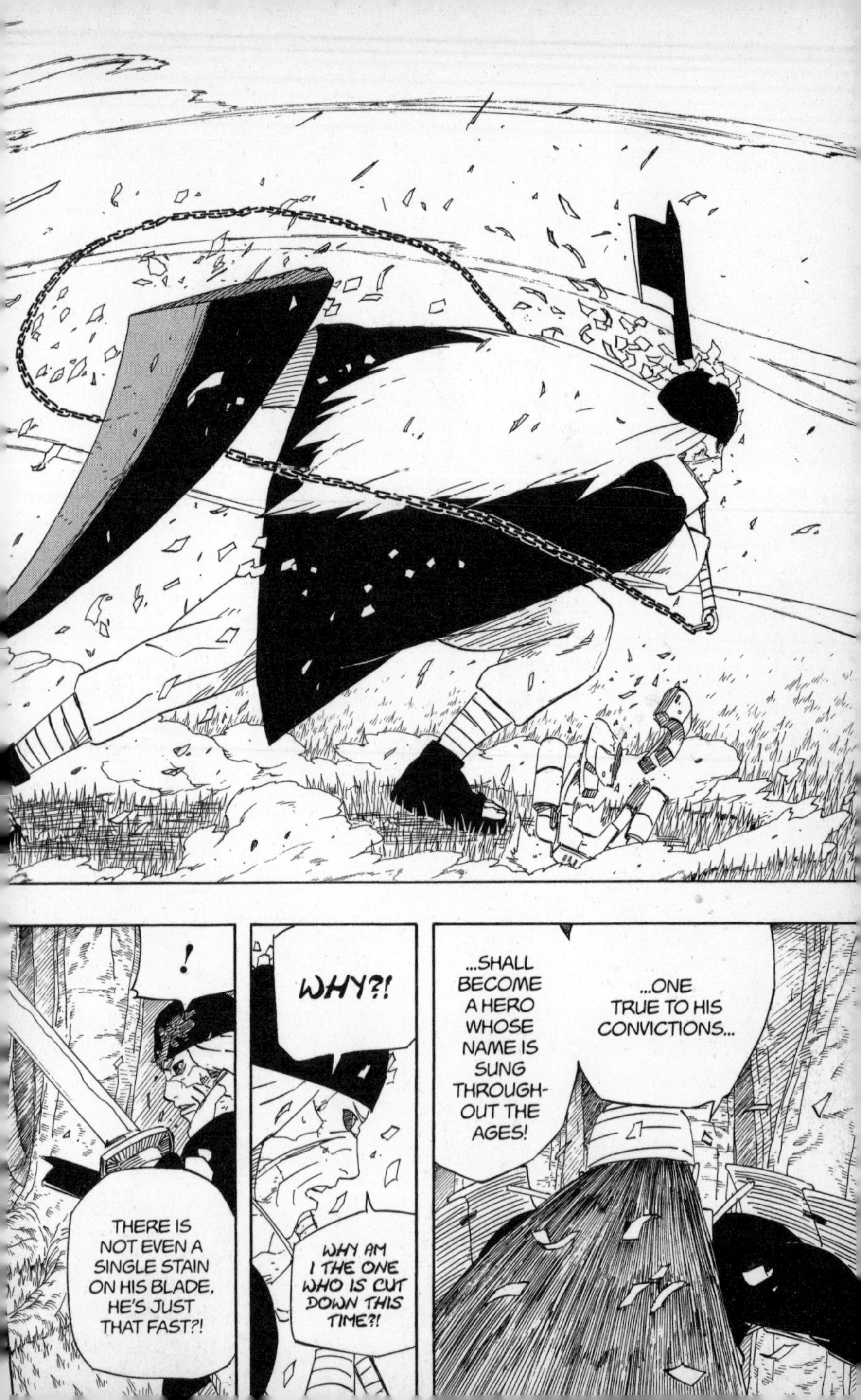
...ONE TRUE TO HIS CONVICTIONS...
...SHALL BECOME A HERO WHOSE NAME IS SUNG THROUGH-OUT THE AGES!
WHY?!
WHY AM I THE ONE WHO IS CUT DOWN THIS TIME?!
!
THERE IS NOT EVEN A SINGLE STAIN ON HIS BLADE. HE'S JUST THAT FAST?!

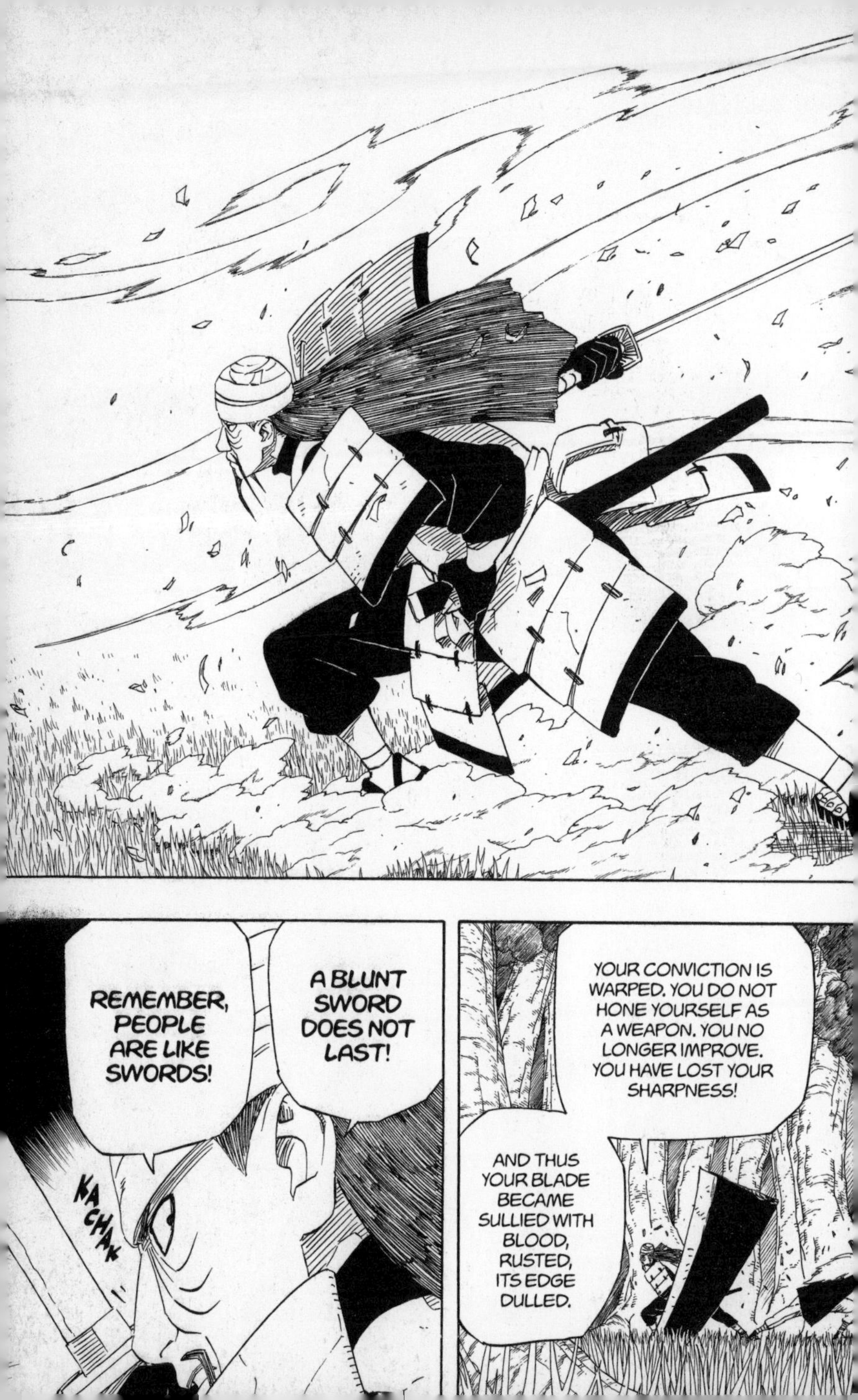
YOUR CONVICTION IS WARPED. YOU DO NOT HONE YOURSELF AS A WEAPON. YOU NO LONGER IMPROVE. YOU HAVE LOST YOUR SHARPNESS!
AND THUS YOUR BLADE BECAME SULLIED WITH BLOOD, RUSTED, ITS EDGE DULLED.
A BLUNT SWORD DOES NOT LAST!
REMEMBER, PEOPLE ARE LIKE SWORDS!
KACHAK

Number 532: Mifuné vs. Hanzo, Decided!!

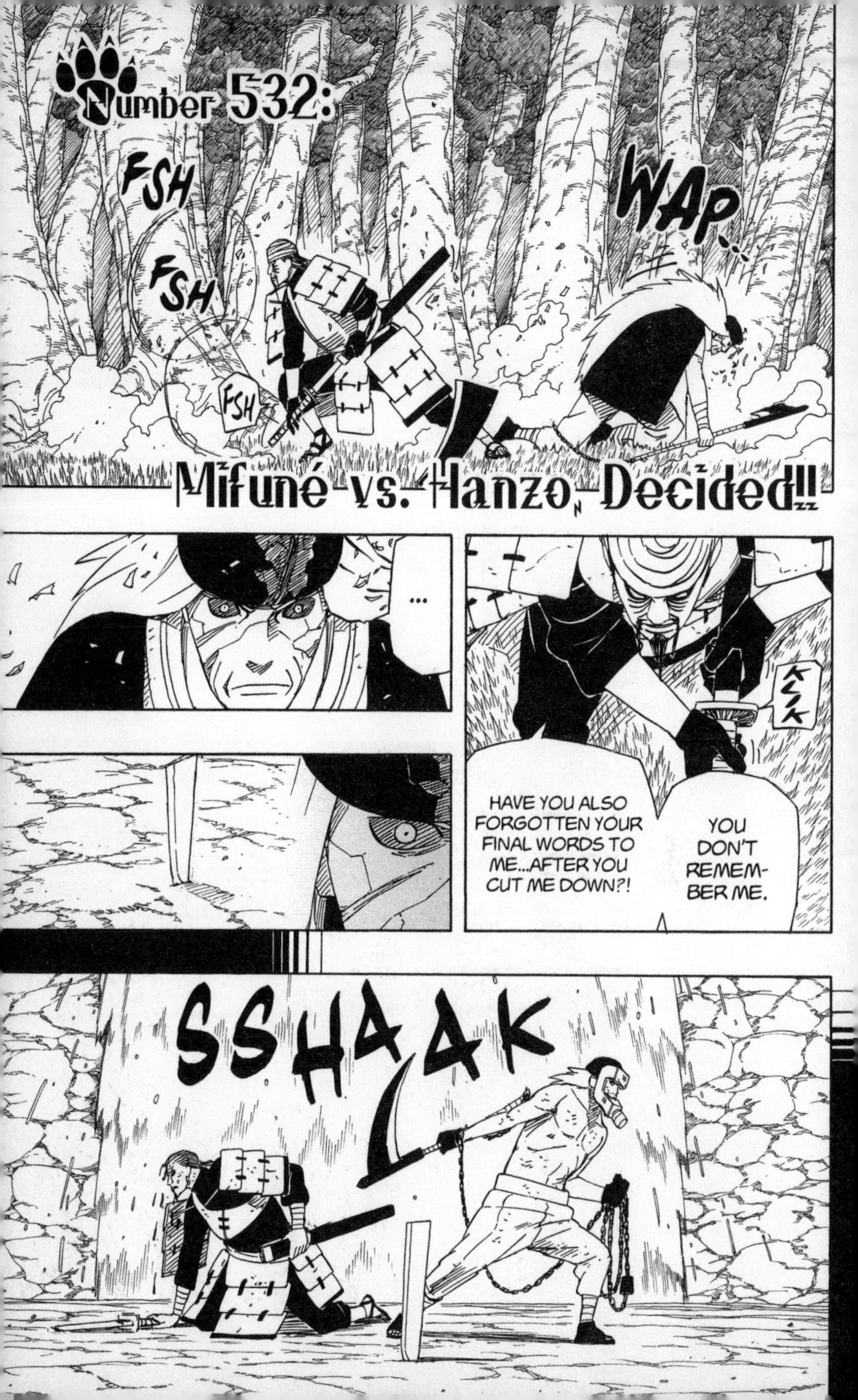
WAP...
FSH
FSH
FSH
KLIK
YOU DON'T REMEM-BER ME.
HAVE YOU ALSO FORGOTTEN YOUR FINAL WORDS TO ME...AFTER YOU CUT ME DOWN?!
...
SSHAAK

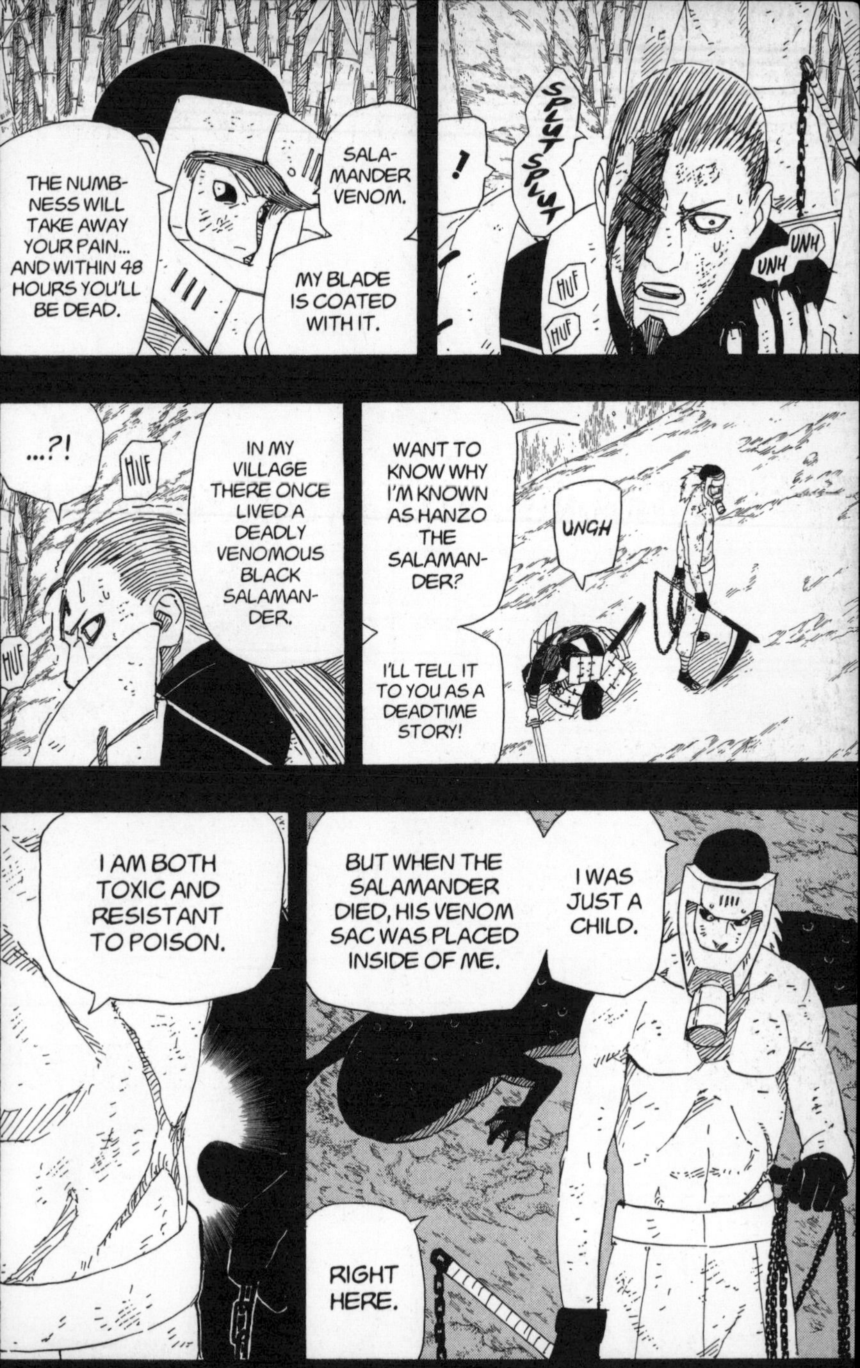
!
SPLUT SPLUT SPLUT
HUF HUF
UNH UNH
SALAMANDER VENOM.
MY BLADE IS COATED WITH IT.
THE NUMBNESS WILL TAKE AWAY YOUR PAIN... AND WITHIN 48 HOURS YOU'LL BE DEAD.
WANT TO KNOW WHY I'M KNOWN AS HANZO THE SALAMANDER?
UNGH
I'LL TELL IT TO YOU AS A DEADTIME STORY!
IN MY VILLAGE THERE ONCE LIVED A DEADLY VENOMOUS BLACK SALAMANDER.
...?!
HUF
HUF
I WAS JUST A CHILD.
BUT WHEN THE SALAMANDER DIED, HIS VENOM SAC WAS PLACED INSIDE OF ME.
RIGHT HERE.
I AM BOTH TOXIC AND RESISTANT TO POISON.

READ THIS WAY

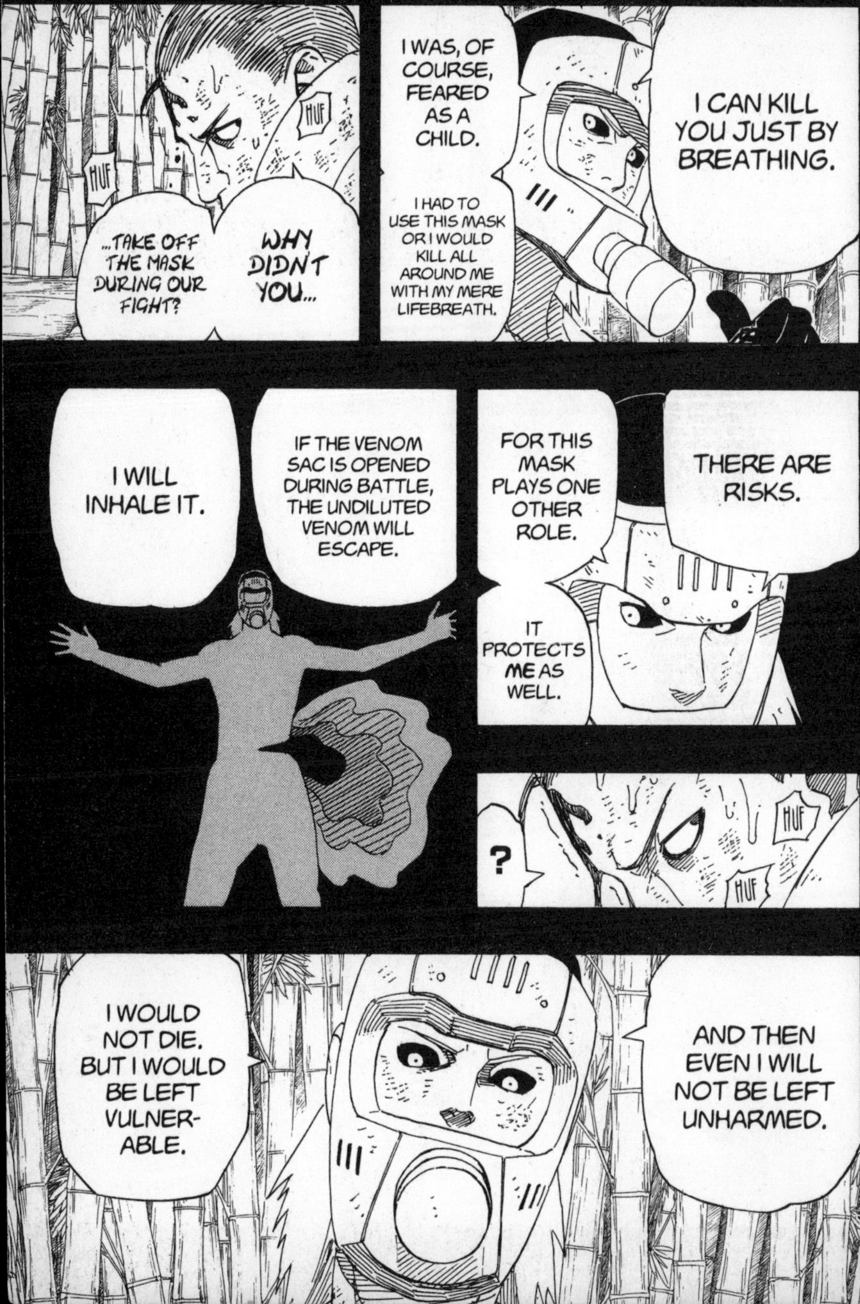
I CAN KILL YOU JUST BY BREATHING.
I WAS, OF COURSE, FEARED AS A CHILD.
I HAD TO USE THIS MASK OR I WOULD KILL ALL AROUND ME WITH MY MERE LIFEBREATH.
HUF
HUF
WHY DIDN'T YOU...
...TAKE OFF THE MASK DURING OUR FIGHT?
THERE ARE RISKS.
FOR THIS MASK PLAYS ONE OTHER ROLE.
IT PROTECTS ME AS WELL.
HUF
HUF
?
IF THE VENOM SAC IS OPENED DURING BATTLE, THE UNDILUTED VENOM WILL ESCAPE.
I WILL INHALE IT.
AND THEN EVEN I WILL NOT BE LEFT UNHARMED.
I WOULD NOT DIE. BUT I WOULD BE LEFT VULNER-ABLE.

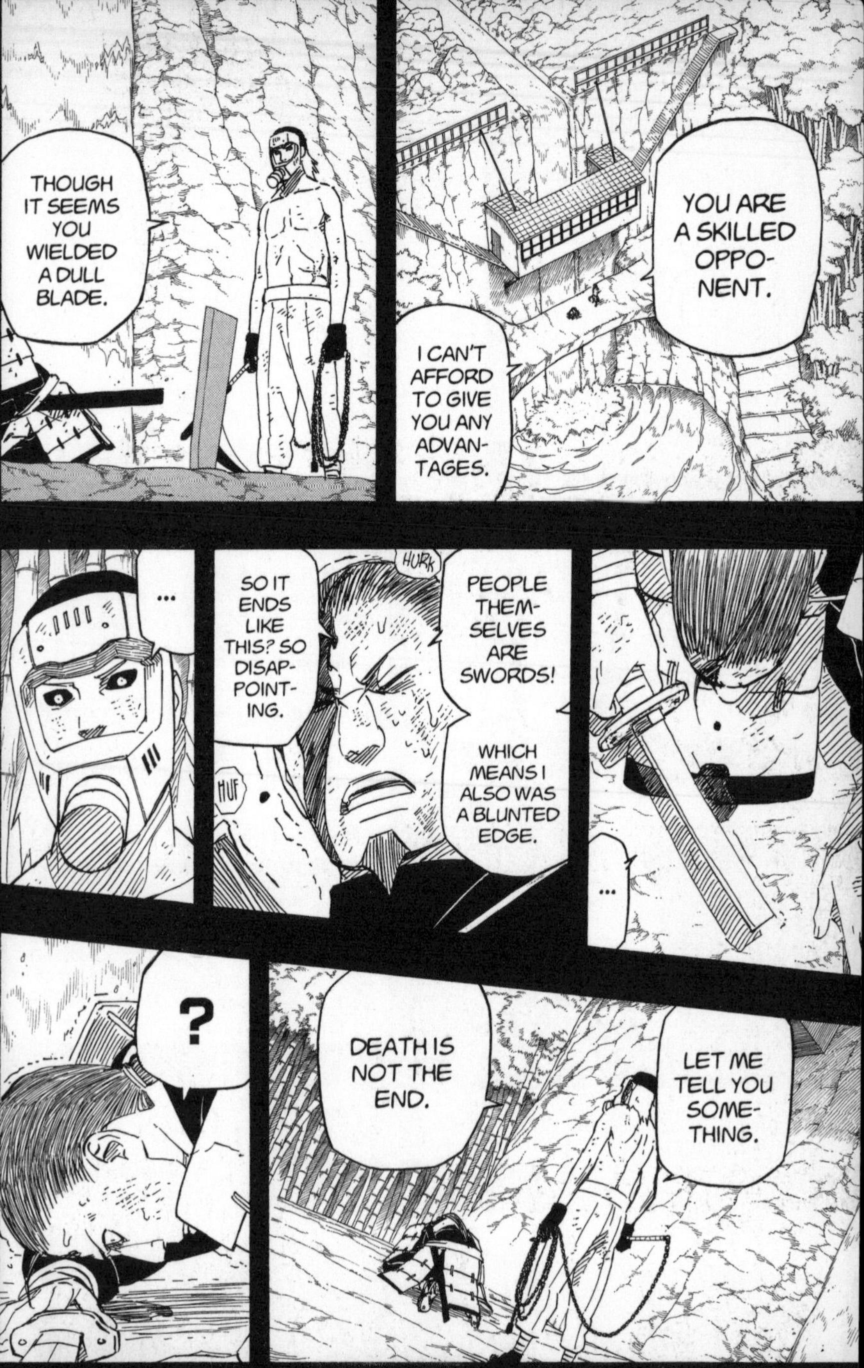
YOU ARE A SKILLED OPPONENT.
I CAN'T AFFORD TO GIVE YOU ANY ADVANTAGES.
THOUGH IT SEEMS YOU WIELDED A DULL BLADE.
...
HURK
PEOPLE THEMSELVES ARE SWORDS!
SO IT ENDS LIKE THIS? SO DISAPPOINTING.
WHICH MEANS I ALSO WAS A BLUNTED EDGE.
HUF
...
LET ME TELL YOU SOMETHING.
DEATH IS NOT THE END.
?

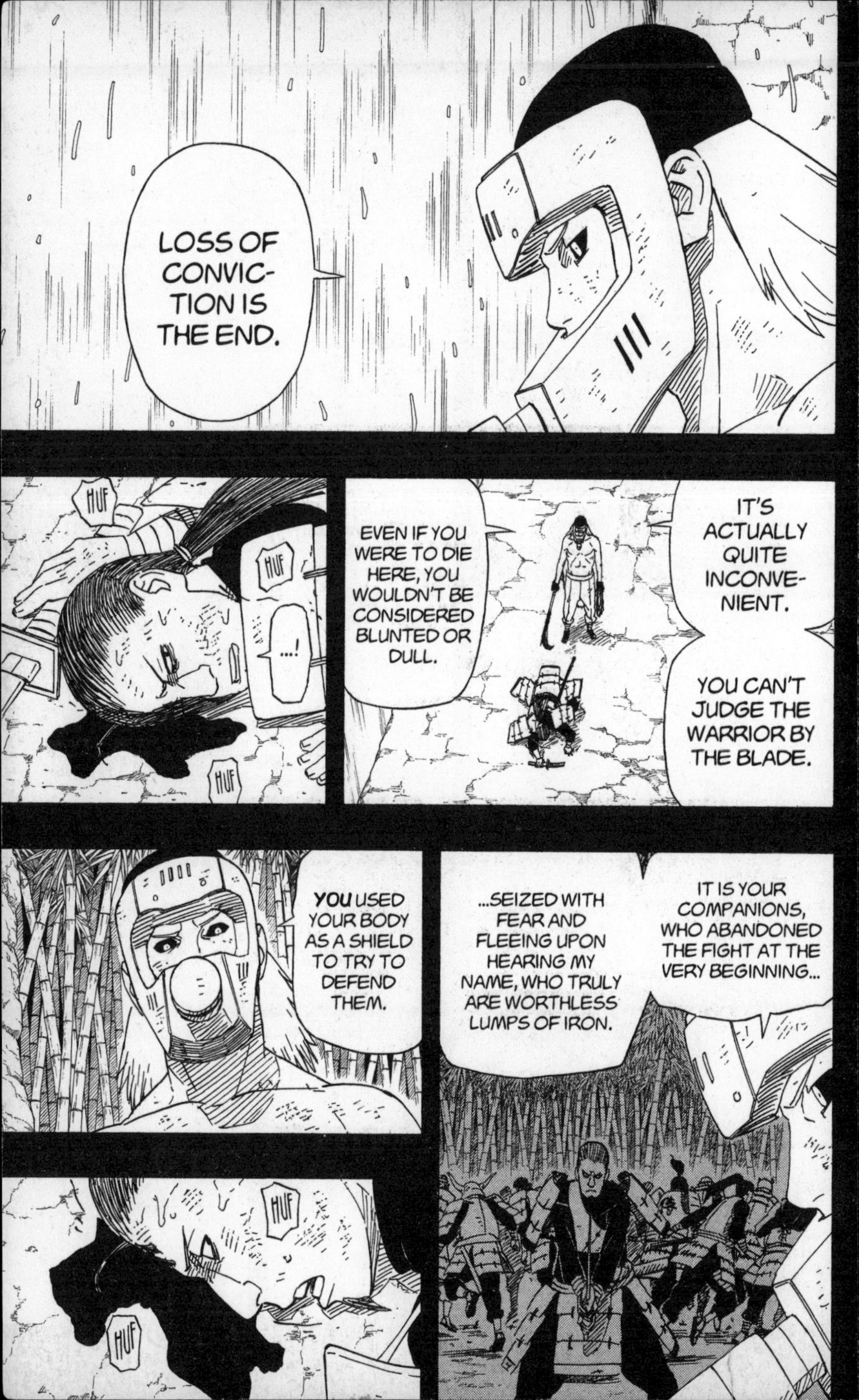
LOSS OF CONVICTION IS THE END.
IT'S ACTUALLY QUITE INCONVENIENT. YOU CAN'T JUDGE THE WARRIOR BY THE BLADE.
EVEN IF YOU WERE TO DIE HERE, YOU WOULDN'T BE CONSIDERED BLUNTED OR DULL.
HUF
HUF
...!
HUF
IT IS YOUR COMPANIONS, WHO ABANDONED THE FIGHT AT THE VERY BEGINNING...
...SEIZED WITH FEAR AND FLEEING UPON HEARING MY NAME, WHO TRULY ARE WORTHLESS LUMPS OF IRON.
YOU USED YOUR BODY AS A SHIELD TO TRY TO DEFEND THEM.
HUF
HUF

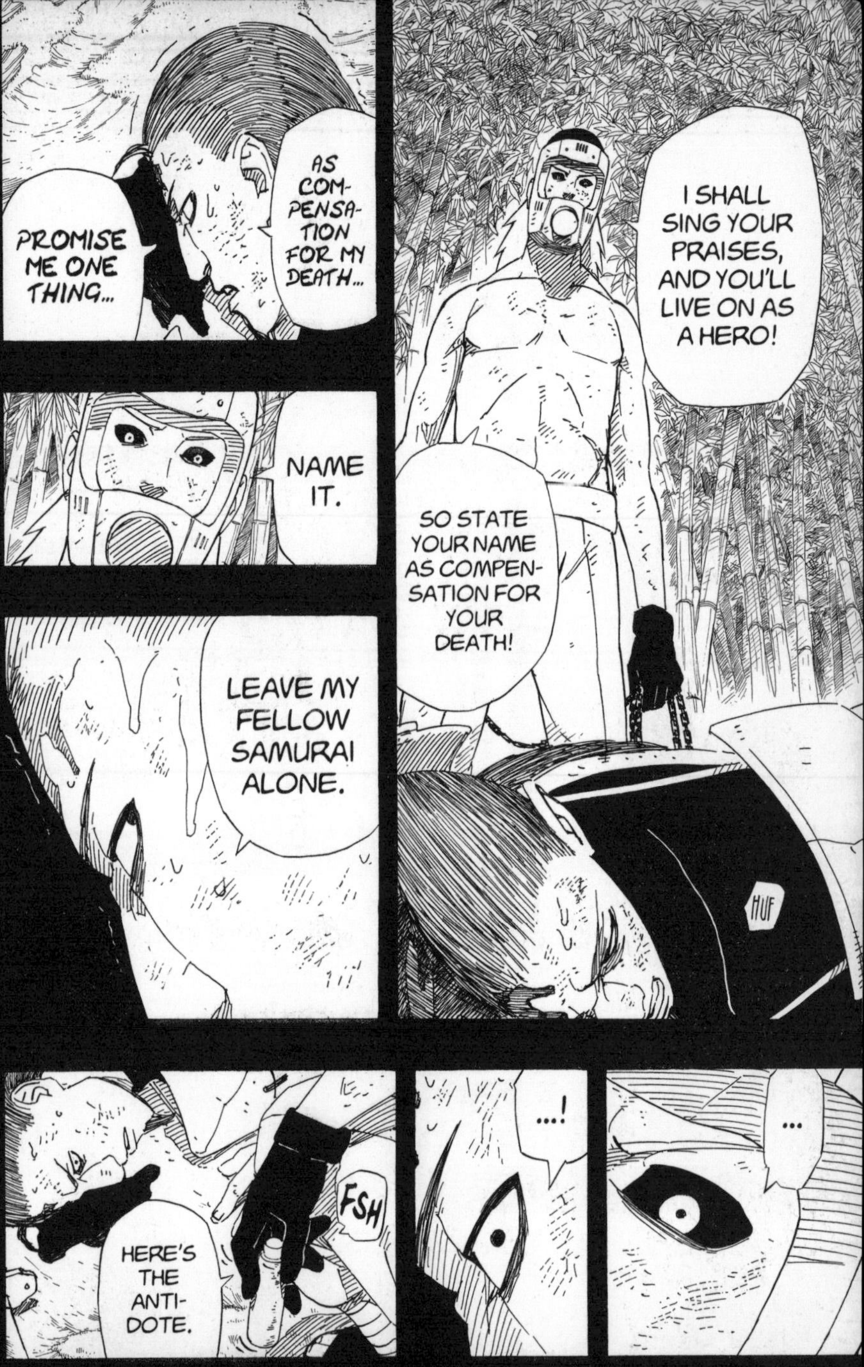
I SHALL SING YOUR PRAISES, AND YOU'LL LIVE ON AS A HERO!
SO STATE YOUR NAME AS COMPENSATION FOR YOUR DEATH!
HUF
AS COMPENSATION FOR MY DEATH...
PROMISE ME ONE THING...
NAME IT.
LEAVE MY FELLOW SAMURAI ALONE.
...
...!
FSH
HERE'S THE ANTIDOTE.

READ THIS WAY

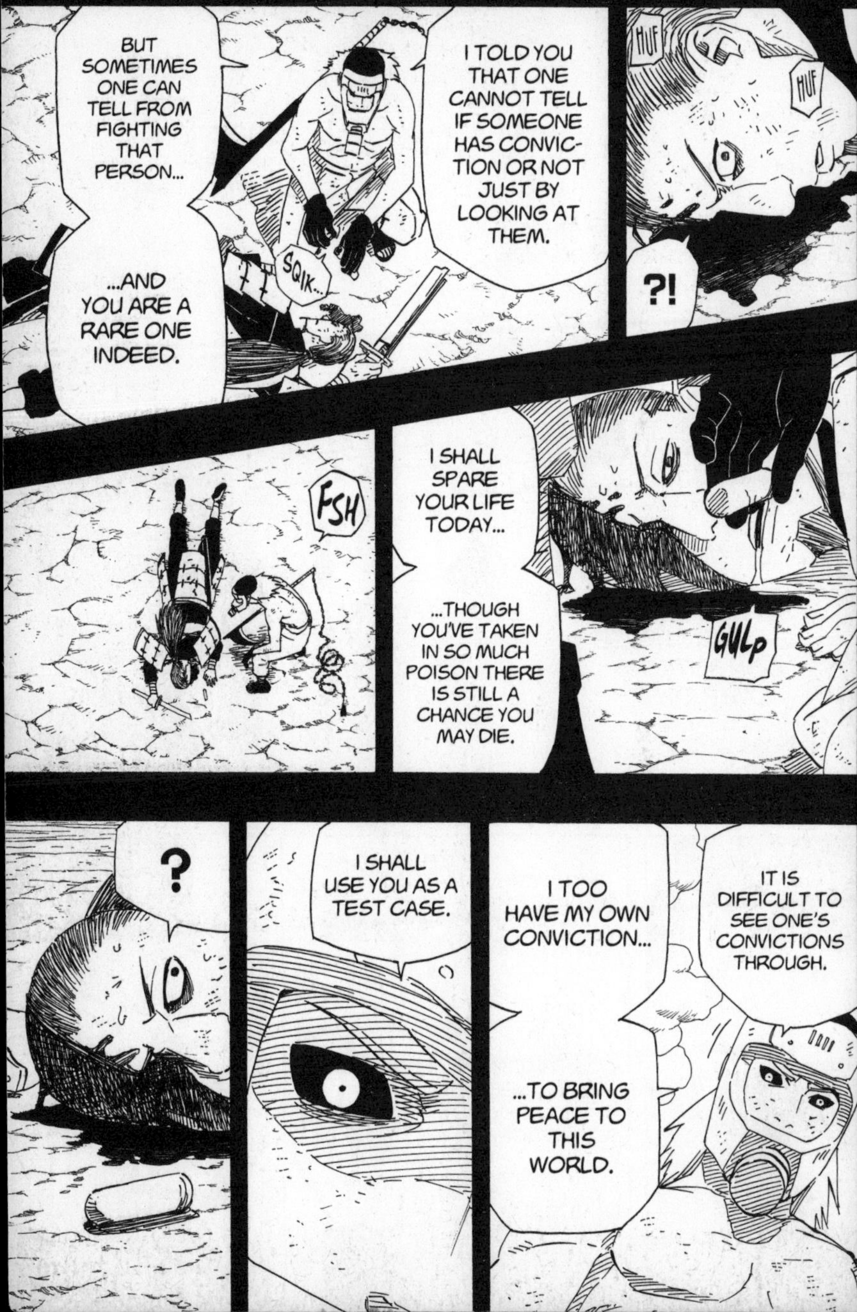
HUF
HUF
?!
I TOLD YOU THAT ONE CANNOT TELL IF SOMEONE HAS CONVICTION OR NOT JUST BY LOOKING AT THEM.
SQIK...
BUT SOMETIMES ONE CAN TELL FROM FIGHTING THAT PERSON...
...AND YOU ARE A RARE ONE INDEED.
GULP
I SHALL SPARE YOUR LIFE TODAY...
...THOUGH YOU'VE TAKEN IN SO MUCH POISON THERE IS STILL A CHANCE YOU MAY DIE.
FSH
IT IS DIFFICULT TO SEE ONE'S CONVICTIONS THROUGH.
I TOO HAVE MY OWN CONVICTION...
...TO BRING PEACE TO THIS WORLD.
I SHALL USE YOU AS A TEST CASE.
?

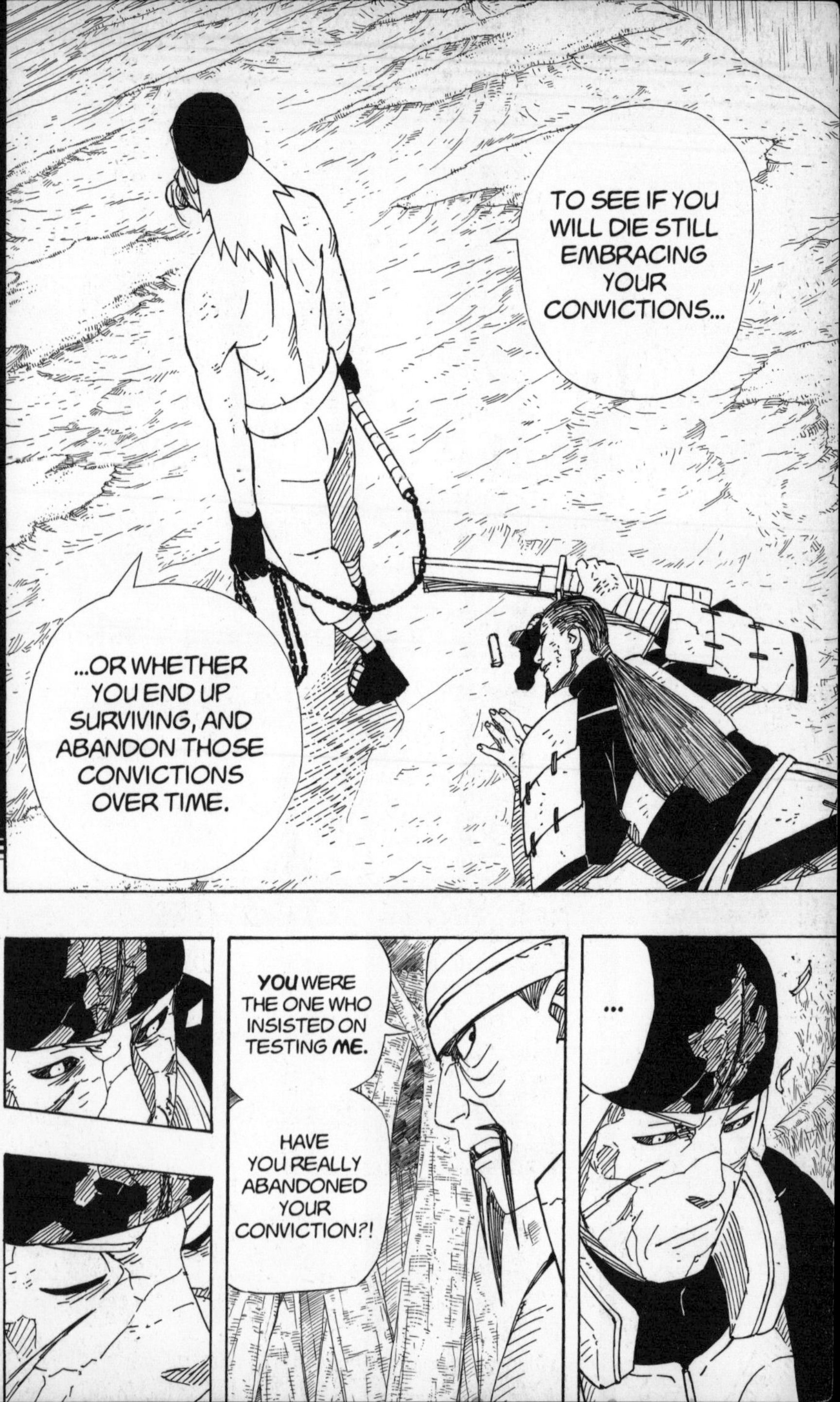
TO SEE IF YOU WILL DIE STILL EMBRACING YOUR CONVICTIONS...
...OR WHETHER YOU END UP SURVIVING, AND ABANDON THOSE CONVICTIONS OVER TIME.
...
YOU WERE THE ONE WHO INSISTED ON TESTING **ME**.
HAVE YOU REALLY ABANDONED YOUR CONVICTION?!

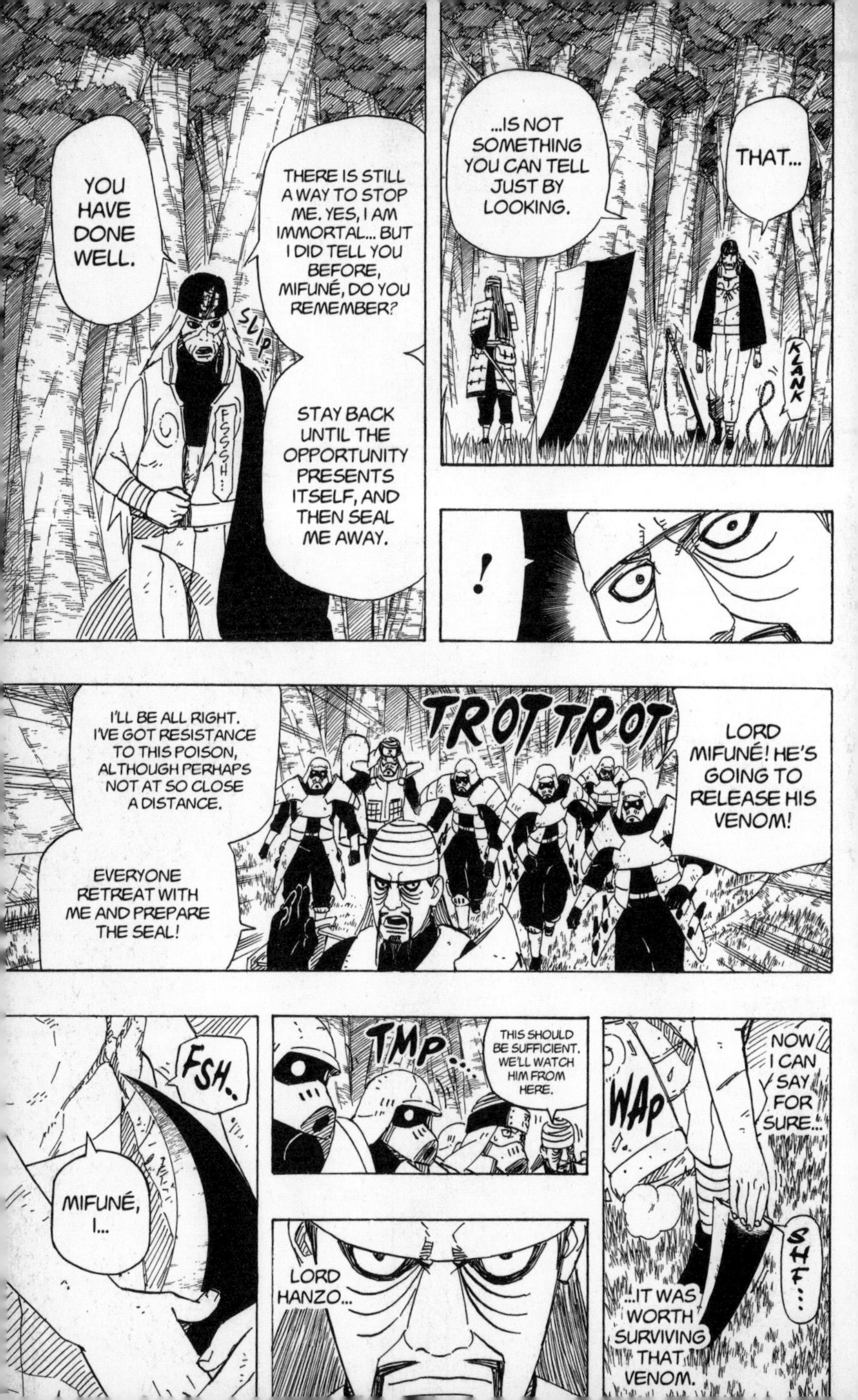
THAT...
...IS NOT SOMETHING YOU CAN TELL JUST BY LOOKING.
KLANK
!
THERE IS STILL A WAY TO STOP ME. YES, I AM IMMORTAL... BUT I DID TELL YOU BEFORE, MIFUNÉ, DO YOU REMEMBER?
YOU HAVE DONE WELL.
SLIP.
FSSSH...
STAY BACK UNTIL THE OPPORTUNITY PRESENTS ITSELF, AND THEN SEAL ME AWAY.
LORD MIFUNÉ! HE'S GOING TO RELEASE HIS VENOM!
TROT TROT
I'LL BE ALL RIGHT. I'VE GOT RESISTANCE TO THIS POISON, ALTHOUGH PERHAPS NOT AT SO CLOSE A DISTANCE.
EVERYONE RETREAT WITH ME AND PREPARE THE SEAL!
NOW I CAN SAY FOR SURE...
WAP
SHF...
...IT WAS WORTH SURVIVING THAT VENOM.
THIS SHOULD BE SUFFICIENT. WE'LL WATCH HIM FROM HERE.
TMP...
LORD HANZO...
FSH..
MIFUNÉ, I...

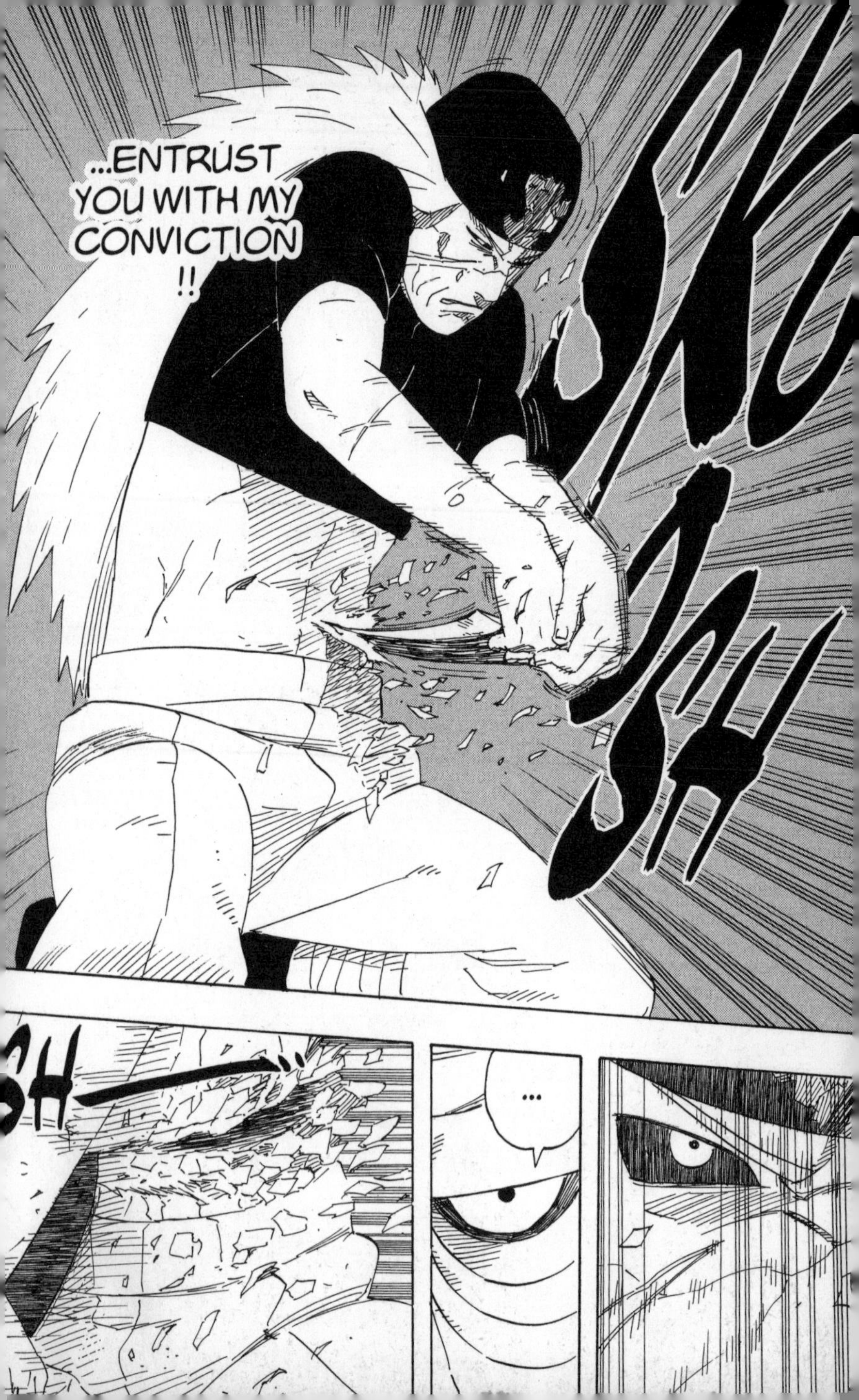
...ENTRUST YOU WITH MY CONVICTION !!
...
SH—

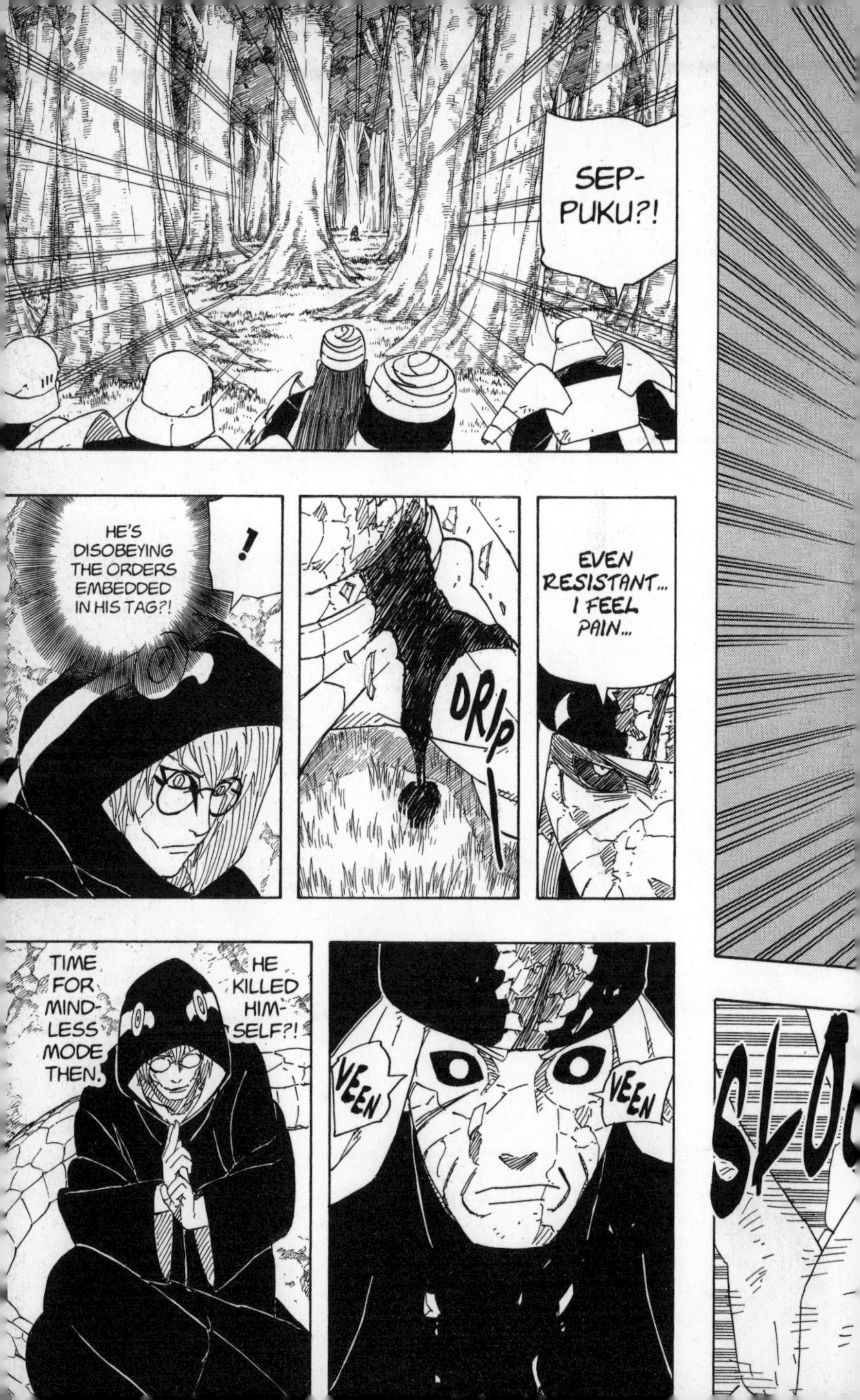
SEP-PUKU?!
EVEN RESISTANT... I FEEL PAIN...
DRIP
!
HE'S DISOBEYING THE ORDERS EMBEDDED IN HIS TAG?!
VEEN
VEEN
HE KILLED HIM-SELF?!
TIME FOR MIND-LESS MODE THEN.

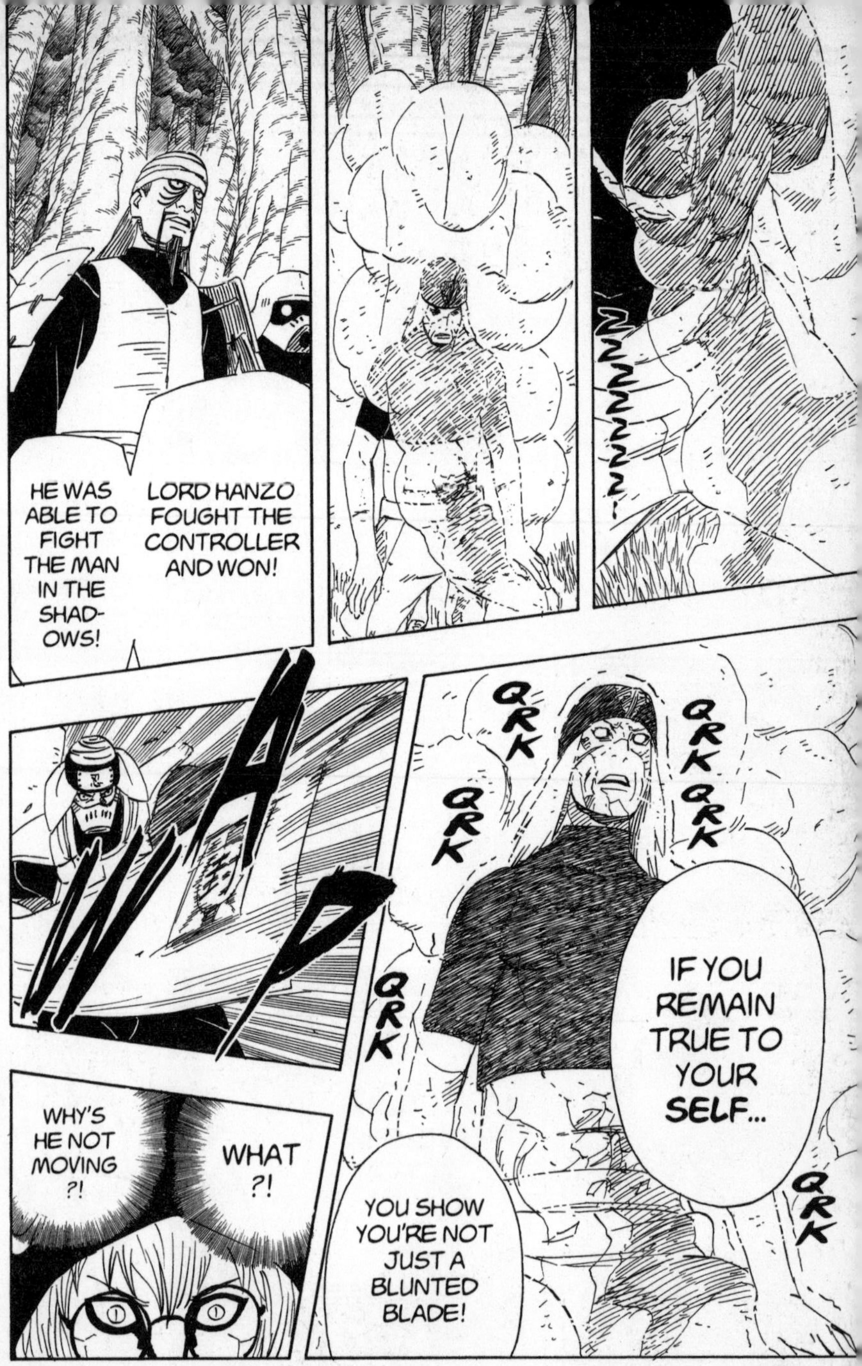
ZZZZZZZZZ
LORD HANZO FOUGHT THE CONTROLLER AND WON!
HE WAS ABLE TO FIGHT THE MAN IN THE SHAD-OWS!
QRK
QRK
QRK QRK QRK
QRK
IF YOU REMAIN TRUE TO YOUR SELF...
YOU SHOW YOU'RE NOT JUST A BLUNTED BLADE!
QRK
WHAP
WHAT ?!
WHY'S HE NOT MOVING ?!

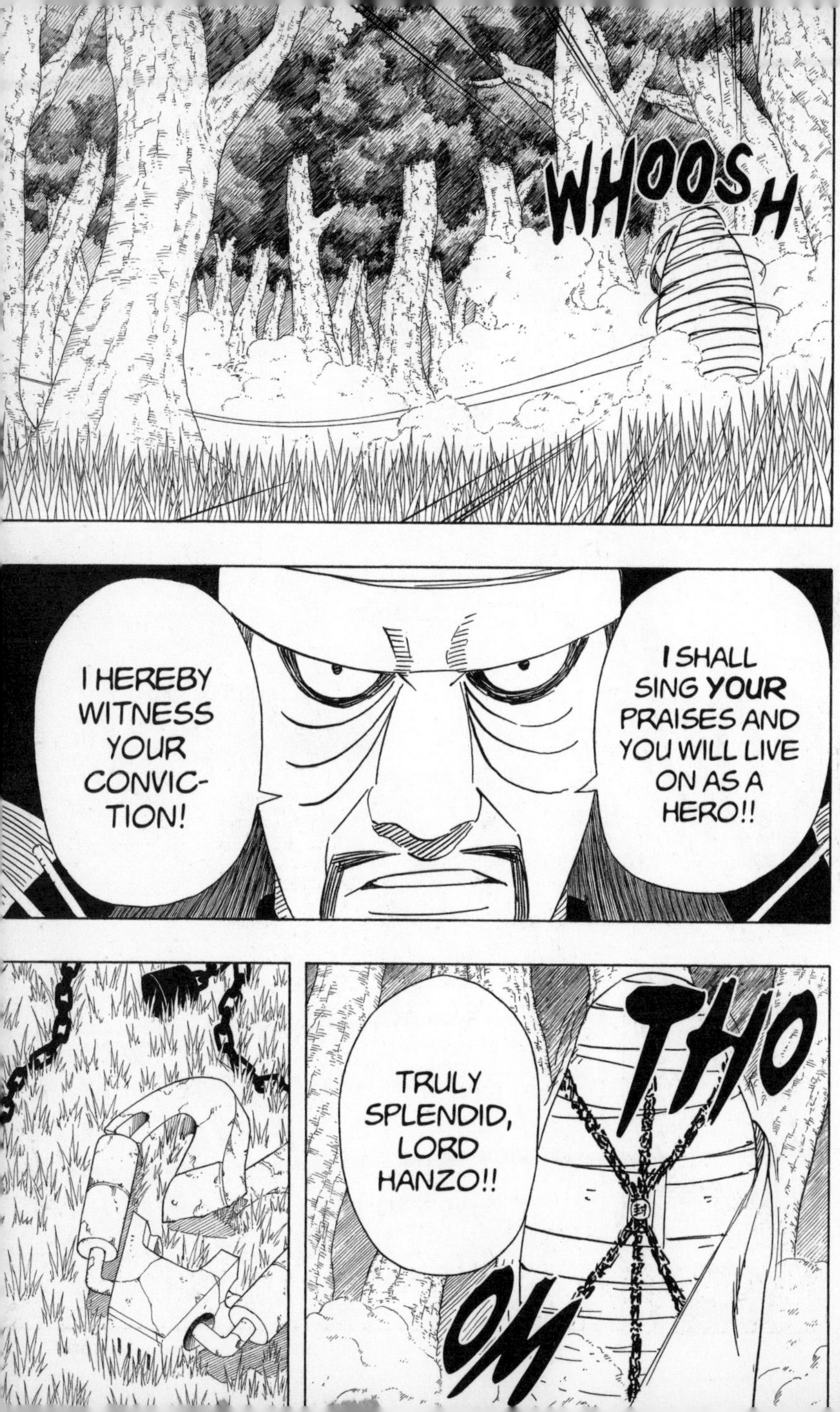
WHOOSH
I SHALL SING YOUR PRAISES AND YOU WILL LIVE ON AS A HERO!!
I HEREBY WITNESS YOUR CONVICTION!
THO
TRULY SPLENDID, LORD HANZO!!
OM

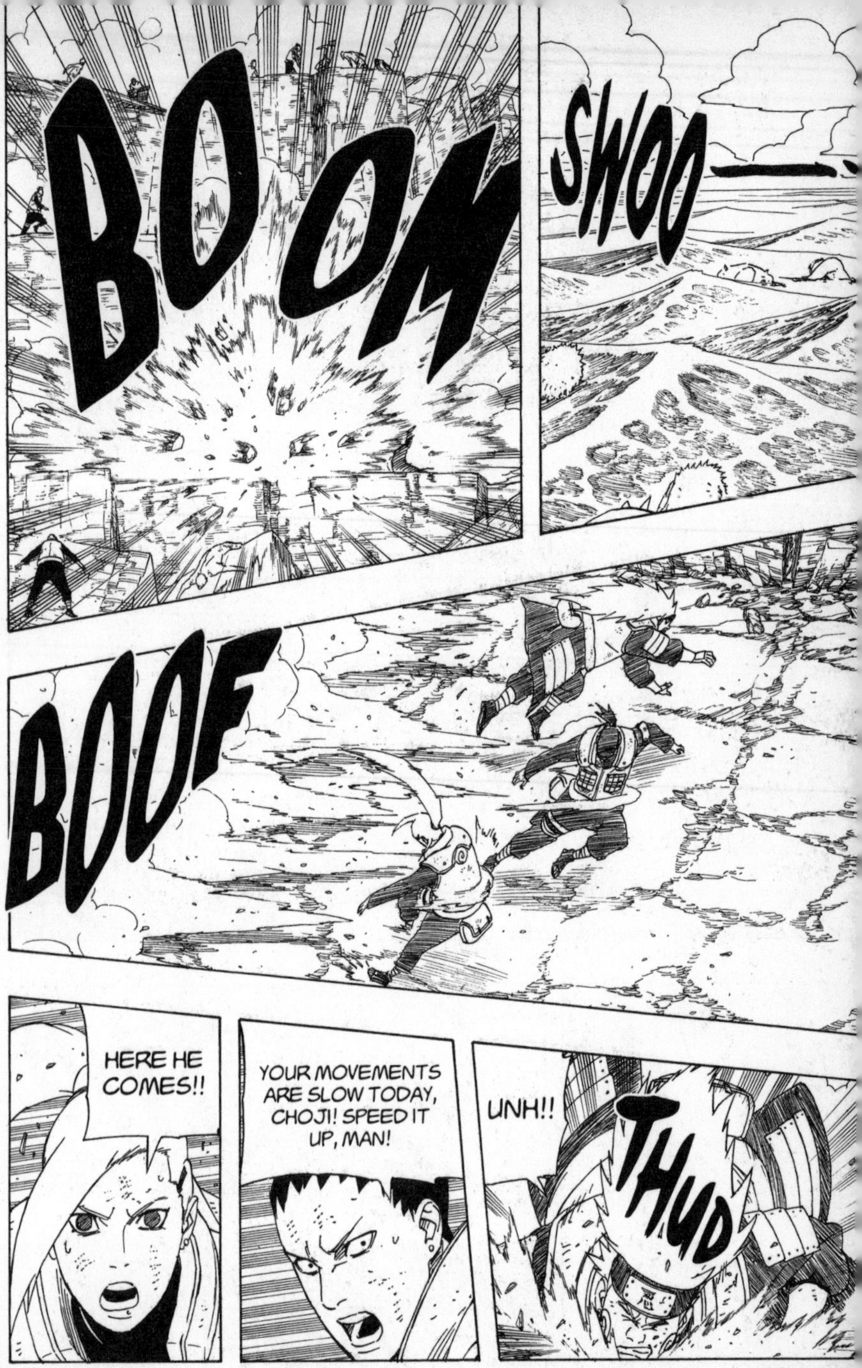
SHWOO
BOOM
BOOF
UNH!!
THUD
YOUR MOVEMENTS ARE SLOW TODAY, CHOJI! SPEED IT UP, MAN!
HERE HE COMES!!

READ THIS WAY

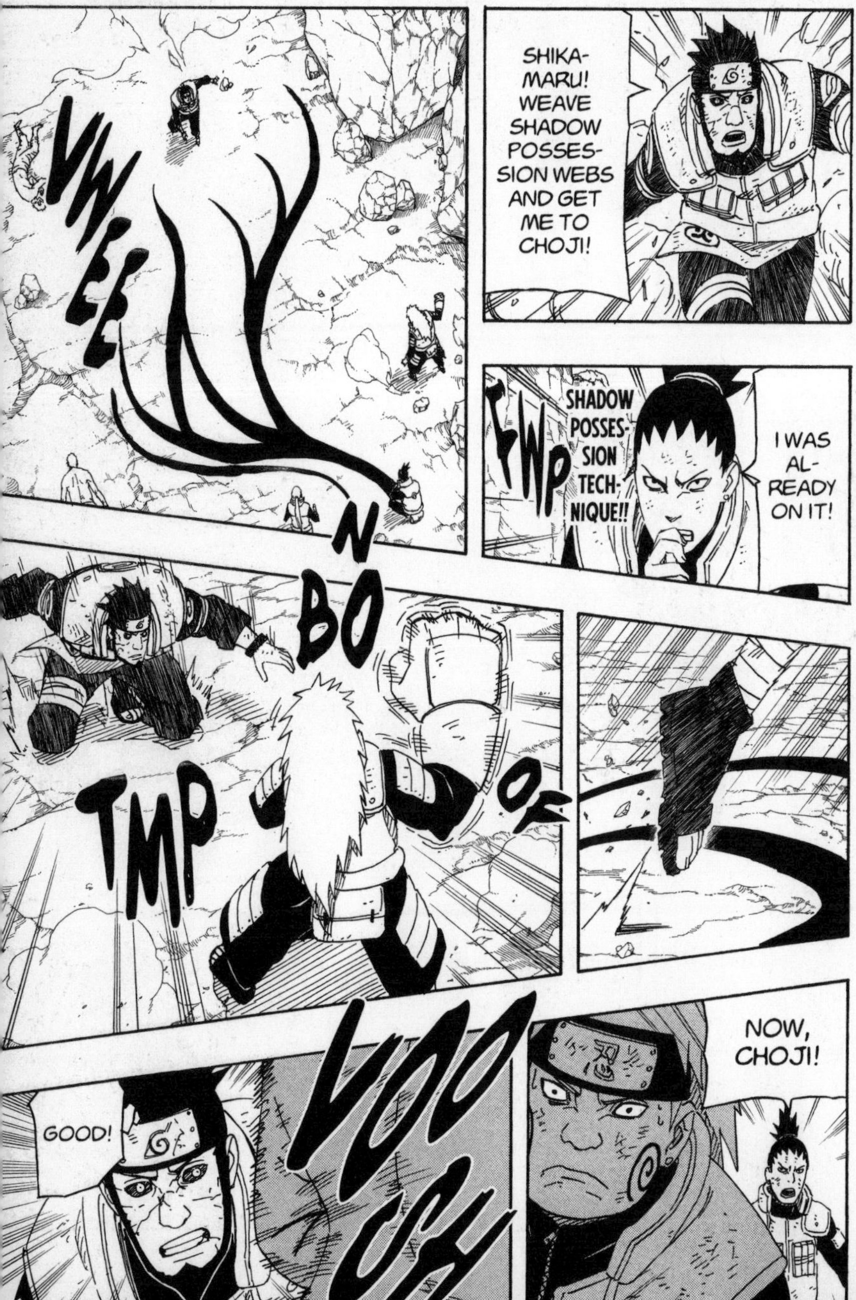

SHIKA-MARU! WEAVE SHADOW POSSES-SION WEBS AND GET ME TO CHOJI!
I WAS AL-READY ON IT!
SHADOW POSSES-SION TECH-NIQUE!!
FWP
VWEEE
NBO
OOF
TMP
NOW, CHOJI!
VOOOSH
GOOD!

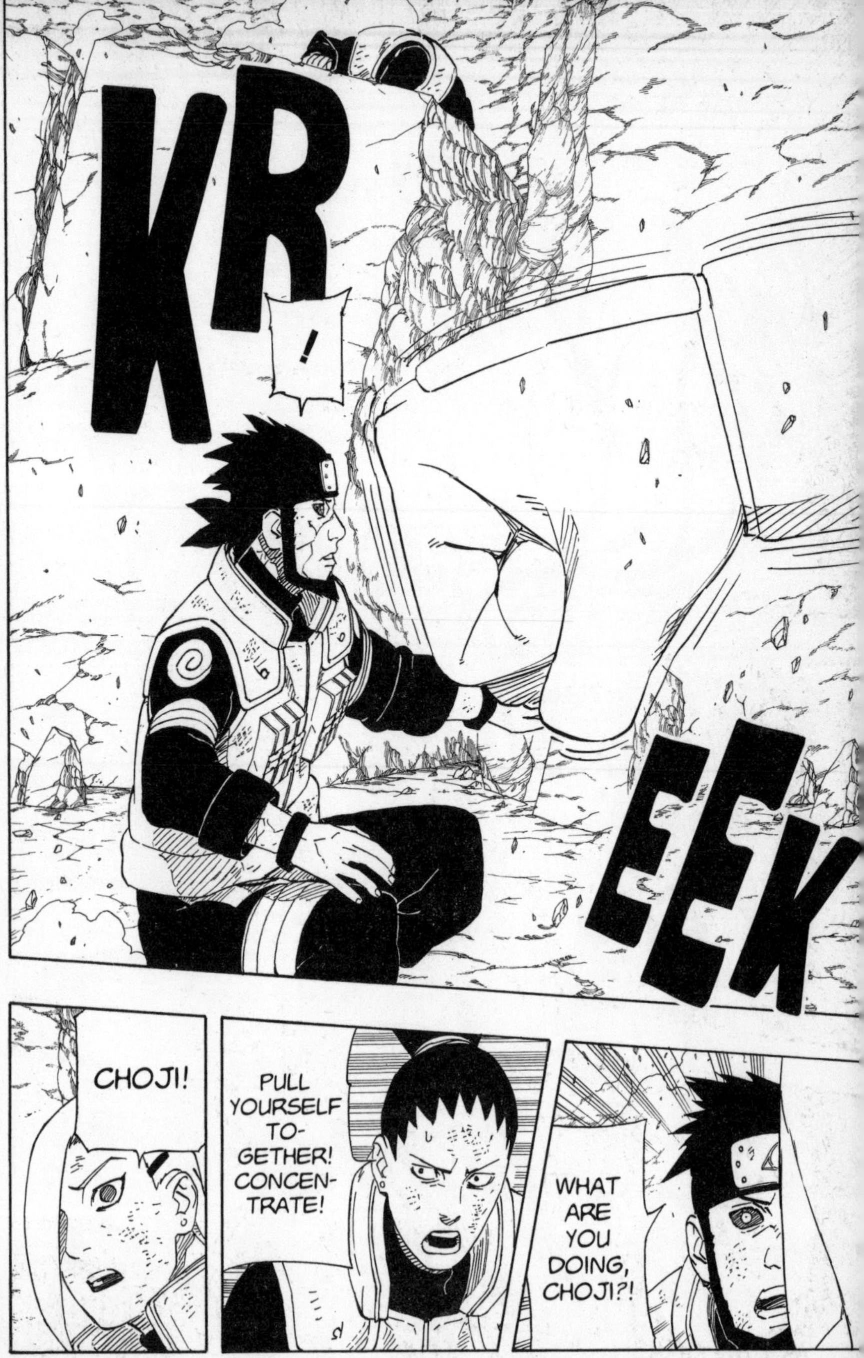
KR
EEK
!
WHAT ARE YOU DOING, CHOJI?!
PULL YOURSELF TO-GETHER! CONCEN-TRATE!
CHOJI!

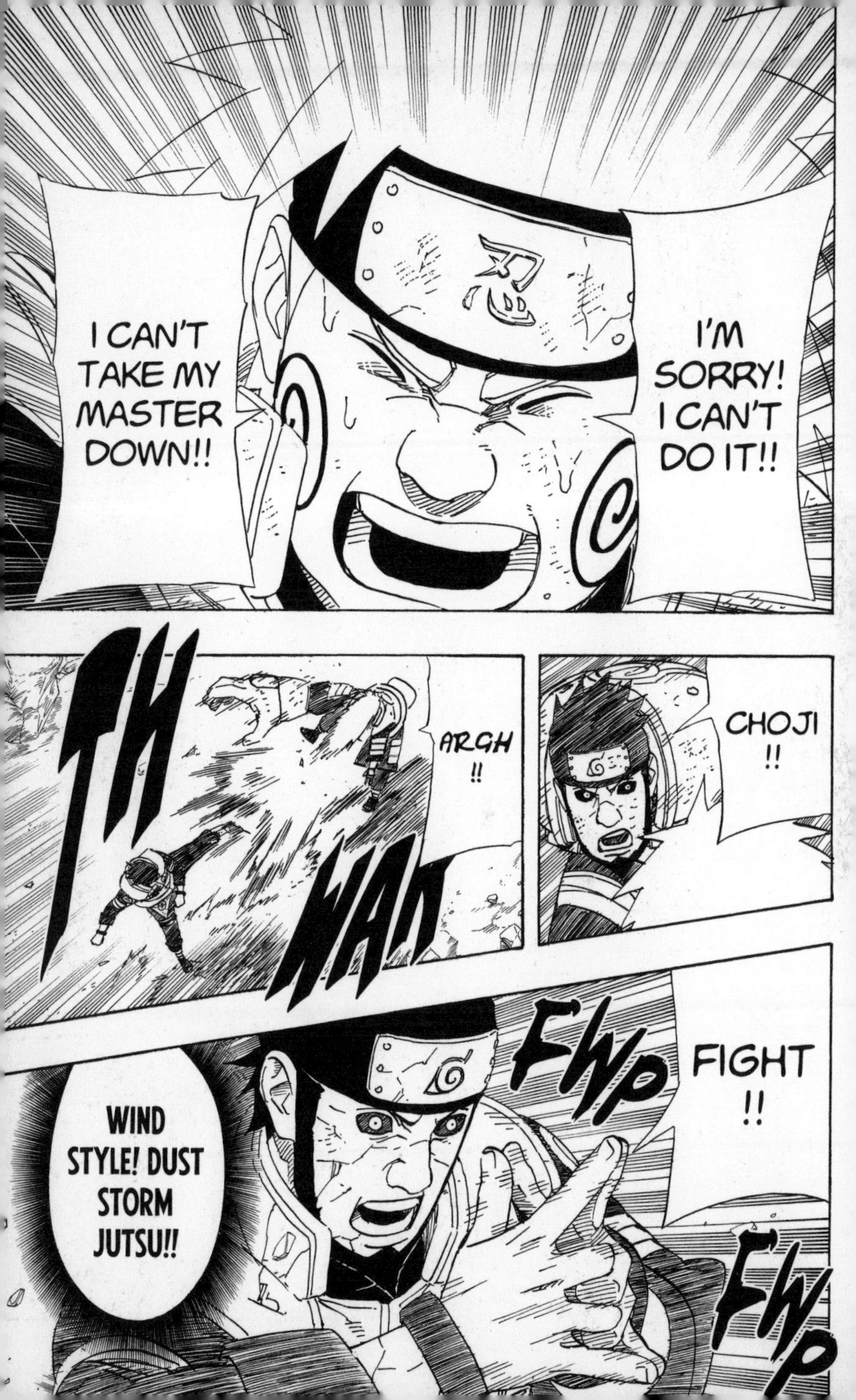
I'M SORRY! I CAN'T DO IT!!
I CAN'T TAKE MY MASTER DOWN!!
CHOJI!!
ARGH!!
THWAK
FIGHT!!
FWP
WIND STYLE! DUST STORM JUTSU!!
FWP

NARUTO

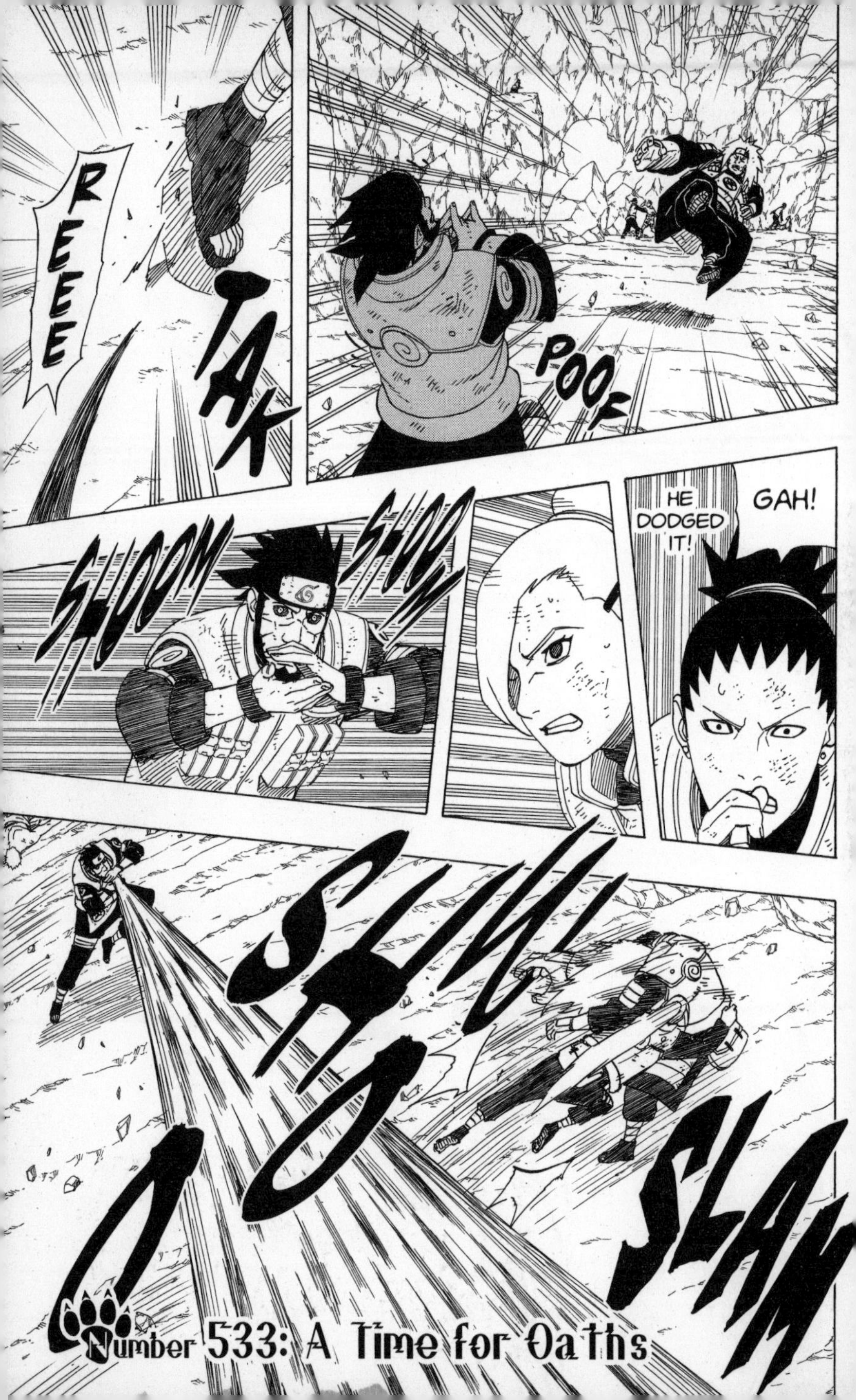
POOF
REEEE
TAK
GAH!
HE DODGED IT!
SHOOM
SHUOOM
SLAM

Number 533: A Time for Oaths

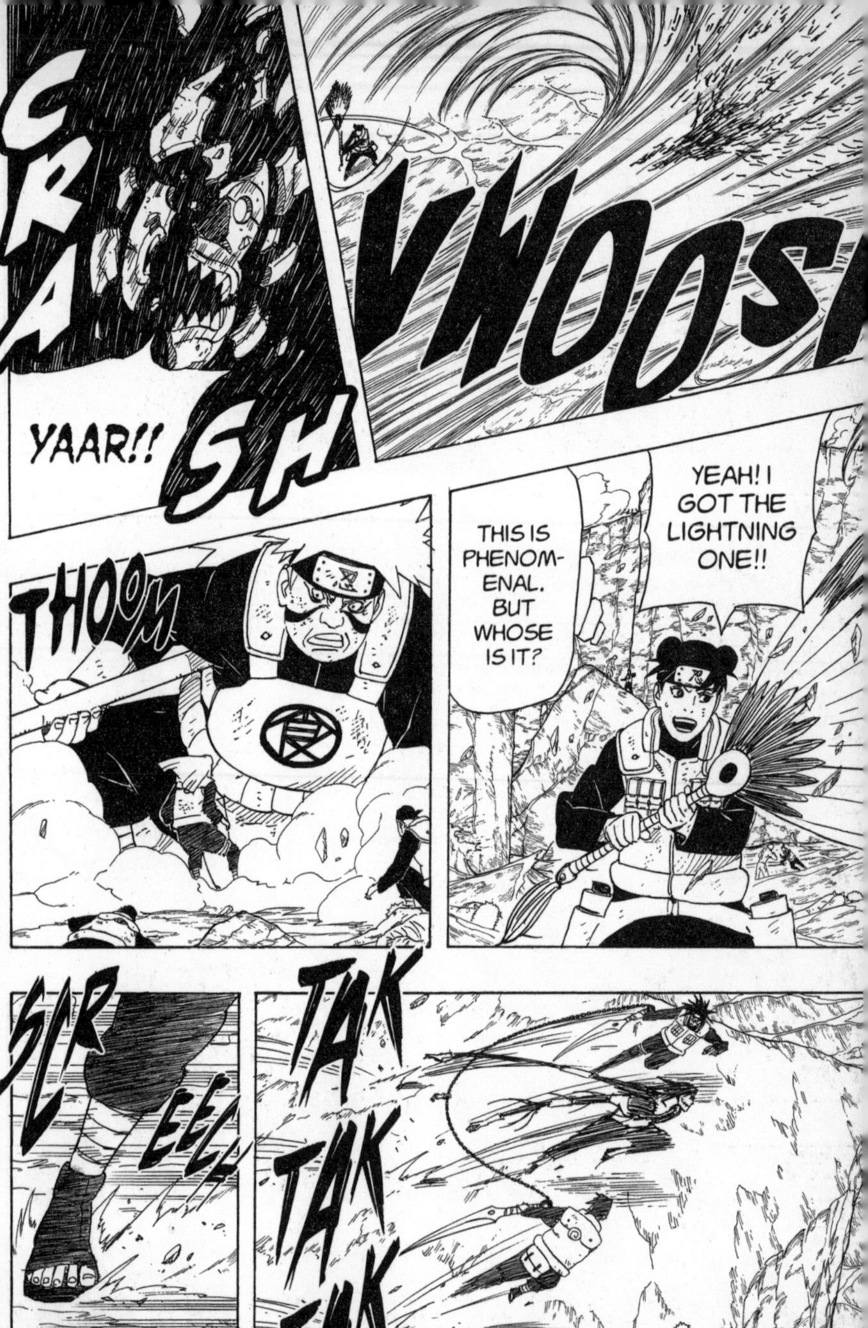
WHOOS
CRASH
YAAR!!
YEAH! I GOT THE LIGHTNING ONE!!
THIS IS PHENOM-ENAL. BUT WHOSE IS IT?
THOOM
TAK TAK TAK TAK
SCREEE

READ THIS WAY

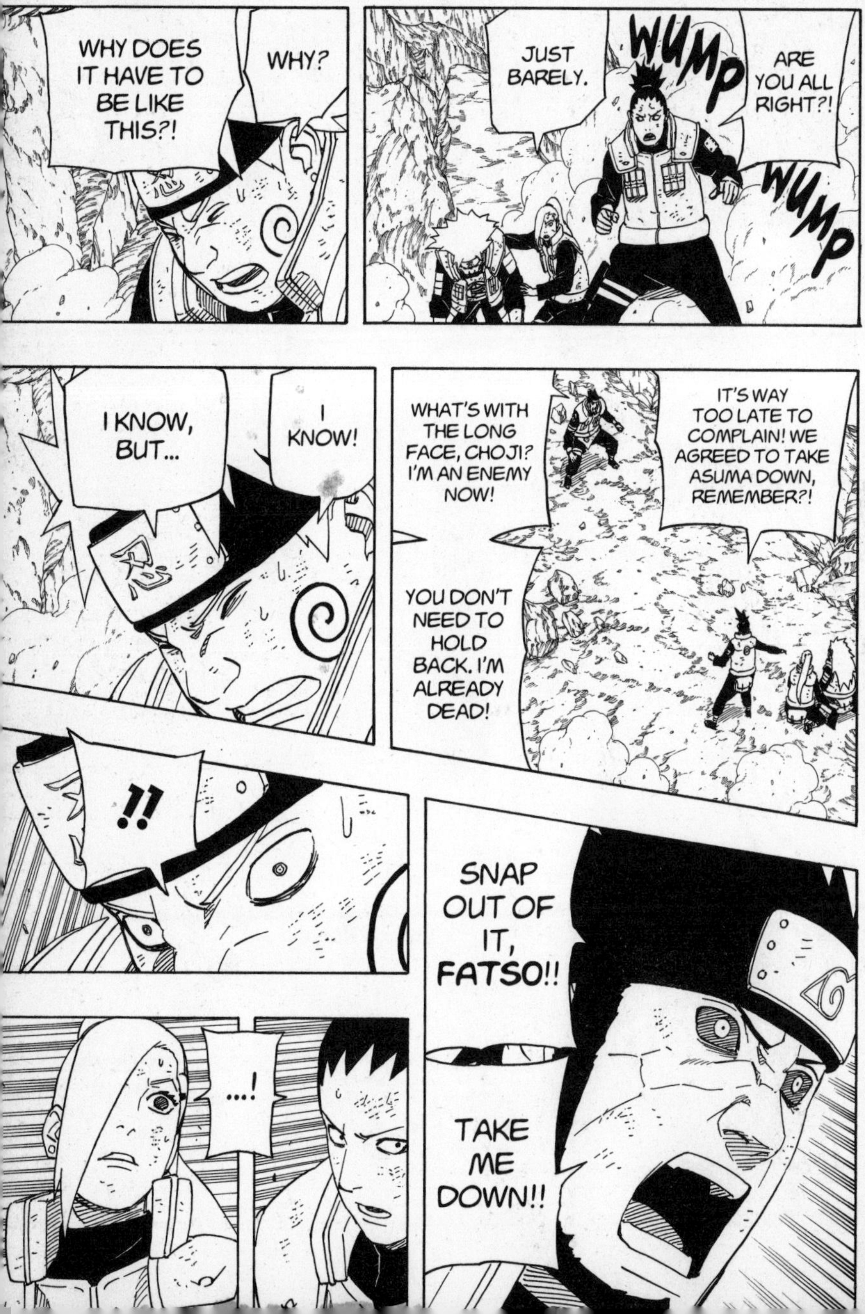
ARE YOU ALL RIGHT?!
WUMP
JUST BARELY.
WUMP
WHY?
WHY DOES IT HAVE TO BE LIKE THIS?!
IT'S WAY TOO LATE TO COMPLAIN! WE AGREED TO TAKE ASUMA DOWN, REMEMBER?!
WHAT'S WITH THE LONG FACE, CHOJI? I'M AN ENEMY NOW!
YOU DON'T NEED TO HOLD BACK. I'M ALREADY DEAD!
I KNOW!
I KNOW, BUT...
SNAP OUT OF IT, FATSO!!
TAKE ME DOWN!!
!!
...!

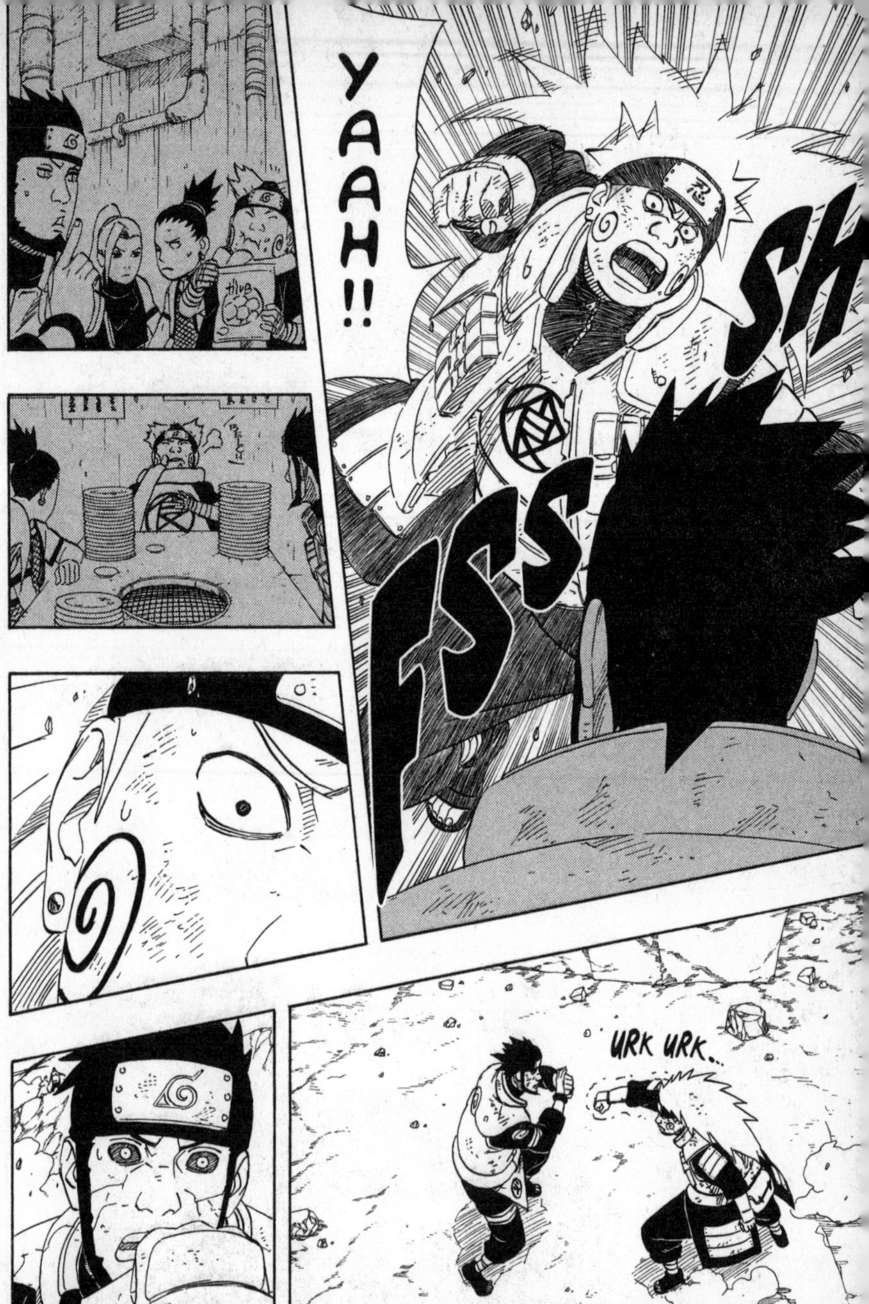
YAAH!!
URK URK...

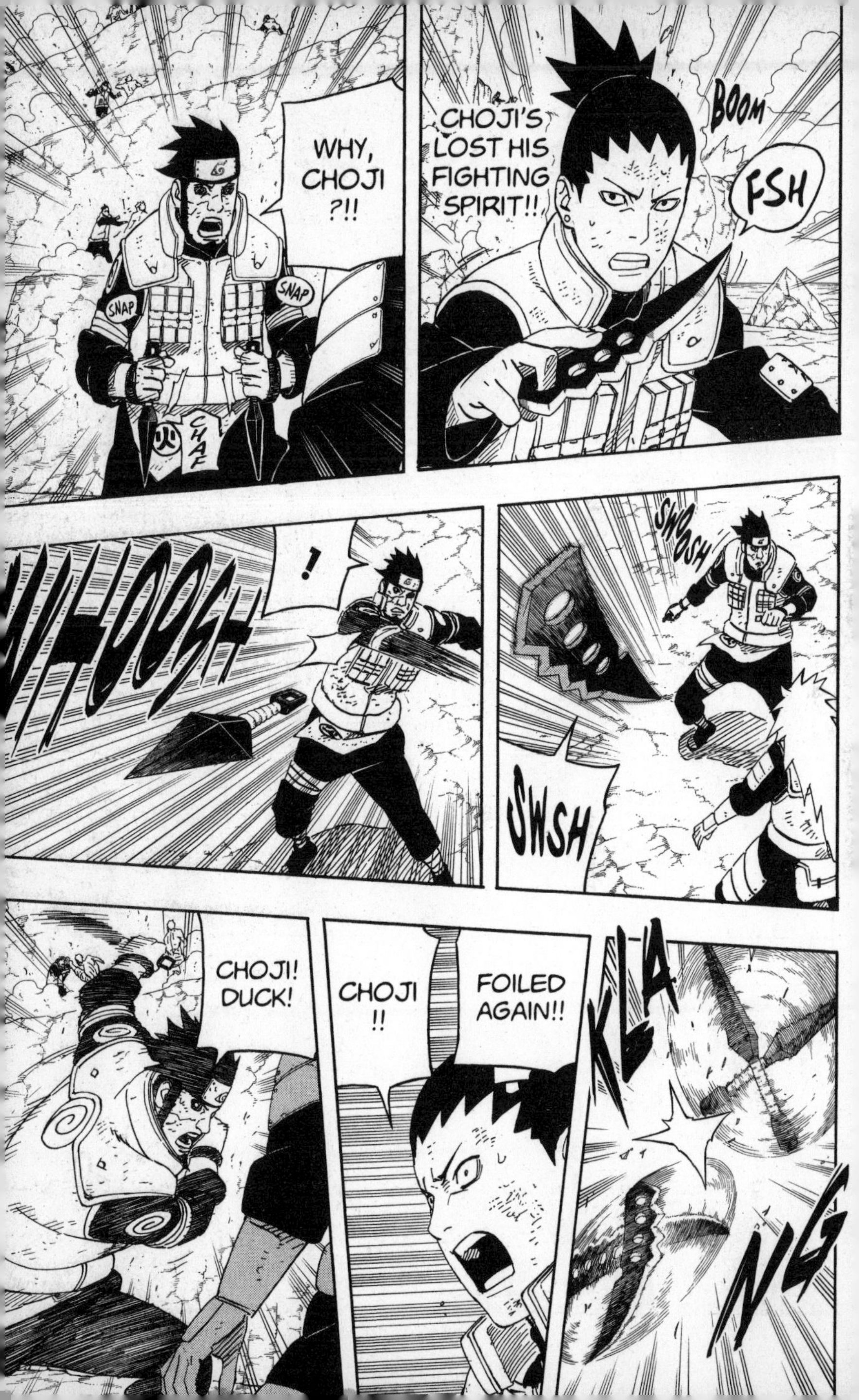
CHOJI'S LOST HIS FIGHTING SPIRIT!!
BOOM
FSH
WHY, CHOJI ?!!
SNAP
SNAP
CHAF
SWOOSH
SWSH
!
KLA
FOILED AGAIN!!
CHOJI !!
CHOJI! DUCK!

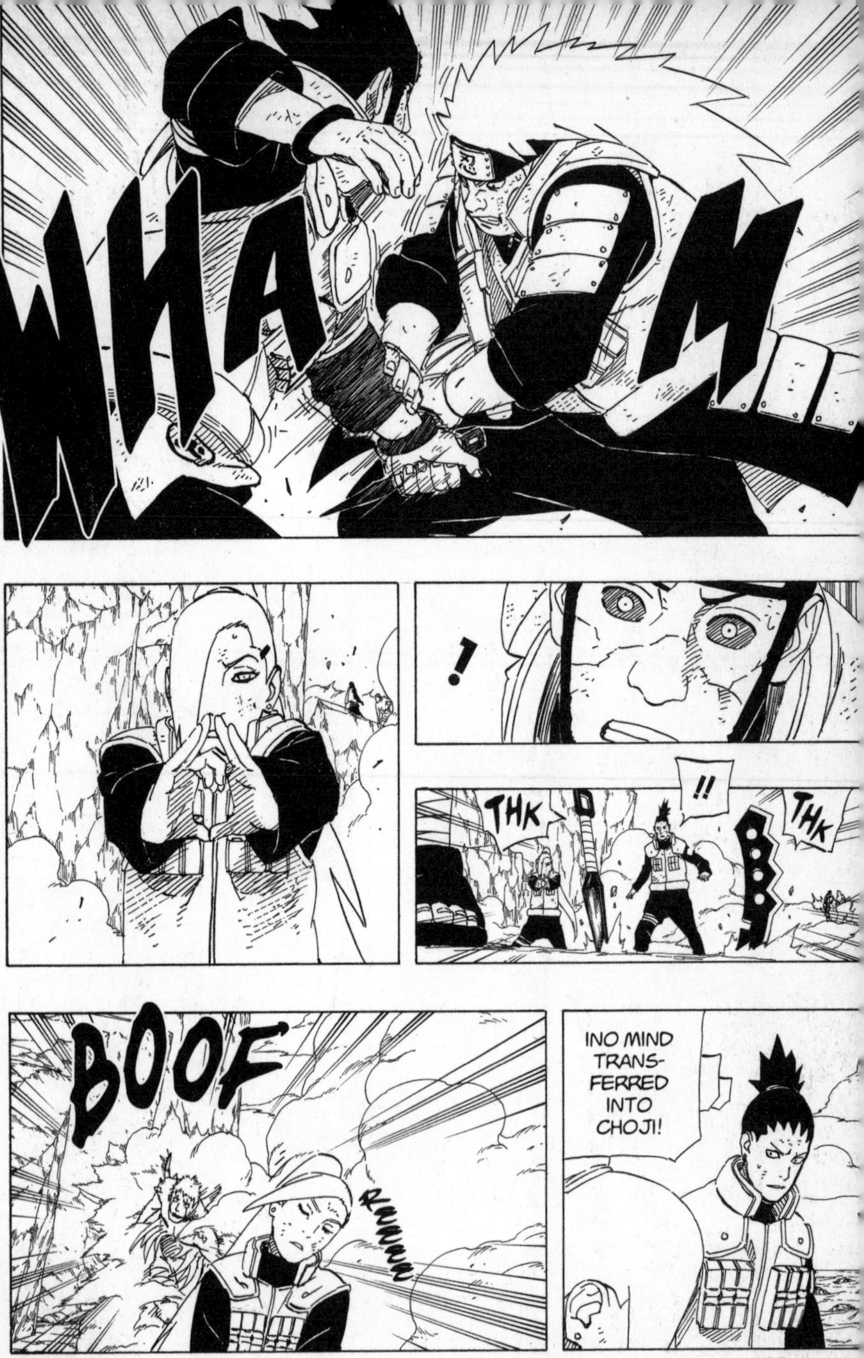
WHAM
!
THK
!!
THK
INO MIND TRANS-
FERRED
INTO
CHOJI!
BOOF

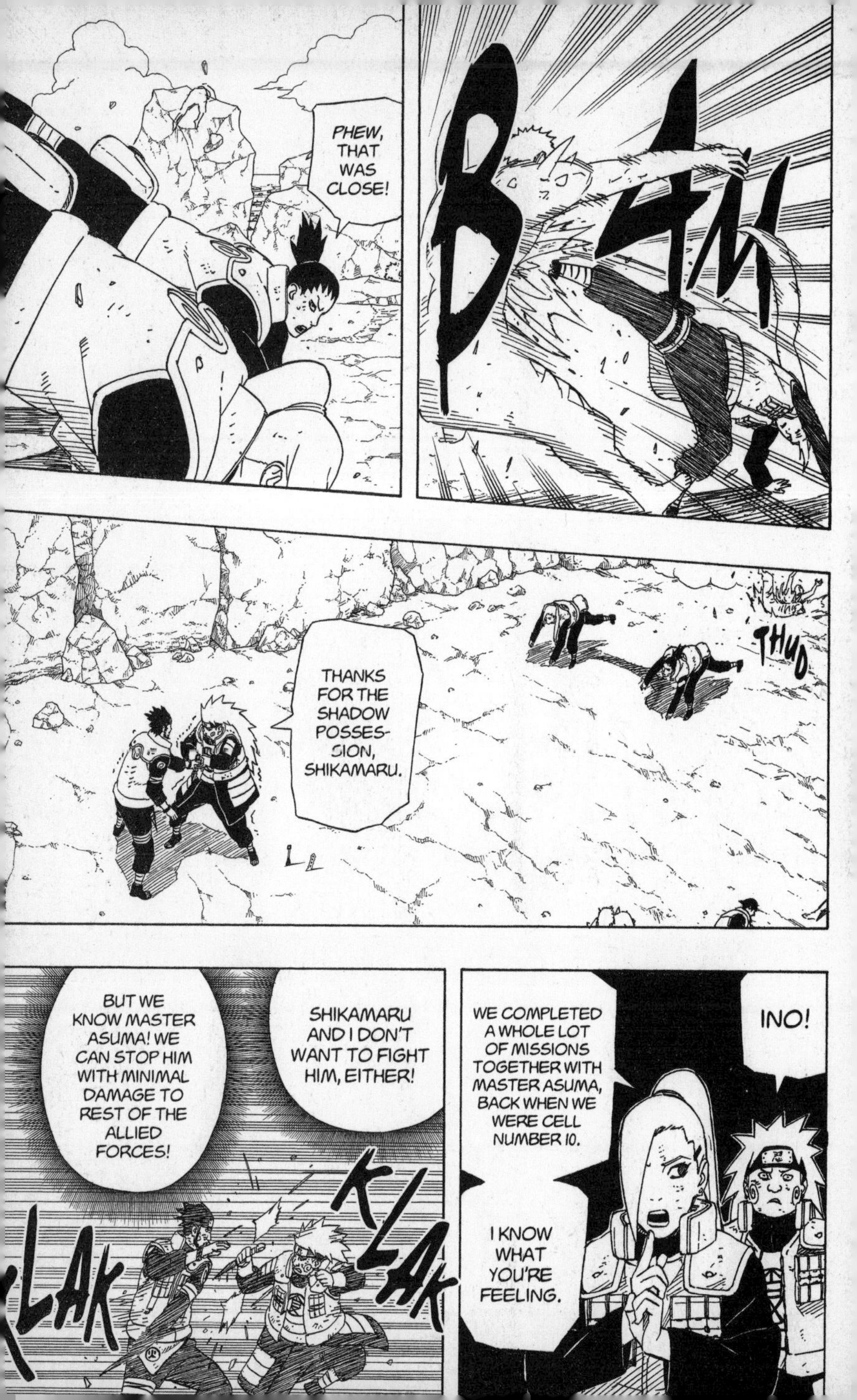
BAM
PHEW, THAT WAS CLOSE!
THUD
THANKS FOR THE SHADOW POSSES-SION, SHIKAMARU.
INO!
WE COMPLETED A WHOLE LOT OF MISSIONS TOGETHER WITH MASTER ASUMA, BACK WHEN WE WERE CELL NUMBER 10.
I KNOW WHAT YOU'RE FEELING.
SHIKAMARU AND I DON'T WANT TO FIGHT HIM, EITHER!
BUT WE KNOW MASTER ASUMA! WE CAN STOP HIM WITH MINIMAL DAMAGE TO REST OF THE ALLIED FORCES!
KLAK
KLAK

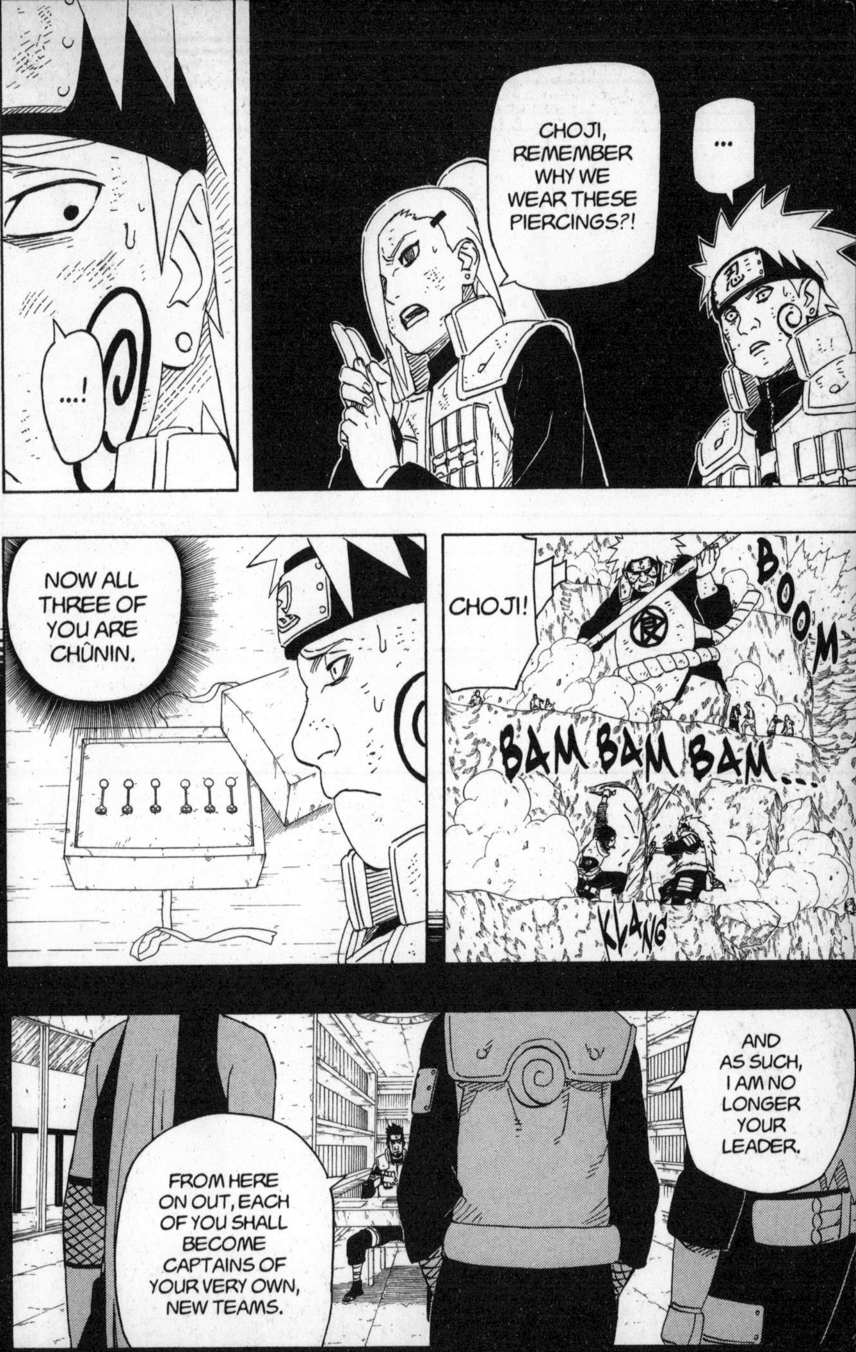
...
CHOJI, REMEMBER WHY WE WEAR THESE PIERCINGS?!
...!
CHOJI!
BOOM
BAM BAM BAM...
KLANG
NOW ALL THREE OF YOU ARE CHÛNIN.
AND AS SUCH, I AM NO LONGER YOUR LEADER.
FROM HERE ON OUT, EACH OF YOU SHALL BECOME CAPTAINS OF YOUR VERY OWN, NEW TEAMS.

READ THIS WAY

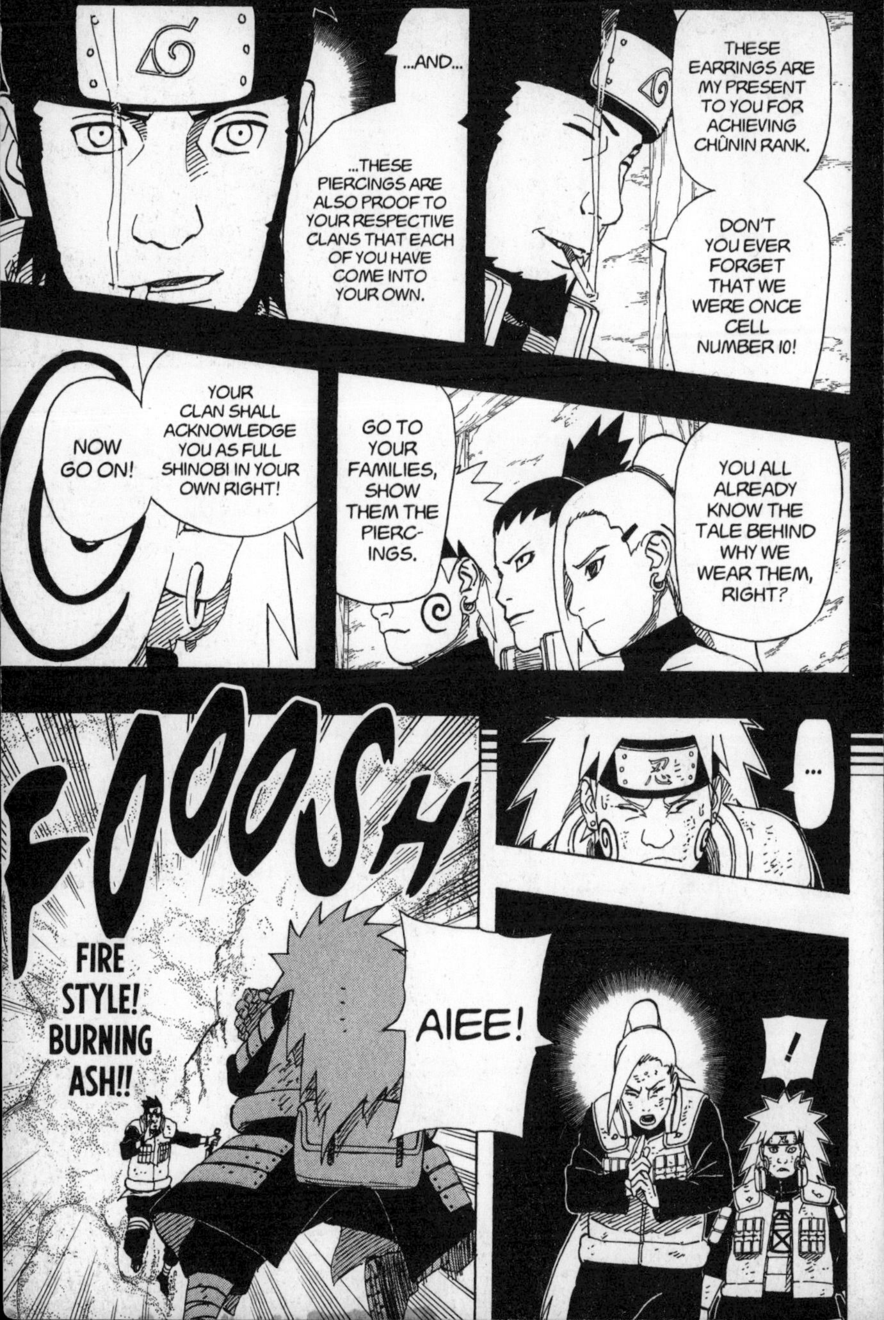

THESE EARRINGS ARE MY PRESENT TO YOU FOR ACHIEVING CHŪNIN RANK.
DON'T YOU EVER FORGET THAT WE WERE ONCE CELL NUMBER 10!
...AND...
...THESE PIERCINGS ARE ALSO PROOF TO YOUR RESPECTIVE CLANS THAT EACH OF YOU HAVE COME INTO YOUR OWN.
YOU ALL ALREADY KNOW THE TALE BEHIND WHY WE WEAR THEM, RIGHT?
GO TO YOUR FAMILIES, SHOW THEM THE PIERC-INGS.
YOUR CLAN SHALL ACKNOWLEDGE YOU AS FULL SHINOBI IN YOUR OWN RIGHT!
NOW GO ON!
...
!
FOOOSH
FIRE STYLE! BURNING ASH!!
AIEE!

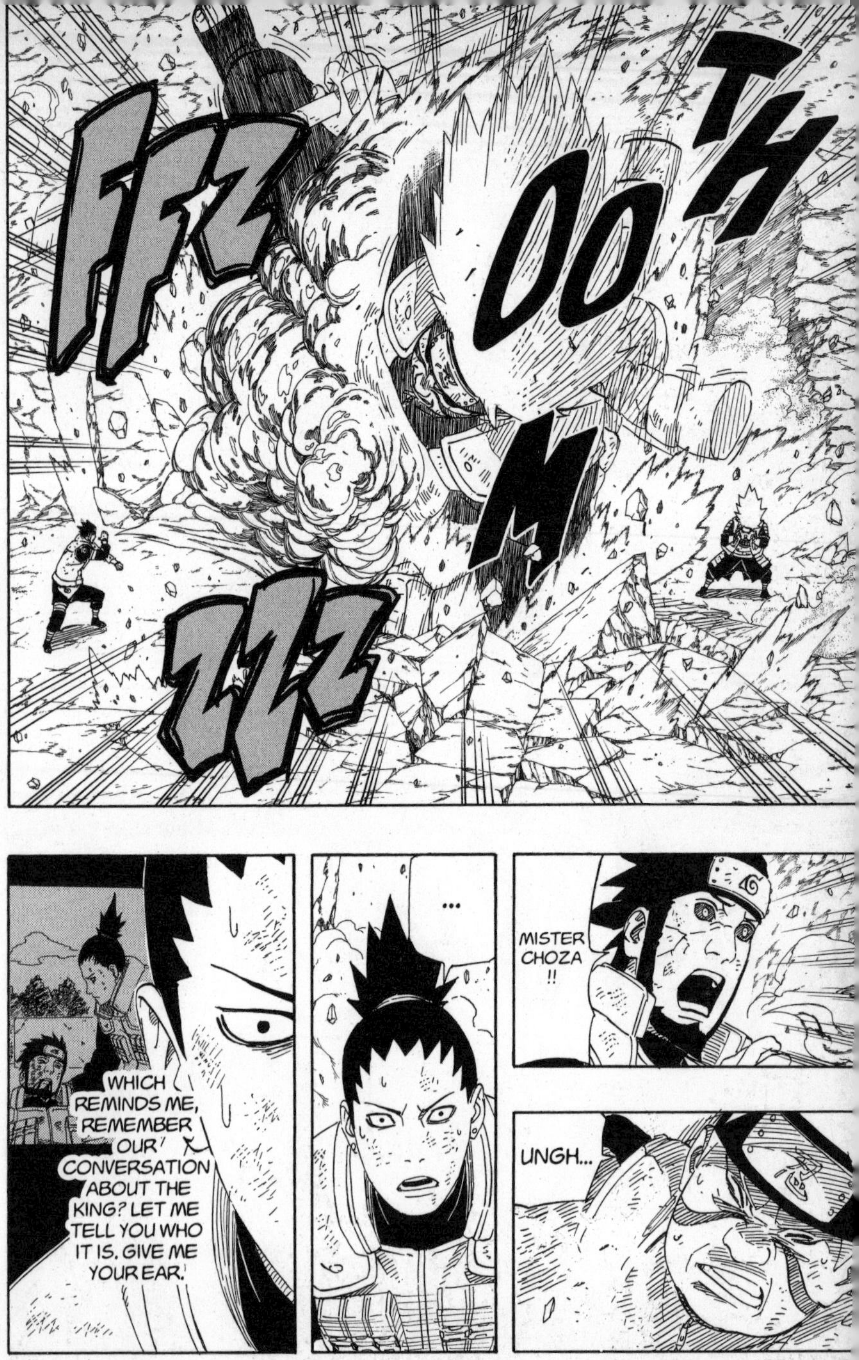
THOOM
FFZ
ZZZ
MISTER CHOZA !!
UNGH...
...
WHICH REMINDS ME, REMEMBER OUR CONVERSATION ABOUT THE KING? LET ME TELL YOU WHO IT IS. GIVE ME YOUR EAR.

READ THIS WAY

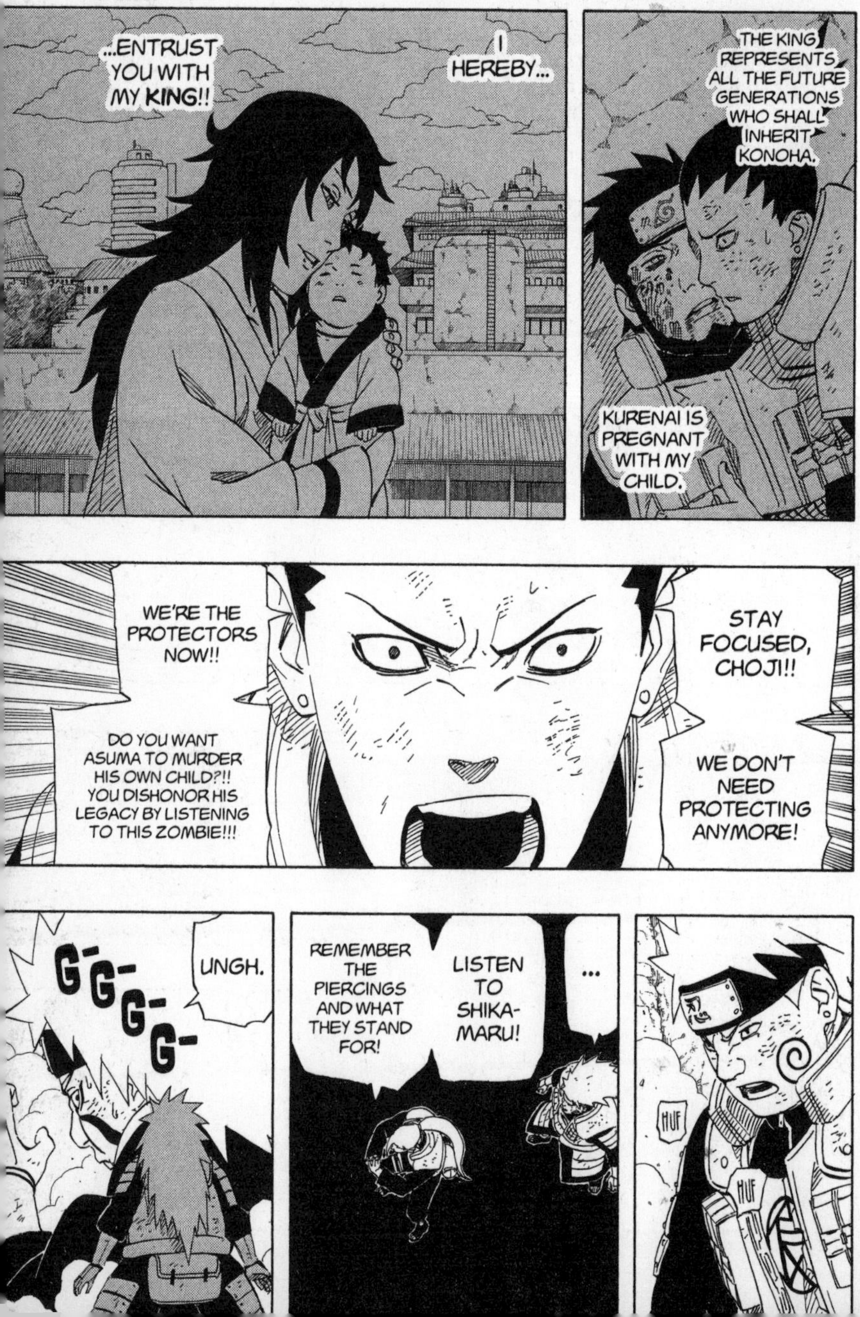
THE KING REPRESENTS ALL THE FUTURE GENERATIONS WHO SHALL INHERIT KONOHA.
KURENAI IS PREGNANT WITH MY CHILD.
I HEREBY...
...ENTRUST YOU WITH MY KING!!
STAY FOCUSED, CHOJI!!
WE DON'T NEED PROTECTING ANYMORE!
WE'RE THE PROTECTORS NOW!!
DO YOU WANT ASUMA TO MURDER HIS OWN CHILD?!! YOU DISHONOR HIS LEGACY BY LISTENING TO THIS ZOMBIE!!!
HUF
HUF
...
LISTEN TO SHIKA-MARU!
REMEMBER THE PIERCINGS AND WHAT THEY STAND FOR!
UNGH.
G-G-G-G-

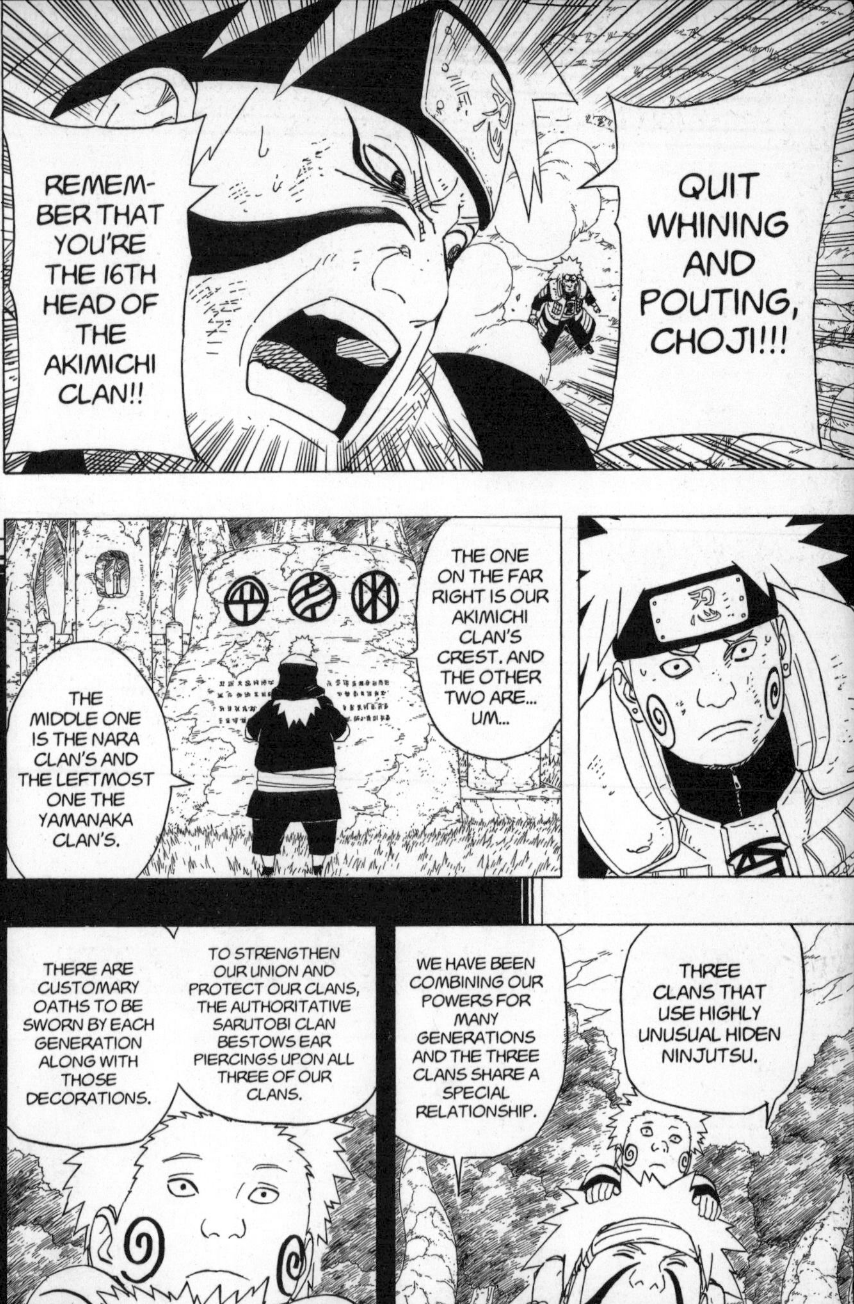
QUIT WHINING AND POUTING, CHOJI!!!
REMEM-BER THAT YOU'RE THE 16TH HEAD OF THE AKIMICHI CLAN!!
THE ONE ON THE FAR RIGHT IS OUR AKIMICHI CLAN'S CREST. AND THE OTHER TWO ARE... UM...
THE MIDDLE ONE IS THE NARA CLAN'S AND THE LEFTMOST ONE THE YAMANAKA CLAN'S.
THREE CLANS THAT USE HIGHLY UNUSUAL HIDEN NINJUTSU.
WE HAVE BEEN COMBINING OUR POWERS FOR MANY GENERATIONS AND THE THREE CLANS SHARE A SPECIAL RELATIONSHIP.
TO STRENGTHEN OUR UNION AND PROTECT OUR CLANS, THE AUTHORITATIVE SARUTOBI CLAN BESTOWS EAR PIERCINGS UPON ALL THREE OF OUR CLANS.
THERE ARE CUSTOMARY OATHS TO BE SWORN BY EACH GENERATION ALONG WITH THOSE DECORATIONS.

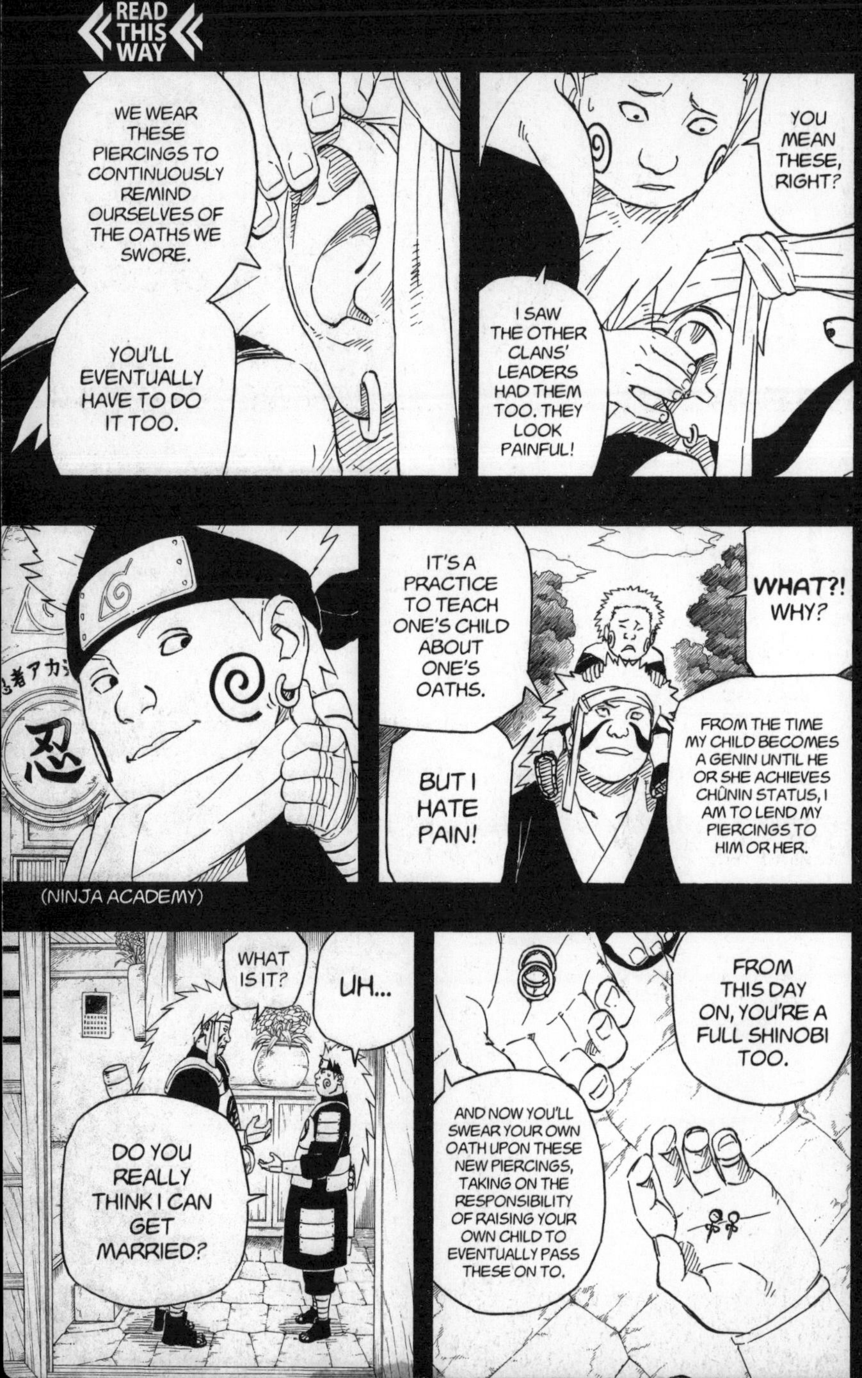
READ THIS WAY
YOU MEAN THESE, RIGHT?
I SAW THE OTHER CLANS' LEADERS HAD THEM TOO. THEY LOOK PAINFUL!
WE WEAR THESE PIERCINGS TO CONTINUOUSLY REMIND OURSELVES OF THE OATHS WE SWORE.
YOU'LL EVENTUALLY HAVE TO DO IT TOO.
WHAT?! WHY?
IT'S A PRACTICE TO TEACH ONE'S CHILD ABOUT ONE'S OATHS.
FROM THE TIME MY CHILD BECOMES A GENIN UNTIL HE OR SHE ACHIEVES CHŪNIN STATUS, I AM TO LEND MY PIERCINGS TO HIM OR HER.
BUT I HATE PAIN!
忍
(NINJA ACADEMY)
FROM THIS DAY ON, YOU'RE A FULL SHINOBI TOO.
AND NOW YOU'LL SWEAR YOUR OWN OATH UPON THESE NEW PIERCINGS, TAKING ON THE RESPONSIBILITY OF RAISING YOUR OWN CHILD TO EVENTUALLY PASS THESE ON TO.
UH...
WHAT IS IT?
DO YOU REALLY THINK I CAN GET MARRIED?

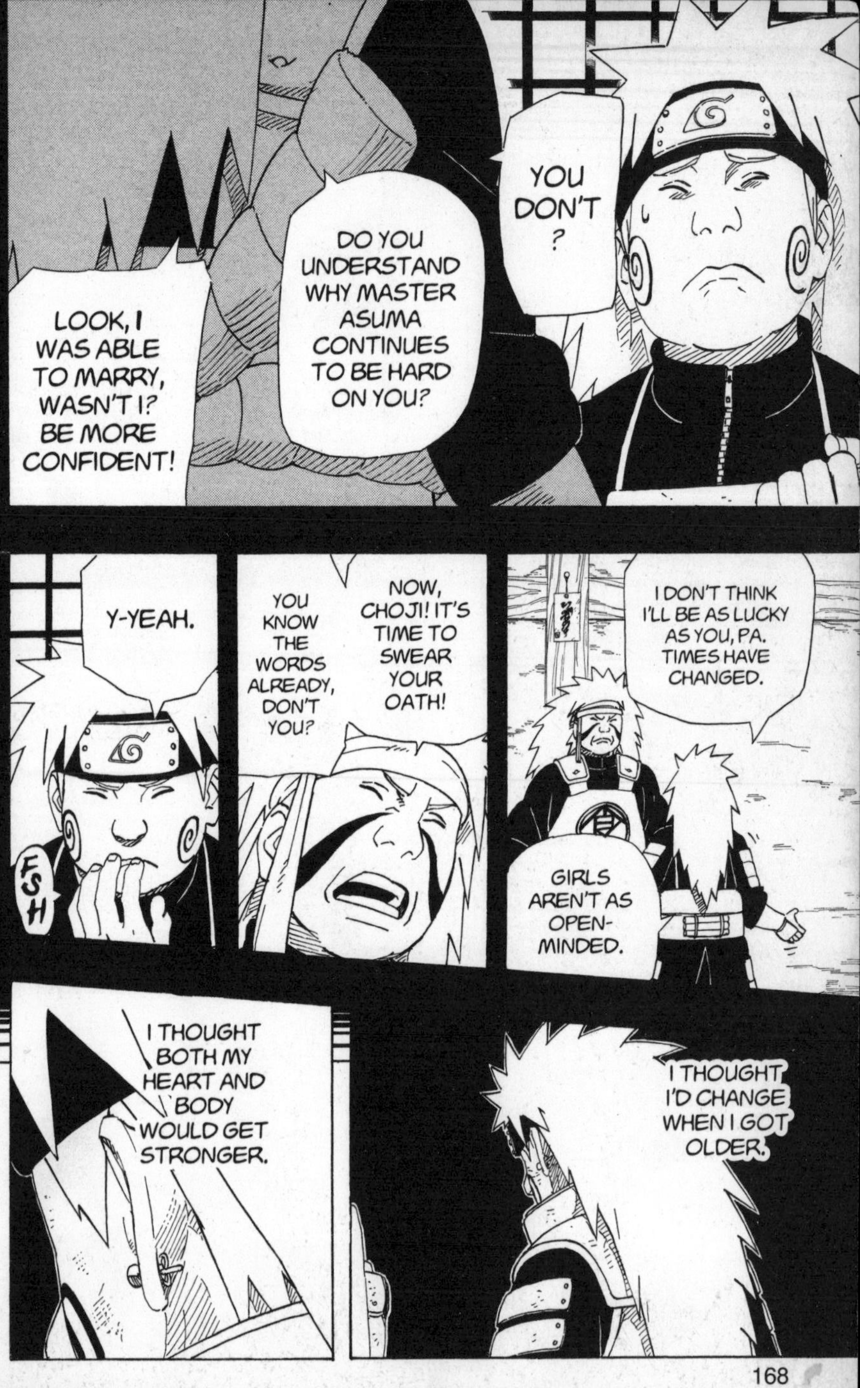
YOU DON'T?
DO YOU UNDERSTAND WHY MASTER ASUMA CONTINUES TO BE HARD ON YOU?
LOOK, I WAS ABLE TO MARRY, WASN'T I? BE MORE CONFIDENT!
I DON'T THINK I'LL BE AS LUCKY AS YOU, PA. TIMES HAVE CHANGED.
GIRLS AREN'T AS OPEN-MINDED.
NOW, CHOJI! IT'S TIME TO SWEAR YOUR OATH!
YOU KNOW THE WORDS ALREADY, DON'T YOU?
Y-YEAH.
FSH
I THOUGHT I'D CHANGE WHEN I GOT OLDER.
I THOUGHT BOTH MY HEART AND BODY WOULD GET STRONGER.

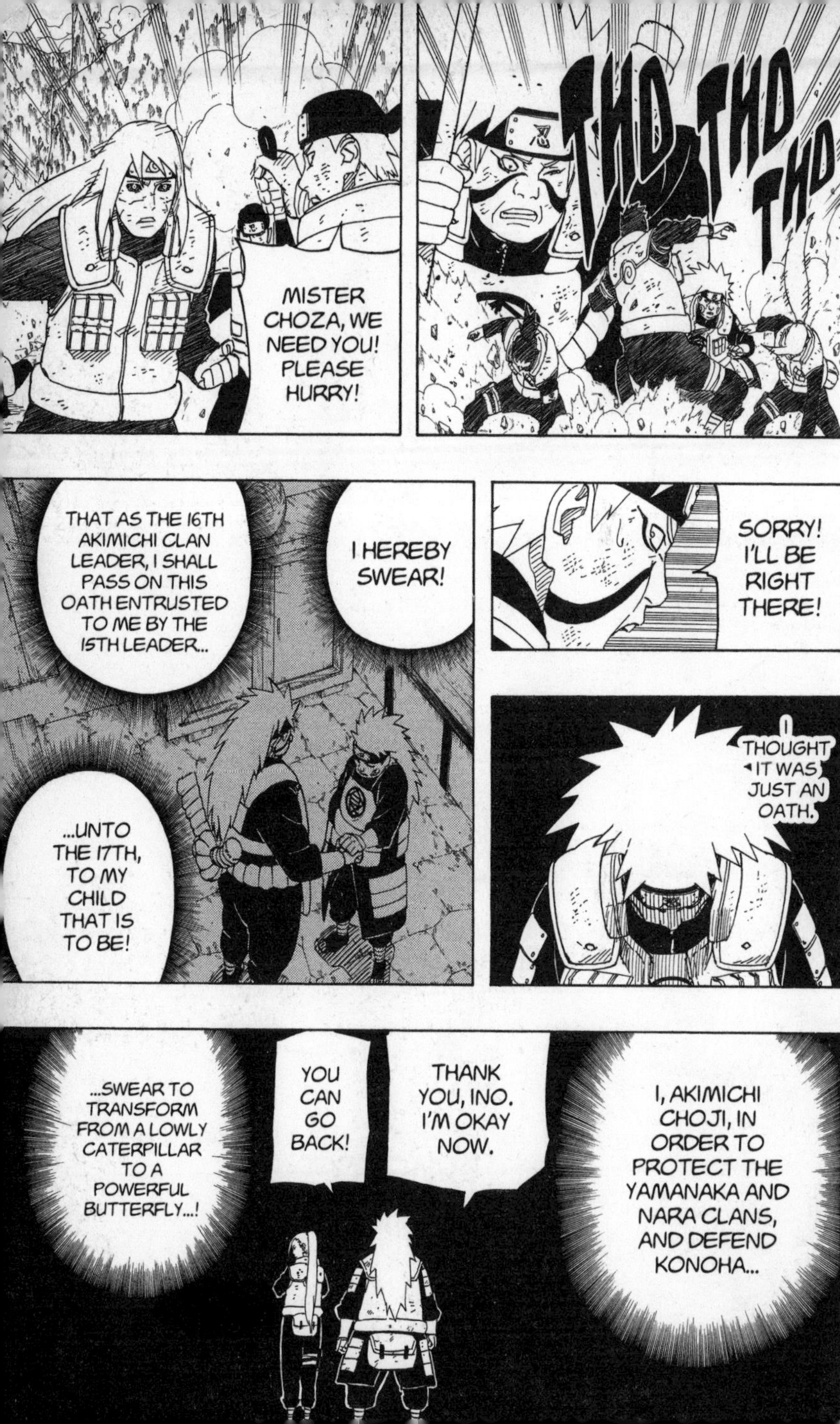
THD THD THD
MISTER CHOZA, WE NEED YOU! PLEASE HURRY!
SORRY! I'LL BE RIGHT THERE!
I THOUGHT IT WAS JUST AN OATH.
I HEREBY SWEAR!
THAT AS THE 16TH AKIMICHI CLAN LEADER, I SHALL PASS ON THIS OATH ENTRUSTED TO ME BY THE 15TH LEADER...
...UNTO THE 17TH, TO MY CHILD THAT IS TO BE!
I, AKIMICHI CHOJI, IN ORDER TO PROTECT THE YAMANAKA AND NARA CLANS, AND DEFEND KONOHA...
THANK YOU, INO. I'M OKAY NOW.
YOU CAN GO BACK!
...SWEAR TO TRANSFORM FROM A LOWLY CATERPILLAR TO A POWERFUL BUTTERFLY...!

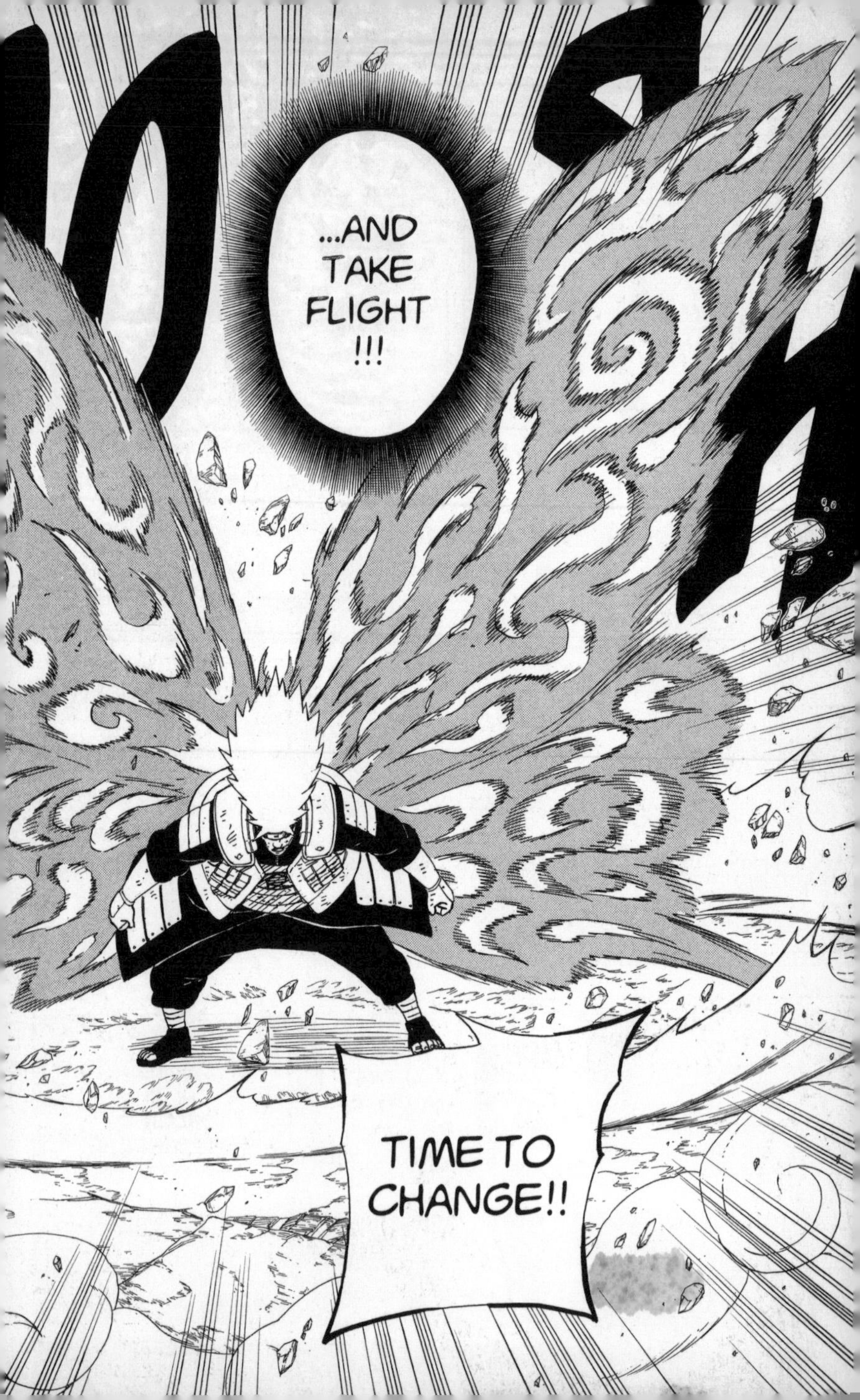
...AND TAKE FLIGHT !!!
TIME TO CHANGE!!

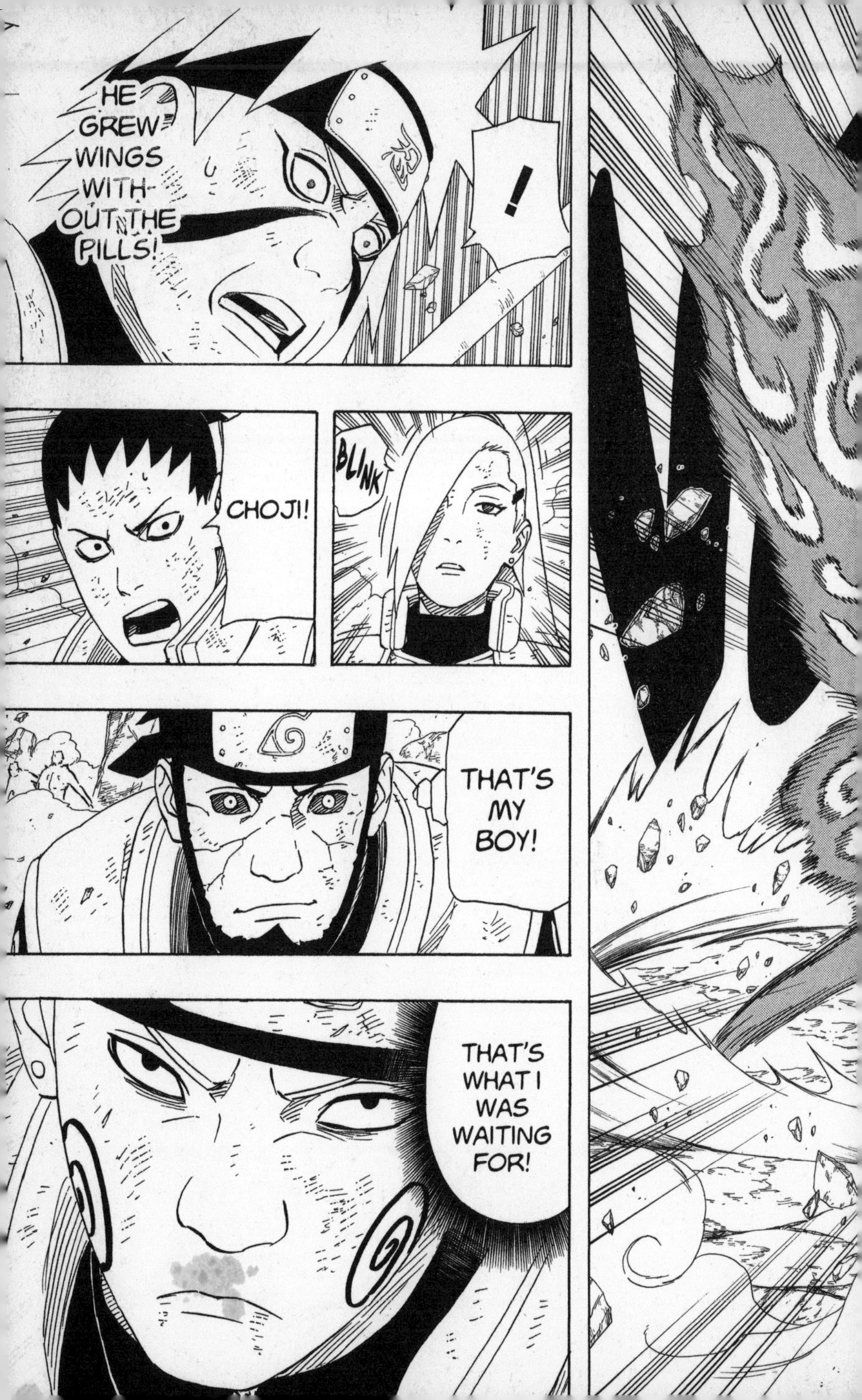
!
HE GREW WINGS WITHOUT THE PILLS!
BLINK
CHOJI!
THAT'S MY BOY!
THAT'S WHAT I WAS WAITING FOR!

NARUTO

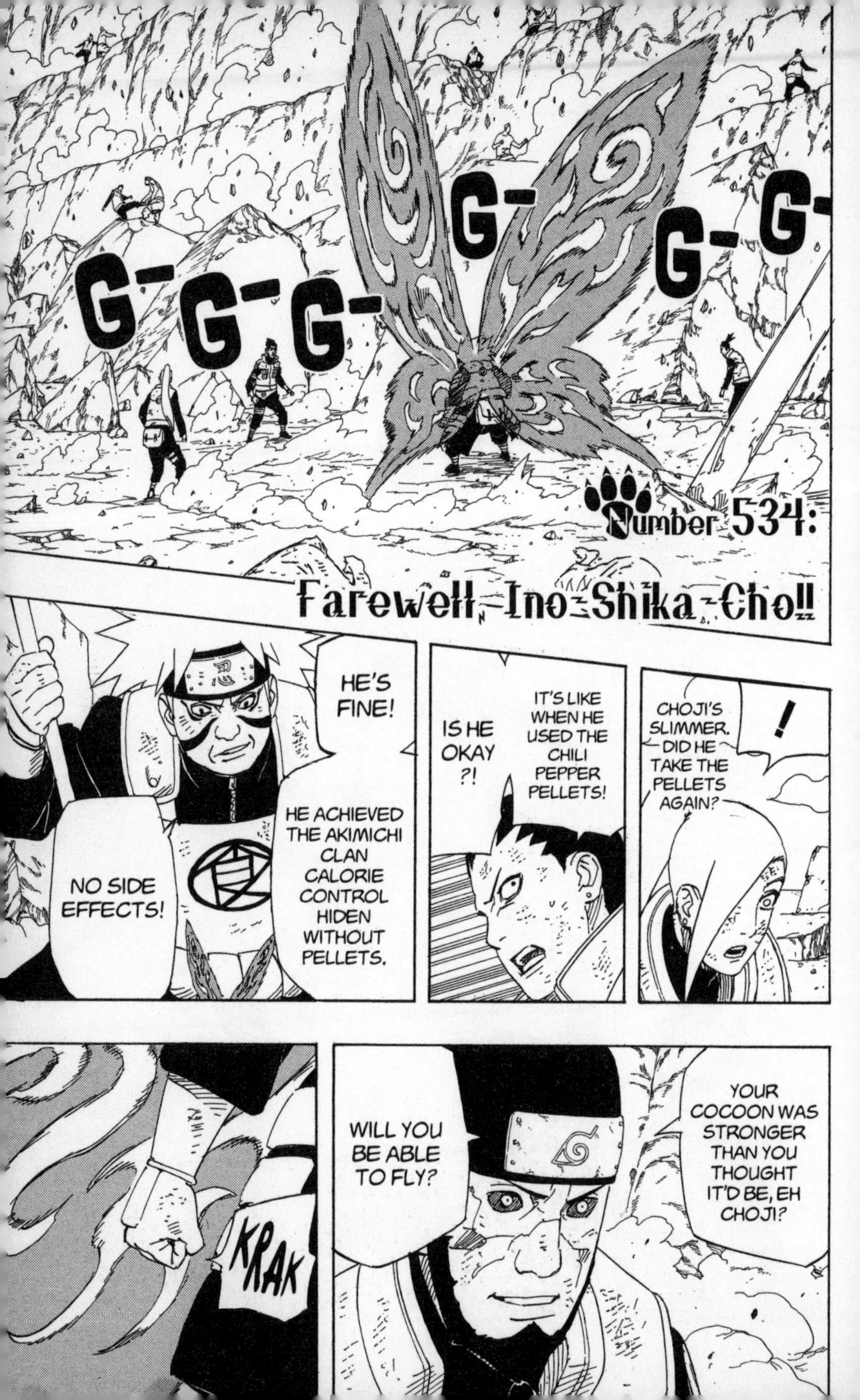
G-G-G-G-G-G-
Number 534: Farewell Ino-Shika-Cho!!
!
CHOJI'S SLIMMER. DID HE TAKE THE PELLETS AGAIN?
IT'S LIKE WHEN HE USED THE CHILI PEPPER PELLETS!
IS HE OKAY?!
HE'S FINE!
HE ACHIEVED THE AKIMICHI CLAN CALORIE CONTROL HIDEN WITHOUT PELLETS.
NO SIDE EFFECTS!
YOUR COCOON WAS STRONGER THAN YOU THOUGHT IT'D BE, EH CHOJI?
WILL YOU BE ABLE TO FLY?
KRAK

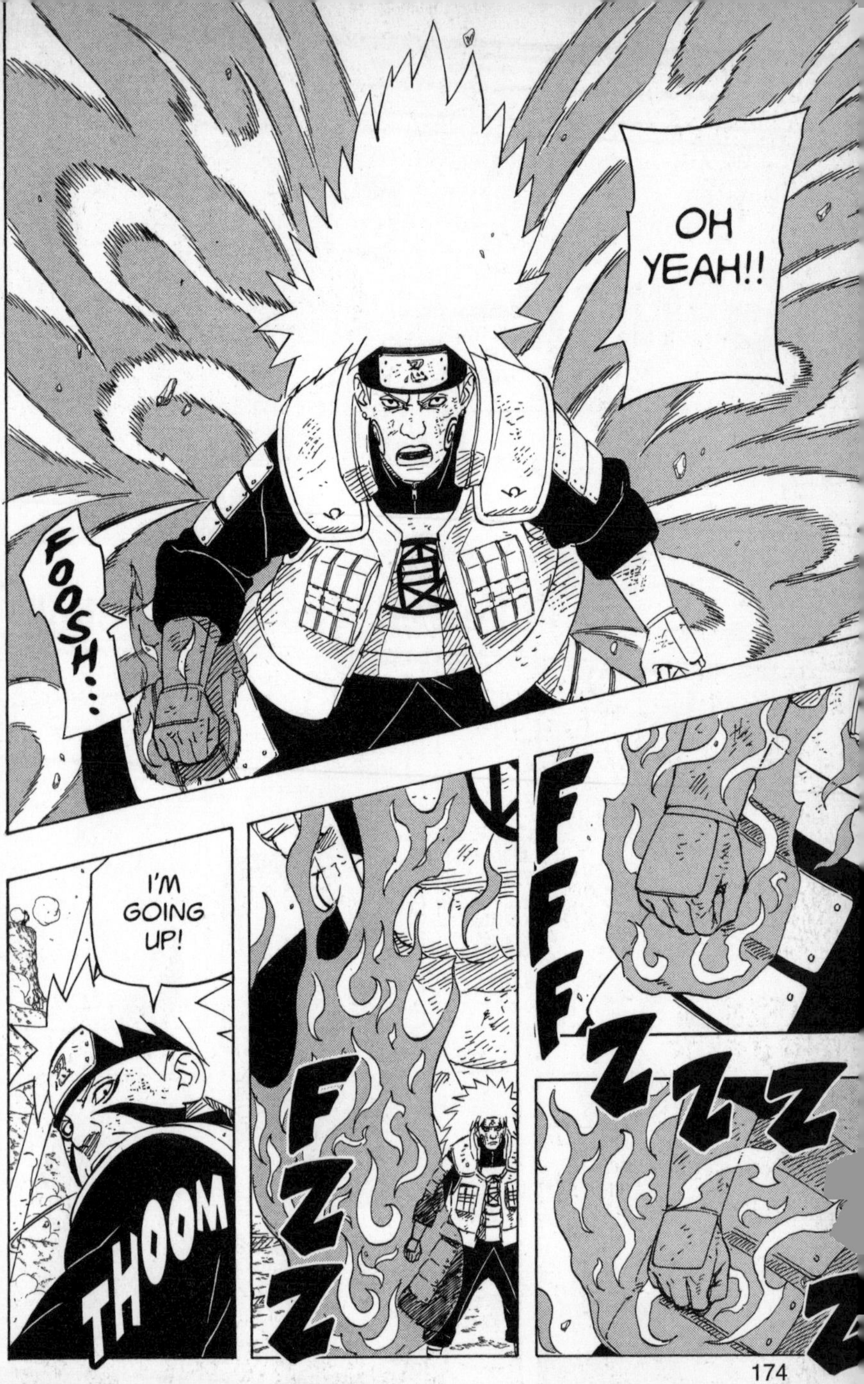
OH YEAH!!
FOOSH...
FFFFZZZZZ
FZZZ
I'M GOING UP!
THOOM

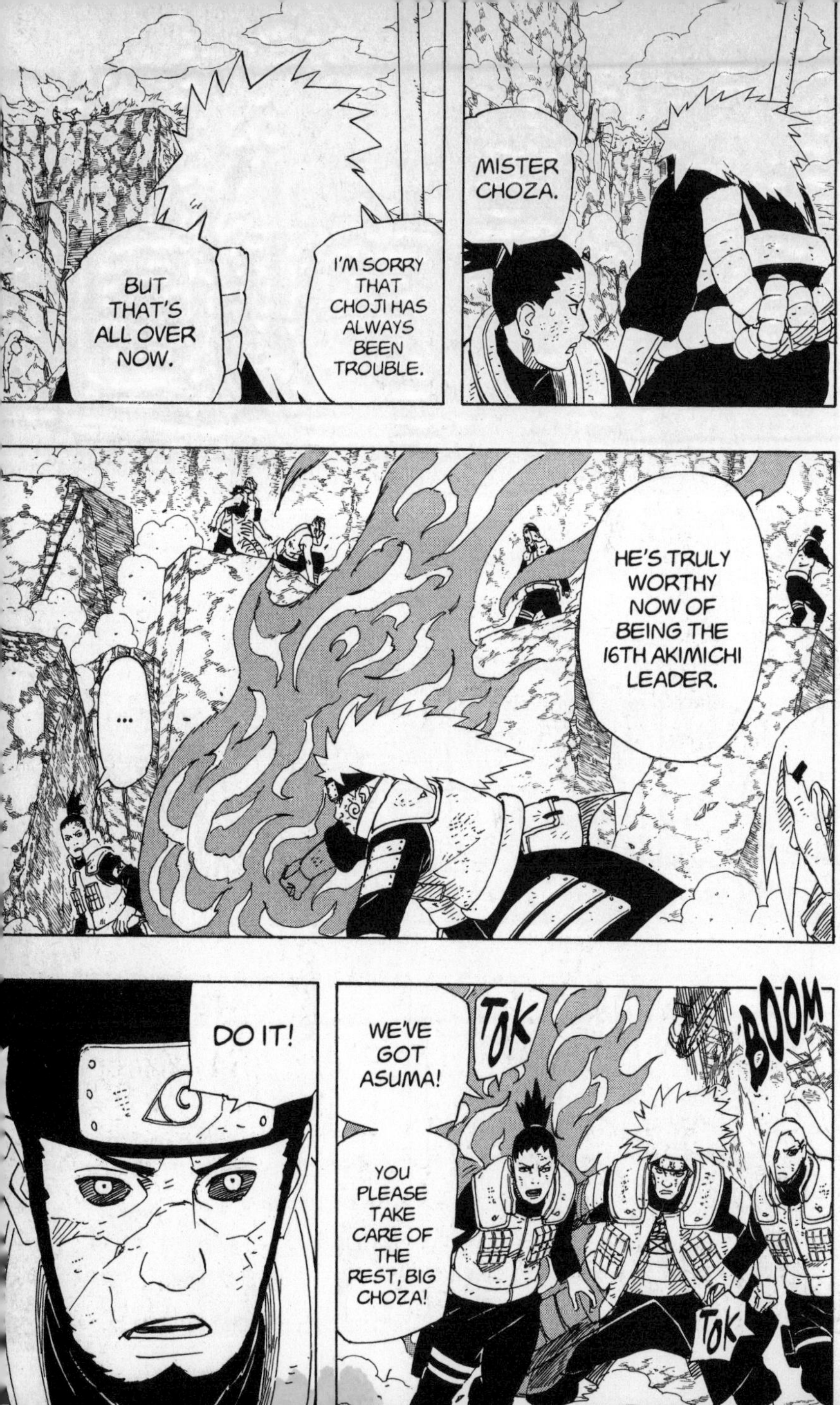
MISTER CHOZA.
I'M SORRY THAT CHOJI HAS ALWAYS BEEN TROUBLE.
BUT THAT'S ALL OVER NOW.
HE'S TRULY WORTHY NOW OF BEING THE 16TH AKIMICHI LEADER.
...
BOOM
TOK
WE'VE GOT ASUMA!
YOU PLEASE TAKE CARE OF THE REST, BIG CHOZA!
TOK
DO IT!

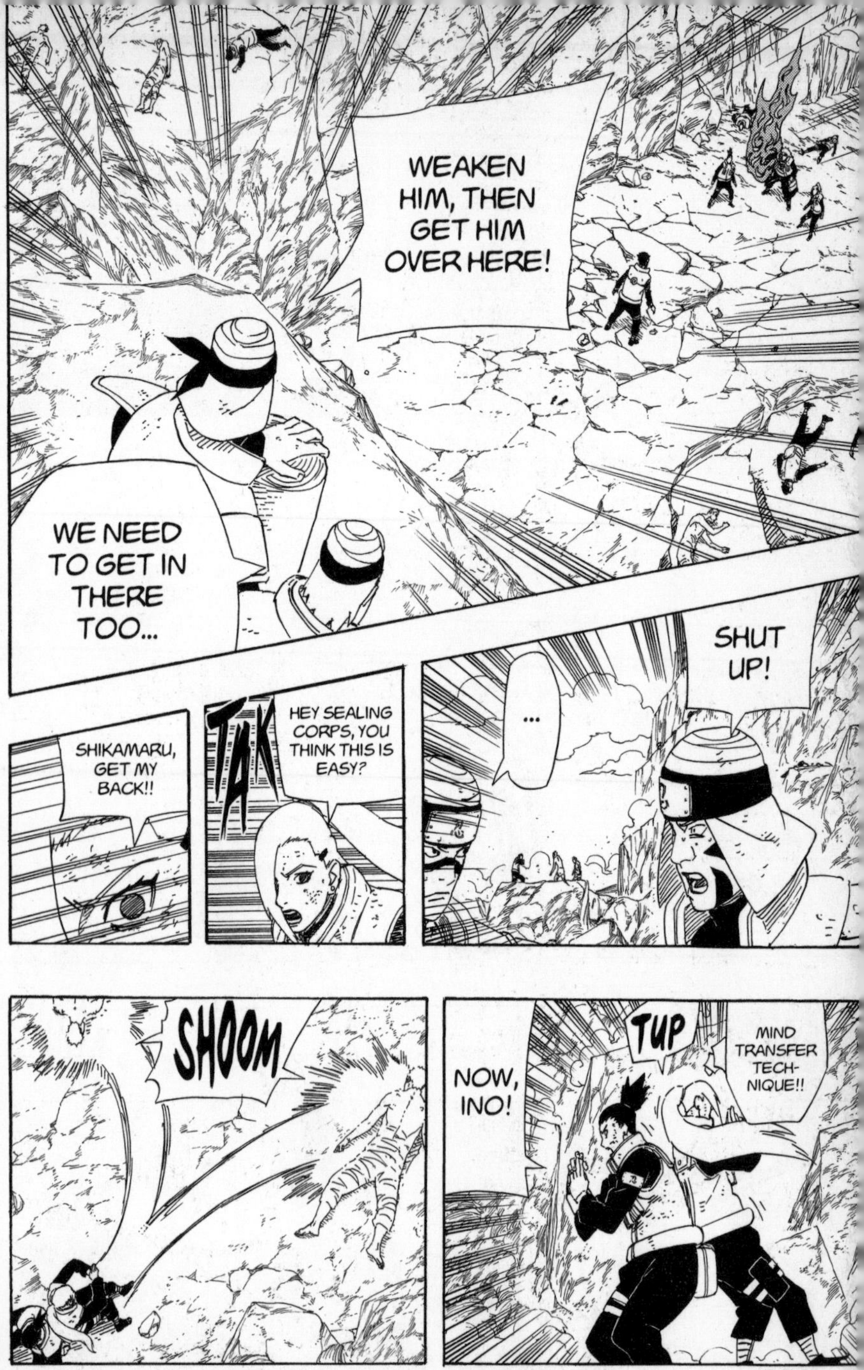
WEAKEN HIM, THEN GET HIM OVER HERE!
WE NEED TO GET IN THERE TOO...
SHUT UP!
...
TAK
HEY SEALING CORPS, YOU THINK THIS IS EASY?
SHIKAMARU, GET MY BACK!!
MIND TRANSFER TECH-NIQUE!!
TUP
NOW, INO!
SHOOM

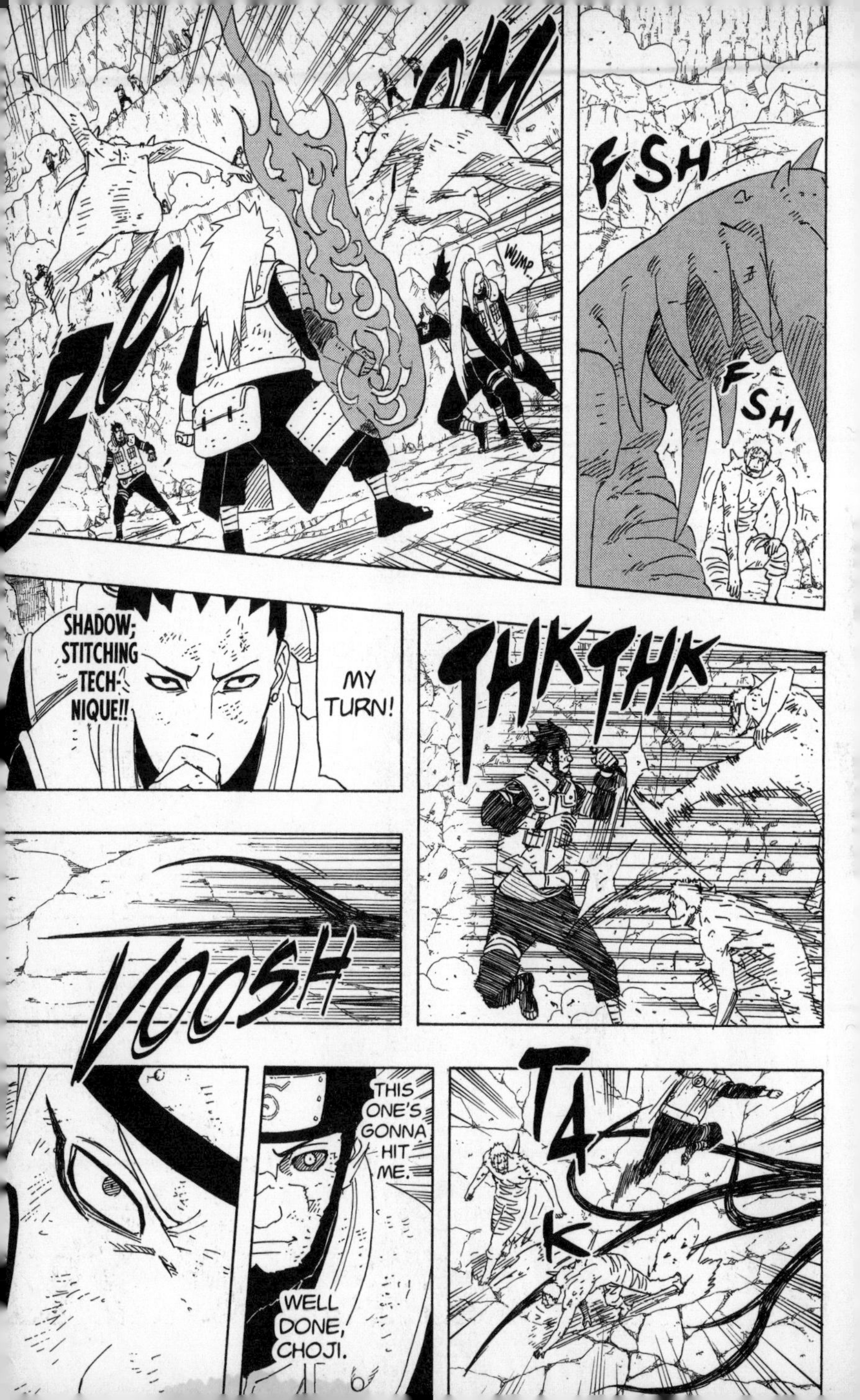
FSH
FSH
OM
WUMP...
BO
THKTHK
MY TURN!
SHADOW; STITCHING TECHNIQUE!!
VOOSH
TA
K
THIS ONE'S GONNA HIT ME.
WELL DONE, CHOJI.

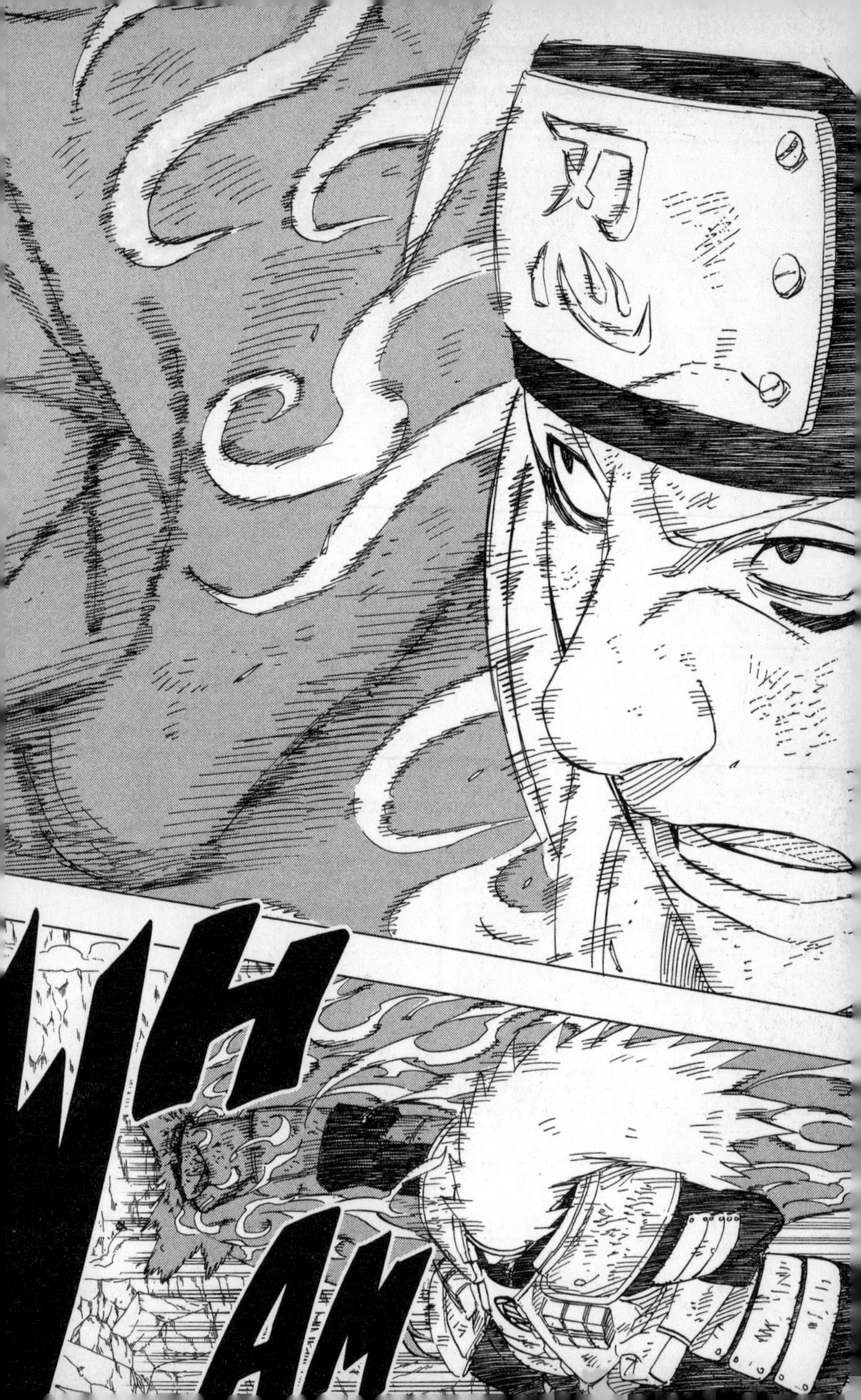
WHAM

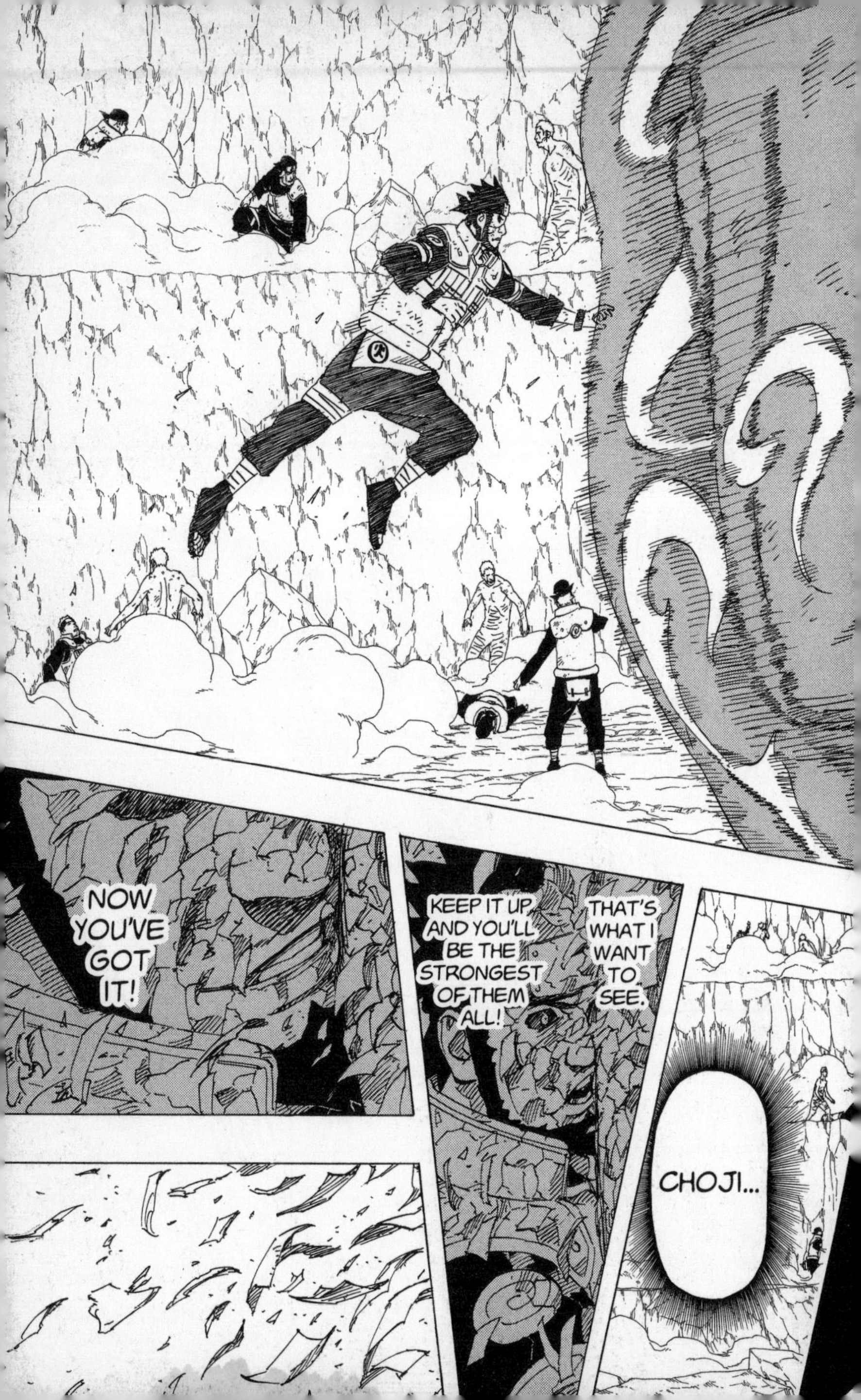
CHOJI...
THAT'S WHAT I WANT TO SEE.
KEEP IT UP AND YOU'LL BE THE STRONGEST OF THEM ALL!
NOW YOU'VE GOT IT!

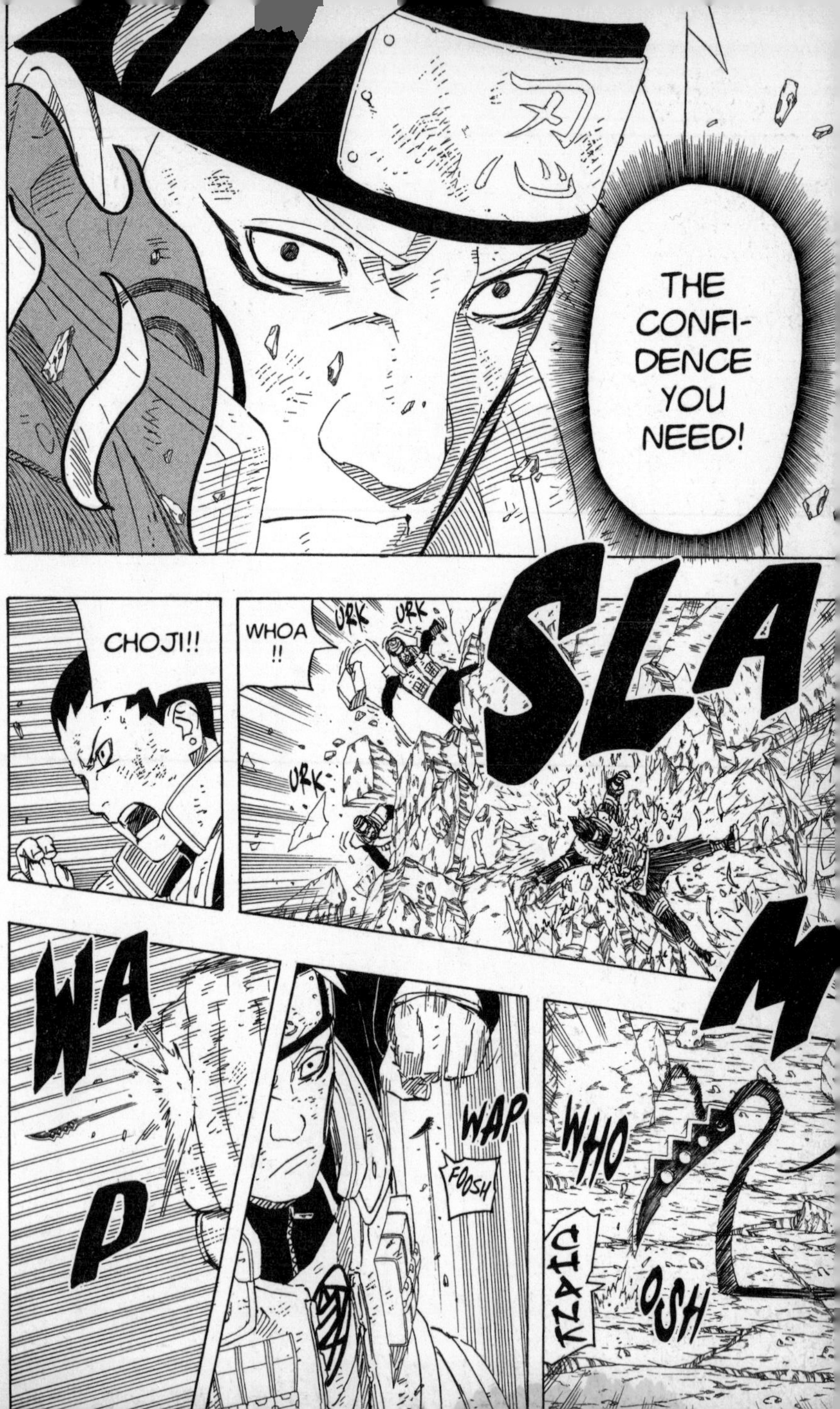
THE CONFIDENCE YOU NEED!
SLAM
URK
URK
WHOA !!
URK
CHOJI!!
WHOOSH
WAP
FOOSH
WAP

READ THIS WAY

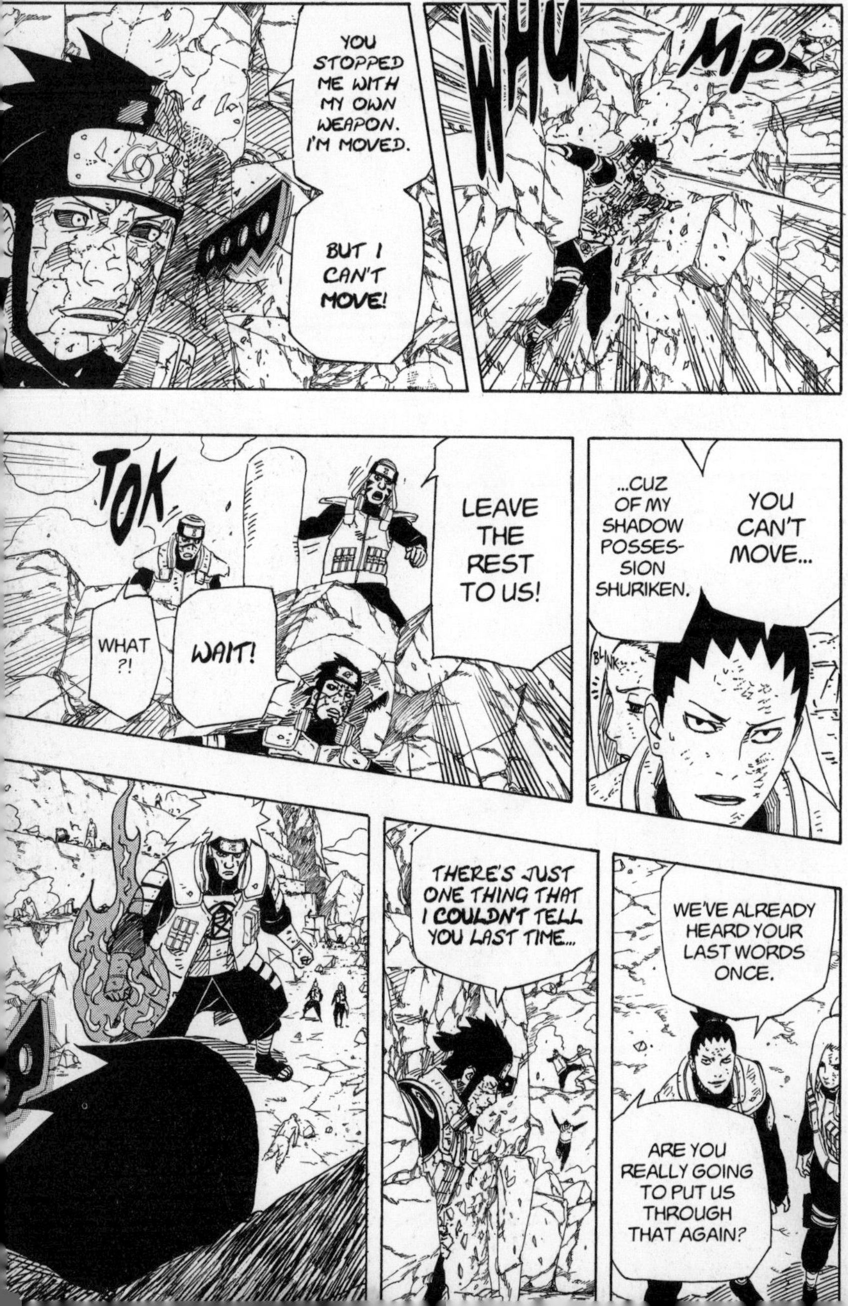
WHUMP
YOU STOPPED ME WITH MY OWN WEAPON. I'M MOVED.
BUT I CAN'T MOVE!
YOU CAN'T MOVE...
...CUZ OF MY SHADOW POSSESSION SHURIKEN.
BLINK
LEAVE THE REST TO US!
WAIT!
WHAT ?!
TOK
WE'VE ALREADY HEARD YOUR LAST WORDS ONCE.
ARE YOU REALLY GOING TO PUT US THROUGH THAT AGAIN?
THERE'S JUST ONE THING THAT I COULDN'T TELL YOU LAST TIME...

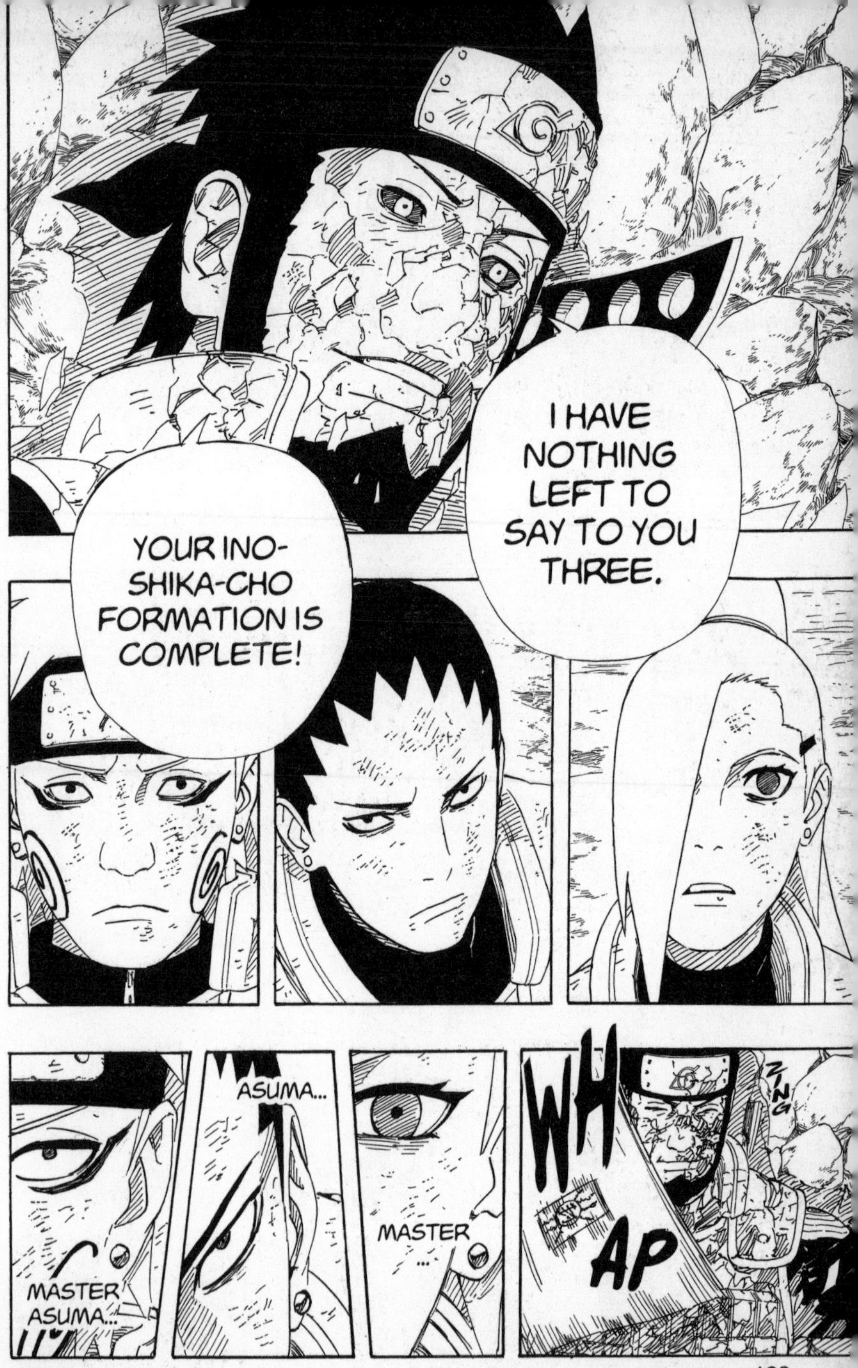

I HAVE NOTHING LEFT TO SAY TO YOU THREE.
YOUR INO-SHIKA-CHO FORMATION IS COMPLETE!
ZING
WHAP
MASTER ...
ASUMA...
MASTER ASUMA...

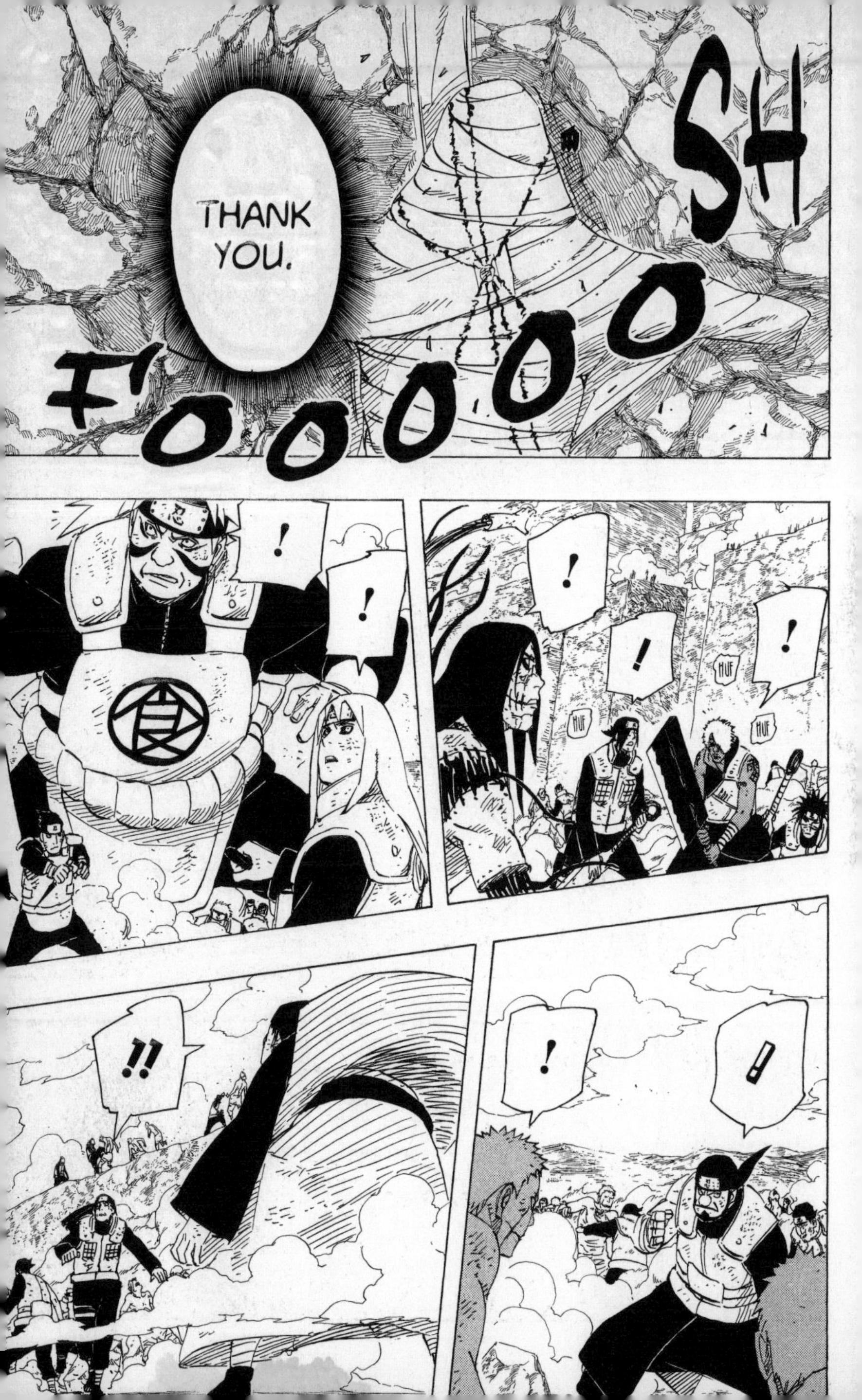
THANK YOU.
F'OOOOOSH
!
!
HUF
HUF
!
!
!
!
!
!!

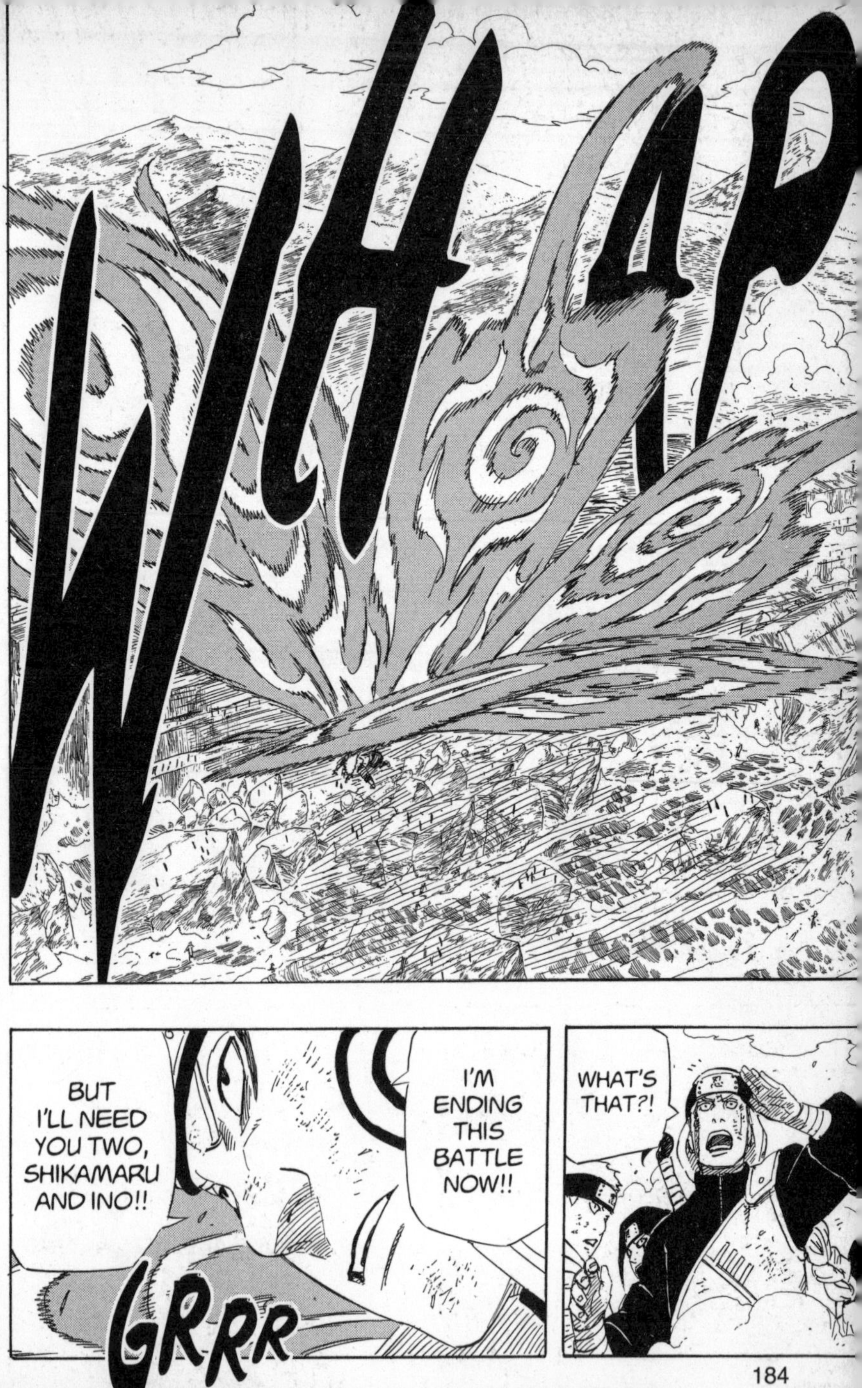
WHHAP
WHAT'S THAT?!
I'M ENDING THIS BATTLE NOW!!
BUT I'LL NEED YOU TWO, SHIKAMARU AND INO!!
GRRR

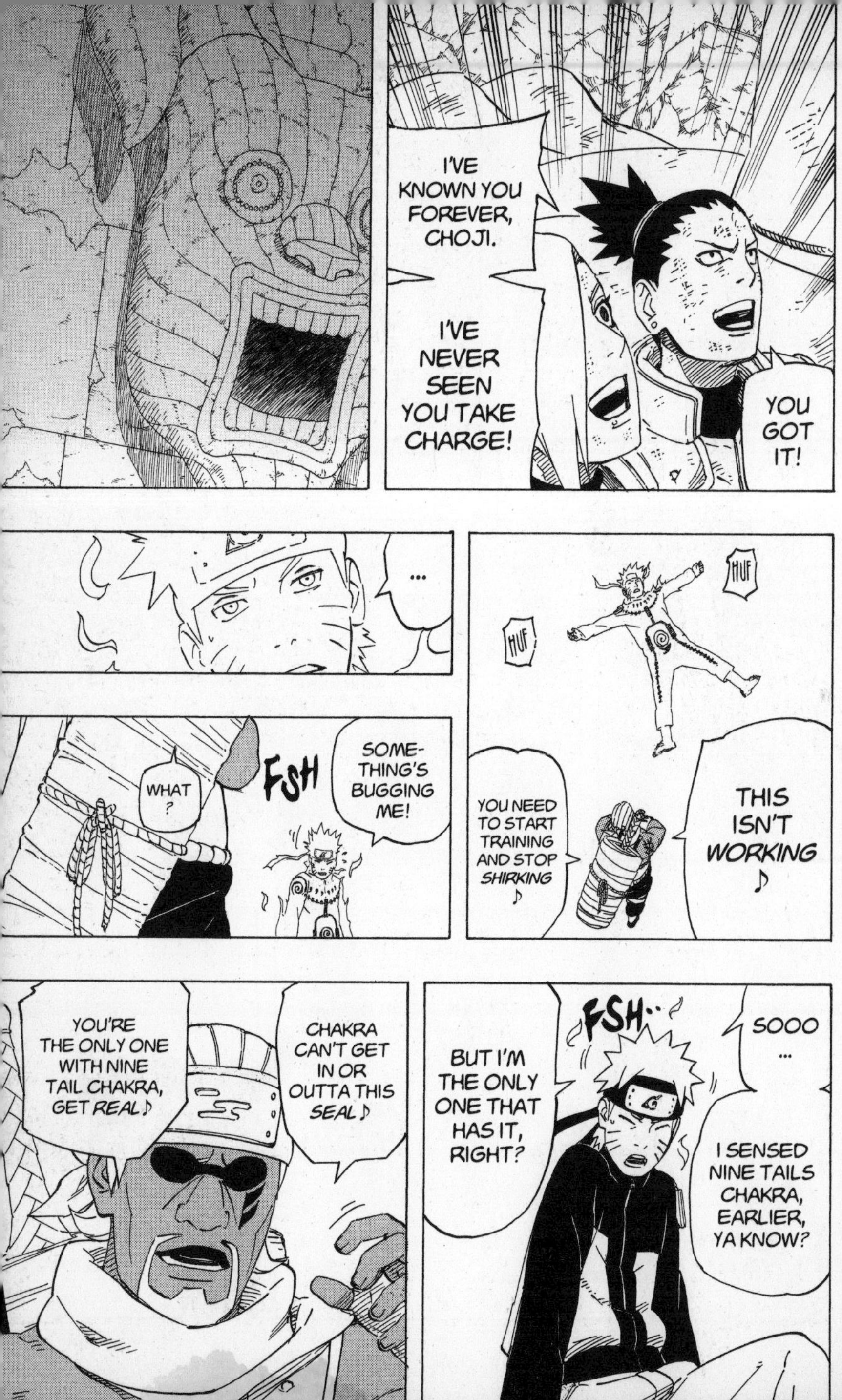
I'VE KNOWN YOU FOREVER, CHOJI.
I'VE NEVER SEEN YOU TAKE CHARGE!
YOU GOT IT!
HUF
HUF
THIS ISN'T WORKING ♪
YOU NEED TO START TRAINING AND STOP SHIRKING ♪
...
SOME-THING'S BUGGING ME!
FSH
WHAT?
SOOO ...
FSH..
I SENSED NINE TAILS CHAKRA, EARLIER, YA KNOW?
BUT I'M THE ONLY ONE THAT HAS IT, RIGHT?
CHAKRA CAN'T GET IN OR OUTTA THIS SEAL♪
YOU'RE THE ONLY ONE WITH NINE TAIL CHAKRA, GET REAL♪

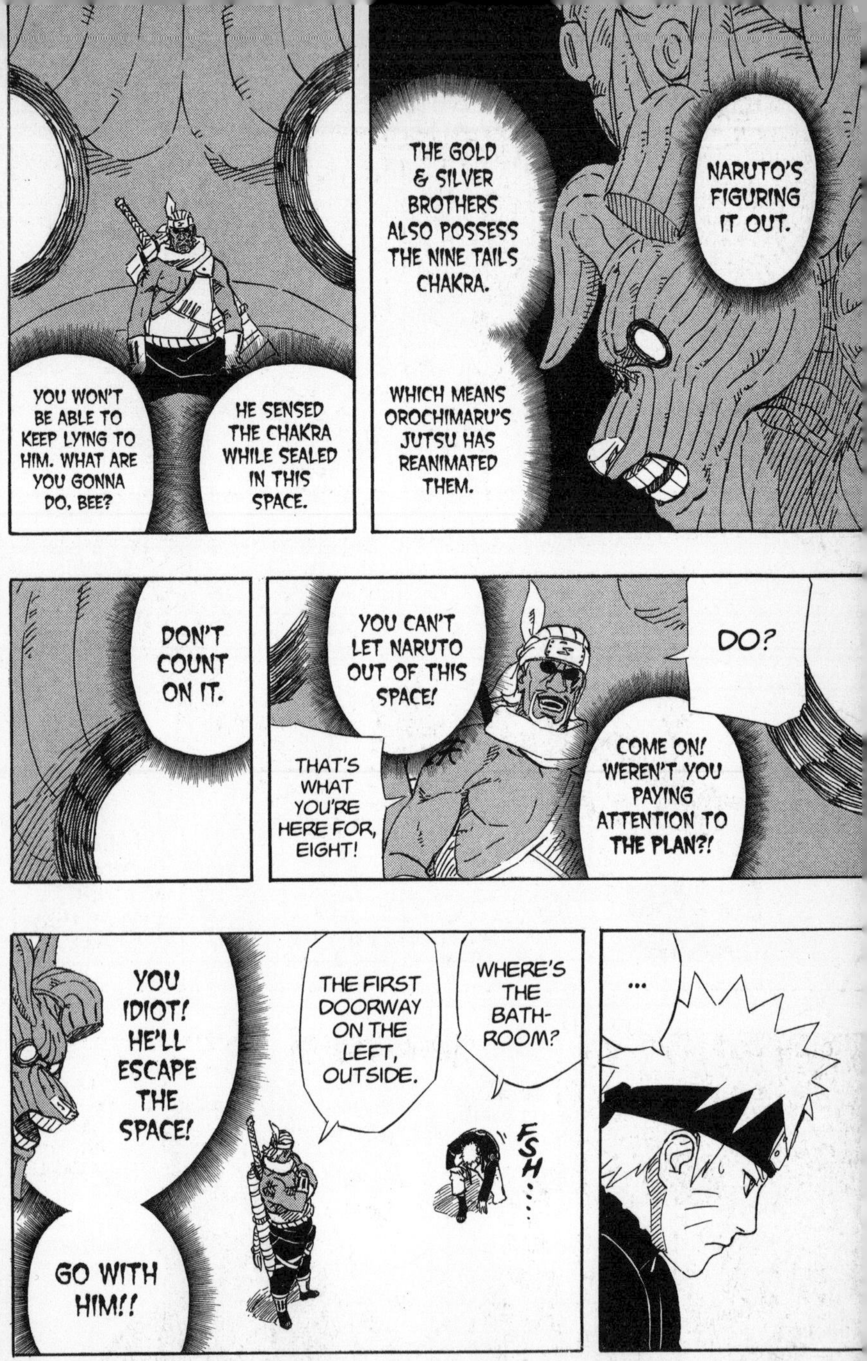
NARUTO'S FIGURING IT OUT.
THE GOLD & SILVER BROTHERS ALSO POSSESS THE NINE TAILS CHAKRA.
WHICH MEANS OROCHIMARU'S JUTSU HAS REANIMATED THEM.
HE SENSED THE CHAKRA WHILE SEALED IN THIS SPACE.
YOU WON'T BE ABLE TO KEEP LYING TO HIM. WHAT ARE YOU GONNA DO, BEE?
DO?
COME ON! WEREN'T YOU PAYING ATTENTION TO THE PLAN?!
YOU CAN'T LET NARUTO OUT OF THIS SPACE!
THAT'S WHAT YOU'RE HERE FOR, EIGHT!
DON'T COUNT ON IT.
...
WHERE'S THE BATH-ROOM?
THE FIRST DOORWAY ON THE LEFT, OUTSIDE.
FSH...
YOU IDIOT! HE'LL ESCAPE THE SPACE!
GO WITH HIM!!

READ THIS WAY

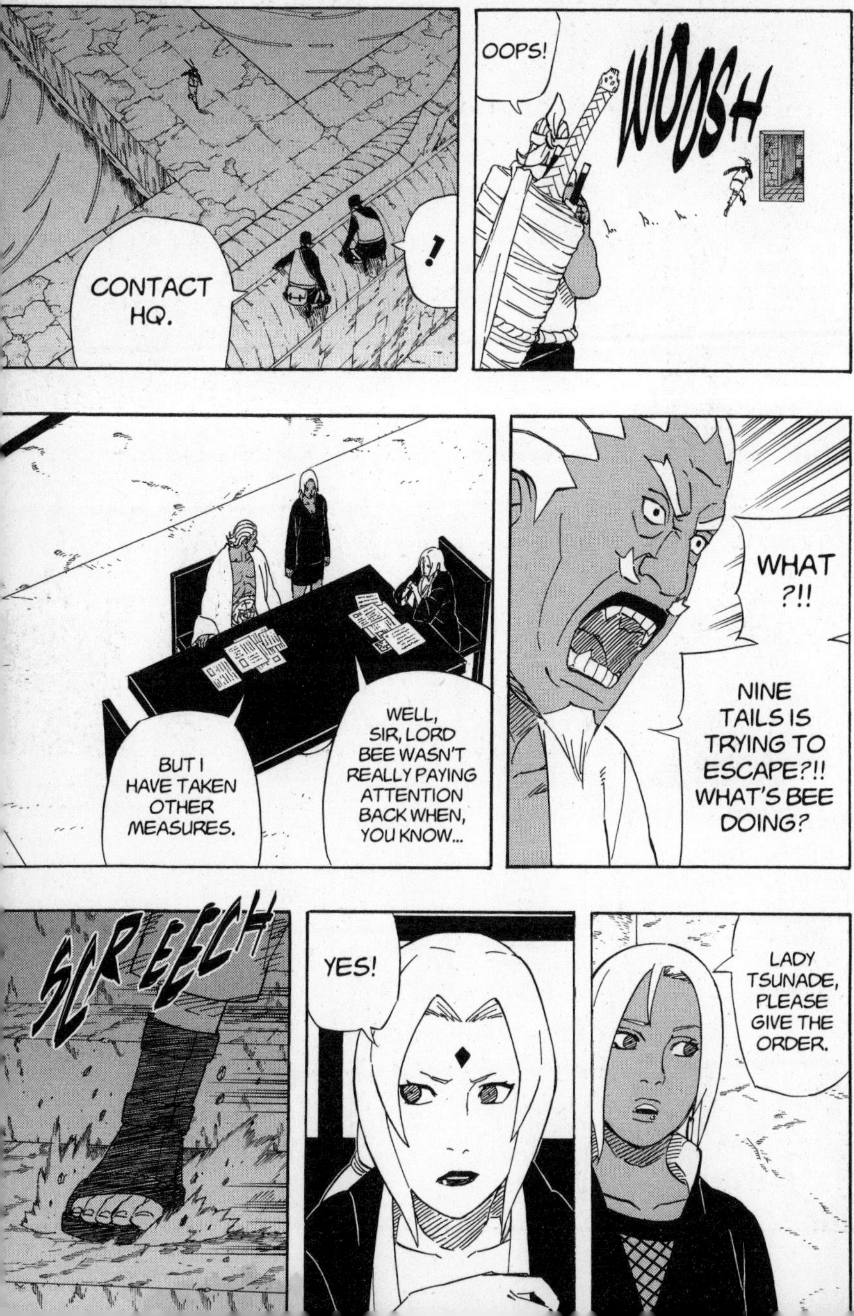
OOPS!
WOOSH
!
CONTACT HQ.
WHAT ?!!
NINE TAILS IS TRYING TO ESCAPE?!! WHAT'S BEE DOING?
WELL, SIR, LORD BEE WASN'T REALLY PAYING ATTENTION BACK WHEN, YOU KNOW...
BUT I HAVE TAKEN OTHER MEASURES.
LADY TSUNADE, PLEASE GIVE THE ORDER.
YES!
SCREECH

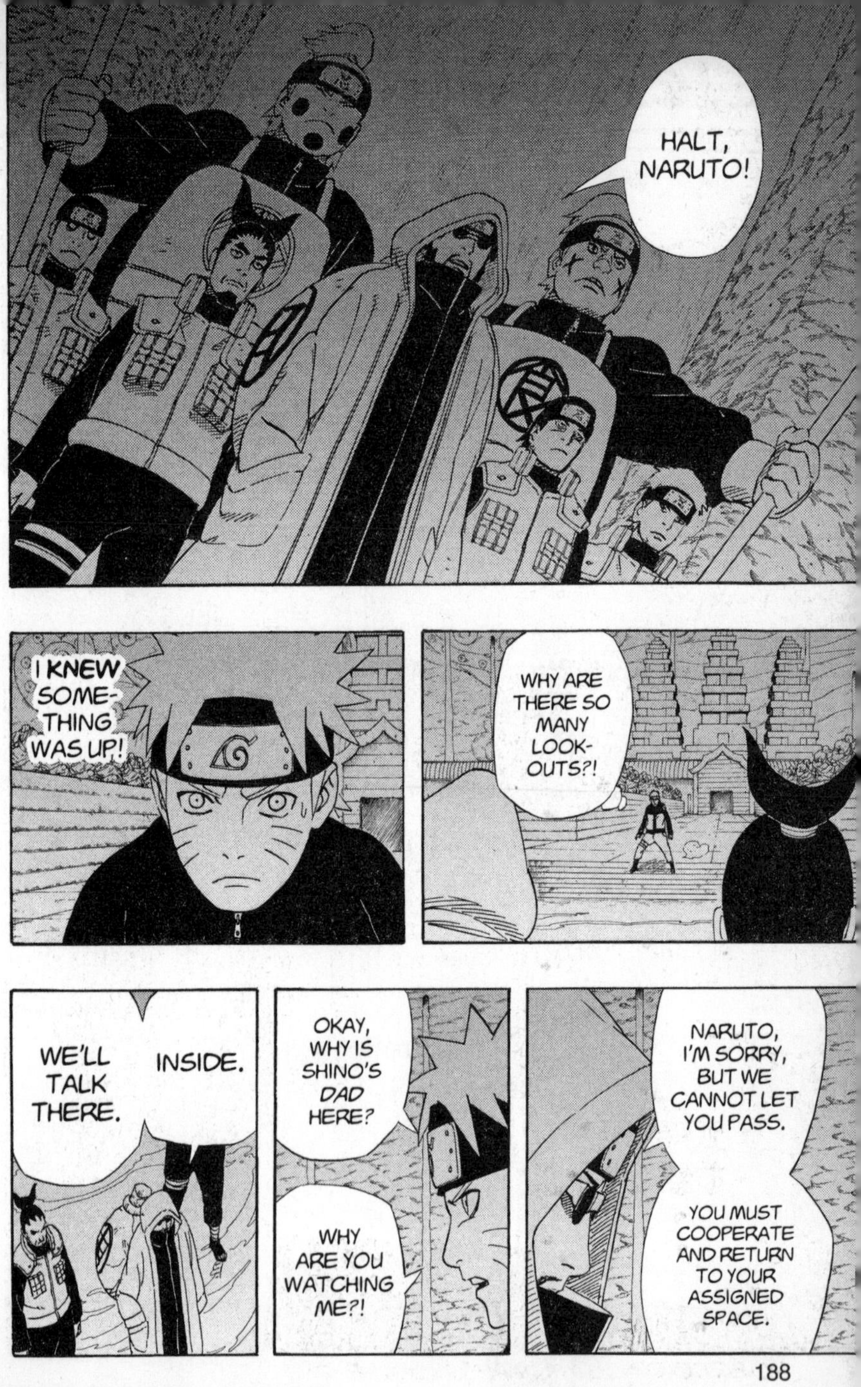
HALT, NARUTO!
WHY ARE THERE SO MANY LOOK-OUTS?!
I KNEW SOME-THING WAS UP!
NARUTO, I'M SORRY, BUT WE CANNOT LET YOU PASS.
YOU MUST COOPERATE AND RETURN TO YOUR ASSIGNED SPACE.
OKAY, WHY IS SHINO'S *DAD* HERE?
WHY ARE YOU WATCHING ME?!
INSIDE.
WE'LL TALK THERE.

READ THIS WAY

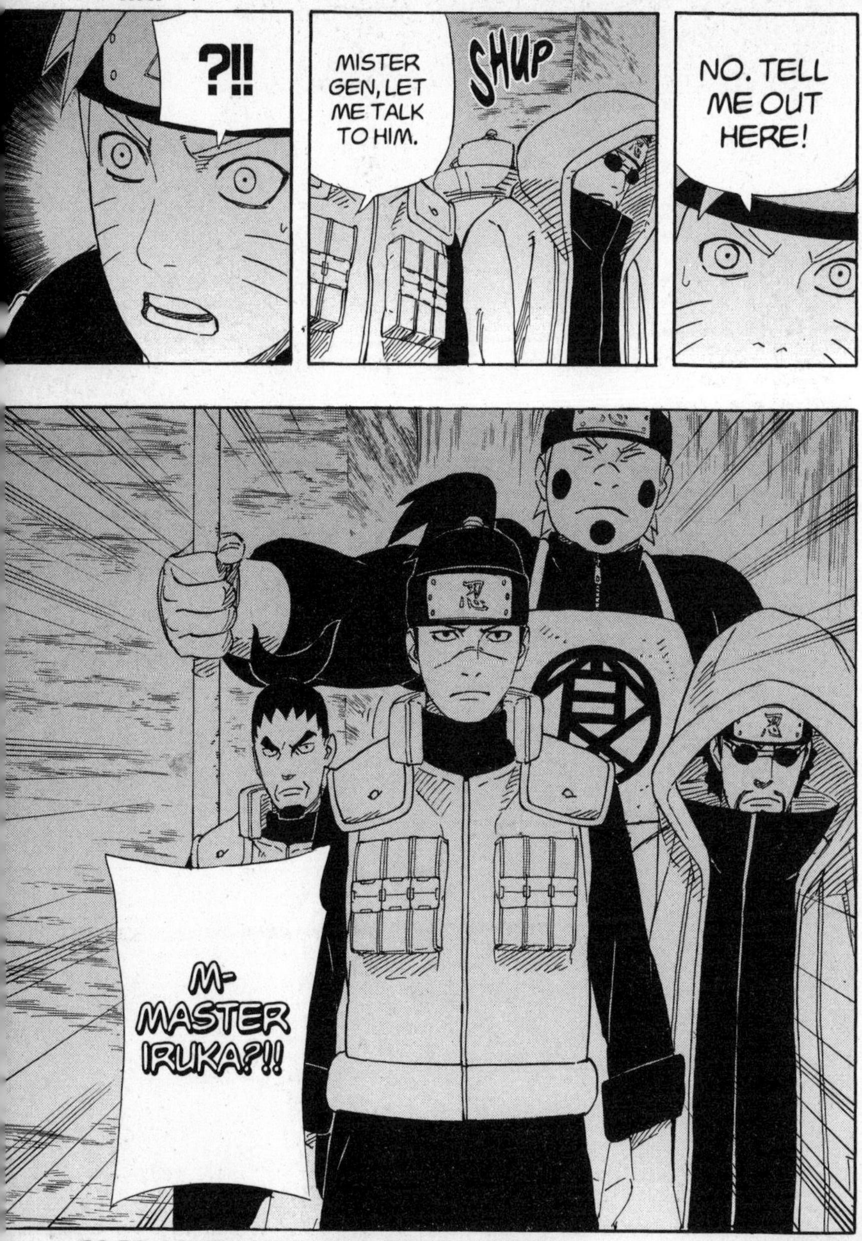
NO. TELL ME OUT HERE!
SHUP
MISTER GEN, LET ME TALK TO HIM.
?!!
M-MASTER IRUKA?!!

TO BE CONTINUED IN *NARUTO* VOLUME 57!

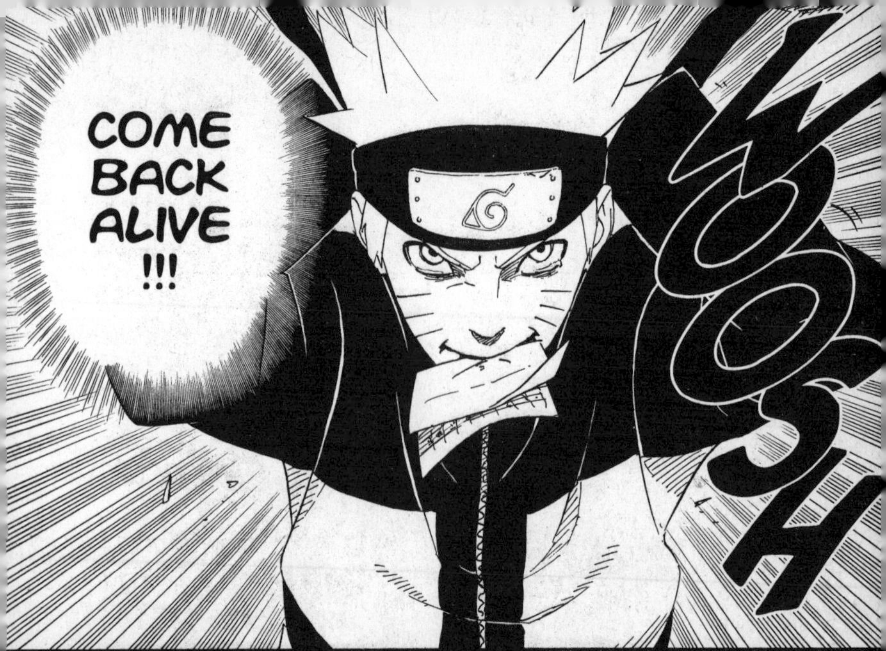
COME BACK ALIVE!!!
WHOOSH

IN THE NEXT VOLUME...

BATTLE

Madara of the Akatsuki joins the fray on the battlefield. His powerful attacks, and a secret plan, take their toll on the Allied Shinobi Forces. Naruto and Bee rush to help their friends, but the leader of the Cloud Village will do anything to stop Naruto from risking his life...even if he has to fight Naruto to do it!

AVAILABLE JULY 2012!